P9-CRC-262

THE TEACHING AND LEARNING OF PSYCHOTHERAPY

THE TEACHING AND LEARNING OF PSYCHO

BASIC BOOKS, INC.
NEW YORK

THERAPY

RUDOLF EKSTEIN, Ph.D.
ROBERT S. WALLERSTEIN, M.D.

Library of Congress Catalog Card Number: 58-13158
Manufactured in the United States of America

Designed by Alfred Manso

First Printing November 1958
Second Printing April 1959

To the students, the alumni,
and the faculty of the Menninger School
of Psychiatry

FOREWORD / Bertram D. Lewin, M.D.

It is with some humility that I undertake to preface this book by Dr. Ekstein and Dr. Wallerstein. Despite my general experience in the field of psychoanalytic education, my immediate experience with "supervision" in the broad sense of the authors is very small. I am the stay-at-home member of the explorers' club trying to comment on the adventures and tough-lived doings of the men who spent years in the Himalayas and near the poles. I can only appreciate and praise their assiduity and their dedication and be grateful for what they have brought back with them for the *Schreibtisch*-scientist.

Supervision, the immediate preceptorial tutoring in therapy, is said to have been a way that originated naturally in the older psychoanalytic institutes of Europe through the simple need of young practitioners to learn practically from older colleagues. Dr. Max Eitingon of Berlin is usually given credit for having made it a formal requirement in the curriculum of the Berlin Psychoanalytic Institute. In the United States, supervision had an independent, or nearly independent, origin in the education of social workers. Today it has become a standard educational device in the psychiatric world, a stand-by in the training of the residents and young clinicians. Here it is comparable to the "assisting at operations" that trains the younger surgeons.

That this educational procedure, too, has its underlying principles and laws has dawned on the sharper educators in the mental fields. There has been much thought, some writing, and, in the formal running of educational bodies, much regulation—not all of it too intelligently planned, for it is easier to make rules than to elicit concepts. Herein precisely lies the merit of the present book. Adolf Meyer once stated a metaphysical truth in a homely way: the present-day task of psychiatry, he said, is to make work and talk coincide. For one must work, and not unimportantly too one must know how to talk, or write. In these pages, work and talk happily intertwine; the ideas are shown in their relation to the facts discovered in the actual supervision of the students.

Once Dr. Ekstein and Dr. Wallerstein have told us, the fact that the supervision procedure is a method of teaching and learning, and that the canons of learning apply to it, seems something always self-evident. Yet, the empirical correlates of this remark are many, complicated, sometimes difficult to perceive; and here is where the reader will profit from observing with the authors the unraveling of tangles in the "learning process." It is to the authors' credit too that they claim no finality for their studies. Indeed, as in so many other psychological matters, it is impossible to set any limits ahead of time. When, for example, one has completed an account of the ecology of supervision under the excellent auspices of the Menninger Foundation, problems of other environments remain. Finally, after having viewed the learning situation and its supervision variety *sub specie aeternitatis*, there remain the factors of a universal nature—indicated but not explained by the remark that they "come from the unconscious."

The authors of the present book through their records and their thinking have given us a glimpse of unexplored areas, and it is to be hoped that their dedication and informed explorations will persist to further inform us and to further clarify the practical and theoretical paths of an important field of education.

PREFACE /

This is a monograph about the theory and technique of the supervisory process—and specifically about the learning and teaching of psychotherapy through supervision. It grows out of a ten-year collaborative experience of the authors and their many colleagues in doing, in learning, and in teaching psychotherapy within the Menninger School of Psychiatry. It originated with a Psychotherapy Supervision Council fashioned initially as a vehicle for the teaching of psychotherapy to students in the clinical psychology training program, for the teaching of the skills of supervision to a supervisory group of staff psychiatrists on the faculty of the Menninger School of Psychiatry, and for the systematic study, by a workshop method, of the theory and technique of supervision itself. Shortly thereafter, the trainee base was broadened beyond the psychology internes to the psychiatric residents, and a systematic (though experimental) training program, focused on the transmission of psychotherapeutic skill as a teachable body of knowledge, became established as an integral part of the educational activity of our Topeka setting—first in a supervisory seminar at Winter VA Hospital, and subsequently in a similar seminar at Topeka State Hospital.

To these tasks the authors have brought a diversity of experience and training; the senior author in clinical psychology, social work, and psychoanalysis; the junior author in medicine, psychiatry, and psychoanalysis. They have trained students representing the various disciplines engaged in psychotherapeutic work in a diversity of clinical settings—a Veterans Administration hospital, a State hospital, and a private sanitarium; a hospital setting for adults and a residential treatment setting for children, as well as outpatient settings for both, a mental hygiene clinic for adults, and a guidance center for children. The range of experience and training brought by the many collaborators to this enterprise, as well as the diversity of the clinical settings and of the clinical material in our Topeka psychiatric community, justifies, we think, our feeling about the generic, rather than parochial, applicability of our examples and the implications we draw from them.

In setting down these experiences in such a form as this, a number of problems become quickly apparent. One that has been pointed to by nearly every one of our friendly readers and critics is that however carefully we try to select our clinical examples with due regard to representativeness and typicalness, the students seem to them to emerge as uniformly "sick," and in real need of psychotherapeutic help themselves. Our clinician readers will, of course, be constantly tempted to look at problems that emerge between people, when one helps another, as psychotherapeutic problems, and thus see patients rather than students. In some cases this may accurately reflect the state of affairs, but the seeming universality of the phenomenon is, we think, an artifact. Our students have been almost all beginners in psychotherapeutic work and, for the most part, have been psychiatric residents. In their strained efforts at empathy with their psychotherapy patients, they overidentify with their patients' illnesses and tend to present themselves through their own "similar pathology," just as medical students may at times learn in part through a process of fantasying themselves the victims of each of the ailments whose characteristics they are trying to master.

Thus, one student complained quite seriously to his supervisor that he would be quite unable to treat the first patient assigned to him in psychotherapy, since by chance his patient suffered from conflicts similar to those he sensed in himself, and seemed no more anxious nor, to the student, really any "sicker" than he himself. In presenting his dilemma in this fashion the student seemed to have shunted aside completely his awareness that he himself was a physician and psychiatric resident, functioning effectively at his highly complex job and with a stable and gratifying home life, while his patient was a nomadic, autistic individual, precariously maintaining a marginal extramural adjustment. Perhaps if the bulk of our students were social workers, not psychiatrists, we might be faced with a different characteristic maneuver, the tendency to see psychological and intrapsychic problems as social problems that could only be solved adequately through social action, slum clearance, increased wages, or enhanced welfare benefits.

It is, however, not only the students who have a need to accentuate their "pathology" as a stumbling block to learning. Supervisors, too, will tend to bring their more difficult "problem-cases" for discussion with their colleagues, for it is with these that they feel most acutely their own needs—to learn supervisory skills. But they have other underlying motivations, as well. Since supervisors, especially beginning supervisors, are more secure with their skills as psychotherapists (which are prior skills) than with the new skills they are trying to acquire as teachers of psychotherapy (as supervisors, that is), they will tend to bring in students who should better be patients, since they themselves would rather treat than have to teach. In part, too, the supervisor who brings up the "problem case" is testing to the limit both his consultant and the program within which he operates. He is asking, "How can anyone teach so-and-so? He's so sick." In asking this, he is also trying to learn the answer.

Thus, for these many reasons our students may at first glance appear uniformly quite "sick." Our language, too, may enhance this impression. We speak of "resistance" to learning and can assume too readily that resistance implies pathology rather than being our way of describing a specific idiosyncratic patterning—the way a particular individual attempts to master a new experience and to incorporate the new without doing too much violence to the old. Which brings us to another problem that arises with the writing—and the reading—of such a book as this. The impression could readily emerge that the teacher's task is to point out and help remove the many blocks to learning, the emotional involvements, the blind spots, the ignorances, so that then, unencumbered and undistorted, true didactic learning could proceed. This would be, however, like saying that the analyst's task in psychoanalysis is to overcome the resistances and lift the repressions so that then the pathogenic infantile trauma can be recovered, and thus the cause of all the trouble exorcised.

Though such was an early-day view of psychoanalysis, it has since been increasingly seen as a constantly interacting process in which concern with defensive constellations and with instinct-derivatives are only the alternating sides of the same coin, and at the end of which a process has been worked through, a process in which each of the aspects of mental activity has been seen in all its interlocking relations with the others, and none is by itself the single "cause." It is one of the chief purposes of this monograph to make clear how we apply this way of conceptualizing to the study of problems in the learning and the teaching of psychotherapy.

In trying to do this, we are, of course, mindful that the therapists of whose learning we speak are for the most part beginners, and the problems with which we deal are those that are most characterstic for beginning students. True, we have chosen some examples of learning dilemmas from the work of more advanced students, and we have tried, as well, in a number of instances to follow our beginning students through to levels of partial resolution of difficulties and to successive levels of integration of psychotherapeutic skills. Nevertheless, they are mostly beginners with beginning problems. It would take another text, and a different one, to portray the characteristic learning patterns and strategic dilemmas of the advanced practitioner. Such a text would be closer to the rich clinical literature concerned with case studies which, from one point of view, can be considered as descriptions of learning problems in which the performance of the therapist is less the issue than the specific technical and theoretical problems posed by the disordered mental functioning of the patient.

Which brings us to another point we wish to make. Though psychotherapy is the skill that is being learned and taught, and though many of the clinical examples illuminate various problems of the theory and technique of psychotherapy, this is a text about how to teach it and how one learns it; it is not a textbook of psychotherapy. We assume that the would-be teacher has himself mastered the fundamentals of psychotherapeutic skill, has himself become an effective practitioner, and is now faced with the problem of how to transmit these skills to another, how to supervise rather than how to do psychotherapy.

Nor, despite its excursions into the area of the social setting within which the learning and teaching of psychotherapy takes place, and its statements concerning the social issues inherent in any therapeutic community, is this in any sense a sociological text. For example, in the first chapter we state our concept of the clinical rhombus, a diagrammatic presentation of some of the lines of interaction within a clinical community. This is not meant to be a statement about the sociology of an institution and of the interpersonal relationships within it. The clinical rhombus is meant rather as a psychological concept, using the interpersonal interactions as the screen upon which to project the magnified image of the internal dilemmas confronting each of us who strives to fulfill a variety of functions—therapist, teacher, researcher, administrator, and perhaps at some point, patient—within a clinical community. In the same way, the second chapter is not meant as a general statement of the principles of sound administration. Rather, it is an attempt at a specific understanding of the meaning of the administrative function in a clinical community and of the impact of administration on the psychological interactions of the different participants in that community.

We have referred a number of times to our many collaborators and the range of their experiences and their interests that permit us to view our own particular applications to the learning and teaching of psychoanalytically-based psychotherapy as directly rooted in a fusion of insights derived from psychoanalysis and social work, psychiatry and clinical psychology. Some of these colleagues have, through their cogent criticisms or the direct submission of material for possible use, helped shape portions of our manuscript in ways for which we are very grateful. They are Drs. Joan Fleming (of Chicago), Seymour Friedman, Vincent Mazzanti, Aaron Paley, Irwin Rosen, Helen Sargent, and Mrs. Judith Wallerstein. Other colleagues (representing every one of the clinical professions within our psychiatric community) who have read portions or the whole of the manuscript in its various stages of preparation and have given much helpful advice are Drs. Gerald Ehrenreich, Carl Epstein, Bernard Hall, Harold Meyers, Gardner Murphy, Lewis Robbins, and Herbert Schlesinger, and Messrs. Arthur Leader, Arthur Mandelbaum, Lester Roach and Mrs. Marcia Leader. In addition, there have been the many participants in the various supervision seminars in which the theories and techniques presented here have been proposed, disputed, and refined. From the earlier group that met at Winter VA Hospital, we want to mention particularly Drs. Victor Bikales, Allen Enelow, Seymour Friedman, Bernard Kuhr, Henry Lihn, Robert Luttrell, Vincent Mazzanti, Aaron Paley, Helen Sargent, and Herbert Schlesinger. From the more recent group that still meets at Topeka State Hospital, we particularly mention Drs. Alfred Bay, Austin Des Lauriers, Antonio Fueyo, Joseph Jensen, Robert Jones, Sam Lacy, Roberto Moulon, John Scofield, William Simpson, Fred Wagner, and Howard Williams. Even in the choice of our title we acknowledge our indebtedness to one of our sources of insight—in this case, social work. For it struck us when we decided upon the title how similar indeed it was to that chosen by Bertha Reynolds for her work, *Learning and Teaching in the Practice of Social Work.*

None of this, of course, would have been possible without the enabling support of the administrators of the Menninger School of Psychiatry and of the various affiliated clinical centers who have provided a hospitable home for the growth and development of these ideas and practices. Nor could this report of the work have emerged without the unflagging help of our secretaries, Mrs. Dorothy Diehl, Mrs. Winnie Siegal, and Miss Marjorie Strouts, and of our medical librarian, Miss Vesta Walker. Throughout the preparation of our manuscript we have had the friendly assistance and thoughtful guidance of our publisher, Mr. Arthur Rosenthal. We appreciate, too, the permission granted by the *Transactions* of the Kansas Academy of Science to reprint a portion of an article by one of us previously published in that journal, and the permission granted by the *Psychoanalytic Quarterly* to quote from a paper by Dr. Bertram D. Lewin.

Lastly, we have our debt to acknowledge to all those who have unknowingly furnished the clinical material and all the springboards for the elaboration of the ideas of this volume—the students and the supervisors, who, while they themselves learned, at the same time furnished the basis on which we have all learned. It is to them, the students, the alumni, and the faculty of the Menninger School of Psychiatry, that this book is appreciatively dedicated. We hope that we have adequately disguised the identity of each, and have used each example only to illustrate a generic, rather than a unique, problem. We would feel satisfied that we have accomplished this particular task if each reader would find in his own sphere individuals and situations that fit each of the described problems just as well as the particular individuals from whom they happened to be drawn.

The authors do not ascribe any of the deficiencies of conception or of execution of this work to any of the individuals whose help we have gratefully acknowledged.

RUDOLF EKSTEIN
ROBERT S. WALLERSTEIN

CONTENTS /

III. *The Learning Process*

IV. *The End Phase*

I / *The Training Setting*

I / The Basic Model of Supervision

Ich habe nicht die Absicht Ihnen die Philosophie beizubringen, sondern das Philosophieren. (I do not intend to teach you *the* philosophy, but how to philosophize.)

—IMMANUEL KANT

In 1798 Immanuel Kant published his important treatise, *The Strife of the Faculties,* in which he described—from a decidedly partisan point of view—the long and hectic struggle between the upper and lower faculties in the German university system of his day. This struggle he conceived as that of democratic libertarianism against the arbitrary demands of authoritarian state power.

The upper faculties comprised those of theology, law, and medicine and primarily prepared their students to become servants of the autocratic Prussian state, whose instruments they were. These faculties were to provide a civil servant class, a *Beamtenklasse* of theologians, lawyers, and physicians through whose dedication the structure of absolute Prussian state power was to be fortified. For this reason the state authorities felt it essential to control these three faculties completely and to prescribe their curricula rigidly so that the graduates could enter their chosen callings with a thorough identification with the ruling principles of the state they served. The students were certainly thoroughly imbued with the best available technical skills in order to fulfill most adequately their service functions to the state.

Understandably enough, the state authorities of that time (not yet having learned totalitarian techniques) paid little attention to the lower faculty, philosophy, since it had no direct vocational—and service—reference and was, in fact, only a prerequisite to entrance to one of the upper—directly professional—faculties. This faculty, not controlled by the government, achieved real freedom of scientific inquiry, so that ideas of research and of freedom in the expression of philosophical and scientific thought could flower. Kant, of course, belonged to the lower faculty and recorded the intensive strife between the two systems. As we know, this ended—at least temporarily—with a sweeping victory for the democratic ideal of scientific freedom. We also know, though, that the very same conflict persists in many ways in our modern professional educational systems, and that the optimal solution is far more complex than that espoused by Kant. Therefore we, too, are tempted at times to project our awareness of this conflict into the past and far away, and to cast the issues into those simpler, more heroic terms; or to point it out only in present-day totalitarian countries conceived to be the true enemies of free expression and creative development.

The old strife between submission to the needs of the state and the preparation for state jobs on the one hand, and complete academic freedom as the only tenable basis for free inquiry on the other, has given way in our time to something more subtle, a shadowy, almost unrecognizable successor to the heroic battle which Kant described. The battle slogan of today may be "liberal education versus practical education" or, on the level of the professional school, teaching "creative expression versus technical skills." Put this way, we are suddenly confronted with a dilemma, as *both* "creative expression" and "technical skill" represent aspects of our teaching ideal.

Thus the current issues concerning the problems of training in psychotherapy are in many ways more complicated revivals of the old conflict. As soon as we start to ask ourselves seriously what the content of a modern psychotherapy training program should be, whom we ought to select for such training and according to what kinds of principles, and, last but not least, what the most productive teaching methods might be, we are caught in the seeming self-same conflict of creative expression versus technical skills. At such a point we wonder if we ought to train practitioners in psychotherapy who are to cure the multitudes of sufferers from emotional illness and to fill the posts in hospitals, clinics, social agencies, and private practice, or if we should train researchers, explorers, curious people who are out to develop new methods and theories and will help us make the advances so essential in this new, still largely unexplored, field.

For the most part, the conflict remains unsolved within the present-day framework of psychiatric training. Residency training programs are necessarily planned to meet the needs not only of the students but also of harassed hospital administrators who are confronted with large numbers of suffering patients, immense social pressures, and small budgets. The development of theory, the stimulation to research, to an attitude which focuses on the individual patient and not on the large numbers, is left to a very small teaching group which seems to be in constant conflict with those who must and should see the other side of the coin. The strife of the faculties somehow goes on and can be found in all present-day professional training centers whether they train for psychiatry, clinical psychology, social work, or psychoanalysis.

Our own contribution presents an attempt at a solution of this dilemma through the development of supervision which—unlike Kant's more partisan viewpoint—is oriented equally toward both needs. The development of methods of supervision for training in psychotherapy depends however on the solution of a number of difficult social and psychological problems which we wish to bring closer to the reader by making use of a psychiatric fable about a dedicated professional community, existing somewhere unnamed. The reader may suspect that we choose this imaginary community in order to project safely our own experiences and thus to barricade ourselves behind the well-known disclaimer that "the characters in this play have no relation to anyone living or dead and all similarities are purely coincidental." This may be so, but we suspect that the reader—if he has ever worked in such a community—will find that we are describing universal problems applicable, to a large degree, to his own setting as well. The psychological problems thus universally encountered are but reflections of our modern social structure, a new edition of earlier, less complex conditions as they prevailed in the Prussian state during the days of Kant.

In our fable, there exists a nearly ideal professional community. We say "nearly ideal" because, although all individual members—and each of them in his particular way—are striving toward the collective goal of the whole dedicated scientific and professional group, the separation of functions in this community has created a number of divisive problems which prevent the group from reaching its ideal. For simplicity's sake we will mention only three of the different groups or classes of people in this community whose functions affect most directly the training experiences of our student psychotherapists.

We mention the teachers first, since this volume deals primarily with the teaching of psychotherapy. Let us assume that, to some degree, the teachers do indeed think of themselves as the most important, though they suffer from the chronic suspicion that the others belittle them and would like to see them relegated to the last position. Who knows if the teachers thus express a neurotic defensive need or if they correctly estimate reality? Their self-concept includes the image of themselves as the proud carriers of a classical tradition, who selflessly and enthusiastically give their skill and their idealism to the students, and who strive constantly toward the perfection of their own skills as well as of the functioning of the setting in which they work. There is in them, however, the latent, and often manifest, complaint that they are not given proper support, that they lack modern tools, that they have too many students and too few teaching hours, and that the other groups in the community alternately disturb and ignore them.

The image that they hold about these other groups that we will also discuss as affecting the life of the student psychotherapist—the organizers and the searchers—is not a reassuring one. They see in the organizers, whom in modern language we call administrators, simply timetable people who want to make things run smoothly according to a schedule and a table of organization; who kill initiative and spirit and count hospital beds and admission and discharge rates without respect for individual difference and individual experience. When the administrators are seen as looking beyond these narrow horizons, it is only in their function as promoters, who need to sell their program to the supporting public, which they do by propaganda, by fund raising, and by a constant effort to make things bigger, seemingly without regard as to whether they meanwhile become any better. The teachers would nonetheless be quite happy if they were harassed only by the Procrustean bed of the organizers.

But this professional community is more complex, and the teachers must also meet the onslaughts of the searchers. Teachers, in their depressed moments, view searchers as people without regard for tradition, for established procedure, or for a sound basis for the order of things; they see the searchers as living a parasitical life, free from schedules and responsibilities, whose predilection is for unreliable experimentation at the expense of both students and patients. Their research is seen as a provocative deviation from the standard in order to undermine established authority and to destroy what the teachers are building within the limits of the administrative Procrustes. While the administrators thus starve the body of teaching, the searchers are seen as depriving teaching of its soul. This professional persecution complex which runs rampant in the community in days of stress is shared by each of the other groups with equal intensity.

The self-image of the organizers is that of the bringers of order into the chaos in which the others move; of the givers of leadership to an irresponsible group of individualists who cannot see the whole because of their sectarian and somewhat selfish and self-indulgent interests. In spite of their drive to establish themselves as the unquestionable ultimate authority, they suffer from a constant feeling of inferiority, since they often suspect that the others look down on them as people devoid of real talent or humanitarian interest who have escaped into administration. In their role as promoters they can recover their self-esteem in seeing themselves as the only ones sensitive to the vital social issues at stake. Thus they think of themselves as the community-minded carriers of psychiatric values to the larger world, although here, too, they occasionally feel looked down upon as hucksters who see their task as diluting and popularizing the truth so laboriously gained by those who are really in the know.

The youngest and most esoteric group of the three with which we are concerned is constituted by the searchers. Their self-image—even though they stress their selfless devotion to science and free inquiry and freedom of experimentation—includes the Messianic feeling that they must elevate the others who have not yet reached their own lofty attitude. They see themselves as the only true carriers of progress, of scientific curiosity, and of the never-ending testing of the established dogma. The teachers they see as obstacles to scientific advance, as reactionary and dogmatic indoctrinators of eager youth who thus become lost to real scientific work. They attack the teacher's useless tradition as an obstacle to scientific curiosity. Moreover, they often have little respect for the organizers, whose tables of organization are seen as rigid barriers to creative work and innovations, although they like to exploit the organizer's function as promoter in order to get research grants, the better to serve mankind and science.

Even in a fable there must be exceptions to the rule and of course there are, and they are then usually looked upon with suspicion by their own group so that the constant struggle that we describe—with the understanding that it is here magnified for purposes of illustration—goes on between groups of the community and among the members of each. We will only mention in passing the rivalry—even between people within each of these groups—caused by difference in university degrees, in basic convictions, in salary scales, in professional fields, and in numerous other respects.

These many points of potential friction in our imaginary community are equaled by the intensity of desire for peace and co-existence. The members of the community may, as a first solution, attempt to free themselves from the paralyzing conflict in which they are all embroiled by looking for a powerful arbiter, a father substitute who will control, cajole, appease, and lead the competing factions. It is usually to him that they present conflicts engendered by the self-images presented above. They expect him to intervene vigorously, and, unless he is a paralyzed Hamlet, he will take some action. Their original hope that he will each time side completely with their particular group gives way to recurrent disappointments, and he is seen then as the unreliable leader who deserts one cause in order to support those who at another moment feel most frustrated and dejected. The arbiter's efforts to please everybody, or at least to keep everybody in line, and his shifting interest in the appeals different sibling groups make to him are countered often with a sudden unification of all groups lined up against him.

Thus, the solution of our professional problems does not, as we have seen, lie in the partisan attitude that Kant advocated. Nor does it lie in the infantile hope that the powerful leader of the whole community will solve things. The resolution can only lie in the mutual recognition that the external struggle against the other groups is often but a reflection of the struggle against the inner difficulty one has in carrying out one's own function, in limiting it wisely, and in avoiding unnecessary and destructive encroachment upon the functions of others. The skillful use of one professional function includes the ability to accept integration with, and the appropriate development of, other functions as well. Our supervisory methods, as we wish to present them in this volume, derive from such a functional view of the professional community in which status and power problems slowly give way to coordinating principles through which professional and scientific cooperation becomes possible. Training in psychotherapy, as we envision it, unites these functions rather than separates them, making use of each within its defined limits.

One problem of this mythical community has been mentioned earlier, and it is prevalent perhaps more noticeably in the field of psychotherapy than in other areas of clinical skills. We refer to the different existing "schools of thought" in the field, usually labeled with the names of the school founders. Existing differences in theory and technique arouse deep emotions in psychotherapists who may be—and this is partly in the nature of their work—"overidentified" with their specific views and usually have learned their skills in emotionally highly charged student-teacher relationships of long and intensive duration. The different schools develop their own allegiances and show little respect for each other. Often they give the impression of being isolated little islands with almost no intercommunication system. The student's problem becomes a difficult one in such circumstances; he is apt to find himself in a paternalistic setting, in a master-apprentice relationship, which may produce authority-bound attitudes. This problem is true even in our near-ideal community, but here the attempt is made to change this paternalistic learning structure into a more modern institutionalized one. In such a modern teaching organization the teacher is responsible to student and school alike. This means that the teacher has to give up much of the emotional investment of a situation in which he could be the sole master of a small guild, a school founder, but has rather to work with colleagues under definite rules and goals arrived at through group decisions. Constant difficulties in group situations of this kind, splits of faculties, and the creation of new therapeutic schools, show how difficult it is to give up the master complex and to serve within an institutionalized school system.

The integration of different and differing views in one school organization, coordinated to the needs of the students, is a difficult one. Can one create a teaching setting in which one could carry out professional teaching on the highest level without the disadvantages of patriarchal dogma? Can one maintain a certain uniformity of basic concepts and agreement on basic requirements without destroying curiosity and creativity? Can one leave enough room for deviations and for search for the new without endangering either service to patients or the training of the students?

Our methods of supervision, our views on training organization and how to use its structure, are an attempt to answer these questions. To paraphrase Kant's statement that he did not teach philosophy, but how to philosophize, we do not teach psychotherapy as a series of specific interactions, but how to carry on psychotherapeutic activity. We do not think of students as the extension of the teacher, but wish rather to provide them with a structured learning situation which facilitates maximum growth through a process which frees potentialities in the developing psychotherapist. There must be room for creativity and difference to be tested by the reality of clinical evidence. Although the common denominator consists in the general acceptance of psychoanalytic principles, we accept and desire difference, trial and error, and growing or changing convictions based on accumulated evidence.

As we look at the broad outlines of our imaginary professional community and wonder about the student psychotherapist who is to begin his studies here, we may start to worry about the diversionary pressures which will be exerted upon him by the different social forces and professional functions which we have described. We might then be in danger of overlooking the fact that the student's problem, although it is highlighted and perhaps reinforced by these external pressures, is actually an inner one. The facts of his background, of his personality features, of his strengths and weaknesses, will each have their external counterpart in the professional functions of the existing social structure. Since he wants to learn what he does not as yet know, he turns to the teachers with the expectation of obtaining a firm body of knowledge and a secure skill. Since, however, he is also rebellious and skeptical, curious and potentially creative, he will constantly be tempted to align himself with those in the community who are research minded, who attack the dogma of traditional knowledge. He wants approval and therefore will be willing to comply and become a promoter who tries to make his product appeal to those who judge, so that he may, prematurely at times, be accepted and fully rewarded. His compliance is counteracted, however, by his need to be independent, to run his own affairs, and to guide his own destinies as a learner, and he will thus wish to be his own autonomous administrator.

Each student may then see in the main classes which we have depicted in our imaginary professional community external representations of similar need systems in himself. The learning obstacles created by these need systems can be looked at most helpfully in terms of an inner struggle which is occasionally reflected in and reinforced by certain aspects of the social structure within which the learning takes place. We can, with this awareness, follow the student psychotherapist into his concrete situation in order to see the specific problems of individual learning emerge. The social forces of our imaginary training center are experienced by the student psychotherapist through the specific individuals who guide his development, very much as the pressures of a culture are experienced by the growing child in terms of the demands of his actual parents.

Let us assume that the student psychotherapist has already acquired a certain body of knowledge in this special field through courses, through an adequate study of the literature, through seminars and discussion groups, and is now ready to start the actual treatment of a patient. The usual clinical arrangement would then bring him into contact with the patient whom he is to treat, with the supervisor from whom he is to learn and to whom he is responsible, and with the administrator who maintains a clinical situation with its professional standards and demands in which both clinical services to patients and teaching services to students can be carried out.

One may picture this psychological situation with its inferred human relationships, each of different functional nature, through a diagram, the clinical rhombus.

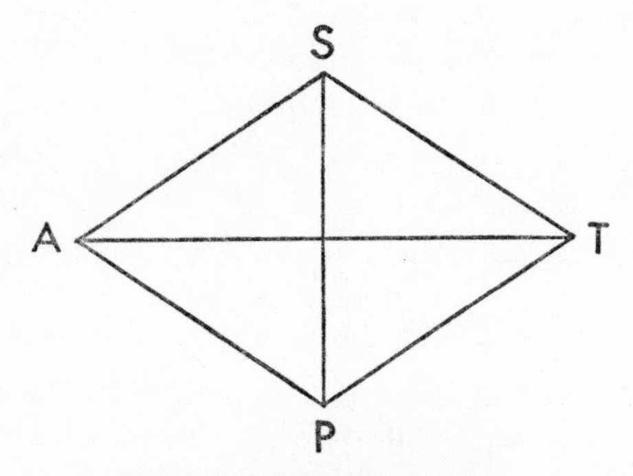

THE CLINICAL RHOMBUS

The therapist (T) will have a certain number of psychotherapeutic sessions with his patient (P). The main purpose of this relationship is the therapist's responsibility to help the patient psychotherapeutically, through the skill which he simultaneously possesses and attempts to improve through his learning experience. The improvement of his skill is guaranteed not only through the experience of actual work with the patient but also through the learning relationship with his supervisor. This relationship consists of regular, usually weekly, meetings with the supervisor (S) which provide the student with an opportunity to discuss the problems of acquiring psychotherapeutic skills. In this limited situation, the student is confronted with two different relationships: in the first (indicated in the line T–P) he is the helper; in the other, the learning relationship (indicated in the line S–T), he is the one who receives help—from the supervisor. This triangular part of the clinical rhombus is but one portion of the total social situation within which the psychotherapist must learn to operate. But even in this limited situation a variety of complexities may be mentioned in order to illustrate the kinds of problems that arise.

The supervisor is directly related to the student but has a quasi-indirect relationship to the patient. On the one hand his responsibility is to teach psychotherapeutic skills to the student, but his additional responsibility consists in maintaining clinical standards and seeing that the patient benefits from the service which is being extended. An interesting situation arises if, rather than identifying with the problems of the struggling learner, he identifies with the problems of the suffering patient and wishes to treat the patient himself through the student. In such instances the student, rather than remaining a learner (and a therapist), becomes only the extension of the supervisor.

This triangular situation becomes even more complicated through the fact that supervision and psychotherapy usually take place within a total institutional setting in which training standards as well as psychotherapeutic standards are maintained and supported by the administrator to whom the supervisor is directly responsible—and to whom the student's responsibility is at least an indirect one. What happens to the nature of the relationships already described if they are enriched or complicated by the administrator (figure A in the left-hand corner of the rhombus) is an aspect of clinical reality which will have its consequences for the total problem of teaching psychotherapy. The administrator's function is frequently overlooked since ordinarily the student has only indirect and infrequent contact with the administrator but deals directly with his clinical supervisor. The student may experience the rules and the opportunities of the clinical setting as basic reality and may overlook its human and changeable aspects personified in the administrator. For the supervisor, the administrator is a much more real factor who constantly influences, for better or for worse, the effectiveness of his supervisory work. The personal aspects of this clinical rhombus will therefore be experienced by each of the participants in a different way, since each of them—student, supervisor, patient, and administrator—has a different place in the hierarchy of interrelationships. We are talking not simply about the variety of human relationships which exist among four people, but about those stratifications of the relationships which reflect the different functions that the participants carry.

This can be exemplified by looking at the four corners of the clinical rhombus from the vantage point of the student therapist, whose work and learning form the chief focus of our interest. As the student in his corner faces the other three corners of his clinical world, he confronts three kinds of problems which, we hope to demonstrate, are but external representations of typical inner situations. He is to help the patient and has to acquire skills in order to cope with the seeming chaos that the illness of the patient, for the most part, represents to him. To the supervisor he brings his own chaos, his own difficulties and lack of knowledge and skill, in order to receive help toward the furtherance of his own processes of increasing mastery and growing competence. And finally, the administrator represents chiefly the conditions and requirements of the clinical situation that the student has to meet, and the approval or disapproval of the work that he is doing. As he goes on with the task of acquiring psychotherapeutic skills, he has to face these same aspects of himself. He has to cope with the archaic, unorganized aspects of his professional self; he has to develop skills, areas of technical and human competence; and he has to struggle with the task of having to live by regulations and of having to live up to professional ideals.

And yet each of these outer relationships represents a fluid rather than a fixed reflection of areas of the student's inner concerns. The patient, while usually representing the disorder that is illness, can also, when he is improving and doing well, be a model of increasing mastery, external evidence of inner growth and maturation. Or he can be seen by the student as a constant reminder for his conscience, that he, the patient, is still sick, and that he has thus far received inadequate help. The patient thus can represent shifting pressures on the student, accentuating by turn any of the areas of functioning with which we are here concerned. Likewise the supervisor, usually experienced as the ego-ideal and the helper, may at times be felt as the strict and judgmental representative of administration, as the personification of the punitive attitudes himself. At some other time, the very same supervisor may be considered to be incompetent and may be seen as the expression of chaos rather than of strength. Even the administrator, whose functions are usually the most stabilized in the student's eyes, may at times appear as the court of reason and of democratic appeal from the harsh judgments and the caprices of the supervisor and may at other times appear as the weak figure whose lack of resolution allows administrative chaos within which teaching and service functions fail to obtain their necessary framework of support.

Thus, we see that the actual reality situation of the student loses its arbitrary aspects and becomes but the series of shifting outer representations of the inner forces and inner dilemmas which are set into motion as the process of learning and doing gets underway.

The student's feelings and thoughts, his conflicts and beginning solutions, as these concern the patient, the supervisor, and the administrator, can all be observed in the supervisory process. While these data are to some extent concerned with external realities as they are graphically represented in the different lines of our rhombus, we must always keep in mind that these data actually present the pattern of the inner learning process.

Similar kinds of observations can be made if we look at the four corners of the clinical rhombus from the vantage point of the patient or the supervisor or the administrator. If we were to highlight the position of the patient in such a clinical situation, we would be describing psychotherapeutic processes primarily. If the administrator were in the forefront of our concern, our observations would be of the psychology of administrative processes. The supervisor's viewpoint, thus focused upon, would bring insights into the problems of teaching.

Our purpose in this book is to highlight the mutual interaction that constitutes the processes of teaching and of learning. The clinical rhombus will be studied therefore from the vantage points of the supervisor (S) as well as of the student therapist (T). Only to an extent that provides relevant insights into aspects of the learning process and the employed teaching techniques will we concern ourselves with the administrator (A). Different chapters of the book will focus upon different segments then, or different connections of the clinical rhombus. At a point at which we are interested, for example, in just what interactions occur between supervisor and student during a particular phase of training, we will be concentrating on the process represented by the line S–T. At that moment we may be paying little attention to what goes on between therapist and patient, line T–P. In another phase, however, we may be very much interested in showing the patterns of psychological relationships between what goes on on the line S–T with what goes on on the line T–P. All these different problems of the supervisory and the learning process will be discussed against the total background schematically represented in the clinical rhombus.

As we go about considering different aspects of the teaching and learning of psychotherapeutic skills, we believe it will be most useful if these are described in a comparatively neutral and nontechnical language. The choice of a neutral language does not, however, imply neutrality in regard to the theoretical framework within which we conceptualize phenomena, nor is it an attempt to convert people who are of a different theoretical conviction. Our understanding of the problems of teaching and learning and of the body of psychotherapeutic skills to be taught is grounded firmly in the psychoanalytic theory of personality and derives from the large body of theoretical and technical knowledge of classical psychoanalysis and psychoanalytically oriented psychotherapy. But the technical language of psychoanalysis, derived from clinical material, is a language of therapy, and its use would mean a casting of the process of learning in concepts which derive from the process of therapy. We could then easily be tempted to see the supervisory process as a psychotherapeutic process. For example, we could see the student's helplessness in the face of the chaos that the patient brings to him as an expression of his id impulses; his fears as to what the administrator will think of him as an expression of his superego strictures; and his expectations of the supervisor as linked to growing ego strength and mastery. Such concepts would indeed help us to see certain common denominators between the patient and the student. There will be ample opportunity to stress the parallels; what seems most necessary, however, is a clarification of that which is different, that which makes the helping process of supervision into a process of learning rather than of therapy. The literature is full of attempts to show that all psychotherapy could be understood as a learning, or, if you please, an unlearning, process. We prefer to show that they are different, that supervision is not a disguised form of psychotherapy. We believe that this can better be made clear if the supervisory process, though it is based on psychoanalytic personality theory, uses a language of its own. If technical concepts can be used more specifically and appropriately, certain problems of clinical teaching and learning can be thereby clarified.

II / Administration and Learning

> Government is itself an art, one of the subtlest of the arts. It is neither business, nor technology, nor applied science. It is the art of making men live together in peace and with reasonable happiness. Among the instruments for governing are organization, technological skill, and scientific methods. But they are all instruments, not ends. And that is why the art of governing has been achieved best by men to whom governing is itself a profession.—FELIX FRANKFURTER

The word *administration* embraces a wide range of meanings which reflect the historic development of different administrative forms varying from concern with the execution of the functions of government to the execution of the will of a deceased person.

Clarification of the meaning of the word administration in any given setting necessitates knowledge of the nature of the program that is to be administered, of the extent of the responsibility and the authority delegated to the person or to the group charged with the task of administration, and of the social situation which limits and supports those who are to execute the program. Furthermore, the administration is anchored not only in the task set for it, in the limits set by those who delegate specific powers to the administrator, but also in the particular personality of the administrator, in his interpretation of his function, in the arbitrary or democratic use of the power that is entrusted to him, in the creativeness of the leadership which he is able to offer. Each of the many possible concepts of administration can represent the model according to which the administration of a clinical setting can be carried out.

In a clinical teaching center, administration is always a complex and multifold function, whose nature cannot easily be delineated, particularly if we wish to derive our portrayal from a consideration of real settings rather than from an ideal definition that only hides the true problems behind overidealizing clichés.

The nature of hospital administration is in a continual process of change, and this holds particularly true for psychiatric settings, because of the many rapid changes they have undergone in recent years. In the old-fashioned state hospital, the superintendent was the undisputed ruler over the hospital community; the existing hierarchical structure facilitated orders reaching down to the lowest echelon, often quite efficiently, but rarely permitted complaints and suggestions to come through to the top, unless one of the occasional scandals broke into public print and perhaps forced the overthrow of the hospital ruler. The feelings of opposition aroused by such authoritarian hospital systems often kept their opponents, especially in moments of stress, from seeing administration as in any way a necessary, much less a highly useful, function. It is true that the social usefulness of the kind of one-sided hierarchical structure that was natural to the nineteenth century hospital can always be debunked by pointing out that some administrators misused the power and authority delegated to them through their appointment by state governments, which in turn were elected by the people. But the misuse of administrative function is not by itself proof that a certain administrative structure should not be used, since any structure allows certain misuses along with the advantages it provides. It is true, of course, that each kind of structure will attract certain personalities who are willing and interested to become administrators within it, sensing that it might meet inner needs they have in organizing their interpersonal relationships, and that certain kinds of structures are more readily turned to personal advantage than others.

However, as long as hospital psychiatry was basically custodial psychiatry, without any very active treatment intent, it required mainly the basic skill of diagnosing patients in order to make proper disposition, to put them into appropriate kinds of wards, as it were, and to run an efficient and humane custodial program for them. The custodial type of patient care will satisfy certain kinds of people and is perhaps even best carried out within a paternalistic, hierarchical structure which—benevolent as it might be—basically looks at patients as eternal children who have to be taken care of, and at the staff as somewhat older children who are old enough to take care of the patients, but in turn must be properly taken care of. Sometimes the patients (and at times even the staff) were suspected, rightly or wrongly, of rebellious intent, and the system usually permitted the administrators to use measures necessary for the maintenance of a docile hospital community. Closed wards, isolation rooms, strait jackets, and such therapeutic devices as hydrotherapy or sedation, could then be used to keep the system quiet whenever any part of the population tended to get out of hand. The administrator's greatest pride might have lain in administering the program at the least cost to the taxpayer. Such a system usually fosters the permanence of hospitalization and of maintained regression, and its administrator must be a unique personality indeed to manifest the psychological stamina which such a task imposes on him—or to enjoy such an interpretation of administration.

There are still many islands of this spirit left, a spirit which considered patients to be essentially hopeless and to be separated from the main body of the wider community. This viewpoint is still embodied in the legal barriers requiring that state hospital buildings be outside the limits of metropolitan areas. But in the main this attitude has changed, and, as we have developed programs for psychiatric treatment even of those who until recently have been considered almost hopeless, our concept of the proper administration of psychiatric clinical centers has changed decisively. The best hospital administrator of former times took care of mentally ill patients with humaneness—but without any real consideration that psychological change might be possible. He sheltered patients and helped them to be useful within the hospital setting. He did not believe in change and growth; he fostered research not about methods of treatment but about methods of classification and etiology. When one begins to think of patients as sick individuals who can change, interpersonal relationships are also seen as carriers of possibilities of change—from regressed and infantile reaction patterns on the part of the patients and from paternalistic reaction patterns on the part of the physicians to patterns which allow for growth to maturity and for equality. The administrator's basic attitudes toward his staff as well as toward the patient population of the hospital must therefore be different, as must also the administrative structure which makes possible the execution of the program which he fosters. A program which is basically oriented to change requires a concept of administration entirely different from the one useful to the custodial program.

This concept of dynamic administration is of increased importance if the clinical setting is dedicated not only to therapeutic service but also to training. The training requirement will inevitably bring students who are but beginners into active contact with all the aspects of the total clinical program, which will pose for the total setting all the various problems inherent in beginning. The students are, to a large extent, dependent; frequently they do not see their dependency on the teachers but struggle against authority as they struggle with their own inadequacies; often they express their struggle by giving a picture of professional and personal incompetence which makes one despair of their inherent capacities.

The administrator who administers a training program for students within a clinical setting must create conditions within which the goals of training as well as of getting people well can be carried on at the best level of quality and with a sense of responsibility that encompasses the student, the patient, and the social forces outside the clinical structure which support it and make it possible. Elsewhere we enlarge on the administrative problem encountered when, in addition to these functions, that of research is encompassed as well. For simplicity's sake, we will restrict our discussion in this chapter to the variety of administrative problems that develop in relation to the establishment of conditions in which the most effective learning of psychotherapy can go on with the simultaneous maintenance of the clinical safeguards necessary to insure the maximum service to the patient population.

In order to develop this problem of administration in relation to the learning of psychotherapy, we shall comment on a variety of administrative modes met in different settings in which psychotherapy is taught. We can take certain prototypical features from various administrators and enlarge them in such a way that they will caricature, more than accurately portray, the people who inspired us to think about the complicated problems of administration. In thus using magnified, exaggerated traits of these various administrators, we may reach an increased understanding of these problems.

Let us assume as our first example that the administrator of a particular clinical setting is one who, though dedicated to running his hospital effectively and with a maximum of hospital service to the patients, nevertheless feels that the learning students basically interfere with the smooth running of the hospital and is likewise unconvinced of the real effectiveness of psychotherapy. It could well be assumed that such an administrator has not much more confidence in the learning process than he has in the psychotherapeutic process. He might trust experience, and he might trust inherent talents which he somehow expects to discover in some of the members of his staff, but essentially he sees administration not as a dynamic process, but as a form of hierarchic government. He is, in fact, the more modern descendant of the administrator of the old-time custodial type of state hospital. This type of administrator usually knows what goes on in every part of his hospital, and perhaps checks in person on the services and on the various aspects of the hospital's functioning. If he is faced with the necessity of establishing some form of psychotherapy training, whether because of pressures from his staff, from the students, or from the social forces which impinge on his hospital, he will do this not as the leader of the program, but rather more in terms of making concessions to what seems to him the passing fashion of the day. We assume that he will do so fair-mindedly, but he will do it without genuine conviction; he will merely provide a climate that tolerates it and within which it must struggle to establish itself. If this is the administrator's philosophy, one may assume that those who belong to the next administrative level will probably think likewise—that they will be very careful before endorsing a training program which is so alien to the top administrator and about which they themselves have many mixed feelings.

In terms of the clinical rhombus which we have elaborated in the previous chapter, we then see a situation arise in which the prevalent administrative ideology would differ from the ideology of the supervisor and from the purposes and goals of patient and therapist, at least as far as the psychotherapy itself is concerned. It is, in such instances, a real question whether the psychotherapy training program could or should exist as a quasi-foreign body within the total clinical setting, and whether it might not create a situation in which the administration itself comes to be experienced by those who attempt to train in psychotherapy as a quasi-foreign body. If one were to do a sociological study in such a clinical center, one would find a situation in which the administration would appear to be walled off from the rest of the clinical body or, alternatively, where the psychotherapy training program would be walled off from the rest of the center. Either situation would not only foster constant tension states between the administration on the one hand and those who represent training in psychotherapy on the other but could well lead to more serious conflict situations stemming from these basic differences which, in the absence of a common ground of shared interest and understanding, would have no constructive solution.

Those who have a great investment in the psychotherapy training might try to safeguard it by keeping the training program small, unobtrusive, and out of sight (and consequently without much influence on the total setting). This training program would be as effective as a private social agency would be in trying to pit its resources against mass unemployment when the government had not created adequate public social services willing to do that which the small private agency at best could only demonstrate in a pilot way. Many large psychiatric centers, we believe, have to overcome just this attitude toward psychotherapy training. This attitude is not necessarily expressed in the special beliefs of the administrator, but may find expression more widely in the very actions of the setting, in its indifference or hostility, sometimes in its ignorance of the effective conditions for adequate psychotherapy training. The administrator himself may even be personally quite willing to attempt a psychotherapy training program and to give it vigorous support, but he may find conditions in the total social structure, in the kind of budget which the community is willing to provide, in the kind of staff he is able to hire, which would necessitate his playing the same role we have assigned to an administrator for whom this role is the core of his professional faith, as it were.

This particular administrator of whom we speak would most frequently be a rather paternalistic person who needs to exert ultimate control over everything; he would delegate authority rather as it is delegated in military or quasi-military organizations. Those of us working in such a clinical setting might often envision the solution of our dilemmas in the fantasy that the setting would be better off without such administration, or with one that pays no attention at all to what actually goes on in its midst.

Let us consider, then, an administrator who might fulfill this hope, who sees his function primarily in terms of favorable community relations, in the finding of adequate financial support for the necessary institutional building program, in participating in regional and national committees, and in doing those many aspects of psychiatric administration assigned to the role of the promoter in our near-ideal community. He might personally feel a lesser investment in the actual operation of the clinical setting itself, and might let the staff function to the best of its ability without intervening much unless a critical situation arises. For him, a critical situation would usually be one that might turn into a political embarrassment. This administrator would not fight training in psychotherapy, but neither would he support it. In terms of our clinical rhombus we would find that the corner of the rhombus which represents the administration is involved primarily with the outer world; consequently, it is clinically isolated from the rest of the organization and contributes little to its ongoing activity. The supervisor wishing to share with this administrator a critical problem concerning a student who perhaps ought to be discontinued in training, or transferred to some other supervisor, might find himself without effective administrative support. He could never establish binding regulations and requirements of the kind which could truly be used as guides for the training program and which would be given teeth by the backing of an informed administration. In fact, the supervisor would frequently feel that the success or failure of his work makes little actual difference to the administration. Whatever success teaching would enjoy in such an organization would come about without the creative help which administration could offer under the optimal conditions which imply an identification of the administrator with the aims of the training.

The danger of this type of administrative structure is twofold. There are some supervisors who will lose courage if not supported, and who will then soon lose their inherent value to the organization. They will do a routine job which will be basically uncreative, since they, too, need someone to look up to, someone by whom to be truly appreciated or helpfully criticized, someone to help them in critical situations as these arise, and someone to help their students when administrative intervention is indicated. Such a system will slowly but surely decrease in its general clinical effectiveness, lose its best staff, and attract less desirable types of students. As another danger, the effective supervisor might slowly become the rallying point of the professional and scientific ambitions of the institution and would soon be considered a power threat by the administration, regardless of how much the administration may wish to tolerate him, since he has become indispensable by virtue of the attraction he offers to staff and students alike. In both situations the integral unity of our clinical rhombus is critically undermined, and whatever training does go on in such an organization is rendered less effective.

The next situation to be discussed concerns the type of administrator who poses a serious problem for all of us who are dedicated to standards of professional competence. We are referring to the individual who undertakes to do administration for negative rather than positive reasons. He has tried himself in various branches of medicine and has perhaps entered psychiatry as a seeming refuge from the rigors of the other medical specialties. He may think of himself as not very effective in any of these efforts, and frequently a good many of his colleagues may agree with his secret feeling that he is a medical failure. Since he has difficulty in working directly with patients and therefore has never acquired the clinical skills which would make work interesting for him, he decides to go into administration. His occupational choice is then not a positive discovery, but rather a negative necessity. He may even have certain talents in administration, or experience may teach him many of the things one needs to know in order to run a program or an institution. A constant feeling of inferiority, though, puts him into a very strange relationship with those who conduct direct training and who are immersed in clinical work or in research. He constantly compares himself with all these, and his own support of the training program will be passive and submissive, carried as it is by a sense of negative identity ("since I can't do any of these, I administer"). This sense of inadequacy will make it very difficult for him to be the positive fourth corner in the clinical rhombus and, although he will secretly admire those who work under him, he will not be able to truly support them, since he doubts his own leadership and thus will soon create doubts in those who ought to be able to look to him for help.

As the psychiatric profession begins to offer specialized training in psychiatric administration and tries thereby to wipe out the vestiges of this disparaging attitude toward administration in its own midst, this kind of administrative complication is apt to appear less frequently. However, though the extreme instance may fortunately become rare, evidences of these feelings are so widespread and so taken for granted that an outstanding (and successful) administrator whom we know did not feel that there was anything incongruous when he said, in evaluating the work of one of his own staff physicians, "He does so poorly at his hospital work and his psychotherapy, and seems so unable to learn, that I think he ought to be encouraged to get out of it, and go into administration or something." It is precisely this social prejudice, that administration is a refuge for the incompetents, that the able administrator must overcome if he is to perform his own task effectively and with respect.

This brings us to yet another type of administrator whose primary respect and identification is with administration as a process. The extreme of this position is the thesis that any lay administrator could run the type of program which we have in mind. If he were but adequately trained in administration, and if he thoroughly understood the administrative process, then he could administer almost any program, and almost without regard to its specific content. The truth of the matter, of course, is that regardless of the program, certain principles and problems of administration would be alike or would show a great many similarities whether the administration were that of a hospital, a factory, a university, or a governmental agency. Based on this premise, it has become commonplace to hire large-scale administrators almost without regard to the type of program which they had previously administered. The current social phenomenon of retired generals who assume major administrative functions in government or in giant industries is a case in point (though this has, of course, other roots as well).

However, if such a "lay administrator," who is trained in general administration but not in medicine, and is therefore without identification with the professional and scientific purpose of the organization, and without special psychiatric conviction, were to come into a clinical setting such as the one that we have in mind, his administration would instantly create problems in the area of psychotherapy training. His first identification would be with the maintenance of the organization, but since he has no direct professional convictions, he would tend to see this in terms of maintaining the equilibrium of the organization, an equilibrium between the different social forces which push toward the fulfillment of their specific interests. He would see this, however, in terms of compromising in accord with the relative strengths of the different component interests, rather than in terms of approximating as closely as possible to the professional purpose and professional ideals of the organization. Such an administrator would state that above all he wants to get the staff working together, that he is not interested in the specific technical problems which he professes not to understand, that these are up to the staff. While he would therefore offer leadership as far as peacemaking is concerned, the working out of compromises, the establishment of work security, benefits for the staff and the like, he would not offer scientific and professional direction. His administrative skill would be truly useful only if subordinated to a type of professional leadership which is clear in purpose, which knows its goals and which offers the staff a set of scientific and professional convictions. We must not assume incidentally that this administrative type is restricted to the "lay administrator," since many physician administrators likewise see their chief administrative function as that of reconciling staff pressures and resolving staff conflicts, without interposing any organized convictions of their own as to the desirable direction such resolutions should take. Where the staff has many strong-willed individuals, this is often the easiest administrative path.

Another and last type of administrator to be considered, more frequently encountered than anyone might suspect, is the kind of individual who cannot limit his administrative function, but must actively intervene and do everything himself. He cannot truly delegate responsibility and authority, although he frequently might be willing to delegate the responsibility without the authority. He would function best in a small setting where he could be the administrator, the teacher, the main clinician, and the community relations expert—the main spokesman for the organization, inside and outside. He would be like the father who runs his family, his business and his life according to the motto: "Father knows best." In a larger training organization, such a person would soon run into difficulties, since he could not truly represent administration, but would want to see himself identified directly with every other function, and could not draw the line between his own function and that of others. He would frequently have to demonstrate that "everything you can do, I can do better," and in order to remain successful would need to surround himself with a mediocre staff that prefers this father type of administrator.

The administrators we have described are largely caricatures, having exaggerated aspects of people in administration whom we have observed or heard about indirectly. If we were to select the qualities that make for an administrator who could administer a psychotherapy training program effectively within a clinical setting, we would demand of him personal maturity, integrity, humility, high professional skill, and a sustained capacity for leadership. We would expect him to "administer" a program, rather than "boss" a group of people. We would expect him to be identified with psychotherapy, understand its purposes and basic skills, and be willing to support such a program of training in integration with the rest of the clinical services which the setting offers. We would not want him simply to tolerate the psychotherapy training program, and we certainly could not work with him if he were to fight it; rather, we would want him to feel this program to be an integral part of his over-all clinical philosophy.

We would not want him to be merely a clinical politician or public relations expert, but to be identified with the clinical functions of the setting itself. In other words, we would not want him to espouse the kind of administration that leaves the staff alone, but rather to work together with the staff, and particularly with the supervisors of the training program. We would want him to be able to delegate authority, as well as responsibility; we would not want him to be merely someone who is identified with "administrative process," with keeping a group of people in harmony regardless of discordant purposes. We would want him to offer creative professional leadership rather than to function simply as an arbiter of conflicting social forces within the clinical community.

What would this ideal administrator need to do for the psychotherapy training program? He would carry the final responsibility and authority for this program. This would include the responsibility both of setting the goals and of establishing the limits of the program, and of promoting the highest standards of training and of clinical service that are then possible. One can perhaps visualize the exercise of this administrative function, characterized through the corner A of our clinical rhombus, if one relates this function to the other corners of the clinical setting. It is desirable to stress at this point that this function of the administrator, while usually resting so far as the final authority is concerned in the hands of one person, will most frequently be distributed among a number of people who exercise a variety of administrative functions within the larger clinical setting. For example, if we think of a large psychiatric hospital in which the therapeutic program includes, of course, more than psychotherapy, we realize fully that that aspect of the administration which is concerned with psychotherapy services and psychotherapy training, as well as the integration of these services with the rest of the training program and the rest of the hospital program, might well be delegated to a clinical director or the chairman of a psychotherapy board. But whatever delegation of duties takes place, we would still need to visualize a unified administration, where it might be possible to trace whatever we talk about back to the top administrator.

The function of this administrator, as we see him in relation to the clinical rhombus, would actually be threefold. He would need to protect the patient, the student-therapist, and the supervisor. This protection, perhaps an imperfect word for what we aim to describe, would require the establishment of a clinical environment in which each of the three could carry out his role, be it the patient who needs help, the student who offers a therapeutic service to the patient and who himself needs to be taught by the supervisor, or the supervisor who himself needs help in order to carry out his training function. The administrator would be responsible for the establishment of an environment in which there is maximum security for each of these roles, or tasks—that of getting well, that of treating while learning a skill, and that of teaching a skill while supervising the clinical work.

In creating such an atmosphere, the administrator would be executing an administrative philosophy in which the highest function of administration is in the service it renders to the individuals being administered (rather than the distortion of administration represented by the reverse situation in which the individuals only serve the needs of the administration). In carrying out these tasks, the administrator would not see himself simply as the special defender of one or the other corner of the clinical rhombus. No sooner does he become overidentified with any one of these roles than he fails in his over-all task. If he sees only the needs of the patients, he will hardly be helpful in establishing a training program and training philosophy. If he is overidentified with the students and constantly protects them for one reason or the other, he will allow clinical irresponsibility and will undermine the training efforts. If he is authority-bound and sees his only function as backing up the supervisor, right or wrong, he will fail to protect adequately the carriers of the two other roles. That administrator will be most helpful to the entire organization who can maintain himself equidistant from each of the functions described.

However, the correct delegation of authority and of responsibility will lead to a situation in which his most direct contact will be with those staff members, the group of supervisors, who carry out administrative functions with him, and who carry as well the main teaching functions. He may, therefore, often feel that his job will be easier if he backs them unreservedly and becomes an unswerving supporter of their authority, rather than if he finds a way that reflects a dynamic approach to administrative problems. Whenever the supervisor comes for help to the administrator, for example when he feels that he has certain problems with a student and therefore wants administrative backing, the administrator must learn to have his ears psychologically attuned to the real problem that the supervisor is having. The automatic espousal of the supervisor's position frequently means no more than taking the problem out of the supervisor's hands, "backing him up," as it were. In so doing, the administrator may inadvertently weaken the very supervisory authority that he wishes to reinforce, since the supervisor may then be in the position himself of seeming too weak to cope with the difficulty, except by calling on the administrator. The administrator should keep in mind that there is usually more than one side to the story; and rather than permit the supervisor simply to externalize the problem, he should, with tact, help the supervisor look for the cause of the trouble. There are administrators who, whenever supervisors are attacked, blindly come to their rescue, as though they had no other administrative capacity than to use their authority to maintain the power structure.

Clinical authority can best be maintained if it remains helpful. It is only too easy to throw the blame for a problem that arises in clinical training onto the learner. Therapists are easily tempted to blame the patient for every failure in doing psychotherapeutic work, to describe the patient as not psychologically-minded, as "resistant" to psychotherapy, or poorly motivated. Rather than being process-oriented, this attitude is authoritarian and blind to the complex interacting aspects of failure. Similarly, the supervisor may find himself in the same boat as the psychotherapist. He may describe the student-therapist as resistant, as unwilling to learn, as "having a problem with authority," as one who cannot take help, and the like. While psychotherapists find it difficult to look at their countertransference problems and their lack of technical skills, supervisors find it equally difficult to look at the problems that they themselves have while teaching, while offering supervisory help. They, too, may have a problem with authority, even though it may concern their own authority, which they may not be able to maintain except through authoritarian devices and, if needed, through the added strength of the administrator who is to back up their decisions.

The administrator should look at the total complexity of interpersonal relationships as they are expressed in the interactions of the clinical rhombus; that is, he should at all times support the proper carrying out of each function, but not necessarily the person exercising that function. This, of course, includes not only an understanding of the relationship between patient and therapist, or between student and supervisor, but also between supervisor and administrator. The very problems that are reflected on the other levels may repeat themselves in the process between administrator and supervisor. Whatever the supervisor may tell about the student may very well reflect the problem that he himself is having with the administrator. The solution of his problem may assist him to offer better help to his students, to become a more effective clinical teacher, and to carry out better the administrative aspects of his teaching, which are to guarantee improved services to the patients.

The administrator usually has the function of reacting to the evaluation of the work of the student through the supervisor and at the same time of evaluating the teaching job of the supervisor and the carrying out of clinical and teaching responsibilities by the supervisor. The administrator will have the final authority, but should use it sparingly. The spirit of the law is more important than rigid adherence to its letter, and the flexible exercise of administrative authority will create a better general atmosphere in the clinical center.

Administrative function is tremendously important. Arbitrariness on the part of the administrator, inability to make decisions, going back on promises, lack of capacity to appreciate the actual work that is being done, inflexible use of regulations, and whatever other faults the administrator might show would instantly be transmitted throughout the clinical community and adversely affect the teaching function and the clinical function. On the other hand, if the administrator is reliable, steadfast, yet flexible and equidistant from the various social forces in the sense described, he will contribute to an atmosphere that permits maximum creativity and allows the teachers to develop in such a way that they will offer the best they can give under optimum conditions. This in turn will be reflected in an enthusiastic, receptive group of students and a patient population that goes through the process of therapy with a minimum of pain and a maximum of therapeutic gain.

This is, however, not all that we expect from the administrator who administers a training program in psychotherapy. His training center, be it part of a hospital, a university, or a community clinic, will constantly face external problems. The functions of the training center will have to be explained to the board of directors, the community agencies that provide the funds, and the public at large which makes use of these services and must directly or indirectly maintain them. Such programs are not only under constant demand, but also under constant pressure and sometimes direct attack. The administrative function has the additional task of mediating these pressures and demands. A good many administrators find themselves so overwhelmed by these outer tasks that they lose touch with the inner professional community. Our expectation of the ideal administrator would be that his own investment would be equally distributed over these different tasks and that he could remain the living link between the professional community and the community at large.

Rare indeed would be the man who could meet all the requirements that we have suggested as essential for the administrator. Someone, to whom we described what we expected of the administrator of a clinical training program, asked us cynically just why we thought an individual who could be this kind of "ideal administrator" that we envision would want to go into administration. And if he did, our critic wondered, could he truly distribute equally his time and interest among responsibilities toward the welfare of the patients, the training of the students, the teaching of the supervisors, and the relationship between this total professional community and the general community outside? Our critic spoke of administrators who exploit the clinical setting for their own advancement—who see in "their" staff tools for programs leading to political power rather than to improved service. How many administrators are there, our critic continued, who can think in terms of staff development, with an objective attitude toward the staff, and be able to identify in part with the needs of each individual member?

It must be said in defense of administrators that, like the students and like the supervisors in the clinical setting, they, too, go through a process of growth, a process in which these stages our critic mentioned will be aspects of their problems in adjusting and in adapting to the multifold tasks of modern administration. As their maturity, their skill, and their devotion develop, they might go through different phases of administration, and they might interpret their function in different ways which will reflect their growing strength or, perhaps also occasionally, aspects of their weakness which cannot be changed. There must be ideal roles for administrators, too, and frequently they may wonder themselves as to how they can move toward the ideal they have in mind. Nor should we forget that all these functions are carried by human beings under shifting outer and inner pressures, so that even under optimal conditions actual performance will be uneven.

To best describe the quandary of an individual who tries to fulfill our requirements for the ideal administrator, we will assume that he has the following dream, which takes its theme from one of the stories in *The Phantasies of a Realist* by the Austrian philosopher, Popper-Lynkeus. According to Freud, Popper-Lynkeus clearly understood the secret of the dream and its function of resolving internal struggle.

The king returns victoriously from war and rides at the head of his army through the streets of his capital. The band preceding the troops plays martial tunes. The population is jubilant, and everyone marches in step together with the troops to the sound of the drums. Even the horse of the king cannot resist the power of the rhythm. As the king watches the masses it seems that everybody walks in step. As the king reflects upon this, wondering about his power, many thoughts occur to him. But suddenly he notices a man among those who march, a man who is entirely out of step with the others and is falling more and more behind them.

The king is actually glad to notice this and he asks one of his officers to fetch the man to his palace. He speaks to this man and tells him that he had never seen a stronger man than he. He tells him that he had observed him at the parade and noticed how—regardless of the king or the troops or the powerful pull of the music—he nevertheless went on in his own way, while ten thousand others walked behind the king like automatons. The king states that he has never seen such a man and wonders how one accomplishes this. The man answers: "I reflected and was lost with my thoughts, and it was reflection which offered the strength to me." But then as an afterthought he adds that he himself is nothing in comparison to another man who has such inner strength that neither rain nor sun can make the slightest difference in his mind whenever he observes nature. If this man wishes it, then the sun remains sun for him, the moon remains moon, the fog remains fog, the mountain is but a mountain. None of them have any language by means of which they can speak to him and alter his mood.

The king wants to see this man, but is told that he has built a high wall around himself. But then the wise man who had walked out of step continues: "But even that man does not have the greatest strength known. He is not able to have a truly equal interest in all people regardless of whether they are beautiful or ugly; and this only one man could accomplish up to this day without delusional help."

The king asks who this man was and what happened to him. Our wise man answers: "Beyond the Gobi Desert once lived Kung-fu-tse. He gave the wisest counsel to the aristocratic leaders of his kingdom, but they did not want to listen to his urging to improve the lot of man and to make him happier. He was accused of just looking out for his own advantage. Thus Kung-fu-tse died as an old man in misery and poverty."

When he hears this, the king throws himself down on his carpet and cries.

With this dream, our administrator thus tries to review the success of his endeavors. As long as he uses his administrative power like the king who comes home from a victorious war, and as long as he insists that all keep in step with him, he falls victim of his own administrative rigidity, since he likewise must keep exactly in step with them. His administration, rather than being concerned with the welfare of those who are entrusted to him, is merely built on the use of power in which everybody else who is "ruled" by him must give up his own individuality and must be in step with the powers that be.

As he wonders about other possible administrative roles that he might take, he starts to admire the man who dares to be out of step, and even to play with the idea that he might allow himself also to be out of step and thus to create a different kind of administrative structure, one which permits him to reflect, to listen to himself, and to support a clinical setting in which similar rights and opportunities are given to the others as well. He finds then, however, that such total self-absorption, if completely out of step, results in his being totally isolated and walled off, as expressed in the story of the man who does not permit his life or his thinking to be influenced by rain or sun, by the moon, the fog, or the mountains; that is, he is out of contact with his fellow men.

These two extremes, the one of being in constant contact with his fellow men but at the cost of destroying all individuality through insisting on their all "being in step," and the one where the administrator finds his freedom by surrounding himself with a wall which then cuts him off from the staff, from his other tasks (though it does leave him alone with his free reflections), are then overcome by a third version of administration.

The wisest man of all "beyond the Gobi Desert" sees his task as the acceptance of everyone within his setting, regardless of whether he is beautiful or ugly, whether he needs help or whether he could contribute more power to the wise man. This attitude toward the staff, the students, the patients, and the community, fails at one crucial point. It disregards the self-protective function of making sure that the administrator remains in power. It is for this reason that Popper-Lynkeus' fantasy, or our administrator's dream, ends with an attack on the wise man. It was not believed that he wanted to perform a function unselfishly, constructively, and in the service of others. A failing dream is not necessarily a prediction as to how things will work out, and in fact is frequently no more than the nighttime expression of the conscience which in waking life expresses itself as the integrity which can bring success.

Let us assume this dream then to be a crisis dream, in which the administrator reviews the different roles that he can play as he tries to administer a program, and in which he sees the difficulties that he is up against as he attempts to grow from a merely paternalistic and authoritarian form of administrating through a process of reflection, at first lonesome and perhaps unproductive, finally to reach a form of administration that is equidistant from different forces and different people, accepting all equally and without selfish, power-enhancing forms of conduct. Such ideal ways of administration are possible, of course, only if the administrator finds himself in a more ideal work situation than that surrounding the wise man "beyond the Gobi Desert"; a situation where, instead of being driven out by the community that does not understand him and that is not yet mature enough to back him, he can indeed get the support he needs.

We must keep in mind that it is the community at large that selects the administrator, pays him, orders him, wants him to be a certain type, supports him, fails him, or fires him. Immaturity in the administrator will frequently be reflected also in those who support him, or help him, or force him to be different. Different social settings attract different types of administrators, and each setting has the kind of administrator it deserves. The ideal qualities we ask for in our administrator make sense only if we go beyond the personal problems, beyond the psychology of the administrator himself to those aspects which are absolutely essential in order for him to function well. Just as we cannot visualize, for example, that our type of psychotherapy could really be utilized in a totalitarian country, we cannot visualize that the administrator we are seeking to develop can become a mass type, typical for all of our settings; rather he should be an exceptional leader who can be attracted and maintained, trained and developed only in settings that are suitable for this task.

For this reason we must concern ourselves also with the features of the institutional setting which the administrator must be capable of developing, the structure which he must devise, and which must be supported by the social forces that delegate the power to him, if we want to fully understand under what conditions modern training in psychotherapy can be carried out. Structural arrangements are the underpinning necessary in order to permit the administrator, the supervisor, the student and the patient to carry out their respective roles. Two excellent chess players need their chessboard and need the chess rules in order to make use of their inner capacities. If they had to play without the board and against external pressures which constantly force them to change the rules and to confuse the definitions of the chess pieces, they could scarcely play the game at all. Our question then in the next chapter concerns the nature of the structure to be developed, the nature of the equivalent of the chessboard and chess rules in a training program for psychotherapists.

III / *The Clinical Setting and Its Structure*

Now let us assume that by some kind of organization we were able to increase our numbers to an extent sufficient for treating large masses of people. Then on the other hand, one may reasonably expect that at some time or other the conscience of the community will awake and admonish it that the poor man has just as much right to help for his mind as he now has to the surgeon's means of saving life; and that the neuroses menace the health of a people no less than tuberculosis, and can be left as little as the latter to the feeble handling of individuals. Then clinics and consultation-departments will be built, to which analytically trained physicians will be appointed, so that the men who would otherwise give way to drink, the women who have nearly succumbed under their burden of privations, the children for whom there is no choice but running wild or neurosis, may be made by analysis able to resist and able to do something in the world. This treatment will be free. It may be a long time before the State regards this as an urgent duty. Present conditions may delay its arrival even longer; probably these institutions will first be started by private beneficence; some time or other, however, it must come.—SIGMUND FREUD

Formal training in psychotherapy usually takes place within a clinical setting. Such settings vary widely in scope and in function; they range through closed and open institutions, residential and outpatient treatment centers, private sanitaria and public hospitals. Each has its own customs, rules, physical arrangements, and spirit that together constitute what we call its structure. The word structure usually implies something fixed and rigid, the permanent strength of the edifice itself. One can conceive of structure, however, as more flexible and variable, the basic set of arrangements that govern the operations of the organization, subject to change as functions and needs shift. In this sense structure is a living reality that carries psychological implications and consequences. The table of organization of the clinical setting is of real significance only as it reflects the inner psychological situation of each participant member of the organization. The strength of the clinical structure does not depend simply upon written rules, clear definitions of functions, stated requirements, or the comprehensiveness of the training and clinical operations, but rather upon the acceptance of these arrangements as statements of psychological realities that guide those who work within their framework.

These psychological meanings and consequences of structure depend not only on the present configurations, but also on how these came into being and how they evolved in constant interaction with the social pressures that helped to mold and limit them. Structure thus embodies the inner psychic problems and solutions, both of those who have created it and those who currently live by it, use it, and interpret it. Even the most inflexible aspect of a given institutional structure, the physical plant itself, expresses the treatment philosophy of those who planned and built it. This recognition has led to the plea that hospital architects should build for a generation rather than a century, so that the treatment assumptions and prejudices of one generation of administrators will not become the strait jackets of their successors.

In studying then, for each clinical setting, the organization and the functions of each of the nodal points of our schematic clinical rhombus, we inevitably interest ourselves not only in the defined nature of the setting and the prerequisites and obligations of those who participate in it at every point, but in the psychological meanings of each of these requirements and privileges as well. We can illustrate our concept of structure best perhaps through the process of historic growth, if we face the reader with the problems encountered when we create de novo an elaborated clinical setting with a psychotherapy program and a training program as well. Two special advantages inhere in this developmental approach. One is the avoidance of the kind of description of structure found in the catalogue of the training center with its stratifications of presumed ideal courses and training facilities, seemingly already fixed in the best possible series of arrangements. Who can truly appreciate the nature of the teaching and learning experience in a training center after having studied its catalogue? The second advantage is that in showing structure in process of formation, one can see more clearly the psychological and social conditions from which it derives and the meanings which flow from it, before these become obscured with time as the structure itself tends to become frozen and as the original conditions which gave rise to it slowly shift and seal over. At this later point the structure is there, a gift from the wisdom of one's predecessors (as proudly stated with an eye to public relations in the training center's catalogue) that has now become a ritual, to be taken more on faith than freshly thought out in terms of its meaning for today. We are not interested in the ritual of structure that develops but in its inner psychological significance, including the meaning of the ritualistic aspects of clinical training and service organizations.

Let us imagine we have a well-trained and dedicated hospital administrator who comes into a new setting and who automatically thereby fills out one corner of the clinical rhombus. His problem if he wishes to introduce a clinical and training program in psychotherapy is how to fill out the other three corners in the best ways that he can, to guarantee the right people in each spot, and to work out the channels of relationship among them so that he provides a structure that guarantees the kind of atmosphere within which therapeutic and training problems can be seen, can be tackled, and hopefully resolved. In doing this he will discover of course that he by no means has an entirely free hand. The kind of clinical rhombus that he can create is to begin with a function of the social reality within which he operates.

The first problem is a power problem: What is the prevailing political policy and climate and what will it back up? Only after such problems are resolved can the administrator concern himself with the technical problems of rendering clinical service and imparting technical skills. He is dependent on the level of the budget given to him by the state legislature or by his governing board. He must take into account the existing standards of medical and psychiatric practice in the particular community in which he functions. He cannot go far beyond the general level of all other aspects of his hospital treatment program. He must adjust his program to the skills and prior backgrounds of both his staff and his students, and finally, his psychotherapy program will depend on the nature of his patient population and the kind of treatment program that the community at large will both tolerate and support. For example, how active a treatment program for delinquent adolescents will the community tolerate if this involves a calculated risk of antisocial and destructive behavior spilling out into community depredations, and to what extent will the community support this program with adequate foster home placement facilities?

The organization of the psychotherapy training program within the institution would likewise depend on other treatment facilities outside the institution. For example, the problems would be entirely different if the psychotherapy training is to be in conjunction with or near a psychoanalytic center where analytic training is also possible and where some of the teachers can perhaps be drawn from the analytic setting, or whether the psychotherapy training must take place in an isolated state hospital, physically remote from either the practice of psychoanalysis or from close contact with the broad stream of general psychiatry.

As we envision such an administrator, we may place him for the sake of the historical development we wish to follow into a hospital that is organized and run in a humane and eclectic tradition. Let us assume that the previous administration stood for a "democratic" point of view, which was reflected organizationally in a minimum of centralized responsibility and the more or less autonomous and individualistic functioning of a staff of variously trained but all well-intentioned doctors, each doing the best job of which he was capable. The previous administrator may have seen his chief function in the employment of the best staff that he could possibly get and in giving each of them maximum freedom for individual expression and creative experimentation, confident thereby that his patients would be getting the best service that his setting could provide. The staff—and the students—in such a setting would of course have differing theoretical convictions and identifications, different levels of skill, and varying kinds of interests in the fields of therapy, of training, and of research.

Actually, each professional person would create an island of his own, a philosophy which is found so frequently in the university tradition, and he might have followers among the student body and thus create his own little school. The old administrator, whom we consider fair and protective of all these different interests, would never permit any one staff man to develop too strong a school of thought or too active a body of adherents which might be experienced as a threat by the rest of the group. The common eclectic philosophy, the fairness, and the "live and let live" atmosphere would, however, not represent a common treatment philosophy nor could it allow the development of a training program in which such a treatment philosophy could be taught. As we describe our own fantasied experiment, we must keep in mind that many of the large psychiatric settings in our country follow just the tradition we have been describing, and we can begin to realize that the new administrator who is dedicated to the proposition that clinical service to patients hinges on a common treatment and training philosophy will indeed meet with many difficulties.

He would of course find many assets in the setting, for whose administration he is now responsible. He would notice that the staff shared a humane attitude toward mental illness and a basic acceptance of psychiatric patients as suffering human beings whom one tries to help. He would be aware of the staff's full assumption of both medical and social responsibility, including, that is, responsibility for the housing, the food, and the recreational activities of the patients as well as their medical care. Since there is, however, no unifying theoretical or even pragmatic treatment philosophy, the hospital is not an organized therapeutic community. Our new administrator would notice that each staff member is in effect the administrator of his own small hospital, perhaps a ward or two, and that there is a minimum of binding group decisions. Excellent therapeutic experiments might be going on here or there, but organized and unified in-service training as well as residency training would be absent. The development of the skills of students in such a situation would usually be a matter of incidental and private master-apprentice relationships among some of the interested staff members who see in teaching an individual responsibility toward the student or resident. The fate of the student in this setting would depend on a combination of initiative and luck. He could perhaps manipulate to get good or bad teaching assignments depending on the relative strengths of his wish to learn and his need to avoid.

In such a hospital neither the leadership nor the group has been identified with an organized set of psychotherapeutic principles. Formal psychotherapy has been rather just one of the many experiments such a hospital could offer. In most cases there would not yet be an attached outpatient facility. This hospital nonetheless would be meeting many social needs posed by its large patient population and would thus be offering a valuable contribution to the community. In terms of training in psychotherapeutic skills and in developing a psychotherapeutic point of view toward patients, such a hospital is, however, quite inadequate, and it is to this condition that the new administrator desires to bring the organization of psychotherapy training exemplified in our clinical rhombus.

All of the above description of the basic hospital setting describes it at its best, with many of the advantages of the well-run hospital. The new administrator may feel quite happy about his new function in spite of the difficulties he will face, and quite grateful to the old administration for the transformation of the institution from one devoted only to the most minimal standards of custodial care to its present modern and humane level of functioning. The new administrator himself, in a previous position, had attempted the well-nigh hopeless job of rehabilitating a "snake-pit" against political pressures which stemmed from social forces that were without insight into the nature of mental illness and as yet opposed to reform.

Our administrator has set himself the task of organizing a clinical and training program built around his belief that for the patients to get the best possible treatment, a psychodynamic orientation must be a central and integral part of the total treatment program, the basic core of the treatment philosophy of the individual staff members as well as the unifying philosophy for the whole institution. He sees formal psychotherapy as an essential function rather than as an additional luxury, and he wants to bring in this psychotherapeutic orientation with supervision and in-service training for both students and staff without, however, undercutting any of the other values that the institution has developed and stood for.

In doing this he faces a variety of problems. The first one would be to fill in the corner of the clinical rhombus that represents the supervisors. Who are they to be and how is he to choose them? What requirements is he to set up for admission to this group and what sort of training should be prerequisite? The administrator can, of course, bring in outside consultants of established reputation and superior skill as psychotherapists and as teachers, say, from the staff of a nearby medical school department of psychiatry or an analytic training center. He will certainly wish to avail himself of such consultant service, but it would be a serious question if he should entrust the bulk of supervisory responsibilities more than temporarily to such consultants. The problems are multiple. Rivalrous tensions will inevitably be engendered between the outside consultants and his own staff, and the development of his own staff members in the acquisition of psychotherapeutic and supervisory skill will be unnecessarily delayed or even prevented. If he were to start with a very weak staff, he may have no other choice.

An alternative and administratively perhaps wiser decision would be to designate all or at least the more senior group of his permanent staff members as supervisors and to use the consultants to help this supervisory group to develop its own skills as well as its supervisory techniques. This will create the first problem. In many training centers, it is assumed that someone who has acquired a certain degree of skill in psychotherapy itself is promoted (without further special training) to a supervisory position, as though supervisory skills develop automatically or are necessarily a function of psychotherapeutic skills. In a good many settings, the graduates of the three-year psychiatric residency program become staff members and very frequently are immediately called upon to take on supervisory responsibilities including the supervision of psychotherapy, which they themselves are still in the process of learning. The high status accorded the function of supervision facilitates the ready acceptance of this role, whatever the inner misgivings of the individual concerned. This premature "expertization" sometimes seems an inevitable consequence of the current rapid growth in psychiatric training programs. And yet we know that not every good clinician, regardless of his skill as a psychotherapist, is equally gifted in matters of training. The administrator's problem is one of setting up a structure that allows for the acquisition of teaching skills as well as the training of psychotherapists.

Our administrator chooses to select from among the most experienced staff members those who volunteer to be supervisors and to give them the opportunity to participate in a seminar in which supervisory techniques are discussed as well as to have individual conferences with expert consultants. In setting up this group of supervisors and in creating rules to govern the working of the group, certain repercussions soon appear. Not all of the members of the senior group will have the same theoretical identification with psychotherapy or with teaching and quite a number of them may be hesitant to join an endeavor in which inevitably the ideas and the techniques of each will be exposed to the eyes of the others. Just before the new administrator came each of them had had his own autonomous setup within the large hospital, and felt beyond criticism. It is helpful therefore if the administrator chooses to set the first group up as a voluntary association, as an opportunity offered those who have the stated prerequisites, such as a completed residency program and, preferably, a few years of actual practice in psychotherapy. While the attendance of this first group of supervisors depends on a voluntary decision, the administrator chooses to take time for this activity and he comes regularly to the group meetings as a symbol of his identification with the stated purposes and functions of this particular group.

In doing so he is mindful of another experience where the administrator allowed such a program of organized psychotherapy supervision to be set up, one which he himself never joined. Soon the supervisors as a group felt themselves at odds with the administrator, rather than the executors of functions delegated by the administrator. To the extent that the administrator's time was taken up with his efforts to deal with external social pressures, he could not identify with the efforts of the supervisors and felt himself caught between opposing inner and outer forces. In that setting, the tension in the line A–S of the clinical rhombus, which existed from the very beginning, made it very difficult to develop the other interlocking aspects of the organizations that the administrator had personally hoped to foster.

In the setting we are now describing and dependent of course on the skill with which the group itself is led and taught, all the eligible staff members begin to participate, after varying intervals. The formula "you can come if you wish" has led to complete voluntary adherence. But the following year, after the group has itself acquired a group cohesiveness and some common body of convictions and skill, it is confronted with the expectation of admission of newly appointed junior staff members, freshly graduated from residency ranks.

The administrator now observes an interesting development. The debate that rages centers around the question as to whether the supervisory group shall admit to its ranks the newcomers to the staff, so junior in experience. Some feel that these newcomers who have not struggled through the issues with which they themselves were occupied during the preceding year would dilute what has been done thus far, and would force the group back to a repetition of elementary issues. They would replace the original proposition: "You can come if you wish" with the new rule: "You can come only if we wish (allow)." In this, not personal, struggle over eligibility for membership, we see a newly developed concern with requirements and prerequisites for the supervisory group, the beginning of group structure. The first rules for the maintenance of standards are being made by the group and, as is frequently the case, are made to start with the newcomers, not with themselves. For themselves the rule is the exempting "grandfather clause." In part this has to do with the older group's guilt over their own too rapid assumption of supervisory authority. Just a year before they had been asked to assume supervisory roles overnight, and a good many of them had discovered during their year of work together that they only played the role of supervisor but had not as yet successfully lived it.

As is usual in such circumstances, social as well as psychological pressures dictate that the newcomers to the staff be sooner or later admitted to the group. They have in the meanwhile not been unaware of the controversy surrounding the question of their admission to the group. The administrator or the leader of the supervisory group may have explained the situation frankly to these newcomers. They may be told that they are welcome now though for a while the wish was to keep them out. The administrator does not necessarily share this point of view, but he identifies with the supervisory group because only in such identification with his senior staff does he help them to develop training requirements that are binding for all and that guarantee the improvement of training as well as treatment standards.

Having come this far, the group has consolidated a phase of its growth into an aspect of its governing structure. Having first made a rule concerning its own standards for admission (albeit a negative rule to apply only to new applicants and to keep out those who don't qualify), the group is now ready also to set up rules which make the functioning of this organization explicit to the students as well as to their patients. Up to this point, the students knew little about the functioning of the supervisory group and certainly not as a policy body making rules to govern the students' work. That is, the organization of function that we call structure diffuses outward. As the group makes rules for others—for the students, for the newcomers to the supervisory group—the group, without being aware of it at first, implicitly creates rules for its own functioning. When periodic evaluations are set up as measures of the adequacy of performance of the students, the supervisors thus create rules for their own participation in these evaluations which incidentally indirectly evaluate supervisory work as well.

Having taken the development of the supervisory group to this point, we can look now to another corner of the clinical rhombus—the T, or the therapists; that is, the students who are now designated as ready to engage in formal psychotherapy. For them, too, prerequisites must be established that represent on the one hand the aspirations of the leadership for the highest level of technical performance possible and that are on the other hand grounded in the existing social realities. What these requirements for formal psychotherapeutic work specifically will be will vary from one training center to another. They will depend on such variables as how highly organized a didactic curriculum exists with perhaps preliminary lecture courses, reading groups, and seminar discussions on the theoretical problems of psychopathology and psychotherapy; and on how much clinical experience in diagnostic work, in ward management, and in the use of a hospital environment is felt desirable to gather before embarking on the more specialized pursuit of specific psychotherapeutic skill as a formal discipline. The requirements for training (and the standards of training) will depend, too, on the therapeutic demands imposed by the needs of the over-all patient population, on the availability of a group of patients suitable for formal psychotherapy, and, last but not least, on the community's willingness to make funds and resources available for the development of such a program. Some communities, for example, may provide only brief and supportive psychotherapeutic services in their clinics, while other communities may stand ready to sponsor services which make intensive psychotherapy available to patients if and when needed. Such decisions as to the type of service that a community may be willing to render, and may endorse, will indeed influence training opportunities. These decisions of course reflect mutual interaction of the agency or institution and the supporting community. The readiness of a community to support a program of intensive therapeutic work depends in part at least on what the professional staff is able to show the community is important; on the effectiveness of the community education, in its best sense.

It is clear then that, in setting the highest attainable standards for its students, the supervisory group can only function effectively if its leadership accurately reflects the basic social reality. One could conceive, for example, of an administrator who would adhere to the ideal that each psychotherapist should have a personal analysis as one of the fundaments of his training. In most training centers today, to adhere strictly to such an ideal would be to frustrate the training program before it could ever get off the ground. The exact setting of the requirements for entrance into this special psychotherapy training becomes then an administrative decision based on a judicial, but not opportunistic, consideration of the relevant variables, both social realities and available training possibilities.

As an aspect of the prerequisites and requirements for embarking on psychotherapeutic work, the question of the varying professional backgrounds of those who are taught psychotherapy within such a setting becomes relevant. The conviction that the proper practice of psychotherapy represents a teachable body of skill acquired through a process of learning under supervision carries the corollary assumption that no formal degree or licensure itself guarantees psychotherapeutic skill. Skill in psychotherapy is something to be taught additional to other specific training, whether in psychiatry, in clinical psychology, in social work, or in other clinical professions. The social pressures that stem from the large needs of the patient body in such a hospital community encourage our administrator to be in favor of the widest dissemination of therapeutic skills. The protected medical and group nature of the setting makes it more likely that responsible training of the representatives of a number of disciplines can go on. For each such discipline, minimal acceptable standards of admission and performance must be set by the supervision group.

The administrator who takes such a stand on training issues may become subject to a variety of attacks. Certain physicians may conceive of psychotherapy as a purely medical activity, to be limited to duly trained psychiatrists. Certain clinical psychologists may resent the imposition of training restrictions and medical safeguards, preferring to exercise the prerogatives of free individual practice. In taking the training stand he does, our administrator of course assumes responsibility only for training and service functions in this particular institutional setting. These functions, and the standards which maintain them, are set within the context of the available clinical resources and of the particular social needs they are designed to meet. The administrator by these decisions does not attempt to enter into any of the wider issues—scientific, political and economic—involved in the questions as to who shall be in independent practice, under what conditions and safeguards, and with what training experiences. Rather he attempts, within the structure of his own setting, to provide the best treatment and training services that it is possible to set up, recognizing that today's knowledge is not broad enough and that today's social needs are too great to enable him to exclude potential contributors as clinicians, teachers, or researchers.

As soon as the psychotherapists have been selected for training, the supervisors must decide on what rules to set up to guide the clinical training program. The administrator noticed, of course, that during the first phases of the development of the psychotherapy and training program, when the supervisors accepted very few rules for themselves, they were not inclined to have many rules for their students either. They were at the beginning cautious in their exercise of the teaching function and afraid that the teacher's prerogative to criticize performance and ask for improvement would be felt by the student as a negative and hostile attack. The supervisors were too recently autonomous practitioners to be as yet at home in an organized structure with rules and standards, and so could not impose on their students what they themselves did not yet believe. Some rules they soon set, however: that each new therapist is to have but one case in detailed supervision at first; that he is to have one supervisory conference a week for discussion of that case with his supervisor; and that he is to submit detailed notes of his interviews with the patient as a basis for the supervision conference. Most other problems may be left open at this point. The supervisory group is perhaps not ready as yet to organize the sources for patients, to raise the problem as to who selects the patient, the supervisor or the student, as to how many patients the student ought to treat without supervision, and whether there should be rules for the continuation or discontinuation of training.

These latter questions, which are usually answered only in the second or third year of the functioning of such a supervisory group, will actually determine the fourth corner of our clinical rhombus, which represents the patient. Questions come up now as to which patients ought to be treated in individual psychotherapy and how they are to be chosen. Should the therapist select his own patients? That is, should he have a "free choice" and what would be the psychological consequences of such a free choice? And how are over-all medical responsibilities to the larger group of patients reconciled with the free choice by the student-therapist of whom he is to take into formal individual psychotherapy? Or, are the patients selected for the student or with him, by the supervisor or by the administrator?

It is interesting to note that in the development of psychotherapy training programs we frequently find the idea prevalent that the resident may select his own patients. This is usually the case when no formal training program in psychotherapy has yet developed and when but a few patients are individually treated, primarily to give the resident training experience and not because the setting has as yet adopted formal psychotherapy as an integral part of its total treatment program. This principle of "free choice" of patients is often strongly defended by the beginning psychotherapist and justified on the basis that to treat a patient psychotherapeutically, one must be able to "empathize" with him. In these beginning phases, psychotherapy is thus experienced very differently from other forms of medical treatment. The young surgeon would regard as most alien the idea that on a surgical service, rather than doing surgery where necessary (and under direction), that he be allowed to select his own interesting surgical case without regard for the needs of all the others. This does not necessarily reflect a cynical attitude to psychotherapy, however. It is rather an expression of the technical ignorance of the beginning psychotherapist. Before skill in it is acquired, psychotherapy is often not thought of as a serious treatment method. The beginning therapist therefore doesn't really feel that it makes much difference whether a particular patient is treated or not. Only as he develops psychotherapeutic skill does the student develop a psychotherapeutic conscience.

As the training program develops, our administrator will gradually guide his supervisory group toward a point of view in which patients will be selected according to their needs even though the student may at times see this as an imposition upon him rather than as a protection of his training status and a protection of his patients as well. Each of these rules will have psychological consequences which will be reflected in the problems that arise in individual supervision. Each rule, and even the explicit absence of a rule to cover a particular situation, represents an aspect of the structure governing the setting that has its psychological implications and that can be meaningfully worked with if these implications are clearly grasped.

In this sketch of a possible historical development we have followed the first steps in the various degrees of structuralization from the initial chaos, the eclectic hospital in which the staff and the students (the residents) each find their own ways, and make their own arrangements with patients and with each other, to a beginning orderliness, a beginning useful structure with a growing knowledge of the psychological consequences of each structural crystallization. As we followed the administrator, we have seen the initial step as a sort of "power struggle" in the newly created organized supervisory group, especially between the older and the newer, and over all the issues of admission, of status, and of prerogatives. Only as this struggle is settled, and a sense of responsibility for their own regulation develops among the supervisors, can energies be fruitfully directed outward toward the student body, who in turn can then be helped to develop a similar sense of responsibility toward their patients.

At the beginning much of what the student-therapist does with the patient will be self-protective and, at times, at the patient's expense, thus tending to undermine the whole treatment process. For example, a student faced with the need to study intensively and over a considerable timespan for important certifying examinations may all too easily play into one side of his patient's conflict about committing himself to a prolonged treatment situation with all its potential for change, which is both desired and feared, and tend to help the patient resolve this conflict in the direction of terminating treatment. For these reasons, concomitant with the rules needed to safeguard the students and the teaching process are the rules devised to protect the patients and the treatment process. Thus our clinical rhombus slowly takes on recognizable outlines, and out of the original anarchic situation emerge the rudiments of a training philosophy necessarily side by side with the rudiments of a treatment philosophy.

The further development and the full exploration of the psychological meanings inherent in each aspect of the rhombus (each corner and each interrelating line) will be the content of all the remaining chapters of this book. Here we can close on a note of caution: what we wish to convey is that structure is not a rigidly fixed set of arbitrary arrangements but rather something flexible, with a developmental history in the past and with constant possibility for change in the present as new psychological circumstances create new needs. Although when seen cross-sectionally at any point in time, divorced from its antecedent growth process, it may appear as a stabilized, "frozen" set of arrangements, it should never become so. When structure does in fact become frozen, or when it proceeds to the extreme of overstructuralization almost for its own sake, it no longer serves its original purposes but acts as a rigid restraint that stifles creativity in the name of tradition or of orderliness. There are examples of institutional settings which maintain permanent and inflexible hierarchical supervisory relationships in regard to each employee and at every level where supervision may ultimately become a stifling ritual rather than a helpful and creative endeavor.

We are committed to the view that structure itself is no more than the expression of an adapting, ever-changing, ongoing process which requires constant redefinition, constant clarification, and which must be used by a leadership attuned to the needs of the clinical community, to the needs of those who represent the different functions in our clinical rhombus. Our administrator must continue then to see his function as a dynamic one. His only tradition must be one that is oriented toward growth, toward development, toward exploration and experimentation, and he must free himself from the constant danger of stagnation and an identification with the status quo. We have invented then a rather ideal person, and there will be few in reality who will live up to the hero of our story. Thought models though are always ideal. Their relation to reality has to do with the opportunity which they offer toward the change of reality. They also may help us understand and measure the existing reality of a clinical setting and its training opportunities and find the levers toward its improvement.

IV / *Training for Research*

> . . . by its nature, it [Science] must prize the search above the discovery and the thinking (and with it the thinker) above the thought . . . the act of judging [is] more critical than the judgment.—J. BRONOWSKI

As we construct our hypothetical, ideal professional community, in order to gain some insight into the social structure of a clinical setting in which therapeutic functions are combined with those of training and research, we become aware of potential difficulties existing among the different groups that comprise such a community. Each group may at times feel unsupported and perhaps even opposed by the rest. Training and research functions especially may frequently appear as sharply dichotomized, as opposing wills that seemingly cannot be combined. The teachers may feel strongly that they are the carriers of tradition, of established and proven knowledge, who are to transmit this tradition and knowledge to the new generation and to enforce standards of theoretical and technical accomplishment through the giving or withholding of licenses for the future clinicians. The researchers on the other hand, out to devise new improved methods and to question the old ones, may appear as constant skeptics and doubters, as the destroyers of tradition and of the firm clinical basis which the teachers try so hard to establish.

The suggestion was made that an ideal professional community would develop teachers and researchers who would have respect for each other's functions, and rather than standing in each other's way, would supplement each other creatively. Ideally speaking, each teacher of psychotherapy conceivably might also have research interests, while those who are mainly occupied with research would not be without teaching responsibilities. Let us assume then, although even in the ideal community this will be only approximately true, that a mature generation of teachers and researchers are allied in their tasks and have essentially mastered the problem of properly integrating training and research functions.

What problems would this group of leaders face as they together participate in developing training in psychotherapy? This of course raises many questions concerning the available student material, their needs and wishes, as well as concerning the social obligations that the training program tries to fulfill. The vast social demands that are made today on the clinical professions, living proof of a new approach to the emotionally ill individual, require primarily a basic training in technical skills geared to meet these demands. We are tempted therefore to train technicians (technically skilled clinical workers) at a rapid speed and must constantly wonder about the requisite equipment which they will need in order to perform their tasks competently. These social pressures tend to force us into the creation of "trade" schools rather than "professional" schools. These pressures are reinforced, too, from the side of the student group undergoing a costly and prolonged specialty training at a time in life when the need to set up a family and to establish a secure earning power vies with this wish to achieve specialized professional skills. Both social pressures and student pressures will operate therefore to turn us into teachers who satisfactorily meet the basic requirements of professional training, who train competent technicians, and yet who never set into motion the type of training necessary for developing research in the field of psychotherapy.

In addition to the demand that is placed upon us by society and by students who have remained students at a time when others are fully established in the economic world, we must also face other limiting facts of life. One of these has to do with the natural limitations of individual creative endowment which one will find in any large student population, and which will tend to push the teachers into the leveling direction of paying most attention to the needs of the larger group of average students, thus encouraging a technological orientation toward the entire training program. Another fact of clinical life, perhaps even more serious, has to do with the difficulty of teaching psychotherapy in such a way that not only are basic techniques taught, but that curiosity and research spirit are encouraged, are reinforced, and indeed are a part of the teaching atmosphere.

Let us assume then that we have overcome the social pressures from all sides, that we can deal successfully with the political aspects of the problem and confront ourselves only with the technical difficulties that will arise when such training proceeds in an optimal atmosphere, one which encourages us to combine training for psychotherapy with training for research. We think then of a type of professional training that freely permits its students a range of choices. Basic to the freedom of choice would be the absence of any inherent value system. To be a researcher is not necessarily better than to be a clinician, nor the reverse. Each—researcher and clinician—may be making a different and complementary contribution to the whole body of scientific work. The supervisor's goal should be to help each student explore and define the degree of choice available to him. Whichever pathway the student ultimately chooses, whether from inclination or inherent limitations, it should not be with an unnecessary inferiority complex, so long as he fulfills his chosen role with integrity and competence.

A good many of our students will not or do not wish to grow beyond the technician who acquires therapeutic skills but who essentially does not make creative, in the sense of new, contributions. But even they would benefit from training in which no sense of final answers is given, which helps them to identify with an attitude toward psychotherapy that leaves room for new learning and that encourages them to be constantly curious about the psychotherapeutic process even though what they find may never be more than rediscovery. Rediscovery, too, has creative aspects. Training should never rely solely on imitation, and on the uncritical absorption of current techniques even though the results of such training may permit the practitioner to get by and even to make a useful contribution.

One might think that such a basic attitude toward training should not be too difficult to put into effect. Unfortunately, there are a variety of circumstances caused by the nature of our training methods which make it difficult to live up to this spirit as our guide. Clinical training is still primarily based on the master-apprentice model. The supervisory relationship, a prolonged and intensive experience for both teacher and student, creates for a good many students patterns of dependency and of imitative needs which are not conducive to skeptical inquiry and to experimentation. The fact also remains that in spite of the youthfulness of psychotherapy as a technique and as a science, a vast amount of technical experience has accumulated which has to be transmitted to the student, and naturally must keep him dependent upon his teachers for a long time. The knowledge and the skills that he acquires are not merely intellectual but are based on his capacity to use himself in a total sense, and necessitate an involvement which requires commitments and convictions of a completely different type than is true in most other scientific fields.

Let us look at one simple example, the technical language employed in our field. The psychotherapist is usually deeply identified with his own theoretical frame of reference, and quite blind concerning other competing frames of reference. While the particular conceptual framework that guides him creates the basis for his understanding of his patients and for the development of his techniques, this same theoretical structure at times constitutes the very blind which he cannot remove in order to see possible new solutions. That theory is at times in the way of the absorption of new discoveries is of course not unique to psychotherapy, but the overcommitment of the psychotherapist to his frame of reference is perhaps typical for our field. As long as scientific achievement is concerned with objective facts, at a comfortable distance from our immediate emotional interest, we are willing to look objectively at the concepts as well as the tools of the specific science. One cannot quite imagine, for example, that the pathologist would be emotionally so involved with his microscope that he would not be willing to look through another microscope of a presumably improved design. He has no particular emotional investment in his theoretical concepts or in his practical tools, although the history of science reminds us that this was not always true even for the natural scientist. One need only recall the bitter struggle that went on between those who fought for the respective truths of their theses in which either the earth or the sun was considered as the center of the universe. This struggle between the followers of Ptolemy and Copernicus has now given way to a more sophisticated understanding of theory in which it is clearly understood that the choice of the center of the universe is an arbitrary one decided not on the basis of what is "final truth" but what is practical for the development of simple descriptions of lawful relationships.

Language is the chief working tool of the psychotherapist, and as such very much a part of himself. While most sciences see the reclarification of their concepts and their organizing theories as a constant task, we find in our field a confusion of words remindful of the myth of the Tower of Babel. This overcommitment to one's own chosen language, this lack of distance from the tools of communication frequently gives rise to the impression that different psychotherapeutic schools are like medieval guilds with their trade secrets and their private rituals. Thus an impression is created that none of them is capable of the objectivity it takes to create a research atmosphere and to train new psychotherapists in the spirit of research.

It has often been said, and this most likely constitutes a correct observation, that the younger psychotherapists will adhere to such passionate overcommitment toward their own point of view more than the more experienced ones. A young psychotherapist needs for reasons of inner security to attain a conviction; as a matter of fact, the first struggle of the learning psychotherapist often consists of an attempt to retain his scientific objectivity without making any emotional commitment, to fight off the kind of involvement necessary if he is to learn to empathize with suffering people. How then can one expect the student-therapist to overcome the objectifying distance of his earlier academic training and at the same time be research-minded in the best sense of the word?

So much is the psychotherapist a part of the very psychotherapeutic process that should also be in the center of research interest that the question has frequently been raised as to whether the therapist himself could be a researcher so far as his own processes are concerned, or if it would not be more advantageous to have such processes studied by others on the outside, as it were. This viewpoint clouds the distinction, however, between the research that is primarily discovery—new concepts, new insights—and the research that is primarily verification—the nailing down of relationships suggested by the hypotheses generated in the discovery phase. Most formal academic training in research problems and research methodology is geared to the sharpening of skills in the processes of verification and amplification. This is of course an essential aspect of psychotherapeutic research and has deeply influenced the kinds of formal psychotherapy research projects about which we will say more later. However, to this date the most powerful advances in psychotherapy theory and technique have come from discoveries—the discoveries individuals have made in and during their own psychotherapeutic work. Most of the clinical research in psychoanalysis is of this kind.

The psychoanalytic setting is usually thought of as an essentially empirical situation. However, Ezriel * and Kubie † have cogently stated the case for considering the psychotherapeutic situation itself as the model for clinical research, a situation which permits the therapist to study, "experimentally" as it were, the very processes in which he participates. For the psychotherapeutic interview constitutes a situation, structured in certain ways with certain mutually interacting expectations built into it, which permits the therapist to make certain observations and to compare the ways in which different patients react to this situation which is held relatively constant. The therapist's own interpretive interventions can be looked at as experimental manipulations in which the patient's responses can be viewed as the reaction to the induced alteration in the setting which the interpretation brings about. The effect of each interpretation can be anticipated through prediction and then observed. Similarly, any variation introduced into the structure can be observed for its effect upon the patient and the way in which he responds.

A part of the teaching of a research attitude in psychotherapy consists then in helping the student to see that the psychotherapeutic situation is at the same time the model of the clinical research situation. The student thus learns not only to use a technical instrument for its healing potential, but he learns to become a simultaneous observer who can use the technical instrument as a research tool as well. A great deal of the research that he will be doing will be remindful perhaps of the repetition of the experiments of the early pioneers in Newtonian physics in a course on physics, constituting actually nothing but repeated demonstrations, or at best rediscoveries. The supervisor will not want to be merely imitated, will not require that the student blindly obey him, but rather will make suggestions that the student ought to regard as setting the conditions for an experiment. The student who uses the

* Henry Ezriel, "A Psychoanalytic Approach to Group Treatment," *Brit. J. Medical Psychology*, 23:59–74, 1950; "The Scientific Testing of Psychoanalytic Findings and Theory," *Brit. J. Medical Psychology*, 24:30–34, 1951; "Notes on Psychoanalytic Group Therapy: Interpretation and Research," *Psychiatry*, 15:119–126, 1952.

† Lawrence S. Kubie, *The Use of Psychoanalysis as a Research Tool*, *Psychiatric Research Reports*, 6:112–136, American Psychiatric Association, October 1956.

supervisor's suggestions should not follow them compliantly but should use his own observational powers in order to see how well they work: In other words, he should test the suggestion against experience. A most important asset of any supervisor would be to possess the kind of humility that would permit the young therapist to experience every one of the supervisory suggestions as a permission for experimentation rather than an order which he must execute. The natural skepticism of the student should be fostered rather than merely experienced as doubt about the supervisor.

There may indeed be some students for whom research constitutes a slogan under whose banner they can legitimately defy established methods. They may oppose any form of supervision under the pretext that there should be freedom of action in the name of experimentation, freedom of science and of research, and the possibility for new discovery. There are some students who come into psychotherapy training with a Paul Bunyan complex, the conviction that they need not use tried and proven techniques, that they need no supervisors, no professional mothers and fathers. They feel that from the first day they rock the psychotherapist's cradle in which they find themselves they have an immense strength which permits them to go out without help and to discover therapeutic solutions unhampered by their supervisors.

There is another group of students for whom research has another special kind of meaning. They cannot allow themselves to become committed to a therapeutic method; they cannot trust it nor can they really trust themselves or their teachers. Such students, the Don Juans of psychotherapy, try one method after the other, are at first as over-enthusiastic as Don Juan about a new love, then abandon the method in disgust. They are then particularly bitter toward those who have become identified with one method and have learned to use it successfully. These psychotherapeutic Don Juans believe they are researchers while they are only searchers without inner identity, without the capacity for personal commitment necessary if one wants to learn a psychotherapeutic method. Even if they are brilliant and often voice penetrating criticisms of established methods, their nuisance value may outgrow their usefulness, and they may prove equally disappointing to their teachers and colleagues. The supervisor's problem with this type of student is a very difficult one, since search for a personal identity or for an inner commitment to a group can only with difficulty be brought into focus in the supervision if it is disguised as an objectified research interest. One of the most difficult problems in both psychotherapy training and psychotherapy research today has to do with the fact that motivations so frequently stem from a need for this kind of search rather than from a true inner preparation for research.

An example of the way in which such an objectified research interest can pose a severe learning block is seen in the work in supervision of Dr. Z. Dr. Z is a psychologist with a primarily academic and research-oriented background, coming to a clinical setting for experience in therapy with an eye toward an objective validation of the subjective data of interpersonal interactions. He is a staff member, with status and prestige, and an individual given to scrutinizing critically whatever is offered him as a proposed worthwhile educational experience—including the psychotherapy supervision that he has been asking for. When assigned to his supervisor, Dr. Allen, he asked of the administrator just how good Dr. Allen really was. Dr. Z then called Dr. Allen and asked him if he knew that he was to supervise Dr. Z.

When the first actual supervisory hour devoted to Dr. Z's new patient took place, Dr. Z presented his material in a pedantic, somewhat dull and almost inaudible manner. In response to a question as to how he felt about taking this particular patient, Dr. Z stated that he agreed this would be a difficult and troublesome case. When asked then what questions he had about his own material and his technical work with the patient, Dr. Z asked a series of clarifying, minor medical questions, about which he as a psychologist could not reasonably have been expected to be informed. In a final effort to engage Dr. Z in the interaction with him, so that they could together formulate the questions around which Dr. Z really needed help and might be brought to seek it, Dr. Allen asked how this present experience doing therapy compared with other aspects of Dr. Z's previous professional experiences.

This was a signal for Dr. Z to state that he had done his doctorate work in a well-known university center of "learning theory"; to satisfy himself that Dr. Allen was poorly informed about the theoretical aspects of "learning theory"; and to expound how he had previously treated a patient according to "learning theory" somewhat differently than he expected to treat the current patient in this setting with this particular supervision. He would, however, strive to maintain strict scientific objectivity in his comparative evaluation of these different therapeutic approaches, be willing to prove one against the other, or perhaps to find the Achilles heel in both. He then ended with a slip of the tongue. In trying to bring the discussion back to a seeming compliance with the proprieties of hierarchical responsibility, he turned to Dr. Allen with the intent of asking, "What are your further recommendations?" What he actually asked was, "What are your further qualifications?"

Perhaps this slip, with its sudden revelation of the underlying attitude of condescension, epitomizes most clearly the psychological tone that Dr. Z strove, successfully so far, to envelop his "supervisory sessions" with. It is clear that the banner of research-minded objectivity becomes a screen behind which deep objections to new learning are mobilized. Yet Dr. Z sought this experience in order to learn. Beneath the aggressive assault was the real anxiety over admitting, openly to the supervisor, that he felt lost in this bewildering situation of coming face to face with the psychological world of another human being. Perhaps the supervisor could have recaptured the initiative in the situation, and have begun to restructure it more helpfully to real learning on the part of the student, if he had responded to the dissertation on the comparative merits of the different theoretical "schools" of psychology and psychotherapy by some such statement as, "I see that you have had a variety of different experiences in the past; and that certainly might be confusing for you now and make it a little more difficult for you to try to learn something here."

Thus, the supervisory process, ideally utilized, will constitute for the student a form of self-discovery, a constantly critical evaluation of what he is doing, of what he is taught, and will help him toward those inner commitments he needs in order to learn the use of psychotherapeutic techniques. At the same time, it should maintain in him the objectivity of the participant-observer who constantly checks his tools and his powers of observation, and is always ready to challenge methods that are not fruitful. The student will then move through different stages in his use of supervision and supervision will finally be replaced by consultation as he develops the capacity for independent psychotherapeutic work.

If the student has arrived at that stage, he should be ready for serious research work if he so desires. This expectation is expressed in the requirement of many institutes and other training centers that the student submit at this time a clinical paper with research implications. His former supervisor may have now become the collaborator. Such a development can take place only if the group of supervisors is essentially free of the need to develop followers and to surround itself with a "school" that is to produce dependent admirers rather than independent co-workers.

If supervision is used as a method of unfolding the best capacities of the student, one which will not destroy his initiative and his curiosity but will discipline him, it will have contributed to the creation of a research atmosphere based not on rebellion and fruitless search but on genuine and mature capacity for new discovery which will lead to the improvement of our healing techniques.

During the process of supervision, special capacity for research, special gifts in the field should come to the attention of the supervisor and he should be able to encourage the student to develop these. This raises the question as to what kinds of criteria can be used to determine that the student can now be a researcher and an experimenter with method. The first evident criterion, as already stated, is that he have attained a sufficient level of technical skill so that he knows well the problems of his area of research and the methods that he is experimentally deviating from. In addition, however, to this question of the level of technical skill, wherever it is set, is the problem of ascertaining and recognizing the "creative impulse," the feeling on the part of the supervisor that something different and original comes back from the supervisee, that the supervisee is now ready to put his own ideas to experimental trial. Yet the whole learning situation is so complicated that each of these factors can also be utilized as a resistance; that is, the supervisee can look at the supervisor's efforts to bring him to the requisite degree of technical skill as an attempt to make him conform to traditional molds and to stifle his creativity before it ever gets a chance to unfold.

Here, as has been stressed, the question of timing is uppermost—to decide when a man is ready and can be allowed to get away from "ordinary supervision" yet with the proviso that certain controls over his efforts remain. These are questions of the skill, tact, and timing of the supervisor, which permit rebelliousness to sublimate into research. This leads to the problem as to the kinds of teachers, of supervisors, who can create this proper atmosphere for the inculcation of research curiosity while at the same time upholding traditional teaching standards and knowledge. This should, incidentally, be possible even for those supervisors who are primarily clinicians and teachers and who themselves do not contribute creatively beyond the creative aspects that go into any psychotherapeutic or supervisory effort.

Finally, there is an administrative structure which must be provided that does not stifle research creativity, but that also does not prematurely allow a bright but unpolished young researcher to run hog wild. That is, appropriate administrative safeguards must be built and this in the face of the fact that the would-be researcher often views administrative regulation as a hampering and uncreative guidance. This relationship between administration and research is necessarily a two-way system of interacting responsibilities. The administrator provides an atmosphere that maintains and supports research activities, even to the carrying out of experimental procedures that may need to be defended before the board of trustees, the legislature, or the public. On the other hand, the research endeavor is at all times responsible to the administration. It is not the proprietary interest of a single individual or a group of individuals within the setting, but an opportunity delegated to the researchers on behalf of the whole to which they are always responsible.

One would wish that the attitudes and methods described above would be part and parcel of every clinical setting, even those which are primarily service-oriented. In some of the larger training centers more can be expected during the training period. We have come to a stage of development of psychological science where clinical research has developed beyond the individual case study to a point where more formal group research can be realized. Different disciplines, as exemplified perhaps in the diagnostic team of psychiatrist, psychologist, and social worker, are working together, are coordinating their data, and are making advances in methods and in theory of psychotherapy. The interdisciplinary approach has enabled us to develop systematic methods, and to work out formal designs that permit project research in such areas as the carrying out of prediction studies, studies of outcome, studies of psychotherapeutic processes, the re-examination of theoretical tools, and the constant redefinition of our basic psychotherapeutic concepts. Wherever such organized project research is being carried on it seems absolutely appropriate to introduce the young student of psychotherapy at the earliest moment to research activity within his reach that can be carried out by him as part of his training. He would need to become acquainted with basic research tools, with research methodology, and be able to take his place in certain of the technological aspects of the research program which he could carry out under supervision. Such research activity may never be more serious for him than experimental college courses in chemistry or in psychology are for the young students. These activities would not necessarily prepare the student for a research career but should help him to gain proper perspectives on his own work, and perhaps to discover for himself professional choices which he had not been aware of before.

Many of our young colleagues go through practical training without being exposed to choices which could decidedly alter their professional goals, and might influence some of them toward much-needed research activity in our field. We thus suggest that the research attitude implied in the understanding and use of the therapeutic situation is not sufficient and must be supplemented by newer research methods utilized now in group and project research, and by a thorough acquaintance with certain aspects of research methodology applicable to the clinical field.

There is one kind of question, which one might think hardly warrants emphasis but which nevertheless comes up again and again in discussions concerning clinical research programs, that we should discuss within the framework of this presentation. Many researchers who tend now toward the clinical field have acquired their research training and attitudes in university settings, with their stress on academic freedom and absolute freedom of experimentation. They profess themselves embarrassed and shocked by the attitudes of the clinically trained researchers who do not seem to permit much diversity of approach, even in their research enterprises. One could think of the more academically trained researchers for example, wishing to utilize in one and the same clinic or hospital a variety of different psychotherapies, based on different theoretical systems, and opposed to each other in many ways of technique and management. Ideal research, so they may claim, would need to allow for a full range of experimentation. The clinicians would soon rise in armor against the chaos created by this state of affairs and the impression would then be given of a power struggle in which one form or way of work must prevail.

The nature of the problem posed may perhaps be elucidated by recourse to the current model of medical research. The surgeon for example, intent on working out a new operative procedure for the alleviation of, say, severe congenital or coronary heart disease, must of course have a thorough grasp of the established knowledge and the established medical and surgical procedures that he intends to modify or make advances upon. If he then devises a new method, this must be given adequate clinical trial on animals and the reasonable success of the operative procedure ensured. Only then is trial with human beings warranted, and even then the stricture is usually enforced that these be patients who are desperately ill and who, without the operation, would have a very grave prognosis. This strictness of standard and of control is of course a consequence of the general elevation of standards of professional activity in medical schools and in postgraduate training centers brought about in the wake of the Flexner report in 1910. This report was of course not directly concerned with research at all, but rather with teaching. Its importance lay in its insistence on standards of competence for medical activity and medical teaching.

A psychiatric researcher might say in regard to this model that we have no analogue in psychiatric or in psychological research. In the first place he would aver that we have no such agreed-upon established body of knowledge that we all accept and share, and can use in common to build upon. Secondly, we have no animals upon whom to try our psychotherapeutic experiments. If one maintains that there is such an agreed-upon established body of knowledge, that is only the arbitrary and dogmatic dictum of the man who has the power to say so. If research is to be soundly based upon an established body of knowledge, from which the researcher is to take his point of departure, the fight then rages over what is accepted as established.

Many of the leading psychoanalytic theoreticians such as Glover * and Waelder † acknowledge quite candidly that most of the basic tenets of psychoanalysis, in which analysts all have such strong conviction, have nonetheless not been "proven" in the same sense as many of the principles of physics and chemistry have been. Glover, for example, states, "There are no agreed-upon definitions of basic concepts," and again, "The second point, namely, that in any given case interpretation is an essential part of the process of psychoanalytical investigation and that nevertheless there is as yet no effective control of conclusions based on interpretations, is the Achilles heel of psychoanalytical research."

Adding to these difficulties is, in general, the slowness of consolida-

* Edward Glover, "Research Methods in Psychoanalysis," *Int. J. Psa.*, 33:402–409, 1952.

† Robert Waelder, "The Function and the Pitfalls of Psychoanalytic Societies," *Bull. Phila. Association for Psa.*, 5: May, 1955.

tion of advances in psychological science. When widespread acceptance of a point of view prevails, the main body of clinical and research interest is well past that position. For example, the upbringing of children today is decisively influenced by views of childhood developmental processes which prevailed in psychoanalysis some thirty years ago, and which have been extensively modified and supplemented since.

The decision therefore as to what constitutes appropriate and acceptable research directions ultimately becomes an administrative—and political—one. The administrator must make the most soundly based decision he can as to what he feels the agreed-upon body of knowledge to be, that the researcher must work from and not ignore, and what the prerequisites are then for doing research based on this body of knowledge. This is certainly a decision that will seem arbitrary to some, yet in order to adequately safeguard clinical services, such a decision must be made. Even within that decision, though, basic postulates that are commonly accepted can be tested cautiously one by one, so long as ways are devised to fully protect the welfare of the patients.

This is different from the more usual academic setting, say the psychology department of a university, in which a variety of theoretical schools of thought can well be represented. In fact this diversity can be looked upon as leading to useful interactions and as providing the greatest freedom for teaching and research. But the moment that clinical services are offered, and the welfare of patients is at stake, a problem arises that the administrator must face, which requires the establishing of standards for clinical service based on his own theoretical convictions and his own training philosophy. In this setting, the administrator may well decide that certain "schools" are not based on sufficiently validated theoretical or empirical criteria to allow their propagation and use in conjunction with clinical material.

Imagine the kind of problems that would arise if patients in the same clinical setting were in fact treated partly by psychoanalytically trained therapists and partly by Rogerian nondirective therapists. Competing schools of thought in our field must therefore develop their individual clinical settings. This does create problems of its own, since it becomes then the more difficult to adequately compare therapeutic techniques and therapeutic outcomes, but this seems an unavoidable difficulty. The belief that a young psychotherapist ought to be schooled in a variety of methods, very different from one another, in order thus to acquire a broad-minded research attitude and to avoid a premature commitment to a particular point of view, sounds ideal but is actually unfeasible, and nihilistic in its effect. It stems, we believe, from ignorance about the nature of training for psychotherapeutic work.

Perhaps our absolute frankness concerning this state of affairs, a frankness to be shared with the students whom we supervise, will give us the distance necessary to enable us to combine training in basic therapeutic skills with the acquisition of a research attitude and to thus truly develop training for research in psychotherapy, which has become the number one problem in the clinical field. An additional, most pressing problem becomes that of communication between research centers, especially between different "schools of thought," so necessary in view of the dangers of isolation and the development of ingroups in our field. The supervisor's responsibility is to help keep the channels of communication open for the student in spite of his own commitment and in spite of the special tasks that the student faces that have been described above.

It has become quite clear through this chapter that research enterprise will always be surrounded by controversy since it questions the established dogma and it searches eternally for the new. Inherent in it is the fact that emotional storms get aroused. The problem for the researcher is whether he can engage in this activity without being himself driven to provoke storms. That is, can creative work not be a rebellious repetition of infantile attitudes? Can it be a truly mature struggle that is not a re-creation of unresolved earlier psychological dilemmas? If our scientific goal is not that of adjustment to society's norms, but that of increasing mastery and adaptation, part of adaptation is making the environment adapt to our own growing skills and needs, and this becomes the area for research to carve out new knowledge and new methods.

V / The Professional Identity of the Psychotherapist

> At times it may flatter the teacher when his students are proud of him. He who is a true teacher must rather wish that he may be proud of his students. If the work of the novice is to praise the master, it will be necessary that the student himself some day become one.—THEODOR REIK

If a psychotherapy training program were to succeed completely in helping its students acquire all the basic psychotherapeutic skills known today, and if this program would do no more than that, it would have failed to fully accomplish its chosen task: the training of psychotherapists. For in professional training the acquisition of skill by itself would not be enough. What would still be missing is a specific quality in the psychotherapist that makes him into a truly professional person, a quality we wish to refer to as his professional identity.

In earlier history, for example in the stable caste society within which the medieval guild flourished, a man's occupation was so much a part of himself that it became literally a part of his personal identity and self concept. He was described by the occupation he held, and perhaps was even named after it. The division of labor and the simplification of part processes resulting from the technological advances of modern industrial society have brought a mechanization of the concept of occupation, the psychological consequences of which are perhaps best described by the word "job." The man today who holds a job in order to make a living may think of it not at all as a part of himself but rather as an acquired external skill that he may be quite willing to exchange for some other skill when it is profitable to do so. The job has only the simple meaning to him of providing a way of "making a living." The climate of our modern age is one in which men and women have grown accustomed to the idea of exchanging one type of job for another, and can do so easily as a part of their adjustment to the industrial operations of varying supply and demand. The occupational history of many people in our culture contains a variety of entirely different job-choices and reflects a real capacity for change at least so far as occupation is concerned.

This capacity for change is, of course, less true whenever the training period in which the basic skills are acquired is an extended one, and becomes even less when the training is based on highly personalized methods of instruction. It is least of all in those occupations that we designate as *professions*. Professional training, if it truly succeeds, leads to a psychologic amalgamation of the person with the function that he is to perform. We speak then not of having a job, but of being a member of a profession. Professional people are strongly identified with what they do, they derive pleasure and pride from the status which their function affords them in their community, and they find it difficult to think in terms of change even if greater economic security is offered, because their deepest satisfactions stem from carrying on their profession which has become part of their life. This sense of professional identity is an essential attribute in a profession such as psychotherapy, and its acquisition must be considered one of the important training goals. Professional identity is a higher form, a later acquisition than the self concept. It is an extension from the self concept, perhaps more easily given up under stress, such as severe illness or social upheaval, but nevertheless an important ingredient without which the professional function would unduly suffer.

How does such a professional identity come about? It originates, of course, in the process of training, the nature of which will be reflected in the kind of professional identity, the type of professional self concept that the individual subsequently develops. Professional identity, which is a reflection of the inner experience of an individual, is matched externally by the recognition of society which identifies a man as belonging to a certain profession. Professional identity in most cases will then be a reflection of the entire professional group, its belief in itself and its status in the community, and its capacity to develop appropriate training methods that assure the continuity and the professional growth of the group.

When we talk, however, about the professional identity that arises out of psychotherapy training, we are faced with a variety of social problems inherent in the nature of the development which people go through in order to become psychotherapists; problems not only in terms of skills, but also in terms of professional identity. As long as Kubie's * call for a special training program for a new professional grouping of psychotherapists is not heeded, and the indications in the present social structure are that it will not be heeded soon, the identification with psychotherapy as a profession will be merely part of a larger professional identity characteristic for today's practitioners in this field.

We have no statistical data available, but we assume that the greatest number of psychotherapists at the present time are being developed within the psychiatric ranks of the medical profession. There are also large numbers of psychotherapists whose original or rather primary profession is in the field of clinical psychology or of social work.

Some elaboration of the specific problems related to their more primary professional identification, which people have in acquiring their additional professional identity as psychotherapists, might give us some better understanding of the special training problems involved. Members of the medical profession seem at first glance to have the easiest problem.† Their clinical training, marked from the outset by their taking the Hippocratic Oath, should make it easier for them to accept fully those aspects of psychotherapy that involve the assumption of therapeutic responsibility—the willingness to stick with the individual patient as long as necessary, the impetus to help to the utmost

* Lawrence S. Kubie, "The Pros and Cons of a New Profession: A Doctorate in Medical Psychology." Texas Reports on Biology and Medicine 12:692–737, 1954. Reprinted in *Medical and Psychological Teamwork in the Care of the Chronically Ill*, edited by Molly Harrower, Charles C Thomas, Publisher, 1955. (In this article Dr. Kubie proposes the name "medical psychologist" for the individual to be trained in psychodiagnostic and psychotherapeutic work.)

† After writing this chapter we came across a very cogent statement of the same professional identity problems of the psychiatrist that we deal with, entitled "Psychiatry in Medicine: Intra- or Interpersonal Relationships?" (Harvey L. Smith, *American Journal of Sociology*, 63: 285–289, 1957). The nature of the dilemma dealt with is captured elegantly in the title itself.

of one's ability, and the standing by a professional ethic ingrained in every medical practitioner through a tradition transmitted to us for approximately 2,400 years.

But it is only from the vantage point of today's securely won position that the status of the medical practitioner looks unassailable. Medical science had to live through a long struggle before society gave it the position it has acquired in our modern day. It had to establish itself against many competing forces, and it achieved slowly the powerful status it now has. The man who is today identified as a physician is an automatic participant in this present-day public respect and acceptance which forms a powerful external reinforcement of his inner sense of professional identity. It is always easier to accept oneself if one is accepted by others. Every young physician who goes into psychiatry benefits then not only from his rigorous medical training, from the medical ethics to which he subscribes, and from the identification with his fellow physicians, but also from the social status of the total medical community which, all together, will characterize his professional identity in terms of his feelings about himself and his experiences among his fellow men.

Strangely enough, though, he cannot fully inherit this professional identity without having to repeat in his own professional development some of the historic early struggles of medicine, because of the newness of psychiatry as an accepted medical discipline. It was only a little over a century ago, at a time, in 1844, when psychiatric practice was confined wholly to the custodial care of institutionalized patients, that thirteen superintendents of state hospitals gathered together to found the forerunner of the American Psychiatric Association (called the Association of Medical Superintendents of American Institutions for the Insane) and to establish its official journal, then called the *American Journal of Insanity*. From this position, confined to the care of the clearly "insane" entrusted to our state institutions, has developed the remarkable widespread current acceptance of psychiatry as a vehicle for bringing relief to all manner and degree of the mentally and emotionally ill. Magical expectations have arisen concerning the wonderful benefits that psychiatric knowledge can bring to patients and to mankind at large.

This exaggerated acceptance is inherently ambivalent. He who expects magic of this newest branch of medicine is ever ready to express his disappointment, and frequently hides deep doubt and suspicion about the new below the surface of his admiration. This uncertain attitude toward psychiatry exists not only among the population at large but can be detected also within the medical profession itself. Psychiatric practice is often felt by the more somatically anchored colleagues to smack of the machinations of the charlatans. The young psychiatric resident who is to acquire a professional identity finds himself confronted from the start with all these doubts that are a part of his environment and of himself and that frequently make it difficult for him to fully accept himself in his psychiatric specialty. While he has chosen psychiatry, he has done so against inner doubts, and might find himself in many communities in a position where he nevertheless has to crusade actively for the new psychiatric spirit and science. The political struggle for the reform of state hospital systems, for the development of community psychiatric services, for funds for psychiatric research, will all devolve upon those whose own professional identity as psychiatrists is but insecurely consolidated and beset by inner doubts.

Most of this doubt and anxiety, while obviously a part of the young resident who is to become a psychiatrist, is hidden under the surface. The façade of his professional self-awareness is a deceptive front of strength and vitality, and is constantly fed by increasing public demands and overt admiration. We hear about the serious shortage of trained psychiatrists, about the many positions which could easily be filled provided the training programs could keep up with the demands for personnel; young psychiatrists who have completed their residency training, and have met the minimum requirements for their specialty board examinations, find the community wide open. Every one of them is confronted with every conceivable choice and is pushed not to defer the choice. Such strong social demand, and the comparative ease with which it is possible to make a prosperous living in this field today, creates a kind of confidence dangerous for the professional self concept, since even a minimum of skill is seemingly adequate to meet present-day needs. One might almost say that the many choices the young psychiatrist has today will at times keep him from further specialized training and from the development of a professional identity which includes the wish constantly to grow, to learn, and to make contributions to the field. He may become prematurely satisfied with mediocre performance which is, however, sufficient to ensure social status and economic security.

These are not all the problems that confront the young psychiatrist.

An even more vital problem deals with the fact that his basic psychiatric training, as he goes beyond general medicine, itself includes so many subspecialties, so many differing influences that he finds it hard to grow beyond where he can be more than a jack of all psychiatric trades. Psychiatric residency programs require basic training in diagnostic work, in ward and hospital management, in somatic therapies, in neurology, in working with the related professions, and also in psychotherapy. The psychiatrist's professional identity is then a multifold one, and this poses a special problem for him as he goes about acquiring psychotherapeutic skills. He may think of psychotherapy as but one of many skills that he wants to acquire, alongside, for example, the capacity to apply insulin subcoma or to read skull X-rays. Or he may wish to choose psychotherapy as the final subspecialty which will represent the bulk of his work, the very one function he wishes to exercise. Obviously, there will be many degrees to which psychiatrists will become involved with psychotherapy. The American pattern of training permits such different degrees, and usually does not give the student much help in terms of coming to grips with the inner decisions and inner commitments to be worked out. In professions that have a simpler structure this problem may be a much easier one to solve. A psychotherapy training program, as part of a general psychiatric residency program, must be devised in such a way as to permit a process in which *ideal professional self-realization* is possible, and in which freedom of choice exists, so that the young psychiatrist can incorporate into his professional self concept those identity aspects that will indicate to what degree he wishes to and is able to become a psychotherapist.

As we turn to the group of clinical psychologists who today contribute a considerable number of workers to the field of psychotherapy, we find that their special problems in forming a cohesive professional identity are colored by the specific history of clinical psychology in this country, its present social position, and its current vigorous struggle for full recognition as a profession. The clinical psychologist seems to start out with a disadvantage in developing a stable professional identity concept. Rather than being able to rely on the more than two thousand years of tradition of the profession fathered by Hippocrates, the clinical psychologists seem to have to rely on the myth of Prometheus, who was punished by the gods for stealing the sacred fire which he wanted to bring to the people. The clinical psychologists are frequently in the position of fighting for the right to do psychotherapy and are often considered as transgressors by the medical profession, similar to the manner in which Prometheus was judged by the gods. Their self concept thus frequently includes both the heroic feeling that they bring much-needed clinical services to people, and the underlying suspicion that they are nevertheless doing something wrong. This suspicion is, of course, nourished by the vigorous struggle in many medical quarters, which, mindful of the need to defend both their standards and their status, suspect that the clinical psychologist aggressively attempts to go beyond the place which they want him to fill.

This struggle, of course, has differences of intensity, as well as of quality, in different parts of the country, but it is truly reflected in the training problems that everywhere confront clinical psychologists. Psychotherapy training may frequently be bootlegged, may be incomplete, or may not be free of a certain feeling of second-class citizenship and a constant demand, tactful or aggressive, for desegregation—even where carried out under the auspices of a responsible clinical setting with medical supervision.

In the attempt to do psychotherapeutic work the clinical psychologist may see the enemy outside his own group, in order to remain unaware of the training problems for which he must shoulder full responsibility. Clinical psychology is a very young profession, a young science, and—not unlike the position of psychiatry in medicine—not in very good repute so far as the other special fields in psychology are concerned. Its primary emphasis on service and application, the qualitative nature of its insights, and its failure to follow the established models of experimental design stressed in university psychology departments are heavily criticized by other psychologists. This criticism is, in part, accepted by the profession of clinical psychology itself, which feels less mature, less scientific, and often attempts to imitate those within the field who have more prestige and status in the value hierarchy of science. These facts are reflected in the training dilemma of the clinical psychologist. In order to receive his doctorate, he must go through a basic, academic training that leaves little room for clinical opportunity or experience; with training requirements that differ greatly from what is actually demanded in the field, and with ideals for scientific research that, at least in part, will not be directly applicable in clinical work. The clinical psychologist who tries to attain a professional identity and sees himself not fully accepted by the academic psychological world or by the psychiatric world, and certainly not by the community at large, will need to fight aggressively in order to attain his desired professional self concept.

It is against these cultural and historical facts that the clinical psychologist comes to the field of psychotherapy. He usually brings to it an intense research interest and research background which together with his gift for psychological problems and his devotion to learning and teaching should give him many assets in developing and utilizing psychotherapeutic skills, could he but overcome the identity dilemmas discussed above. One wonders whether the spirit of Hippocrates and of Prometheus can come together and provide an ideal which might guide both, the psychiatrist as well as the clinical psychologist, as they work collaboratively in developing psychotherapy as a skill, a scientific profession, a research opportunity, and a social obligation.

The experience of social obligation is certainly a powerful aspect of the training of social workers and their growth of professional self concept. In fact they often feel that they labor under seemingly Herculean tasks in securing community support for their programs of bringing social services and social needs together. In some ways the social worker's basic training seems to give rise to certain advantages from the point of view of the formation of professional identity. The scope of social work seems more clearly defined and its specializations are more clearly worked out in terms of the basic requirements which make up the pattern of social-work training. If the social worker, for example, were to choose case work as his basic function he could truly involve himself during his training in the development of this specific skill, and he could truly identify himself with his case-work teachers without feeling many other areas competing for his allegiance, his capacity for identification, and his devotion. Unlike the psychiatrist or the psychologist, the social worker is less torn among multiple purposes and may find it correspondingly easier to grow toward a unified professional maturity in his selected direction. In this he holds an advantage perhaps over the clinical psychologist and the psychiatrist. As an individual, the social worker is oriented toward institutional work and his professional identity contains the capacity, the willingness, the very wish to see himself as a part of an organization. He sees himself neither as an independent private practitioner nor as a scientific research prima donna. He has learned rather to work in a group and his professional identity concept contains to the fullest extent the idea of social responsibility, social service, and social interaction.

Social workers are also at a training advantage because the integration between the curriculum of the professional school and the field work in an established social agency is usually better worked out than is true for most schools of psychiatry and clinical training programs for psychologists. This integration permits a clearer definition of training purpose, and the establishment within that purpose of meaningful training requirements which are geared to delimited goals, the acquisition of definite skills. In particular, the social worker acquires the skill to work through the agency; that is, to use the opportunities and the services as well as the limitations of the social agency as functions of the helping process.

But there are also disadvantages which create obstacles in the achievement of a consolidated professional identity, obstacles which will also stand in the way of that part of the social worker's identity that has to do with his development as a psychotherapist. One obstacle of course concerns the very position of social work as a profession in our society. Although social work is much older than clinical psychology, it faces the very same struggles regarding acceptance by the other clinical professions, and by the community at large. Social workers have grown from a beginning marked by the tradition of Lady Bountiful dispensing "charity" among the lower classes and it has been difficult for them to demonstrate to the community their true skills, their professional self-development, and the deeper meanings of their function. An inordinate amount of time must be used in order to develop appropriate community relations, to prove that a given agency renders a useful service to the community, and that the community ought to support adequately both the agency and the social work profession.

This is particularly true when it comes to the introduction of new "intangible" services in which psychological help is given rather than direct relief or "tangible" help. One need only recall the struggles in the large metropolitan centers when fee services were first introduced, and when social workers as well as clients found it difficult to accept the idea of a fee for social service, for counseling, or for the types of psychotherapeutic help now rendered in many agencies throughout the country. This struggle is by no means ended; it still goes on in communities throughout the nation, and is in part a continued reflection of how the social worker feels about himself in this new role, as well as of the degree of community acceptance of it. It is for this reason that social work, in spite of the comparative clarity of function which it has achieved, is nevertheless constantly reclarified and redefined. The many panels at social-work conferences concerning the nature of the field of social work reflect, in part, the continuous struggle social workers have to establish and to maintain their function. Thus, for example, some social workers insist that their function never should go beyond "case work," while others willingly assume "psychotherapeutic" responsibility.

The same struggle is experienced in interprofessional relations and has brought about the usual and seemingly chronic adjustment problems between social workers and the other clinical professions. Social workers until recently had little use for or contact with clinical psychologists, and felt themselves to be in a dependent position in relation to the psychiatrists. While clinical psychologists frequently "fought" the psychiatrists, social workers were more willing to maintain the status quo. Nevertheless, they felt frustrated by the fact that the psychiatric profession as a whole had not yet learned to use social work as an interdependent profession, but saw in it merely an "auxiliary" function. Problems of this kind will be felt whenever social workers are used for psychotherapeutic work. Their professional identity concepts as far as psychotherapy is concerned will contain their inner need to see themselves intimately connected with an organization, and to establish certain types of relationships with the other clinical professions.

Social agencies have developed organizational patterns which frequently include a well-established and extensive recording system as well as a supervisory structure quite different from those established in the other clinical professions. The other professions often experience the social workers as being unduly and even permanently dependent on their supervisors. Supervision is not only an integral part of the training in social work school but remains a permanent pattern in most agencies. It is often maintained even for those who supervise, who then in turn become dependent on case-work consultants employed by the agency, or on outside psychiatric and psychoanalytic consultants. A great deal of time is usually required for the maintenance of process records on each case, which is often viewed by the other professions as an overritualizing of work, an overdoing that cuts down on spontaneity and on effectiveness. The social workers themselves have of course seen these problems and are working on them, but nevertheless the impression remains that they seem to do too much of the work that psychologists and psychiatrists seem to do too little of.

We have mentioned earlier that social workers see themselves as the designated instruments of an agency, and they have learned to work through the agency structure. Their allegiance and their identification with the supervisor becomes more than personal. It constitutes really an institutional allegiance, and the organization for which they work has a completely different place in their inner lives, in their working armamentarium, than does the hospital or the clinic for the psychiatrist or the clinical psychologist. This interesting phenomenon, a part of the social workers' professional identity, will have a direct bearing on the type of service and on the type of psychotherapy which they are able to render. Their clients do not simply come to them, as one may go for treatment to a psychiatrist in private practice, but they seek the services of an agency, and what they evolve with their worker is in part a reaction to the institution to which they come for help. Social workers have learned to understand this aspect of the helping process which is defined by the institutional setting, and they have taught us to increase our psychotherapeutic effectiveness through paying attention to the effective use of this very phenomenon. All settings that provide clinical services and make use of clinical teams have now come to understand that the nature of the psychotherapeutic process is deeply influenced by the setting in which it occurs. At times this has led to a sort of professional anonymity for the worker; he may submerge himself as it were in the agency and offer the agency's service rather than his own. This is indeed a weak facet of an identity concept in that the social aspect, the connection with the agency, the clinic, or the hospital may be overemphasized at the expense of the private aspect, the core of individual therapeutic help.

The point has been developed that the primary profession in which one was trained before the decision was made to become a psychotherapist, or to use one's skills largely as a psychotherapist, will be instrumental in defining or limiting the type of professional identity that one will be able to develop. This means that there will be differences in the way in which psychotherapists will experience themselves, differences which go beyond individual personality differences and the therapeutic processes which they themselves may have lived through as a recipient of help, differences which are based rather on the social and cultural aspects of professional life that have been discussed.

We can perhaps capture this range of difference in somewhat exaggerated form if we can visualize the kind of question that a member of each of these professional groups might have uppermost in mind in seeking employment in a clinical setting—beyond the salary question common to all, of course. The psychiatrist might wonder what scope exists for autonomous functioning and for the assumption of administrative as well as clinical responsibility. The clinical psychologist might ask about opportunities for research inquiry into psychotherapeutic processes and clinical problems. The social worker might inquire into the adequacy of the supervision system and the clarity of clinic function and purpose.

We have paid attention up to this point to three main professional groups as they are found in today's modern clinical settings. But there are also others who have found their way to the profession of psychotherapy. For example, clergymen, marriage counselors, and workers in sociology and anthropology have joined the growing ranks of psychotherapy. The nature of their capacity to help others, and their concepts of their professional selves as they become psychotherapists will likewise depend in similar ways on their primary professional identification. This will be particularly true for religious leaders who have always seen themselves as helpers of the troubled and who will have their own special problems in developing the type of helpfulness which is called psychotherapy. Still another group of helpers—nurses,* recreational therapists, occupational therapists, and vocational guidance counselors, who may all use themselves psychotherapeutically—would need to be discussed as well if we are to understand fully the effect of primary professions on later professional identifications.

We have already indicated that as yet there are very few training programs in which primarily psychotherapists are developed, the most notable exceptions being the group of psychoanalytic institutes devoted to training in a highly specialized psychotherapeutic skill, psychoanalysis. (And psychoanalysis, like psychotherapy in general, is a spe-

* *A Way to the Soul of the Mentally Ill*, by Gertrud Schwing (International Universities Press, Monograph Series on Schizophrenia No. 4, New York), is an example of pioneering psychotherapeutic work by a nurse with schizophrenic patients.

cialized professional function with its own specialized professional identity.) Psychotherapy is indeed a new and still incompletely delineated professional grouping within a number of larger (and more clearly defined) professions. Training in psychotherapy is usually given as one of the many training requirements for professions that include this skill but expect much more of the trainee as well. If one thinks in terms of organized public acceptance, conveyed by officially recognized schools, public diplomas, and state licenses, then the profession of psychotherapist does not, in fact, exist. Public licensure and public recognition is extended to the larger professional function but not to psychotherapy in itself.

Whenever the attempt is then made to develop an adequate psychotherapy training program within one of these larger training frameworks the initiator of such training will soon struggle with the fact that the student, be he a psychiatric resident or a psychological intern, finds great difficulty in trying to meet the many requirements of his training. The psychotherapy teachers will feel themselves in conflict with the total broader purpose of the school, and usually will have to resign themselves to the idea that adequate psychotherapy training can only be fully attempted on a post-residency basis. We must expect then that psychiatric residency programs as well as clinical psychology programs will succeed in teaching only the rudiments of psychotherapy, and preferably teach it in such a way as to offer choices to the young professional person who may then be free to extend his training beyond his formal residency, and to acquire later the skill and the professional identity which mark the psychotherapist. It may well be that out of such post-residency training efforts, which consist usually of in-service training for the staff in different clinical settings, will grow an adequate body of experience and the professional convictions that will lead to the establishment of training programs in which psychotherapy will be the main aspect of training, comparable perhaps to the technical training of psychoanalysts in present-day psychoanalytic institutes.

We have suggested earlier that an inner professional *identity* is partly related to being externally *identified* as a psychotherapist, to being accepted as such by the general public and by other professions. The other side of the coin has to do with the inner *process* by means of which such professional identity comes about. The external side of it rests in the feeling of being accepted by others, of having met the requirements, in other words of being identified as what one wants to be. The internal side has to do with the process by means of which such an identity is established, the *process*, if you will, *of identification* with the teachers of psychotherapy. It is for this reason that the teachers of psychotherapy have a very special meaning for the future psychotherapeutic practitioner. When we speak about identification with the teachers we may think of the many shades of meaning of this term. For example, identification may refer to a wish to emulate the teacher, to be completely like him, or to be his devoted follower. It may have to do with the attempt to imitate him and to absorb fully his patterns of working. Frequently the wish to identify in such a fashion with the teacher may carry so far during the learning process that the learner may forget his own individuality, and become simply an imitator, one who literally swallows everything that he receives from his teacher. Such a process will lead to imitation and dependency but not to a genuine professional identity, which must be based on the capacity to maintain one's individuality. It is quite clear that various phases of this process of identification will be very much in evidence as learning proceeds, and that different students will go through differing kinds of identificatory processes according to their differing personality needs, and their differing ways of learning.

What will then be extremely important are the wishes and expectations of the teacher as he sees students identifying with him, a process by the way which frequently is carried out in negative motions, in struggles against such identification. There will always be teachers whose impetus to teach is based very much on the need to gain followers and imitators, who through their total identification with the teachers give the latter strength and purpose. The goals of such teachers may be to surround themselves with small "schools," groups of students and followers who meet their emotional needs for acceptance. It is not only the student who needs to be accepted by the teacher, but those of us who teach psychotherapy know very well that we too have potent needs for acceptance. The more primitive needs for acceptance are based on the wish to see the student as an extension of oneself, a projection of one's power, a proof of one's skill, and such needs will inevitably interfere with the teaching process. Teachers of psychotherapy will be more genuinely effective and will achieve more mature identifications in their students if they have been able to free themselves of the archaic aspects of such needs for students, and have been able to refine these needs in such a way as to permit the students to identify with them not only as persons but as carriers of a method and a function. Such a philosophy will foster growth toward maturity, toward individuality, and toward true collaboration.

Our field, undefined as it is in large part, competitive as it is, and beset as it is by rival ideologies, does not make it easy for the teacher to develop an attitude toward students in which his own main identification is with the teaching and learning process. Most psychotherapists have learned, and have fully accepted the philosophy that one helps patients in such a way that they can develop their own purposes rather than live according to the needs or wishes of the therapist. Teachers of psychotherapy, however, find it more difficult to develop the notion that they ought to help students develop their own best psychotherapeutic capacities and styles rather than become merely imitators of the techniques and skills of the teacher.

The teacher of psychotherapy is not in a position to prescribe to the student the manner in which the student ought to work out his problems of identification with the teacher. The teacher of psychotherapy should be able, however, to leave these choices to the student. Some students may not be able to learn to work like their teacher, unless they feel they are like him, unless they can constantly incorporate him as it were, and think of themselves as particular students of his. This indeed is part of the history of any young science in which the scientist finds it necessary to describe himself in terms of his teacher, as an Aristotelian, a Darwinian, or a Freudian. This self-description has often been less the goal of the teachers and much more the need of the students. In the field of psychotherapy training, the intensity of this need to create a professional identity concept, an integral part of which is that one consider oneself as belonging to a certain group or a school of thought, derives from the prolonged and individualized and emotionally highly charged training.

It is for these reasons also that the problem of identification with the teachers will become increasingly complex as the learning process unfolds. Identification does not depend just on conscious intent. Identification is in large part an unconscious process that makes frequent use of primitive and deep-seated psychological mechanisms which powerfully influence the mode of learning. We can think of students who have all kinds of special problems as they struggle to identify with their teachers. One kind of student may find it possible to carry through such identification only if he has the permission to identify as it were. He overidealizes his teacher, cannot really think of himself as somebody who could possibly ever be as good as his teacher and who would be privileged to do the same things that the teacher is doing. Whenever he wants to assume responsibilities like those his teacher carries, such a student can do so only by securing permission from the teacher. When he has received this permission, he may suddenly need to see the teacher devaluated; may need to debunk the teacher and base his own self-acceptance, actually his lack of self-acceptance, on the debunking mechanism. It is as if he were to say to his teacher: "I can now do what you do since I have discovered that I have overestimated you. You're really not very good yourself." Another kind of student, because of deep-seated emotional processes mobilized during learning, may feel that if he were permitted to do the same things as his teacher, he would really be doing something forbidden to him, something intimate which is permitted only to the elder generation. One can see then that frequently archaic unresolved emotional problems may interfere with the mature development of identificatory processes. Frequently we will find students who need personal psychotherapeutic help in addition to supervisory help, in order to make the fullest use of their learning opportunities.

The best teachers of psychotherapy will be those who, beyond their secure skill which they teach and beyond a need to proselytize, are capable of offering real choices to their students on the road toward mature professional self-realization. They will be teachers who do not need to overidentify with their students but rather can identify fully with the process of teaching itself. They do not seek extensions of themselves in their students, although they will be deeply gratified if they have taught successfully. The most successful teacher will be the one who can help independent minds to develop, and who may then find that some of his students may later be his friends and his scientific co-workers. Teachers should get their deepest gratifications not from the fact that their point of view prevails, but rather that they have developed methods of teaching which insure growth in knowledge and guarantee collaborators who stimulate them to test and to further develop their scientific assumptions. The best teachers will be eternal learners, and as such they will help their students to identify with their activity and their own process of constant growth, rather than with static opinions that become frozen dogmas of limited usefulness. Teaching and learning are then the mutually interdependent two sides of the coin, if it carries the permanent value of genuine professional identity.

II / *The Beginning Phase*

VI / *The Supervisor Meets the Student*

There is no learning without your wanting it and your starting it.—NATHANIEL CANTOR

The problem of beginning is a multi-faceted one. Both supervisor and student begin their work together, each with his own set of anticipations concerning this new experience. If we bring the problem to its common denominators, most likely true for all such beginning processes, we may assume that each participant hopes to master the new situation in the same way that he has mastered previous ones, and at the same time is concerned lest this new situation turn out differently and that he may not be able to master the new with the methods of old. Were he to bring a past consisting of failure experiences to this task, then the situation could be a reversed one. The wish then to meet the new by making it into the familiar that one can master, and the concern that old methods will not apply might well occupy the minds of both participants. The beginning phase of supervision will be a reflection of this struggle, whose goal is to restore the new situation to an old and familiar one, with the difference that the struggle now will mark a process between two people who have gotten together for a stated professional purpose.

In a previous chapter we traced the emergence of administrative structure in a clinical setting and we followed a development in which gradually each of the four corners of our diagrammatic clinical rhombus took on recognizable shape which could be translated into human relationships and acquired meaning. Each individual, representing one of the roles defined by the nature of the rhombus, enters into a direct or indirect relationship with individuals representing each of the other functions. These various beginnings often take place simultaneously. Thus—at least in the kind of organization we have in mind—the physician in training begins psychotherapeutic work with his patient about the same time that he will begin as student with his supervisor. This chapter illuminates the part of the rhombus represented by the line S–T (Supervisor-Therapist); that is, we wish to study the beginning of supervision, or, to be more concise, the setting up of the supervisory process, the practical arrangements between supervisor and student before the latter has even attempted to work directly with his new patient.

The supervisor and the student meet at first to outline their objectives, to establish certain routines concerning time and space, concerning the recording of material, and of course concerning the selection of appropriate cases for treatment. As we study their beginning with each other, and follow what transpires between them, we must not lose sight of the fact that this is not a private experience deriving from a private commitment but has to be understood within the framework of the total training structure characterized through the clinical rhombus. The difference between a private master-apprentice relationship and the type of supervision which operates within a defined structure the purpose of which is to regulate the training program can best be illustrated by describing the actual beginning work of a student and his supervisor.

The student in question, whom we will call Mr. Y, has had a frequent experience in relation to the training center which has offered him training. He has often been dissatisfied, and has many times expressed the opinion that he expected something more or something slightly different from what the training center had actually been able to offer him. He has been slightly critical and usually disappointed. As soon as he met his supervisor, Dr. Baehr, a new supervisor who was just learning how to teach but could rely on a stable knowledge and tested skill in psychotherapy, he repeated this pattern which had characterized his earlier relationship to the training center. The difference now, which hopefully could be used to help the therapist and the supervisor break the barrier separating the student from the training center, consisted of the fact that they now had the support of a fairly well-developed training organization with a structure of defined obligations and responsibilities within which they could find their roles and examine the nature of whatever problems might arise. The facts were that the administrator at this time had assigned the young therapist to the supervisor but he had not as yet selected a patient for consideration by the supervisor and the therapist.

The psychotherapist called his new supervisor and arranged the appointment at a mutually convenient time. The first question that arose between supervisor and therapist had to do with the mechanics of choosing a suitable patient. Mr. Y quickly expressed his conviction that this should be the sole responsibility of the supervisor. Mr. Y characterized the administrator's engagement in this process as an unnecessary intrusion on what he thought should be a more private and personal arrangement between himself and the supervisor. He was unprepared though for his own participation in the final decision concerning the suitability of the patient. In fact he said to the supervisor, "I thought you would arrange all that for me." Then he sat back. He thus expressed his compliance and deference to the supervisor as well as his plea that he be taken care of properly. We also see here a well-known and often-repeated tendency to reduce the learning relationship to one where there are only two people and where the facts of the existing reality, the administrative rules and limitations are denied and criticized. A one-to-one relationship is familiar and would facilitate the student's mastery through the methods of old.

The supervisor referred to the participation of the administrator in the process of selecting appropriate patients for assignment. The student who happened to know that his supervisor also had administrative control over a ward suggested that it was his understanding, as a matter of fact his expectation, that the supervisor would and could quite immediately provide a patient for him from among those for whom he had administrative responsibility. When the supervisor again pointed to the initiating role of the administrator in the carrying out of this function, the therapist responded with an expression of disappointment. "Naturally I am a little bit disappointed." He followed this with a statement that he should, after all, have expected this. He then told the supervisor through a flood of complaints how his various previous experiences in this particular clinical setting had each started with much enthusiasm and promise, and had often ended with the feeling of being just a little disappointed, a little let down.

In vague outlines we see emerging here the learning problem which this particular therapist expresses through this beginning experience with the supervisor even before he begins to work with the patient. As he has in the past, perhaps he will continue to be just a little bit disappointed. He constantly seems to experience unhappiness over things that are not going quite as well as he had hoped and expected. The teacher, the supervisor, will turn out not to be omnipotent, and may always give less than the student had anticipated. Enthusiasm may characterize the beginning but it must then be followed by disappointment. He had looked forward to the coveted psychotherapy training and supervision, but even before he sees his first patient he has given the supervisor a glimpse of things that may come. How must the supervisor feel about a student for whom he as the teacher can expect to be but a new disappointment?

We are thus not only concerned with the responses that the student creates in himself as he meets a new situation, but also with the feeling of disquiet and obligation which arises in the beginning supervisor. Our supervisor began to wonder about the reality grounds of the student's feelings. Perhaps the supervisory structure was unduly rigid and the therapist is its unwitting victim. Indeed, the arrangements which had been set up by the administrator for patient assignment were as yet far from ideal. Actually they were a necessary compromise with the vested interests of individual staff members who up until recently had unchallenged jurisdiction over the management and treatment of patients assigned to their sections, and only now had to learn to cooperate with the psychotherapy training program in order to guarantee the patient supply for training demands.

At this point, the supervisor explained apologetically and in detail why the patients on his section for whom he had administrative responsibility were not directly accessible to the therapist. And he implied, out of his guilt-enhanced identification with the complaint of the therapist, that he as the supervisor had some reservations about the wisdom of these restrictions which seemed so arbitrary but that that was the way they were set up. We can readily see just what happened to the supervisor here. Rather than recognizing the particular pattern of expectation in new learning situations, namely, that the student would tend to "be a little bit disappointed," the supervisor here could not separate himself from the student and judged reality then in the very same way that the student did. The inner problem of the student, rather than having been seen as such, became a reality problem, and the student and his supervisor for a moment felt united against the "arbitrary" administration which frustrated them both and could be considered responsible for their shared disappointments. The supervisor then, rather than representing the administration, rather than identifying himself with the training structure, condemned the structure, the very tools which he needed to use in order to help the student. In taking sides with the student in the latter's attack upon the non-ideal structure, the supervisor was of course trying to deflect any attack on himself as a non-ideal supervisor. After all, he himself was just a beginner in his task, and he was understandably sensitive to any attack, to any criticism of his possible supervisory shortcomings. Rather than seeing the complaining attack that the student made upon him in its true light, he warded it off, and thus, rather than freeing the young therapist, restricted him, so that the student therapist was no longer as free to bring into the conference these very obstacles which stood in the way of his acquiring therapeutic skills. How could the therapist even get mad at the disappointing training organization or its representative, the supervisor, if the latter so clearly agreed with the rightness of his complaint?

At this point one can see how therapist and supervisor were struggling with the same problem, namely, how they could begin to work together and effectively within the rules and limitations of a structure which was not of their own making. They both have to discover that in order to work together they must learn to use the training organization which at this point they have been experiencing only as an obstruction to what might otherwise be an ideal relationship. They have combined forces against this obstruction, against the third party intruder, rather than seeing it as the tool which would guarantee their working together. Instead of seeing the protection of the institution, its attempt to guarantee proper safeguards for training, they found themselves engulfed in the entanglements of institutional "red tape."

What would be an alternative in this situation? The supervisor, being first of all a psychotherapist, might easily have fallen into the trap of overpsychologizing, and have offered a statement to the anxious and disappointed therapist to the effect that he seemed to be the kind of person for whom things were always "a little bit disappointing" in order to hint at the nature of the presumed underlying personality problems, the unresolved neurotic conflict of nurture, never enough milk from the mother and never enough wisdom from the teacher.

This indeed would be an angry quasi interpretation, an attack disguised as psychotherapeutic help, and it would redefine the relationship in the light of an entirely different purpose. The purpose of this relationship is learning, and learning the purpose must remain, in spite of the underlying personality problems which can so easily tempt one to dynamic conjectures but would lead us away from the path of learning.

If the supervisor, instead of attacking the present administrative setup had just restated that it makes for a bad start if such a misunderstanding exists concerning the selection of patients, and if he had wondered together with the student how he could help him within the existing framework, he would have brought the problem back into the situation between himself and the therapist and thus provided for potential helpful change through the interaction between them.

This example has been chosen to demonstrate how the total setting, including even an arbitrary and seemingly trivial arrangement about the selection of patients, has a direct influence on the supervisor-student relationship and will serve to activate reactions in all students which will permit the sensitive supervisor to formulate for himself correct expectations as to how each student will go about the business of learning from another person.

The psychotherapeutic zeal of the supervisor might sometimes get the upper hand, and he might then be inclined to look at such reactions simply as problems of transference, the pathological repetition of the past. Those of us who watch the supervisor might well be inclined to look at his reactions, too, as a problem in counter-transference. However the example demonstrates that the supervisor now has a new tool for teaching, and does not need to lean so heavily upon his psychotherapeutic armamentarium. This new tool consists in his being attuned to the fact that teaching does not go on in a vacuum, and that the existing social structure, the basic facts of training as they have been developed by the training center although by no means yet worked out in ideal ways, can be used in the service of the teaching purpose.

The arrangements concerning the selection of patients, the best that the institution could develop up to this point, which have been experienced by the student as "disappointing" were simply seized by the student in order to express the persisting feeling that he should get more from the training center than it seems to offer, and that therefore he must look for ways to put the blame for this disappointing situation on the teacher. The supervisor, if he himself were not inexperienced and did not overidentify with the student, would not need merely to see the weaknesses of the system and apologize for its shortcomings, but by accepting its limits and representing it to the student could help the student to use the available opportunities for learning rather than to battle them. He thus would be helping the student to take on somewhat more responsibility for his learning than he would be doing were he permitted to remain in a situation which both he and the supervisor experience as frustration. As his responsibility for learning increases he will start to look for shortcomings in himself rather than in the system. The problem, at first experienced as external, will now be experienced as internal and thus can be truly mastered by the student. We wish to suggest in passing that the supervisor will be able to assume such an attitude only in a system which he can truly represent. If he were to work within an administrative setting in which the administration is either basically opposed to such training purpose or is entirely antiquated and unskillful, he will ultimately either leave the system, or he will tend to restore a quasi private teaching arrangement for himself. In that case he will not get help from the administration, and he will be isolated and "a little bit disappointed" very much like our student in the illustration which has been offered.

There are of course as many patterns of beginning as there are beginning students. If one watches a group of learners as they exhibit their beginning problems in a learning situation, a bewildering variety of uniquely different learning patterns will be revealed. Dr. X for example expressed his way of beginning entirely differently than did Mr. Y. He also came to his supervisor, Dr. Cohn, for a preliminary discussion before he was actually to start with his first patient. While the purpose of this preliminary meeting was to discuss anticipated learning needs, Dr. X soon came to the point of openly stating that his real wish was for personal psychotherapy and not for supervision. He wondered whether Dr. Cohn could be his therapist, either within a formal arrangement or by perhaps converting the supervision conference into bootlegged therapy "which I need more and will ultimately help my patients more." This expression of personal anxiety as he was to start treating a patient, and his professed need for personal therapeutic help implied at the same time that he, Dr. X, did not really need or want supervision, and that he rejected help in the one area for which the supervisory situation was actually designed. This is a rather tempting and puzzling situation for the supervisor. On the one hand he is faced with a left-handed compliment since a colleague confesses to him therapeutic needs, and selects him as the would-be psychotherapist. It seems to express the highest confidence in him as a psychotherapist and as a person, confidence which the supervisor may feel that he cannot possibly disappoint. It also carries with it the rationalization that a positive psychotherapeutic experience would essentially be more helpful for this student than supervision of his therapeutic work. There are quite a number of supervisors who at bottom believe that the personal psychotherapy of the student is indeed the most forceful instrument of teaching. Such supervisors take this notion from early psychoanalytic training in which it was assumed that the personal analysis constituted the real training of the analyst-to-be, while all the other aspects of psychoanalytic training were but embroideries that imitated the established academic (but useless) pattern of training. This notion of psychoanalytic training lingers on as a phantom in some of the abandoned closets of psychoanalytic institutes but essentially of course has been given up.

What could the supervisor do? A demand has been made on him which is highly personal and highly confidential; the rejection of it might have tremendous consequences for further work with this student, while the acceptance of it would destroy the teacher-learner relationship. We see here a kind of beginning where the student states his needs in such a way that they cannot be met within the particular situation. If such interchange were to take place in private practice, our supervisor could accept this student as a patient and treat him. He does not have this alternative in a training situation since he is responsible for every one of his decisions to the administration of the training center. He must work within the limits set, and he will find now that the very limits will give him the levers necessary for the tactful handling of this way of beginning. It sounds like an ominous beginning, one that might actually frighten many a good supervisor. If there is so much illness in the beginning therapist that he even wants to bootleg psychotherapy from the supervisor, can one entrust a patient to him? We see then that the potential reactions that the student would face could all turn out to be destructive ones, and he has thus provoked a situation which certainly could keep him from the benefits of a useful learning experience.

The supervisor needs to think of two aspects in this specific situation which will aid his search for a helpful solution. He must remember that the student who comes for help in learning psychotherapy will often express the need for help in terms which are somewhat different from the ones that the supervisor can meet. This is but an extreme case, namely, one where the student asks for something which the supervisor cannot do at all, and which, if taken at face value would make it impossible for the student and the supervisor to get together constructively. The second point has to do with the fact that the supervisor does not have to make a personal issue out of it, that is, to reject or accept the idea of psychotherapy for this student. And this is exactly what he had in mind when he kindly recognized Dr. X's stated therapeutic needs but reminded him that this particular time was set aside, not only by the two of them but also by the administrator of the training system for supervision of psychotherapy and for nothing else. The question was whether Dr. X was prepared to begin, or if he had so many doubts about supervision for himself that he could not start at all. Did he want to begin with a patient, or did he feel that his overriding personal therapeutic needs would require that he forego, at least temporarily, psychotherapeutic work under supervision? Perhaps the supervisor and the student could meet together a few times in order to talk this over. Out of this interaction, Dr. X was not only able to arrive at a decision that he did want to at least try to do psychotherapy under supervision, but more than that, he realized that one of his difficulties in learning now was his attempt to see the obstacles to learning, the difficulties in making use of the supervisor not in the area of skill but in other areas in which supervision could not help. He soon realized that by taking the supervision tools away from the supervisor, and making a request in terms of psychotherapeutic needs, he pushed the very problem of learning away. It is strange to think perhaps that in order to avoid the problem which is focal in supervision, namely, how to work more effectively with a given patient, the student is ready to confess his weakness in other even more vital areas. One might suggest that he avoids change as a psychotherapist even at the price of confessing all his personal weaknesses. He is not unlike the analytic candidate who works the other side of the same street and wishes to make his personal analytic hour into a control hour; who wants to learn from his analyst how to analyze patients rather than resolve unconscious conflict.

While the supervisor successfully helped this student to overcome the first hurdle, he also got the first glimpse of tendencies which can be expected to develop during the work with this student. He will strive to guard himself against the learning of technical skills by converting the supervisory situation into one where he and his personal needs are to be the center of attention. He may wish to exclude the patient and prefer to expose himself rather than his work. The use of structure will help our supervisor to convert this beginning into one where the focus of the supervisory relationship will be learning rather than quasi psychotherapy.

Another configuration of learning difficulties can be illustrated by the more detailed exposition of a situation as it materialized during the first supervisory conference between Dr. W, the student, and his supervisor, Dr. Baehr. This first interview will not only reveal aspects of the beginning but will permit us to conjecture about what is to come. Supervision, like psychotherapy, is an intensive and time-consuming process designed to help effect inner changes, although the nature of these changes is different in each process. In supervision we aim at a change in skill, a change in the use of the professional self, while in psychotherapy we aim at changes which embrace the total adaptive functioning of the individual. As in every process which involves change, and may be experienced as adventuring into the unknown, the change is both wished and feared. The problem for which help is desired is brought to the helper but at the same time inner resources are usually developed which are to defend the status quo. In effect, the person to be helped seems to want the new, without any essential giving up of the old; to change, and yet not to change. In the initial testing out in which both the helper-to-be and the help-seeker take stock of what each brings to the relationship, one can frequently study the grand strategy of the campaign, the long vistas ahead, and can do so much better than when one has plunged into the detailed week-to-week tactical work. The pattern of the first interview during supervision, not unlike the first dream which the analysand brings to the analyst and which reveals the core of the neurosis, may reveal the way in which the student will go about learning and at the same time opposing necessary change.

The work of Dr. W will give us an illustration of this intensive struggle. Dr. W could be described as a particularly "obstinate" student who always felt resistant to working within any regulation and who brought along the feeling, although not verbalized at first, that it was difficult for him to accept a student role in relation to a supervisor whom he wanted to regard as a peer rather than as a supervisor. The description "obstinate" reveals perhaps what kind of feelings such a student is apt to arouse in his teachers. Dr. W began his contact with the supervisor by forgetting the first appointment. The supervisor phoned a few minutes after the appointed time, and learned from the student that he had forgotten the conference time, that a patient was waiting for the student in his office at that very minute, and that he had to rush downtown following the appointment with the patient in order to see another patient in an outpatient clinic. He wondered whether they could skip this appointment and perhaps start next week. He then added, almost as an afterthought, "Please, don't read my unconscious!" The supervisor felt like replying, "It doesn't seem so unconscious" but controlled his impulse. In lieu of the scheduled supervisory session that week there was a five-minute chance exchange in the corridor.

The anxiety which frequently accompanies the first meeting between supervisor and student may be so all-pervasive and express itself in behavior so obvious that it tempts one to generalize on the obstacles one will expect to meet with the particular student. Nevertheless, it seems quite safe to say, particularly after Dr. W also asked to have his second appointment changed because he had forgotten to resolve the conflict in his schedule with the outpatient which he had wanted to take care of, that we are beginning to see here a significant aspect which will be an underlying feature of future sessions. The first two moves of the student, rather than bringing him into the supervisory situation, express his struggle over the acceptance of supervision and of himself as a learner, and are expressed even before the first actual supervisory session.

An interesting facet of the student's behavior is that it leaves very few choices to the supervisor. He may be tempted to "interpret" the student's behavior, or he may wish to reprimand him, but in either case he will not be really helpful to the student. He may be tempted to remain altogether silent as one supervisor did who waited for his student several months before he took this up with the administration. Preferably, he may hope that he could take this up with his student during the next conference, actually the first one to take place.

When this session did take place, Dr. W, to whom a patient had been assigned previously, did not as yet have any interview material. The supervisor then suggested that this preliminary hour be devoted to questions Dr. W may have, either about the case summary or their prospective work together. Dr. W already had had a factual briefing about the essentials of the training setting at a group meeting together with the other students who had started in this particular program. Nevertheless, he responded to the supervisor's invitation by asking that Dr. Baehr "explain the whole setup" as if he had never heard it before. He succeeded for the moment in reversing roles as if the supervisor had the responsibility now to show his program to the students and to have the student either accept or reject it. Dr. Baehr, struggling with the impulse to point out this reversal in roles, chose to explain in a straightforward and factual manner and hoped that he could thus bring Dr. W face to face with the big question inherent in this new undertaking, namely, whether Dr. W experienced this program as different from his previous endeavors and if it raised any special problems for him.

The student's attitude was felt to be so provocative that the young supervisor seemed to have to lean over backwards in using most of his energy to remain objective and factual. Instead of responding to the student's request for information, as an expression of uncertainty so that the student could react to this recognition, he gave the explanation as though a truly information-seeking question had been asked, only to find that Dr. W sought no information, saw no specific problems, and could indeed see no real difference in this particular way of learning except one which he stated, namely, that "you have somebody that you go to, but, of course, that does not affect me." He had learned that the supervisors of this training program had conferences with a training consultant concerning their teaching problems. In other words, the supervisor who had felt it necessary to describe all the features of the program, even those that did not directly affect the student, found himself suddenly in a situation where his factual explanation was turned against him as a confession of weakness. In effect, Dr. W told him that there was really no difference between this kind of learning and previous learning situations, and if there was one it consisted of the fact that the supervisor had to go to someone concerning the performance of his job. The explanation of the supervisor could be used as a weapon against him.

By now, we may be inclined to look at this situation as if it were a chess game between two people, and we would then have the feeling that the supervisor is at a disadvantage, a number of successful moves having been made against him. True enough, if the supervisor loses, so does the student, but a conflict situation indeed has arisen. The supervisor even now might have been able to turn the tide of events in his and the student's favor. He might have said: "Yes, it is true that each of us has someone to whom he is responsible. Don't you think that that makes some difference?" Thus, Dr. W's multiple-determined remarks could have been taken back to the source of his anxiety so that some significant help for him could emerge in the experience. We notice the aggressive intent in his remarks, which invites retaliation or forces the strict avoidance of retaliation, but what is more important, we must perceive the fact that Dr. W feels threatened in this new situation in which he himself might have to confess difficulties and go to someone for help. It is against this awareness that he defends himself so strongly. At first he must deny any existing differences between this way of learning and former experiences, and when he is brought face to face with the difference, he must depreciate it. The little difference there is gets used to point up the dependency of the supervisor rather than his own.

The next move of Dr. W again was a defensive one. He had, after all, one question. "There are several different ways to take therapy notes," and after outlining several of them, he asked, "Which do you use here?" Even this seemingly indifferent question can be seen as bearing on the same central core of anxiety. Dr. W's secret wish is to avoid the kinds of psychotherapy notes which will reveal his technical difficulties and lack of therapeutic skill to the supervisor. When he learned from Dr. Baehr that "process notes" were preferred in this setting, he asked (although the nature of this type of recording had previously been explained in the group orientation) "What are process notes?" Again, Dr. Baehr explained this, and again he wondered how Dr. W felt about this. To this the student replied, "Oh, that's OK. As a matter of fact, I did have something like it in a group control last year where the notes dealt not merely with verbatim words back and forth, but more with feelings and attitudes." Again the difference was minimized and with it the attending anxiety. Everything was reduced to the familiar and therefore the problem hardly existed.

We will not be surprised to hear that after a variety of similar, rather neutral questions, Dr. W finally got around to the patient, and wondered whether the patient was well motivated for treatment. Only in this way, as a potential problem in the patient whom he had not yet seen, was Dr. W able to state his own problem, namely, the question that he has about his own motivation as a learner. He stated that he had been given conflicting opinions about the patient's motivation; and he was confused in general about the concept of motivation. He elaborated different viewpoints about the concept, and the supervisor, finally attuned to the real import of Dr. W's questions and his inner struggles, decided to say, "How nice it would be for our learning purposes here if we had a patient who everyone could agree, by whatever criteria, was a well-motivated patient. Since things are as they are, we can only attempt to utilize whatever motivation there may be and we may hope that the process possibly could bring out some change." This response is also an indirect message to the student and to his own motivation. Perhaps the student has some slight awareness of the role which he assumed for himself in the learning situation when he remarks then at the end of that conference, "Maybe I am raising straw men before I even start."

This detailed record of the first supervisory hour which took place before the initial contact with the patient demonstrates the deep inner struggle in Dr. W to defend himself in every way against the learning that ostensibly he wants so very much. At first he forgets the first meeting completely; then he forgets to change his schedule, and only after two broken appointments does he find it possible to come to the supervisory conference at all. The next step gives us the impression that he simulates confusion and ignorance while constantly asking that the setup be explained again to him although it had already been fully explained. As soon as it is explained, he now denies the difference and remarks, "It's no different. I had it all before." Whatever difference he must admit is minimized and turned into something quite familiar. Finally, as if to preclude any awareness of his own position as a beginning learner, he sees the whole problem in the patient whom he has not as yet seen, "Maybe, after all, the patient is not motivated."

And yet, if one can allow oneself not to get angry at the surface expressions of the student, one can see behind the provocative fireworks a real longing for help on the part of a student who asks himself desperately whether the new way of supervision, and the psychotherapy to be learned, will be of any value to him. He asks himself whether he can learn under such new conditions and he wants the supervisor to prove to him that it would pay to learn with him. Most of his questions, rather than being about himself, are expressed in terms of the patient and in terms of the supervisor. All the insecurity, all the inner anxiety, is expressed in questions concerning the potential weakness of the supervisor who has to see someone about his teaching, and the possibly poor motivation of the patient.

This indeed will make effective learning quite difficult for Dr. W and it may foreshadow a stormy course in supervision. This preliminary conference between supervisor and student, devoted only to administrative arrangements and not as yet to work with a patient, has already yielded rich material toward the detection of the kinds of problems which one may subsequently encounter with him. This emerging learning pattern of Dr. W, his way of mastering anxiety in a new situation, the wish to reduce the new to the familiar and thus make it harmless, and the attempt to see the problem in the other rather than in himself will characterize the teacher-learner relationship, and will set his task for the supervisor.

This is not the place, at a point when we discuss the "diagnostic" use of the beginning process, to discuss the gradual unfolding—and perhaps change—in the patterns of Dr. W's learning through supervision. The reader may feel pessimistic and may suggest that an individual as anxiety-ridden and emotionally crippled as this student seems to be cannot be helped through supervision. This is not necessarily so; even here, definite learning can occur and desirable changes will emerge. The extent to which this was made possible for Dr. W will become clearer in the chapter devoted to a discussion of the ongoing process in supervision. There, one will be able to follow the extent to which the initial "diagnostic" statements made here were borne out in actual practice and could be used helpfully in the training of this student. We have put the word "diagnostic" in quotes for lack of a better word to indicate that we are trying not only to predict learning patterns but also to suggest supervisory methods for tackling the problem stated in such a "diagnosis."

This interview has also served us while we were following the learning problems of the beginning therapist, to observe the teaching problems of the beginning supervisor, or rather, to observe the supervisor's learning to become a teacher. Actually, this supervisor was not very much older and not very much more experienced than his student and thus found it difficult to cope with an element of competitiveness, a natural struggle for supremacy which he should have avoided as a teacher who is able to accept the student. It was also true that the entire supervisory system which was initiated by our new administrator was new at that time and was comparatively untried in the particular setting. This fact put the new supervisor, who still had a good many misgivings about his new techniques and his new role himself, into a position where he was attempting to sell a teaching philosophy rather than to use it skillfully. Bernard Shaw said that "he who can does and he who cannot teaches." We might paraphrase him and suggest that "he who can supervises and he who cannot advertises his methods." The supervisor may have hoped that his student would quickly accept the new method and would become a sort of propaganda agent for the new teaching technique and the new viewpoint, thus calming perhaps the supervisor's own worries about the new, not yet tried instrument and the new system of responsibilities which he was to represent. The supervisor himself, rather than believing in tackling inner difficulties about his new responsibility as a teacher, may have seen a solution to this problem in the external strengthening of the system, an easier answer than the one of deepening his own skills as a teacher. The latter comment is not simply a reflection of the supervisor's lack of experience but rather a recognition that teaching problems are also political problems. Regardless of how skilled the teacher may be, whatever transpires between him and his student must be understood against the background of the total clinical rhombus. Part of the supervisor's strength, beyond his personal skill, his tact, and his maturity, is derived from the effectiveness of the total clinical setting. The full quality of the teacher will only be brought out at its best if he is supported by an understanding administration that skillfully provides a structure within which learning and teaching can take place.

Specific examples do not always lend themselves to an understanding of their generic implications. Our three students, even though each of them had a different way of introducing himself to his new supervisor, have a variety of features in common. Each of them brings expectations to the supervisor which will not be fully met. Each of them seems to have a pattern of asking for help in learning psychotherapy which stands in the way of full participation. It may seem to the reader that the selection of this material is rather one-sided. He may think of students who seem to collaborate fully and accept every suggestion, but nevertheless even with these he will soon detect that their way of acquiring knowledge from their supervisor contains features which must change during the process of learning if its fullest development is to take place. The learning of psychotherapy requires the complete participation of the student, an emotional and intellectual involvement which aims toward a new integration. The student cannot begin a process of acquisition of skill without his definite pattern of beginning. The supervisor cannot help the student unless the student is prepared to allow for change, for genuine adaptation rather than pseudo-adjustment. Psychotherapeutic skill, unlike other skills, cannot be learned on the surface and without a new sense of deep, inner discipline. The supervisor, aided by the structure of the training center if he can use it effectively, must help the student to be able to use the help under the conditions that are set by the training setting rather than under the conditions that he would wish to impose on the training center. The struggle for the conditions of help in learning might be a private and personalized struggle between two people as would be true in a master-apprentice arrangement. In such a struggle there is only an either-or. If the struggles of the learning process go on under the conditions of structured training, we can provide devices which create the limits, which create the necessary emotional distance, which create the optimum conditions for growth; a growth that finally becomes self-initiated by the student and is not left to immature devices of indoctrination or the chance of running into a teacher to whom one happens to take.

These examples cited to demonstrate the beginning of supervisory work have highlighted the different forms that the inevitable anxiety or concern takes during this period marking the departure from the comfortable known into the new unknown. The patient's reactions of anxiety and curiosity, of hope or despair, of embarrassment and guilt, which he brings at the beginning to the psychotherapeutic situation, is widely known and freely acknowledged. No matter how long it took the patient to bring himself to treatment, to resolve at least that part of his conflict which kept him delaying treatment, at the moment before starting the anxious "so soon?" frequently emerges. And in spite of his decision the doubt emerges again as to whether this was, after all, the right decision. Frequently, as he faces the office of the therapist, at that time practically a stranger to him, the problems of the preceding tormenting weeks and months seem to recede in the background and are pushed aside as it were by an entirely new kind of anxiety. The patient may well feel as some do when they slip into the dentist's chair, and the unbearable toothache vanishes or becomes a quite bearable dull ache; they who now feel that the dentist's intervention might be unnecessary after all. This new kind of anxiety, regardless of what rationalization the patient will offer concerning his questions about the psychotherapist, the expense of treatment, the uncertain outcome of treatment, the hope for other and entirely different methods, is but an indication that one may be more afraid of inner change than of the painful illness.

Why should one be surprised that the student of psychotherapy brings similar feelings to his teacher? As a matter of fact, he will even bring these feelings and these thoughts into the psychotherapeutic situation with his patient, and it is these beginning anxieties, these secret, frequently magic wishes, these doubts and bewilderment about his adequacy and his training for the task ahead that must be mastered somehow. Some students pass over all these initial feelings and are preoccupied with the need to "allay the patient's anxiety." Many a student remains inactive in the initial contact with the patient lest the patient, so goes the rationalization, interrupt treatment, or get too anxious. This aspect of the therapeutic axis, the anxiety of the beginning psychotherapist, the many forms that it takes, its origin, how it may be recognized, and how the supervisor can help the psychotherapist to cope with it in the gradually unfolding supervisory process, has been considered here. The fact that the student begins with his new patient while he also starts working with his supervisor helps us to see these problems in dual form. The fact that the student begins with us in supervision and brings to us a complex grouping of expectations in relation to the supervisor, in relation to the training center, and in relation to the patient offers us useful leverage to bring this whole group of interrelated problems into meaningful focus for the student with corresponding benefit for his patient. The parallels between his beginning therapeutic work and the actuality of facing the problem of beginning in supervision itself can be utilized by the supervisor provided he keeps clear of the danger of confusing the two processes, which have in common the problem of beginning but which differ in their basic purpose.

We may well ask now just what will happen to the beginning phase of supervision after the psychotherapist has actually started with his patient. Up till now we have gained some insight into what it may mean to a young psychotherapist when he starts seeing his supervisor. What does the experience with the patient mean to the therapist? What happens to him when he comes face to face with the actual work situation? How will his problems of beginning show up there in the work with the patient? Is there a relationship between his way of beginning with the supervisor and his way of beginning with his patient? These questions will occupy us in the next chapters.

VII / The Therapist Meets the Patient

Was man nicht erfliegen kann, muss man erhinken. . . .
Dies Schrift sagt, es ist keine Sünde zu hinken.

("What we cannot reach flying we must reach limping. . . .
The Book tells us it is no sin to limp.")

—Quoted by FREUD *

In the preceding chapter we attempted to simplify somewhat the many complex issues raised when the individuals representing each of the functions defined by our clinical rhombus start to work together on their common task. We did this by narrowing our inquiry and focusing on one of the many beginnings, that of the supervisor with his student denoted by the line S–T (Supervisor-Therapist) in the rhombus. We pointed out how different beginnings take place almost simultaneously, for the student of the supervisor is at the same time the therapist of the patient. By now shifting our focus we can illuminate the simultaneous activity taking place in that part of the rhombus represented by the line T–P (Therapist-Patient). And since the student-therapist is thus seen from two points of view, insight can be gained as to how the aspects of his psychological organization relevant to his functioning as a student are similarly or differently reflected in his functioning as a therapist.

* In *Beyond the Pleasure Principle.* The quotation is taken from the version by Rückert of one of the Maqāmāt of al-Harari.

This can be illustrated best if we follow the initial psychotherapeutic interviews of one of the same students whose first contact with his supervisor has already been detailed. For this purpose we select Mr. Y, the eager beginner who has heretofore been chronically disappointed in his various training experiences. With the new supervisor he experienced his first disappointment when he discovered that the former had not made what he regarded as the proper arrangements to select a suitable patient for his consideration. Concerning this issue he had told the supervisor, "I thought you would arrange all that for me," and was somewhat disconsolate when the supervisor referred to the initiating role of the administrator in this selection.

A few days later a patient was referred through the designated administrative channels for consideration for treatment by Mr. Y. According to the clinical summary available to Mr. Y and to his supervisor, the patient was a fifty-four-year-old, widowed male, recently admitted to the hospital because of sleep disturbances and tormenting memories of a fire in which his wife and children had been burned to death. The patient's life had been characterized by considerable instability. His education had been interrupted just short of his graduation from college. He had moved from job to job. He had been married five times, each marriage being of brief duration, and all but the last terminating in divorce over what on the surface seemed to be trivial difficulties. For much of his adult life he drank very heavily. Since the onset of his present illness, some two years prior to this particular hospitalization, he had sought psychiatric help on three separate occasions. Each time he must have presented himself somewhat differently to the examining physician, since three different diagnostic categorizations were made, perhaps reflecting these different emphases. The three diagnoses were: acute depressive reaction, chronic alcoholism, and emotionally unstable character. In view of his frequent change of jobs, of wives, and more lately, of doctors, it is possible perhaps to speculate that the patient soon to meet our neophyte therapist is also someone who has chronically been a little bit disappointed.

The patient dated the onset of his current illness at a time two years before the present hospital admission when he returned home late from work one night to find that the apartment house in which he, his (fifth) wife, and two children were living was in flames, and to make the shocking discovery that they were already dead. In his first hospitalization some two weeks later he was in an acute depressive state, in the course of which he constantly proclaimed his negligence in not coming home on time, and thus not having been present to prevent the tragedy. Throughout the two-year period since that time, the patient continually complained of sleep disturbances and nightmarish dreams. For three or four nights in succession he would go to bed and, in hypnagogic states as well as in dreams, see visions of his wife and children being burned, crying out for help, and dying; more recently, his father, who had been dead for many years, had begun to appear in these dreams to reprove him. He would toss, roll, get up and smoke a cigarette, go for a walk, all in an unsuccessful attempt to dispel these thoughts. During the day he would recognize these as hallucinatory experiences, especially in regard to the father, and call them "crazy thoughts" that he should be able to control. After three or four nights spent this way he would collapse in utter exhaustion and then awaken the next day still tired, groggy, and feeling unable to go to work. Along with the patient, we, too, might recognize the ever-present danger of a psychotic breakdown, and see his repeated hospitalizations as desperate appeals for help in warding off a florid psychotic process.

Mr. Y, after agreeing to begin to work with the patient, called the patient's ward and scheduled the first appointment, for which the patient, on his side, had been prepared by his ward physician. When therapist and patient met, the former introduced himself, saying his name was Y. When the patient quickly asked, "Doctor?" the therapist responded, "Mr. Y." In answer to an inquiry by the therapist, the patient acknowledged that his ward doctor had told him why he was coming here and had, in fact, explained the whole thing to him. He further said that he had gone about finding out who the therapist was. Mr. Y asked the patient what he had found out, and the latter said that he found that the therapist was a doctor on the staff. Mr. Y said that he was not a physician, but a psychologist, and that he was not on the staff, but still in training. When he followed this up by asking the patient what the ward doctor had told him about the therapist, the patient replied stiffly, "Oh, the doctor told me I would be speaking to you; he didn't tell me much more."

What can we see as having transpired in these opening moves between the therapist and the patient? Is there a relationship between the therapist's way of beginning with the supervisor and his way of beginning with the patient? He has told his supervisor that in his learning experiences to date he has come to expect to be a little disappointed. His first patient is a depressed and self-depreciating individual. In response to the patient's anxious endowment of his "doctor" with the curative potential that the title conveys to him, the therapist beat a hasty retreat with his defensive statement that he was not yet a doctor, nor even on the staff, but merely a trainee and a beginner. Thus he has said to the depressed man with his lowered self-esteem, "Look, you may not have a very high opinion of yourself, but don't look to me for too much help with this, because I don't have a much higher self-appraisal myself. After all, I'm a student, just a beginner." He has said in effect, "Don't expect too much, lest you be disappointed," and has in so doing ensured the very disappointment in himself that he wished to ward off. At the very beginning of an intended psychotherapeutic relationship, the therapist protected himself from the demand that he deal helpfully with the patient's presenting problem by the confession that he struggled with a similar problem, which he had not yet been able to resolve satisfactorily in himself. Yet it would be difficult for the patient to voice directly his disappointment in the announced helplessness of the therapist. In depreciating himself, the student therapist had averted the selfsame accusation from the patient. Mr. Y had said so himself, first. He could wait for the patient's next move.

The patient, in his turn, next focused the interview on himself with the statement, "Doctor, I'm not here for a vacation, I'm in good physical shape; I can do a lot of things. The last time I was in the hospital they sent me out and said I was all right, even though I didn't really feel well. They said I should go and work these things off, but they only keep getting worse." The therapist asked what precisely was wrong, and the next pattern of interaction emerged. The patient developed the story of his difficulties; his chronic alcoholic excess, sporadic troubles with the law that derived from his drinking, and then his sleep disturbances, his nighttime visions, and finally the quasi-hallucinatory experiences. "I keep seeing them at night . . . I see my father now. I'm not even asleep and I see them. I was never close to my father, but now he keeps coming back. All those ugly things, too. I don't even know how to describe them. Something like a red belt once, like it was going to come down from the ceiling—and I'm not even asleep. Boy, am I glad when I start hearing the birds singing and see the sun coming up in the morning. You know I can hardly believe that anything went on like that during the night."

The therapist's responses to the patient's material could best be characterized as a "diagnostic" one. His every response (at the points where the narrative temporarily halted) was a variant of the "tell me more" or the "what else" question. With this approach, the therapist could keep his own distance and make no commitment himself, other than the implied promise that later when the patient had ultimately "told all," the hoped-for help would be forthcoming. It invited the patient to commit himself more deeply, while postponing present action by the therapist with the promise of future help.

Of course, the attitude of the therapist at this point could be soundly supported in the theoretical teaching to which he subscribed. The therapist, with his conscious rationale embedded in the matrix of psychodynamic thinking, wanted to be helpful through being "non-directive," a fusion of outlooks derived from his views of psychoanalytic and "client-centered" therapeutic work. In so doing he treated the patient according to his model of the presumed treatment approach to the neurotic, forgetting the insights his own "diagnostic" searching should have made evident, the near-psychotic state of ego organization of his patient. The patient had come to the hospital for help in warding off psychosis, only to have his therapist voice the insistent demand to remember more—and to tell more. At the same time that the patient is enjoined to tell still more, he must be unsure of how much impact what he has just told must have had, since even after his revelation of the terror of his nighttime experience, he was asked "what other thoughts" this led him to.

So we need not be surprised when in the course of the interview the patient began to withdraw. He said, "But then, I'm O.K. during the day," and described how well he had got along with his wife, how excellent was his state of health, and how diligent a worker he was in contrast with some of his lazy, "free-loading" fellow patients. Suddenly the situation had reversed. The patient had withdrawn, asserting his health, and in order to maintain the contact, the therapist had to become, perforce, the pursuer and now prove to the patient that he was sick despite his defensive protestations of health. When the patient referred to his own well-being, the therapist interrupted to state, "You always work off everything during the day, don't you? Maybe you're afraid that by the time you get around to seeing me these things won't look so big anymore like they did at night, and you won't have anything to talk about." And after another such strategic retreat by the patient, the therapist again countered with the assertion that he agreed with what the patient had said previously about not being helped by having a vacation here, and that there were a lot of things that were ganging up on him that they should try to get to the bottom of. The patient said in reply that he didn't really have any big problems. He just didn't see why all these experiences should happen to him. The therapist said that most people see their problems as small when they look back upon them, and are sort of ashamed actually to tell other people about them. But that doesn't mean that they're not very large to the person himself and can't cause him a lot of trouble. In reply the patient started talking about some friend of his who, he said, worried about every little thing.

By now the reversal was complete. At first the therapist held his distance and asked that the patient commit himself. As the patient began to do so, the therapist preserved his own noninvolvement behind his "diagnostic" detachment. When the patient in his turn withdrew, the therapist now moved closer to affirm the patient's illness and his need for help. Perhaps at this point he already experienced warning signs of the patient's beginning to play with the thought of terminating his treatment. Certainly, we can feel that the therapist's affirmation of the patient's need for help stemmed in part at least from a desire to hold on to the patient at all costs, and not alone from a wish to be maximally effective in helping the patient work out his own best decision—whether it would be to stay in treatment or to leave.

How, then, did the therapist propose to help if the patient would only stay? At this point in the interaction Mr. Y asked the patient how he thought he could be helped. The patient thought and said he wasn't sure; that he had tried everything; that he would do anything to really get better now, and that he would be frank and tell everything that the therapist wanted to know. This, Mr. Y said, was a good attitude and the patient was certainly going to have to do a lot of talking about himself. Mr. Y continued by saying that he would see the patient two hours each week and that the patient could stay in the hospital as long as necessary on this occasion. A few moments later the therapist commended the patient for "wanting to go to work on what's wrong with you," and then added, "but you know it's going to be pretty hard work." It was after this setting of the conditions and the climate within which help was being proffered that the interview was brought to a close and the next meeting time agreed upon.

What meanings did the patient read into this move of the therapist? And from what intrapsychic constellations in the patient did these ascribed meanings derive? Certainly, the patient has demonstrated to us through the vivid portrayal of the hallucinated father image the degree of externalization that he must maintain of his incompletely consolidated conscience figures. Superimposed upon the memory of the conflagration with its representation of the woman being consumed in the fire of the impulses, is the terror-arousing figure of the father which seemingly could never be allowed closer and with which the patient seemed never able to reconcile himself. (He has said, "I was never close to my father, but now he keeps coming back.") When the patient came at last to the hospital to be relieved of his depressed state by the succoring mother, he was confronted instead by the strict father in the person of the therapist, who sternly demanded that he work hard to achieve the promised rewards.

Perhaps out of this we can see the logic of the "surprise" with which the patient will confront his therapist in their second session together—namely, his decision to leave both psychotherapy and hospital. For the patient had come fearing a psychosis and seeking help to ward it off. When faced with the new representative of the father who enjoined him not to repress the erupting psychotic process, but to remember ever more and to work hard at it, he chose to flee the hospital again—as he had before. Thus the patient reacted repetitively to a total situation—be it hospitalization or job or marriage—and rather than reveal himself and involve himself with all the feared consequences of that course, he sought refuge in another flight—and began yet another repetitive cycle.

The manner in which he revealed this determination to the therapist in the very next hour confirmed that the patient acted as if the nature of the decision should be self-evident. After a somewhat awkward initial silence the patient began by saying, "There have been quite a few changes, haven't there?" When the therapist confessed his puzzlement, the patient explained that something had come up, that he had always wanted schooling under the G.I. Bill, that unless he registered this very next week he stood to lose some of his G.I. benefits, that learning Spanish and typing would do him good, since he "could use the money" he received while he learned, and the learning could lead to a variety of possible employment opportunities. "Besides, I'm going to work hard at it and that's good for me."

The balance of the hour was then occupied with the repeated, but unsuccessful attempts of the therapist to reach the sources of this decision and, if possible, to undo it and lead his first patient back into therapy, not end it before it had even begun. The patient would say only at one point that he felt that he had talked too much in the first interview and for the rest further elaborated what he stood to gain in security—and in pride—by exchanging treatment for schooling. In the end they parted, the therapist obviously more than a little disappointed in his failure to hold his patient; the patient disappointed that the longed-for help that would make this experience of hospitalization different from the previous ones had not materialized. Too, in relation to the supervisor, the therapist was probably at least slightly aware of yet another disappointment suffered in the sequence of his training experiences—with its reproach to those who did not take sufficient interest to procure a properly ensured treatment case.

As one looks at the over-all dynamics of this first therapeutic contact, one asks first what the therapist's major problems with it are. Certainly, the difficulty does not consist only of the pragmatic consequences—that the patient chose to leave rather than stay for treatment—and how this consequence could perhaps have been averted. For this decision might well be the appropriate and even inevitable resolution of the dilemma confronting the patient at this juncture. Rather the major problem rests perhaps in the fact that the decision to leave seemed to well up as an inner compulsion, made as if it were a judgment against the stand taken by the therapist, rather than a decision, the determinants of which had been brought into consciousness and that became then the outcome of sober consideration by both therapist and patient of a problem shared jointly between them. For instance, the therapist might have acknowledged—as he did—the illness of the patient and followed this with a statement both of willingness to help as well as of awareness of the many problems the patient would have in following through on this offer of help. For the decision to reject psychotherapy need not be only resistance. The patient was fifty-four, his illness was deeply rooted in his character structure and in his behavior, and significant psychotherapeutically based modification would necessitate a considerable investment of time and energy. Under these circumstances the decision to forego psychotherapeutic involvement might well be the wisest one. One could wish only that it would follow such a conscious consideration of the relevant factors, helpfully brought to explicit awareness and focus by the activity of the therapist, rather than be an intuitive, unconsciously based repetition of a need acted upon without insight and therefore without mastery.

Perhaps these are some of the reflections of the supervisor as he reads the process notes of Mr. Y's first hour with his patient, in anticipation of the supervisory conference. What Dr. Baehr, the supervisor, does with this material depends, of course, on his supervisory philosophy as well as his skill. He has available to him not only the process account of his student's contact with the patient, but also his own beginning conference with the student prior to the assignment of the student to the patient. How the supervisor will try to relate the knowledge from these two sources of information in a way helpful to the student, we will be able to follow in our account in the next chapter, "The Supervisor and the Student-Therapist Discuss the Patient," in which we focus comparatively on processes occurring simultaneously along the lines S–T (Supervisor-Therapist) and T–P (Therapist-Patient) of our clinical rhombus.

Before we turn, however, to a consideration of what transpires between student and supervisor when they together discuss the patient, we ought to illustrate more fully the manner in which the range of ways of learning—and specifically of beginning—can be variously expressed, by taking up the beginning therapeutic work of yet another, much different, student whom we have likewise met in the preceding chapter. This is Dr. W, the student who cannot acknowledge that any experience is new, but must rather reduce whatever he sees to the already known and conquered. To him the experience in learning to be offered by the new supervisor is seen as just a repetition of what he has already learned, and the problem posed is merely one of identifying the sameness. How, then, will such a therapist confront a new patient?

The patient referred for psychotherapy to Dr. W was indeed at first glance quite like many Dr. W had seen in his previous general medical as well as psychiatric experience. The patient was a forty-six-year-old man, with gastro-intestinal complaints of eight years' duration. These had started with anorexia and feelings of tension arising first while he was in a combat zone subject to repeated strafings. He became fearful, seclusive, and lost interest in his buddies. The anorexia was soon overshadowed by bloating, abdominal pain, and nausea. He tried to vomit but couldn't. X-ray study revealed no evidence of ulcer.

The patient attributed his growing nervousness to the suffering he experienced working for a commanding officer whom he saw as both incompetent and alcoholic. The patient felt the entire outfit to be constantly jeopardized by the poor judgment of this officer and dreamed of the day when he could wreak his revenge by pushing the officer into the path of a vehicle, or, alternatively, escaping the oppression by obtaining his discharge from the army. Incidentally, the patient had grown up under the domination of a controlling mother who forbade his participation in extracurricular athletic or social activities, manipulated his job choices, and took his pay checks, leaving him enough money to go to an occasional movie. He dreamed constantly of throwing over the yoke of his mother's authority and when he did so in his early twenties he had a few years of "sowing his wild oats." These consisted of spending money more consistently than earning it, drinking, gambling, and running around with women. When he did work intermittently at manual labor, he felt strong and proud in his independence.

Upon release from the army and the restrictive controls he suffered there, he continued to have stomach complaints, felt weak and unable to keep up his former standards of hard work. He felt that he ran into an increasing number of unsympathetic and driving foremen. His discomfort and abdominal pain was only mitigated by his wife's appearance three times a day at his job with his medication. Nevertheless, he worked less and less, and became openly depressed and repeatedly sought hospitalization. His physicians constantly wondered whether his gastro-intestinal complaints were "on an organic or functional basis." Equivocal X-ray evidence of gall bladder disease led to the surgical removal of that organ with little impact on the seeming progressive course of the disability. He finally accepted psychiatric referral, though at the same time he considered psychotherapy to be an implication or accusation that his complaints were only imaginary.

Certainly such a patient was no simple psychotherapeutic prospect. And we have already seen how in his initial contact with his supervisor Dr. W raised his doubts about the quality of this patient's motivations for psychotherapy. Only there we have permitted ourselves to interpret his communication from the standpoint of the interaction of the student with the supervisor, to whom he was really saying, "I know all this already. I've had it all before. So you will indeed have a job eliciting sufficient motivation from me to make me really receptive to what you may have to teach."

But now he approached with misgivings the patient whose motivation likewise was seemingly so dubious. As he came to the patient's ward to introduce himself to the patient for the first time, he espied the hospital's internist making his rounds. He then went first to the internist and chatted with him about the physical findings in the patient. This was in the center of the ward, no more than fifteen feet from the patient who was lying on his back with his head turned to one side as though he were asleep. Dr. W wondered uneasily at this time whether or not the patient heard himself being discussed, but received no clue as to this from the patient. In this discussion of the two physicians concerning the patient, and presumably just out of earshot, the essentially intrusive aspect of this curiosity into the inner events of the other is suddenly projected onto the patient and perceived as the patient's nosiness and eavesdropping, just as in the previous interview with his supervisor Dr. W projected the whole question of the adequacy of the motivation for the process ahead onto the patient.

After he left the internist, Dr. W went over and stood by the patient's bedside and called him by name several times. The patient looked up and acknowledged that he had been sleeping. Dr. W introduced himself and invited the patient to his office for their initial consultation. Dr. W explained that he was the doctor assigned to treat the patient and found out that the patient had been given his name by the administrative doctor on the ward. In the office the patient's first comments were that he was still sleepy, and he ascribed this to the medicine he was taking that made him sleepy. This was not usual, but today he had received some extra medication. He said this was given to him because he had a sick feeling in his stomach.

Dr. W asked the patient to describe this more, but he could do little more than just say it was a sick feeling; he then referred to his throat and described a sensation he had there that caused him all his difficulty. Dr. W said, "I listened to this attentively and encouraged him to go on accepting all that he told me as certainly very meaningful material *to him*." And Dr. W then added, "This description was quite detailed." Here Dr. W had come up against the struggle in himself that was evoked by the manner in which the patient presented his complaints. Dr. W, in accord with his theoretical teaching about the presence of inner purpose in communication when it is looked at in terms of its psychological meanings, tried to accept the parading of somatic sensations as a metaphoric statement of the expectations and the demands of the patient toward the would-be helper. So he tried to accept what the patient told as certainly very meaningful—to the patient; thus emphasizing his own unwillingness to identify yet with a heretofore alien viewpoint. For this viewing of communication as a psychological move in an interpersonal drama has been but uneasily grafted upon Dr. W's earlier and more solid training as a physician who gives sober and literal consideration to the exact grouping of discrete symptoms and signs into distinguishable somatic disease patterns. Thus Dr. W could accept the somatic complaints as a statement of psychologic purpose and meaning only crudely and not quite sincerely, and perhaps began to wonder in himself if he should revert to his more familiar medical orientation built around the "differential diagnosis" of pathological entities.

As the patient went on to develop the chain of somatic events leading ultimately from symptoms to gall bladder operation, to his conviction that something had gone wrong in the gall bladder operation to incite all his subsequent difficulties, and to his suspicion that the offending etiological agent might well be the gas used for the anesthesia, Dr. W came finally to the role of the concerned internist, intent on the question of differential diagnosis of "organic" from "functional" disorder—the very dilemma that had puzzled the previous (nonpsychiatric) physicians who had treated the patient. Dr. W wanted to know specifically which anesthetic agent the patient had had, and could be told only that the patient "couldn't remember anything after walking into the operating room and taking off his pants."

Dr. W was now caught in his own double role. He had tried to maintain the position of the psychologically attuned observer and yet this had given way, and he failed to respond to this last remark as a communication with interpersonal purpose and psychological meaning. Rather, he had become the psychiatrically-oriented internist who seeks to certify the diagnosis of psychogenic disturbance through exclusion of somatic disease process. Are the patient's continued post-operative complaints to be linked to the ill effects on the organism of the particular anesthetic agent used? If so, an organic basis for the disturbance has been established. If not, then perhaps it is functional. In functioning in this "medical" way, Dr. W based his stand on his prior very thorough medical training and indoctrination, and he indeed saw his psychotherapeutic patient in an older, more familiar way. In taking on the role of psychotherapist for the first time, Dr. W truly found nothing new—as he had warned his supervisor that he would not.

In functioning this way, Dr. W overlooked that a number of physician colleagues had already taken the patient through the very same diagnostic and evaluative process before referring the patient to Dr. W for psychotherapeutic help directed toward the emotional difficulties of the patient—emotional difficulties which they had previously satisfied themselves to be significant determinants of the somatic symptoms. Furthermore, Dr. W has precluded his own functioning in a psychotherapeutic frame of reference within which the unfolding complaints and interpersonal difficulties of the patient must be conceptualized as part of a psychological interaction, regardless of the nature of the concomitant involvement of the soma. Basically, Dr. W has not at all grasped that a psychotherapeutic process can evolve, even though the patient has simultaneous needs related to other medical specialties. For he has come prepared only to seek the old in the new, not to see what its newness consists of.

Through this shift in position, Dr. W felt, however, "much more comfortable with him, finding that it was not difficult to talk to him—even though I felt that we had come to no understanding that this was psychotherapy and that he was accepting it." Here, Dr. W's guilt was invoked and he tried to re-focus his role as a psychological participant. He went on to say, "My purpose at the time was an attempt to try to appreciate his feelings concerning this thing, the immediate symptom, perhaps to empathize with him and to refuse to really put any label on this as an imaginary or as a physical thing, but rather to accept that he had much difficulty, and I could appreciate it." But the patient had already taken his cue. "He (the patient) went on to assure me that there was something in there—that he knew it because he could feel it. He said that he had taken medicines quite a long time now, that they had done him no good whatsoever, and that he was sure that there was only one solution left. I asked him what this was, and he said it was surgery."

With this rejection of his good offices, Dr. W became angry and asked the patient if he had any definite idea as to what type of surgery it had to be, and the latter replied that he didn't know, that he thought perhaps his palate was wrong. Dr. W then suggested that maybe the palate had been pushed down and hurt while the patient was under anesthesia during the gall bladder operation. The patient half agreed, nodding his head that this might be so. Dr. W further suggested that perhaps the patient thought the palate ought to be corrected and put back in place or something, to which the response was, well maybe something like that. Surely, Dr. W has not offered these suggestions seriously, but has allowed his anger to spill over into a poking fun at the very holding-onto physiological explanatory mechanisms that he has himself unwittingly abetted. Perhaps in embarrassed recognition of this, Dr. W then abruptly told the patient that he would be seeing him three times a week, and indicated the time of the next appointment. The patient hesitated a little at this point and then said that he might be a few minutes late, as he received his medication at that very hour. Thus the patient served notice that, though he would consent to meet again, the appointments must not interfere with his "real" treatment. Dr. W took this into account and set the appointment fifteen minutes later, and so ended the first interview.

How does Dr. W perceive his first contact with the patient? Or, more precisely, what will he convey to his supervisor as his perception of this interview? For this, we can turn to the last paragraph of his process notes of this first interview. "I felt that the patient had come to the hour a little resistant to starting out with a new doctor and certainly quite cautious as to what I might be like. I tried to sympathize with him and get into the feeling of the distress caused by his symptoms and thus encourage him to accept me and start a relationship. I felt that the essential thing at this time was to start a relationship as a basis for him to come to see me, before the issue of psychotherapy itself and whether or not he wants it would ever be touched on. I felt he knew as well as I that this was psychotherapy, but that it would be much easier to accept without bringing the issue up. I felt that the patient did begin to accept me through the hour, did test me a couple of times to see if I was going to react and perhaps reject him when he displayed his hostility toward psychotherapy, and he then evidenced his acceptance of me by his quite readily accepting further appointments."

Here, then, Dr. W states the version of his first therapeutic interview which he wishes his supervisor to accept. As Dr. Baehr reads the material as offered in the process notes, what impressions come to his mind about the problems of the treatment hour? Dr. W has stated that the patient had come to the hour a little resistant and certainly quite cautious as to what the new doctor might be like. Dr. Baehr knows, however, from his initial supervisory contact with Dr. W before the patient was in the picture, that Dr. W, too, is quite resistant to starting and troubled about the problem of motivation. And from the manner of Dr. W's middle-of-the-ward conversation with the internist, all the while glancing in the direction of the patient and wondering if he overheard, one can feel confident that the patient is not the only one of the pair who is cautious as to what the other is like. Dr. W then states that he tried to empathize with the patient, to encourage the patient to accept him, and to "start a relationship." Here Dr. W has endeavored to put his psychiatric teaching into practice. But he has not yet established his own convictions about the essential differentness of a psychotherapeutic relationship from a social relationship, and so he can say that he feels the essential thing is to "start a relationship"—any relationship—before the issue of psychotherapy itself and whether or not the patient wants it is ever touched on. And so, when the patient responded by revealing the intensity of his own hypochondriacal fixations that were seemingly unaffected by the therapist's offer of a helping relationship, Dr. W's psychological framework rapidly gave way to his earlier more "medical" viewpoint.

Dr. W became, then, the physician bent on differential diagnosis, separating the functional from the organically based disorder. In doing so, he failed to start a psychological process geared to the conviction that psychological understanding can lead to psychological change. He did not explore, as he might have, the patient's expectations of him, and the patient's perceptions of the nature of the help being offered. He did not explore, as again he might have, the whole nature of the psychotherapy referral to him. What understanding was the patient given by his ward physician as to the reason for a referral for psychotherapy? To what extent did the patient participate actively in this decision and to what extent did he simply acquiesce? For the patient is rather a simple-minded and quite literal individual. To him the world of psychotherapy is *all* new. And to this newness he brings wonderment as to how this new intervention can promise any alleviation of his distress. But his new doctor seeks not for the new, but only to rediscover the old; and so they end, the therapist frustrated that the patient now seems unwilling to give up his anchorings in his somatic preoccupations, and the patient puzzled as to why really they shall be meeting together three times a week—especially since he already has a ward physician who handles all needs for medication and care. It will not surprise us therefore that the patient does not come for the next appointment, and when the therapist goes for him after some twenty minutes have gone by, he finds the patient asleep in his bed, claiming he has been hazy with medication all day and therefore forgot the appointment, and finally silent for most of the balance of the hour after the therapist and he go to the office.

How therapist and supervisor now bring together these varying impressions of the process engaged in by one of them with a third person, and how this is done within the context of another process—the supervisory process, which, like a therapeutic process, is aimed at the problems and needs of but one of the participants—will be the subject matter of the next chapter, "The Supervisor and the Student-Therapist Discuss the Patient." In that chapter we will follow a variety of processes that can occur as one attempts to focus comparatively on processes occurring simultaneously on the two lines S–T (Supervisor-Therapist) and T–P (Therapist-Patient) of our clinical rhombus.

VIII / The Supervisor and the Student-Therapist Discuss the Patient

Every piece of work is in fact a realization—piecemeal if you like, but each complete in itself—of our own nature; they are stones on that harsh road which we must walk to learn of ourselves. No wonder, then, that each one in turn is a surprise to us!—THOMAS MANN

In the preceding chapter we were concerned with a number of questions that arise as we study a beginning process between a therapist and his patient, such as: What problems does the patient present to the therapist? What problems does the therapist see in his interaction with the patient, and which ones will he choose to bring to the supervisor? And, what problems does the supervisor see as he reads the process notes of the therapeutic interviews that he may wish to raise with the therapist? As we now study the first session at which the supervisor and the student therapist discuss the interactions of the therapeutic situation between the therapist and his patient (against the background of their own interaction), a new group of questions come into focus: What problems does the supervisor have with the student? And, what problems does the supervisor have concerning the patient? Here we encompass a broadened concern with simultaneous activity along two lines S–T (Supervisor-Therapist) and T–P (Therapist-Patient) of our clinical rhombus; and since the student-therapist is thus seen from two vantage points at once, a unique opportunity is afforded to see how aspects of his psychological organization relevant to his functioning in the one setting are similarly or differently reflected in the other.

For purposes of clarity of exposition of these processes we can best follow the two students, Mr. Y and Dr. W, both in supervision with Dr. Baehr, whose first interviews with their supervisor and then with their patients we have followed in the preceding two chapters.

The mutual disappointment experienced between Mr. Y and his depressed patient has already been seen clearly in our discussion in the preceding chapter of their first interview together. We have seen as well how this experience of disappointment was what Mr. Y had already both expected and feared. The decision to terminate the therapy, which had hardly begun, was communicated to the therapist by the patient at the beginning of their second hour together. It was defended by the patient as a forward and constructive step. Something had come up that he hadn't expected. He had always wanted to take advantage of his schooling opportunities under the G.I. Bill, and now he found that unless he registered this very next week he stood to lose his G.I. benefits. He wanted to learn Spanish and typing, both of which "might do me good," since he "could use the money" he received while he learned, and the learning itself might lead to a variety of higher level job opportunities. He stated his own conviction that "I'm going to work hard at it and that's good for me" and proclaimed as well the support of his ward doctor. The ward doctor, he said, quite agreed that he could take a thirty-day pass so that he could start school (and still return to the hospital if need be) and not lose his G.I. Bill benefits. He further stated that "the ward doctor said it might work out pretty well. . . . Do you think I should do it?" Thus the question was posed for our neophyte therapist, confronting him early with the seeming imminent loss of his very first patient, and bringing to the fore perhaps his ready disappointment in the patient who was declining his help and in himself who felt unable to offer help in a way that would be accepted.

Confronted with this question, Mr. Y answered, "You know you've tried working hard before and it didn't seem to do any good." With this statement Mr. Y threw the weight of his influence against the contemplated decision, the wisdom of which the patient then felt constrained to defend. Here a beginning psychotherapist has lost his psychotherapeutic bearings. The patient has couched a psychological problem about accepting a therapeutic relationship in terms of a proposed "constructive" step in reality. The therapist, interpreting a psychologic move as an already inevitable real move, called on the patient's own history of repeated abortive starts in the past to oppose the present restatement of the same intent. Instead of dealing with the psychologic material psychotherapeutically, the therapist opposed it since it had become a threat of imminent action rather than a communication about treatment. In thus treating a psychological problem as an action problem, the therapist gave way to his own counter-acting, leading to a deadlocked hour in which the patient invoked his pride to bolster a decision that he ended up more committed to than he had perhaps intended.

The last paragraph of Mr. Y's process notes of this interview conveyed the uncertainty of decision of each of the protagonists at the end of the session. "The patient apparently did not want to leave as I started getting up to end the hour, but in an apologetic way started to justify his wanting to leave again. He then admitted that if going to school helped him he would not come back at all. He then said, though, that if I thought he should stay he would. I answered that he did not have to feel guilty about leaving and that he was the one really to make the decision since he knew himself well enough. He got up and said that he would think about this. He then added that he might not see me again, though, and we shook hands. I told him that if I didn't, I certainly hoped that he would get better."

What might have transpired in this hour if Mr. Y had been able to treat the psychologic material as such and not as a call to action, destined to add yet another disappointing experience? Suppose for instance Mr. Y had responded to the patient's initial question "Do you think I should do it?" with a statement that it sounded like a wonderful decision and a brave one too; only that it came as somewhat of a surprise that the patient felt up to it already, in view of the very upsetting experiences he had been through that he had recounted in their first hour together. Could they together have gone on to consider the pros and cons and have thus brought the psychological problems behind the intent to terminate into the psychotherapeutic arena?

It is with such questions in mind perhaps that supervisor and therapist came to their second conference. Mr. Y came in wondering—as his problem in *beginning* with the patient—what he might have done to contribute to his new patient's abrupt ending. He began by stating that the ward physician in fact felt quite guilty over the part he had played (without consulting the therapist) in encouraging the patient to feel very free to go ahead with this attempt to "try it once more on the outside" and "get more training." Indeed, while the therapist had played the role of the ward physician pointing out the "unrealistic" aspects of the projected flight from treatment to training, in view of the previous failures of just such attempts, the ward physician had on his side assumed the quasi-psychotherapeutic attitude of offering the utmost of freedom in which to maneuver. The psychotherapist thus tried to prevent action and the ward physician encouraged free expression—a complete reversal of roles. After thus presenting the ward physician's part in the sequence of events, Mr. Y came around to his own question, couched as his own guilt, expressed variously as "Did I contribute in some way to the patient's abrupt departure? Did I push him too hard? Would a more experienced therapist have done differently?"

The discussion of these questions centered around Mr. Y's handling of the chief dilemma—and chief defense—presented by the patient in his first therapy hour. The depressed and self-depreciating patient had presented as his central theme, "I don't amount to very much. And no one cares especially for me. No one takes care of me. Will you? Can I depend on you? Will you care for me, love me, and guarantee to help me?" Mr. Y had resisted from saying, "Yes, I will," and accepting this total responsibility; although he confessed that he was almost tempted to say, "Please do," when the patient had said (at the end of their second hour together) "that if I thought he should stay he would." In struggling against this temptation Mr. Y had sought some supervisory support when he made sure to see the supervisor for a corridor conversation of a few moments several days before the actual supervisory hour in order to be reassured that he had done the right thing in not saying, "Yes, please stay." He felt, perhaps correctly, that he could thereby have held the patient in the hospital, though he was also well aware of the difficulties such a course of action would create for the total therapeutic situation.

Dynamically, what has now taken place? Mr. Y had been tempted to plead with the patient and say, "Yes, please stay." In this plea would be the unspoken assertion, "I may not be much of a therapist as yet, and I may be a big disappointment to you, but please don't you desert me in turn; don't you disappoint me!" Mr. Y had successfully warded off this extreme, the dangers of which for the psychotherapy he could well sense, and resorted to its opposite, that the patient "was the one really to make the decision since he knew himself well enough." Avoiding the one temptation, Mr. Y tried to clarify the total situation as the patient's dilemma and the patient's problem to be solved. One could well wonder, as the supervisor did with Mr. Y, whether he might not have been more helpful to the patient in supporting him with the problem, in trying to feel with him the dilemma of having this problem, rather than in just leaving the patient with it, which could be perceived as a rejection and a withdrawal by the therapist.

Where exactly did Mr. Y convey to the patient what he had hoped to cover up by not saying, "Please do"—the conviction that he himself was not much of a therapist as yet, and that he must be as big a disappointment to the patient as the patient was to him? This we have already seen in our discussion of the first interview between therapist and patient, when the former introduced himself saying his name was Y, to which the patient asked, "Doctor?," and the therapist had responded, "Mr. Y." The patient, almost ignoring what he had heard then, said he had gone about finding out that the therapist was a doctor on the staff. To this Mr. Y replied that he was not a physician, but a psychologist, not yet a Ph. D., and that he was not on the staff but still in training. Here the depressive mood and self-depreciated tone of the patient had been early met by its counterpart in the therapist confessing from the start his lack of skill and his despair of offering real psychotherapeutic help. The implications of this opening interchange and how it so promptly set the tone of the ensuing two hours, which the therapist then ostensibly battled so vigorously against, were not directly evident to Mr. Y. It was rather the supervisor who, in connection with the whole discussion of what it could have meant to have yielded to the temptation to plead with the patient to stay, asked the therapist to reflect on the possible meanings to the patient in his confession of his beginning training status.

Dr. Baehr focused this issue by asking Mr. Y why he had thought it necessary to elaborate his statement to the patient beyond the factual "I'm not a physician. I'm a psychologist." Why did he have to spell out the poverty of his curriculum vitae as a psychotherapist? Mr. Y felt that this was a matter of honesty but he had indeed been wondering about it and had felt somewhat uneasy as he said it at the time. He said too that maybe his statement stemmed from a certain defensiveness about not being a doctor. What did the supervisor think about it? Dr. Baehr wondered again whether Mr. Y couldn't have stopped at that point; that his statement had given the patient an unnecessary "reality basis" to substantiate his neurotic denial of the therapist's ability to help him. This would indeed make it more difficult subsequently to raise with the patient the latter's many doubts of Mr. Y's abilities as a therapist. Mr. Y said that yes, he could see that. His statement *was* gratuitous. "But after all, I am no great shakes as a therapist. I am new at this." To which the supervisor replied, "Sort of your insurance against failure? To warn the patient not to expect too much or to be too disappointed?"

Here perhaps is the crux of the problem. The inexperienced therapist has been led to overidentify with the patient, a depressed individual who found ample reason to depreciate himself and to be disappointed in what he gets. The patient evoked in the therapist the wish to overidentify and to confess his own sense of inadequacy, a confession by the way which had no place in the therapeutic situation with the patient but had a very real place in his learning situation as a beginning student. Through this displacement Mr. Y confessed via the patient what really belonged with his supervisor, namely his anxiety that as a beginner he felt unable to offer real help. His honest confession was thus indirectly brought to the supervisor through the blunder committed in the therapeutic situation. It had, too, another overtone. When he thus indirectly communicated to the supervisor that "I'm just a beginner," Mr. Y also conveyed "Therefore, don't expect much of me in my therapeutic work." To what extent is Mr. Y, when presenting himself as such a weak and compliant beginner, voicing the same demand to be adequately cared for that the patient made on him? Certainly, from our very first contact with Mr. Y we can posit that corollary to such a demand would be the feeling "And I can expect to be a little bit disappointed in the way you meet this demand." Thus to the disappointments in his patient and in himself would be added the disappointment in the teacher.

Consciously, however, Mr. Y had seen this whole issue as one of honesty and here he had stood on seemingly solid ground. He had been indoctrinated in his didactic course work with the importance of complete integrity and honesty in all dealings with one's patients—and yet he could see that he had gotten into real trouble with his gratuitous self-depreciatory remarks. The statement that this was a question of honesty was made in a way designed to shut off further clarification. Honesty is supposed to be an absolute virtue and never to be compromised. If it leads us into a therapeutic impasse, then somehow that must be the fault of the therapeutic method itself, not of the therapist. But, psychologically considered, honesty just like dishonesty is a trait and an attitude and is motivated, with its well-springs deep in the character structure of the individual just as any other trait that has a specific dynamic function. When this or any other trait is displayed in an interpersonal relationship one can therefore legitimately raise the same questions, "What kind of honesty? How much honesty? Honesty to what end?"

There are a multiplicity of equally honest answers and the problem is rather one of selection of that particular "honest" response (as all responses should be) that is most relevant to the preconscious meaning intended by the patient by his question. The most relevant honest answer to the query "Are you on the staff?" might be a remark that the patient wonders if he is getting the best therapist available and one adequate to his needs. Such a statement by the therapist could only be based however on a realistic acceptance of himself as an individual of much interest, some knowledge, and potential skill, albeit a beginner. That is, can the student therapist be helped to an appraisal of himself based on a realistic assessment of assets and potentials and a healthy acceptance of himself as a beginner? It is only after such a self-acceptance that the beginning therapist can go on to acquire real therapeutic skills. He is then free of the need to ward off both patient and supervisor with the plea "I'm not much. But don't hold it against me. I'm sure to make lots of errors but I'll confess my weakness first so it won't be necessary for you to call it to my attention." If the supervisor can accept the student as a beginner, the student can perhaps begin to accept himself as such (and with the legitimate anxieties of the beginner) and can begin to assume the responsibilities of the novice in applying himself to problems of developing therapeutic skill.

How then did the supervisory hour end? Mr. Y raised the question of his assignment to another patient, since this particular patient might or might not return, probably not. Dr. Baehr left the way open for him to speak to the responsible administrator, but Mr. Y expressed the hope that the supervisor would more actively engage in the selection of this next patient than he had in the first. Mr. Y already felt that inappropriate handling by the ward doctor had helped crystallize the patient's decision to leave. Now Mr. Y added the implication that poor initial selection by the administrator had also played its role in the failure of a therapeutic situation to evolve.

Maybe he could help himself a little. Mr. Y knew of several patients awaiting assignment to psychotherapy and mentioned one in particular that had been discussed at a case conference at which both he and the supervisor had been present. He reflected a moment and said he guessed not, that the patient was too much like the one who had just left. Dr. Baehr pointed to major characterologic differences between the two patients and Mr. Y then said, "Oh yes, that's so. But I guess what I wanted is a more compliant patient than either of these. But that would be more like myself and I don't suppose I could learn as much, in terms of my own goals of wanting to be a therapist, with such a compliant patient, so much more like myself." We need not take this professed self-concept of Mr. Y at face value; he is hardly compliant. Rather we can see that he is asking for a patient whose compliance consists in his willingness to stay with his therapist.

On his way out the door Mr. Y asked if the supervisor would be seeing the training consultant (in the local jargon, the "supervisor of the supervisors"), before their next meeting together the following week. Dr. Baehr said he'd let him know. Here we see the problem of beginning, reflected on yet another level of training and of responsibility. Dr. Baehr was a new supervisor, a fact well known to his student whose remark could be taken as the aggressive counterassault upon the supervisor, "You need supervisory help yourself." Perhaps this would be the only way the disappointing supervisor could overcome his own inadequacies in the eyes of his critical student.

A week later Mr. Y returned for his third supervisory conference. He had no patient and had submitted no material. Dr. Baehr asked him what he wanted to talk about, how he wanted to use the hour. Mr. Y waited momentarily with an expectant air and then asked about the status of the search for a new patient. In effect, what action had the supervisor taken? Dr. Baehr reported that active efforts were indeed being made, though no appropriate patient was available just this week. Mr. Y then asked his second question. Had the supervisor seen the training consultant? And thus Mr. Y came back to where he had left off the preceding hour. Dr. Baehr merely said "Yes," and Mr. Y then went on with "Well, did anything more come out of it?" The supervisor's response to this gambit was "You mean more than we had already said here last week?" A noncommittal remark indeed, which failed really to engage the issue raised by Mr. Y who in turn then veered back to a discussion of the patient he had lost with "I haven't given much thought to the case actually anymore—sort of repressed it. I've been wondering some about when I was going to get a new one. I suppose I have been trying to think *that* case over some more. . . . If I'd known we were going to talk about it again, I'd have come prepared."

In the ensuing discussion of the case, Mr. Y was again naturally concerned with the question of the part he had played in helping drive the patient away from therapy. He went back to the remarks made in the previous supervisory session concerning the recitation to the patient of his lack of qualifications and the depreciation of his own capacity to help the patient. The supervisor remarked at this point on the dovetailing of the therapist's own self-depreciation with the very quality with which the depressive patient faces his world—his self-depreciation. This struck Mr. Y and he said quickly that, yes, that was true but the motivations differed in the two instances; the patient's was out of depression and his own was different. Dr. Baehr waited and Mr. Y went on to say that his own motivation was possibly the warding off of something. When he was asked what that might be, he replied, "Some demands of the patient, I suppose." Here we may wonder, however. We know how critical Mr. Y already was of his relatively inexperienced supervisor; we can see some of the source of this critical attitude in Mr. Y's fear that the supervisor is perhaps justly critical of him. When he said that he was concerned in the therapy with warding off the patient's demands on him, was he also alluding to the supervisory situation in which he might be occupied with simultaneously warding off the felt demand of his supervisor in regard to his work performance, and the awareness of his strong counter-demand on the supervisor for the very kind of care and insurance that the patient had asked of him?

An extended discussion of these issues ended in Mr. Y's remarking, "All I had thought I was doing was that I was being honest—and yet, of course, I did wonder about it as I said it." Here we are back to our discussion of honesty which Dr. Baehr, however, took to new ground when, in talking about how one should key oneself to the real question and in being honest choose the degree and kind of honesty appropriate to the occasion, he stated, "After all, your honesty didn't include a statement that you take these issues to a supervisor for control and yet that too is a statement of fact highly relevant to your position with the patient, just as my also having a supervisor is likewise a fact." Thus, at the very end of the session, the supervisor brought the discussion back to the issue raised by the student at the very beginning, at a time when indeed little could be done with it. Mr. Y acknowledged that he guessed what the supervisor said was so and he certainly could see the absurdity of pushing things to that extreme, and at this point the time was up.

Why did Dr. Baehr wait until so late in the supervisory session to bring this crucial issue out into the open, at a point when not much could be done with it, and why did it then emerge as so forceful a confrontation? Here we are dealing with yet another problem of beginning, that of the beginning supervisor with his own still undeveloped supervisory skills and his own anxieties in the face of his new authority and responsibility. We can speculate as to whether he just did not perceive the importance of this issue until so late, or whether he did perceive it and felt handicapped by lack of knowledge of how to deal with it effectively and helpfully, or whether he was immobilized in his response to this assault because he inwardly accepted the accusation against himself as an accurate representation of the facts.

Certainly the reference to the training consultant and the question as to whether anything more had come out of the supervisor's conference with him was felt on some level by Dr. Baehr as an undermining of his supervisory authority. It touched so directly on the problems and anxieties of the beginning supervisor, with perhaps many of his own feelings about both authority and supervision not clearly worked out. Behind the student's question there would of course be other determinants such as the plaint "I am helpless. What are you and the training consultant between you doing about it?" The uppermost feeling, however, seems to be the many doubts the therapist has about a supervisor who has himself to conform to a higher and more informed authority, a doubt which serves of course to help still the student's inner doubts about himself.

Had the supervisor been able to deal with this issue as it arose early in the hour, a number of ways lay open to bring it helpfully into focus as a learning problem of the student's operating in both the supervisory and the treatment situations. For example, how differently might the balance of the supervisory session have turned had Dr. Baehr stated early, "It is a difficult spot to be in a helping relationship to your patient just as I am to you and to feel at the same time that you are constrained to constantly run and check with a supervisor." Or with a little different emphasis, "Yes, we each of us have to come to our work bringing wisdom from afar. If we wait for that, it'll always work to cut down our own spontaneity. Do you think that in our work we can each forget about it and do the very best we can on our own?"

Here we should perhaps stop this somewhat detailed exposition of Mr. Y's (and his supervisor's) tribulations in learning, which have carried us rather far afield into the individuality of particular problems in learning—and in beginning. Out of the banal observation that we all have learning—and beginning—problems in each new learning and beginning situation that we enter comes the clarification of the uniquely different forms that these problems take with each of us. By way of comparison we can turn now to the work of Dr. W, also in supervision with Dr. Baehr, but at a point where the latter is himself somewhat less a beginner at his supervisory task.

Dr. W has seen his new patient for three sessions between his first and second supervisory hours. In the preceding chapter we followed in detail the events of the very first therapy hour, and could see in the summary paragraph of the notes of that interview, which we quoted, the nature of the problems that Dr. W felt existed between his patient and himself. He called the patient "a little resistant to starting out with a new doctor" and "cautious" as to what the new experience promised. Dr. W felt that his problem was to "start a relationship" with the patient apart from and anteceding the clarification of the specifically psychotherapeutic nature of that relationship. Dr. W ended his note with the hopeful statement that the patient was evidencing acceptance of him by readily agreeing to further appointments.

Their second meeting served to dispel any basis for that optimism. The patient "forgot" the appointment, and when, after twenty minutes went by, the therapist sought out the patient, he found him asleep in bed claiming that he had been hazy with medication all day and therefore had forgotten. The patient was willing to come to the office for the balance of the hour, all the while explaining that he had clean forgotten all about the appointment, though he had been thinking about it earlier in the day. When Dr. W wondered at this forgetting, the patient couldn't explain it any further. He had just forgotten. The rest of the time together was marked by many lulls and pauses; one pause lasted six or seven minutes. The patient ended this pause by a statement that "There isn't much to say." When Dr. W remarked to this that "You don't like to talk about your troubles like this, do you? You forgot to come over, you can't think of anything, and you just don't think it will do any good." The patient answered, "Oh, I don't like to talk about myself too much, it doesn't do any good. But I would like to know how those X-rays I got yesterday came out." Not that the patient had much hope in the somatic realm either. "He used to have some hope and tried to fight it out but he didn't have much left anymore."

Here Dr. W summarized the problems of the hour as follows: "I felt the main issue of this interview was more of was he going to be allowed to be passive. I felt that it really started out wrong by my having to go get him as though this is my wanting him to get better. . . . I think his continued long pauses were bids for a passive position and somehow I felt that the idea was partially put across that I was not going to allow him to be completely passive and I was not going to take all the questioning and interview into my hands and push it."

The third hour the patient was even more stubbornly detached. There was nothing he felt he wanted to talk about. He had said all the things to doctors that he had to say and it hadn't done any good. He began to talk of getting out of here and going to live with his wife's folks, and though this would not be wholly pleasant, he and his wife had "no other place to go." He was unhappy at the outcome of his many contacts with hospitals and doctors and again stated that he wanted to leave and wouldn't stick around long if things didn't help him any more here. In this context Dr. W mentioned the repeat diagnostic esophagoscopy that he knew to be scheduled for the next week. The patient said that they had looked in his esophagus a number of times before and had even taken a couple of biopsies and they had told him there was nothing wrong down there, that it was just his imagination. He didn't know why it would do any good to do it again though he said he would wait around to have it done, but that if then something definite didn't come out of that, he would go on with his wife to her parents' home. In this interview Dr. W felt the patient to be quite "hostile" to him, "probably in retaliation for my aggressiveness last interview in being quiet and making him bring up the subjects."

These then are the reports of the three therapy interviews that Dr. W brought for discussion with his supervisor in their second session together. This meeting Dr. W opened by stating that he hoped his material was in satisfactory form, that he had interspersed it with paragraphs of commentary illustrating how he had thought about the therapeutic problems he had faced, and that he hoped that this was what was wanted. He thought that of all the problems he had met maybe he and the supervisor could talk about "the problem of beginning in psychotherapy." He had been somewhat uncomfortable wondering if he had "done just right" with this. At this point Dr. Baehr picked up this statement and added that he too had been struck by just this problem in the material. Dr. Baehr further said that he thought Dr. W's real concern with this problem, and Dr. W's feeling that he had possibly circumvented rather than dealt with this problem of "how to begin" had emerged very clearly in the summary paragraph Dr. W appended to his notes of the very first interview with the patient.

In this interchange we can see how very differently Dr. Baehr is now responding from the way he did in the interview with Mr. Y. In the discussion of that interview we had noted Dr. Baehr's slowness to deal with the predominant psychological issue posed by his supervisee, despite his apparent clear perception of the problem. Now, in this interview, Dr. W, the supervisee, seems barely to have time enough to state what he regards as a problem area, and no time to elaborate what his conception of the nature of the problem is, before the supervisor has intervened to say that yes, it is indeed a problem; he has seen it, too, and identifies it by chapter and verse. How do we explain the seeming difference in Dr. Baehr in the two situations? For one thing the interview with Dr. W took place some two months later than the first one with Mr. Y. In the meantime Dr. Baehr had been discussing his own problems in teaching with the training consultant, and no doubt Dr. Baehr's propensity to be aware but not to intercede had itself been the subject of discussion. An inhibition of action was thus followed by a phase of possibly excessive action.

And perhaps yet another factor was involved here. Mr. Y had presented himself as a weak and self-depreciated student, fearful of the always-to-be-expected disappointment, saying in effect "I'm so inadequate. Please don't hurt me." To this the supervisor, reluctant to add yet another blow or to confirm the ever-ready expectation of disappointment, had responded in kind, saying, "Indeed I won't." With Dr. W the supervisor has been dealing with a different kind of fellow. Dr. W had openly expressed his considerable doubt that supervision had anything new or different to add to what knowledge he already had acquired, and almost as openly had been wondering about his need or wish for it. In this instance Dr. Baehr lost no time in jumping in to administer a blow on behalf of his beleaguered position under the guise of a helpful confrontation within the supervision. Thus we can see how the learning problems of the student come to interact with the teaching problems of the supervisor. In fact, the kind of learning problems posed by the student and brought to recognition between himself and the supervisor will inevitably be influenced by the teaching problems of the teacher, just as we take for granted that the transference problems posed by the patient and dealt with in the therapy are inevitably influenced by the countertransferences of the therapist.

In the face of this assault by his supervisor Dr. W, who had initially broached this whole problem of "how to begin" in therapy, retreated and said that he didn't understand what was meant. It then devolved on the supervisor to suggest that they look at the submitted material together and review such statements as that the therapist "tried to sympathize" with the patient, or that he tried to "start a relationship" *before* the question of "psychotherapy, whether or not he wants it" was raised. Dr. Baehr wondered what this meant, and how one could start a relationship, without an understanding that this was to be a professional and a helping relationship, or did Dr. W have some other kind of relationship (viz: a social relationship) in mind? Could one build a relationship *in vacuo* without clarifying what the relationship was for, what expectations the patient had, who had sent him, what they had told him, etc.? Such questions had nowhere been asked of the patient. To all this, Dr. W listened and then replied that there was really *no difference;* that all that was exactly what he had done implicitly all through. Maybe it just didn't come out properly in the material. At this point Dr. W reasserted himself and his position, and it was now the supervisor's turn to retreat. Dr. Baehr said that if that were so, fine. He had just wanted to sharpen the focus a little. Dr. W said that he was quite sure that the patient really "knew" that this was a professional helping relationship that he was driving at, that this had "really" been in the air, but that, true, the patient had not had an opportunity to bring up his feelings about this. Dr. W acknowledged that he had "deferred" this, perhaps out of fear of losing the patient, perhaps out of other reasons. But he saw all this now, and wished to get on to consider the second interview.

The second hour was the one in which the patient had forgotten to come, he was asleep in bed; and when he finally came, had little to say, his words being punctuated by long silences. The supervisor asked what aspect of this material Dr. W wished to take up first. Dr. W wondered how the supervisor felt about his formulation of the central problem of this hour as one of the patient's passivity and his attempt to force the therapist to "take over." Here Dr. W saw the therapeutic process with the patient as marked by the same struggle of conflicting wills tugging with one another that had characterized his own interactions in the supervisory situation with Dr. Baehr. Again, Dr. Baehr felt constrained to explain. He said that he would paraphrase the patient's position in this hour as one that said in effect "What am I doing here? Why do I come? Please clarify this or else why go on?" Dr. Baehr suggested that in these terms the patient could be seen as responding to the unasked questions of the first hour.

And again, Dr. W had his reservations. He said that maybe that was so but couldn't it just as well be looked at as the patient saying "I've surveyed the situation; I'm looking for somatic help—surgery—which you are not giving me. There's no help here of the kind I want, so why should I go on with this?" It's as though Dr. W has two maneuvers within the supervision session. He either denies and wipes out the difference, and therefore of course cannot see the new; or he disputes it and offers a plausible alternative. The supervisor is caught in the first instance by an impulse to prove that there is a difference and in the second instance by a need to prove his own view. He fell in with this invitation and agreed that yes, Dr. W could indeed formulate it that way, but it was a way that would give him less therapeutic leverage. Maybe it's not that the patient has thoroughly explored the psychotherapeutic possibilities and rejected them; maybe he had not yet been enabled to really explore them. Maybe in fact he *does* want help and *is* motivated. In saying this Dr. Baehr was well aware of how difficult it was for Dr. W to see evidences of motivation in others—or in himself.

To all of this Dr. W quickly said O.K., and shifted his ground to a consideration of the third interview, the one in which the patient was so hostile. Perhaps this interview was just a continued expression of the patient's resentments against the other protagonist in the psychotherapeutic struggles. Dr. Baehr remarked that the patient added a new twist to his theme, "I'll stay around to be esophagoscoped but if nothing definite comes of that, I'll go off to my in-laws." Dr. W said that he had indeed felt uneasy about how he had introduced to the patient the idea that another esophagoscopy was contemplated. He realized now, he said, that he had used this to hold the patient—"at least you'll stay until next week for the esophagoscopy"—and held him with the promise of a somatic therapy, not psychotherapy. "I guess I was really more afraid to lose the patient than I had realized all along." Dr. Baehr seized this acknowledgment and said in reply, "So you hold him by avoiding trying to clarify your own relationship with him and your own offer of potential help. Rather you defer all this, and now the things you've deferred in hour one come back in hours two and three." At this point, at the close of the supervisory session, Dr. W acknowledged ruefully, "I guess I see now some of what I was doing in the first interview. Gosh, it's hard to deal with these patients."

In assessing what took place in this supervisory session we can perhaps be somewhat encouraged by this closing interchange between the supervisor and his student. This very "stubborn" pupil, to whom nothing is new, who denies and wipes out the difference between each new learning experience and the old, seems to have been pushed back bit by bit to see the pattern of interrelation between his interventions in one hour and the patient's material in subsequent hours. He has begun to see too how the net effect of his own impact on the psychologic world of his patient has been other than what he had consciously intended it to be. In having to see his own technical limitations, he has indeed indirectly acknowledged his need for help.

However, we can also say that the supervisor has sidestepped the main learning problems unfolded by his student in this early work together. When the student either minimizes—or disputes—the difference introduced by the supervisor, the latter seems drawn to counteract, to join the dispute, or alternatively to withdraw his own suggestion. What he fails to do is to come to grips in any way with the mechanism itself which blocks whatever accretion of technical skill the supervisor may have to offer; the mechanism, that is, of failing to see the newness, of needing to wipe out the difference. As with his other supervisee, Mr. Y, Dr. Baehr is perceptive of the interplay which he duly notes and records. But just as with his other supervisee, in his response to this learning dilemma, Dr. Baehr is hesitant. Even as he to some extent engaged in it, Dr. Baehr must have felt the impossibility of arguing or truly convincing Dr. W by his logic, of being able to *prove* that after all there is a difference. Wouldn't Dr. W just care to see it? Dr. Baehr indeed wanted to avoid the reversal of position from a point of view characterized by the supervisor's feeling "I have the (teaching) goods. Let's see if you can use them," to a point of view characterized by the student's feeling, "Let's see what you offer and prove to me that it's good or any different."

How could one then avoid such a reversal? Here we again come to the supervisor's teaching problem, his hesitation at actively entering the psychological world of his student even at the very point where ostensibly the student asked for this entry—at the point of clinical inadequacy and lack of psychotherapeutic skill. If well done, whatever the immediate response in resentment at painful exposure, one could hopefully await the ultimate appreciation of the student that a meaningful relationship could be established in which there would be a difference—and would be learning. But as with the student and his learning problems, we must give the supervisor time to detect and to work out his own problems in teaching. Certainly the seeming difference with which the supervisor handled these initial interviews with the pair of students, two months apart, gives way on closer inspection to a picture of a more basic similarity in supervisory approach.

At this point we have followed our patients, our therapists, and our supervisors well past their various beginnings with one another, and have seen how our shifting attention from one point and one interconnecting line of our clinical rhombus to another has enabled us to illuminate psychological connections among these different simultaneously occurring processes. With these beginnings well launched we can next turn our attention to the kinds of learning problems and problems about learning that arise in these processes.

III / *The Learning Process*

IX / *Supervisor and Student—Problems about Learning*

Was Du ererbt von Deinen Vätern hast,
Erwirb es, um es zu besitzen.
("What thou hast inherited from thy fathers,
Earn it, to make it thine own.")—GOETHE

The supervisory process embodies two major purposes. One is to maintain the organization's standards of clinical performance through the knowledge (and supervision) of the nature and the quality of the professional service. The other is to help the student-therapist toward the acquisition of increased professional skill—in this case, psychotherapeutic skill. The major obstacle to the smooth growth of psychotherapeutic sensitivity and competence (and hence, of improved clinical service as well) is the mobilization during the process of learning of idiosyncratic patterns that determine the way in which a given individual learns—the ways in which mastery is sought and the specific difficulties that limit its effectiveness. These "learning problems" encompass the whole complex of ways of acting and responding within the psychotherapy situation that are determined not by the objectively ascertained needs of the patient but by the characteristic, automatic—and therefore, at times, inappropriate—patterns of response of the would-be helper.

Hence, supervision that is focused on the nature of the difficulties in the therapy resulting from a therapist-patient interaction (and to which *both* may bring inappropriate and, from the standpoint of adaptation, unskillful patterns), inevitably asks for introspection and a willingness and capacity to change on the part of the therapist, as well as on that of the patient. The area and range of change sought—and hence the purpose of the relationship—is different. In the case of the patient the decision to seek therapy is an acknowledgment of some failure or at least dissatisfaction in his personal life and is a tacit agreement to offer the whole gamut of his relevant life experience to joint scrutiny. The entire range of his "personal problems" thus may become grist for the psychotherapeutic mill. In the case of the learning therapist the entering into a supervised relationship implies a willingness to offer to joint scrutiny the sector of himself that comprises his professional helping functioning, in order to achieve his goal—learning and increased psychotherapeutic skill. The change ostensibly sought is limited thus to one area, that of manner of use of oneself in a psychotherapeutic relationship but within that area the change desired may be equally far-reaching and "deep."

In the social work literature this distinction is made in terms of consideration of the "professional self" apart from the "personal self." Change in the personal self is accomplished through a process such as psychotherapy. Change in the professional self is primarily a function of supervision (as well as of other training devices). And the two, although complexly interrelated, do not necessarily march together hand in hand. If the favorable change in adaptive functioning brought about through a successful psychoanalysis by itself included the desired concomitant changes in the professional self (the combined increased sensitivity, flexibility, and skill), then every cured analytic patient could claim his right to be a practitioner. Patently, this is untrue. Then where is the deficit? It is not merely in *lack of knowledge* of theory and technique, because lack of knowledge in that didactic sense would require only the appropriate comprehensive arrangement of didactic material—lecture and seminar courses—to fill the breach. However, the carrying out of psychoanalysis under supervision is also an established and essential part of the process of training. And the purpose of this is more than to facilitate situations in which meaningful questions of technique arise and demand solution. Rather, the supervision situation is a laboratory in which the characteristic problems of the student in working with the analytic material can unfold in a setting in which he has help in differentiating the technical skill-problems of the objectively most appropriate therapeutic maneuver from the problem—the learning problem

—expressed in his own predilection for handling the given situation in one particular way and not in another. And, in addition, yet another strand may be interwoven. The counterpart of the predisposition to react in a particularly patterned way toward the patient—*the learning problem*—may be projected into the relationship with the supervisor as a characteristically limited way of reacting and of learning, and pose therefore a specific *problem about learning*. The more the student is a beginner, the greater will be this tendency to suffuse the problems he has with his patient with his own subjective distortions and present them through the inhibiting difficulties—the problems about learning—that he has with his supervisor.

Psychoanalytic training, as at present constituted, makes one further basic assumption. And that is that a significant degree of help with personal problems (an analysis, either completed or at least a certain point in its progress attained) must be reached before one can undertake supervised analytic work (with its focus then on the problems in learning). Hence, personal therapy by no means automatically solves the learning problems; though to the extent that the problems about learning derive from unresolved neurotic residues stirred up on assuming the learning relationship vis-à-vis a supervisor who represents administrative authority, these should at least be considerably diminished.* It may be that in certain individuals both learning problems and problems about learning are so pervasive and tenaciously rooted in the ramifying complex of personal problems that it will only be possible to pay fruitful attention to them after considerable resolution of the underlying personal problems. Such individuals should not do therapeutic work, whether supervised or not, until after a preliminary period of personal therapeutic help.

Our own experience is, however, that in order to do certain types of psychotherapy (not psychoanalysis) personal therapy is not an essential concomitant or prerequisite—except in such cases as those just referred to. The supervisory process itself undertakes to offer help with the learning problems and the problems about learning as they unfold, and is predicated upon the capacity of the individual supervised to

* Problems about learning are not just the problems between the student and the supervisor, evoked around the process of supervision itself. For example, the problem of professional choice and professional identity, what one wants to be professionally and hence what one wants to learn, is also a problem about learning.

make effective alterations in his professional self, without necessarily significantly changing his personal self. The two are not necessarily parallel. Nor is this a surprising observation to us. We are all aware of therapists who in their professional lives handle with competence and equanimity problems that they have not completely resolved in their personal lives. One may find it possible to face the mobilized anger of a psychotherapy patient expressing his irrational, hostile, and hurtful impulses and yet be immobilized by the hostile condescension of an aggressive salesman (equally "irrational" behavior and equally determined by unconscious drives).

The ability to thus handle problems effectively in the one circumscribed area (professional helping) and not in the wider area of the interactions of daily living is basically no different from the commonplace observation that competence in one area of professional helping does not certify to competence in another—even adjacent—area. A skilled psychoanalyst might be much less effective as a face-to-face psychotherapist. Or a social case worker doing both psychotherapy and case work might be much more effective in the one endeavor than in the other. In this sense skill problems cannot be automatically translated, and each kind is learned separately—best, under supervision.

For purposes of heuristic clarity we will here separately consider problems about learning (problems between supervisor and student) which will be discussed in this chapter from learning problems (problems between therapist and patient) which will be deferred until the next chapter. In doing this we are temporarily separating two interrelated lines of our clinical rhombus, S–T and T–P. In the subsequent chapter on the parallel process we will see how the events transpiring on the one line are so often projected onto the other, so that what is in one frame of reference and for one purpose the student's problem about learning is at the same time reflected in the other frame of reference (with its different purpose) in the learning problem the same student displays.

Why should problems about learning emerge with such regularity? The word *problem* implies, of course, the double-sided nature of the dilemma. In coming for supervision the would-be therapist to some extent signifies his willingness and desire to learn. (Even when he comes only because it is required, he has, in the pursuit of some professional goal, placed himself in a learning situation in which supervision is one of the necessary elements). And we say that he learns through becoming aware of and working toward the resolution of the problems his learning poses. That these are "problems" means that a counteractive resistance is evoked. Much as we want to learn, learning implies change, and however much desired, change is simultaneously feared. Thus in this overdetermined manner the "problem about learning" becomes the focus of the struggle to change one's level of professional functioning, and is at once the vehicle of the change and the measure of the resistance to the change.

That is to say, the problem about learning is not only to be seen as an obstacle on the pathway to increased professional skill; it is rather the very road the student and teacher have undertaken to travel together toward their common goal. And it will be a different road depending on the different character make-ups, and differing ways of learning and of teaching that each student and supervisor bring to their joint endeavor. In this sense there is always a problem about learning in the most "normal" of student-supervisor interactions, if by problem about learning we mean the predilections and idiosyncrasies brought by each to the interaction, which together determine what will be learned and how it will be learned. Every new supervisee will have to work out how he can learn best from his new teacher, how to present his material, how to seek answers to his questions, and what kinds of help his teacher can best offer him. The supervisor has the same "problems" about his new student. In the mutual finding out and testing process that ensues as the supervision gets under way, affective components are inevitably mobilized (as in all meaningful human relationships) and these are the "problems about learning"—the particular ways in which this student will try to learn from this teacher, ways that both determine and limit what will be learned and how this learning will be accomplished.

These problems about learning are as manifold and diverse as the range of human personality differences itself. To bring a number of them together in a chapter like this, in order to sample the variety and to follow some of the ramifications of their unfolding, is by no means to attempt an exhaustive listing. For this entire volume is in actuality a process of watching the emergence of all varieties of problems under various guises—as problems of crises, problems with the structure and with the administration, problems in the parallelisms seen in the simultaneous relationship of the student-therapist, to the patient on the one hand, and to the supervisor on the other, etc. In this chapter a number of learning situations not elsewhere considered under distinctive headings will be brought together and followed in order to underline the flexible adaptive range required of the supervisor striving to be helpful and the diverse paths by which interactions between two human beings, the teacher and the student, can lead to the common goal—improvement of the student's professional self-awareness and skill.

This study of the problems about learning of a variety of students will in fact reveal clear—and diverse—learning patterns, more or less as distinctive for each individual as is his total character patterning. For illustrative purposes these patterns can be categorized by various shorthand appellations that, however, do not do justice to the complexity of the phenomena subsumed or the nuances through which they manifest themselves. Nor should it be thought that naming these patterns implies psychopathology in the way that psychiatric diagnostic categorization does. Psychopathological implications have meaning within a psychotherapeutic framework which provides the leverage for exploring that meaning in the life of the individual. Within a teaching and learning framework we see ways of learning (problems about learning), each imposing its own patterning upon the knowledge and skill that is taught and learned. When an individual's manner of learning is crystallized and pronounced, it may be named as the representative of a class, and as is always true of the more extreme case, may illustrate more sharply what is present in all.

Such, for example, is the designation of the pattern of "learning by vigorous denying." This has characterized a number of different students who have felt the need to ward off the impacts of the supervisory and teaching experience—as exemplified by Dr. W who fought off each new perceived difference by an attempt to reduce it to the familiar. Yet despite this constant denying and perhaps through the struggle precipitated around it, Dr. W does learn. Sometimes the strength of the denial may be sufficient to cloud the perception of what is, in fact, actually being learned. In the formal evaluation of Dr. Z in his work with his supervisor, Dr. Allen, such a "surprise"—that is, surprise to the supervisor—could be detected. Dr. Allen had been struggling, seemingly unsuccessfully, all through the supervisory process, to help Dr. Z focus on a complex of inhibiting difficulties that prevented him from really becoming meaningfully and helpfully involved in the emotional life of his patient. Dr. Z, a psychologist with a primarily academic background, preferred to play the role of the "objective scientist" attempting to evaluate and compare the different psychotherapeutic schools. He stoutly maintained that his psychological distance from his patient was essential to his true "objectivity." He had to deny constantly that any help could accrue—in fact, quite the reverse—from allowing himself to take in and try out the ways of looking at the therapy interaction offered by the supervisor. Yet, in the heightened focusing of the evaluation process, two things became clearly discernible. One was that all along, while denying, Dr. Z had nonetheless been learning, with severe—and unnecessary—difficulty perhaps, but learning and changing a little. The other was that he himself was more aware of this than the supervisor had been. In his evaluation of the supervision experience, he acknowledged the cogency of the viewpoint represented by the supervisor all along, and indicated his own awareness that if he expected to help the patient at all—and, incidentally, learn anything about systems of psychotherapy as well—he would have to effect changes in the nature of his interpersonal operations—become more "involved"—much as he disliked this and had to deny the need for it.

A different example is that of Dr. V's pattern of "learning by submission." Dr. V was a student who conceptualized his own inner psychological world and his relationships to objects in a rigidly hierarchical arrangement, with definite roles and patterns of behavior enjoined by the stratification. The patients were "below" and could be manipulated and directed, and Dr. V experienced his basic difficulty with his patients in his hostile need to control them. Supervisors were "above" and were, insofar as his own resentments at his position in the hierarchical structuring permitted, to be related to submissively and dependently. Dr. V thus presented a basic pattern of submissive acceptance, except when punctuated by outcroppings of his underlying stubborn hostility. This submissive acceptance leads to an imitative taking on of the external trappings of the supervisor's presumed directions, without the truly effective learning that comes from the growth of insight and the internalization of the at first externally perceived learning dilemma. The submission may be but another form of resistance—and a more "acceptable" one than hostile rebellion—and at the same time be in itself a first step on the way to effective learning; in other words, the particular individual's learning pattern. In the two patterns cited to this point, in the one case the learner fights and denies; in the other he submits. Both of these are equally reflections of a stage on the way to learning—a stage before the individual is able to accept the posed dilemma as his own, but must experience it as something external, arbitrarily imposed by the supervisor.

Still another variant is the "mea culpa" attitude of Dr. U. Dr. U was a serious and gifted student with an introspective bent and a ready psychological mindedness. As difficulties emerged in his work with the patient, Dr. U tended characteristically to respond with embarrassment and ready acknowledgment. In fact he would magnify his own failings to the point of caricature and point out how they ramified widely into many areas of his personal life. Actually, this ready acknowledgment, quick insight, and intensely expressed desire for change became in itself a major defensive maneuver and learning block. He was way ahead of the supervisor in diagnosing his own "psychopathology" and in assuming a total "mea culpa" attitude. How could anyone else find fault where the hapless sufferer had already indicated his even greater awareness of the seriousness of the difficulty?

This whole learning pattern was the subject of discussion throughout the supervisory process and was brought to more explicit focus at the mid-period evaluation. What emerged clearly was Dr. U's expectation that the supervisory process was inevitably an aggressive assault—albeit, ultimately for his own good—in which he was each time "beaten" by the supervisor; and which he even helped set up each time in such a way that this expected outcome would be sure to eventuate. It was as if Dr. U was stating that he had to "learn by being beaten," though this was both painful and embarrassing, especially as it came so clearly into awareness. The rest of that hour was occupied by a discussion of the oppressive and uneconomic nature of learning in this manner. Was this the way Dr. U had to learn or was a different pattern of learning possible to him? For one *can* learn with almost any pattern, although with more or less difficulty depending on the pattern, and the danger must be guarded against that the supervisor's narcissistic needs lead him to push the student to learn imitatively in the supervisor's image or to push the student into a pattern in which he acknowledges gratitude for supervisory help, while covering up the denial and the struggle against it. Here again, with an awareness of these possible pitfalls, the supervisor is in a position to help the student face his own learning blocks, and bring about those shifts in his pattern of learning that he himself is ready for.

Sometimes the problem about learning is posed in the most elementary and concrete terms, though behind these stand all the same complex character (and learning) configurations brought by each professional student to his supervisor. The beginning supervised work of Dr. T exemplifies such a problem, which we have come to call "the problem of finding a problem," and will be presented at some length to illustrate the intricate network of difficulties that ramify from the naive and concretistic (and seemingly "simple") attitudes that characterize this way of learning. Dr. T was an individual whose learning difficulty unfolded according to the model, "I am not really responsible for bringing in my own problems in learning, for by definition they are 'scotomata' and that means that I can't see them. Rather it is the supervisor's job to tell me where they are and point them out to me."

This characteristic of throwing himself on the bounty of the supervisor began to emerge in the preliminary meeting arranged to set up the program of the supervision ahead. In response to an explanation of the nature and obligations of the work to be done together, Dr. T said enthusiastically that this was just what he had been long waiting for. Though he had never before done process notes, he had, while working with a previous supervisor, attempted to take verbatim records during the interview hour. In response to this statement, his supervisor, Dr. Daniels, outlined factually how process notes (done after the hour, incidentally) differed from such verbatim recordings. Dr. T said again that he had never really had this kind of supervision before. As a matter of fact, he had been quite disappointed in both his previous psychotherapy training and his previous experiences in supervision, all of which he seemed quite willing to discount completely. He said that in these previous experiences either the entire session was taken up in reading his material to the supervisor, leaving no time for any discussion, or the supervisor's comments were such general statements as "You're doing fine! Keep it up." When Dr. T would ask, "Keep what up?" he would be told, "Just what you're doing." Or the supervisory time was taken up in theoretical discussions of "ego psychology"; that is, taking the patient's statements and elaborating on them in terms of their interesting place in the patient's system of defensive and adaptive mechanisms, rather than "in *telling me* what it meant in terms of my relationship with the patient."

Dr. T then went on to state quite explicitly that he felt that his first two years had for the most part been wasted as far as acquiring psychotherapeutic skill was concerned, and that he was in something of a mild panic as he contemplated finishing his residency training within another year—wondering whether he could truly acquire the sought-for skill by then. He said, "I've been reluctant to say this, because the first time I expressed such feelings to my section chief it went down on my record that I was insecure." He then followed the confession with an open statement of his great expectations, "I sure look to this supervision to finally give me what I have been wanting. I have a lot of hopes."

Here Dr. T was already sketching the broad outline of how he expected to relate to the supervisor, the part he visualized for himself in the process, and the fantasied expectations of the benevolent, admired, and omnipotent teacher. For his part, Dr. Daniels allowed this picture to develop without yet joining issue with any of the implications expressed. He could, for instance, have dealt with the statement, "I have never done process notes," with a recognition (beyond the information-giving statement of what process notes are) of the anxiety at working in an unfamiliar system. Again at the end, in response to "I have great expectations here—of you," Dr. Daniels had an opportunity to begin to clarify the difference between the fantasy and the roles each would have to play, in order for really effective learning to ensue with some statement as "That's a tall order for me, isn't it?" By avoiding joining issue at this time, Dr. Daniels avoided, too, the arousal of anxiety in his student (and in himself), only to postpone the consideration of these problems (and the anxiety that would sometime have to be liberated in connection with them) to another occasion.

A good example of such an occasion arose in a supervisory session several months later. This was at a point rather far along in the psychotherapeutic work with a mildly depressed and quite severely hypochondriacal patient. It illustrates well the full development of the difficulties in learning tentatively delineated in the very first hour together. By this time these problems had been brought to explicit focus, particularly at the time of the mid-period evaluation which had taken place about a month prior to the supervisory session to be cited.

During this formal evaluative review both student and supervisor had agreed on the existence of serious problems in learning which inhibited the effectiveness of Dr. T's psychotherapeutic work and acted to block change in the direction of increased skill. In keeping with his way of seeing and presenting himself, Dr. T could infer the existence of his difficulties from his very evident lack of progress in learning; but what the underlying problems were, he did not know, though he did wish most earnestly to be told if this were possible. Dr. Daniels agreed on the existence of the difficulties and the problems, and pointed to the very helplessness about where or how to begin to identify these, and the expectation of having them magically detected (and dissected) via a process of "spoon-feeding" as in itself a major problem about learning. Dr. T was not in full agreement with this. He recognized that he had difficulties in his therapeutic work and in detecting problems in it for discussion. He realized, too, that he did bring to his supervisor the expectation of learning by "spoon-feeding" and that this *was* a problem of some magnitude to him. He was not quite willing to accept the interrelatedness of these—to him—still discrete problems in the two relationships, that with the supervisor and that with the patient. Supervisor and student agreed to focus during the second period of supervisory work on the resolution of this difference in viewpoint.

For the supervisory conference to be here discussed, which took place about a month following this evaluation, Dr. T had submitted two interviews with the patient that represented probably the poorest samples of his work from the entire period of time that he had been treating the patient. Dr. Daniels began by asking what problems he had had that he wished to discuss from these hours. Dr. T paused, thought briefly, and then said that he had been surprised at the outcome of his "presentation of the realities of his current situation" to the patient. He had not expected such apathetic acceptance. Dr. Daniels asked, "Surprised? You mean it was so totally unexpected?" Dr. T said no, not quite; that a number of possible responses on the part of the patient to the planned therapeutic maneuver had been considered together; and that, after all, he shouldn't have been *surprised* at the response; this was the way the patient was. This apathy was his total response to life. Dr. T should have known. It was just the patient. Dr. Daniels said he took this to mean that Dr. T could visualize no other response really possible to the patient. Dr. T said yes, that was right.

Dr. Daniels said that that would leave no particular problem for them to discuss together. Dr. T was puzzled. What was meant? Dr. Daniels answered that, well, if everything was so inevitable, determined wholly from within the patient's character structure, then no matter how Dr.

T had played out his role, really no matter what he said, or who else said it, or with whatever level of skill, it would all still have been the same. Was this really what was meant?

Here Dr. Daniels had in a rather heavy-footed manner brought the whole logical conclusion of Dr. T's stance vis-à-vis his learning situation crashing down at him. Does this strong attack derive from Dr. Daniels' conviction that only in this way can Dr. T truly become aware of how attempting to learn by "spoon-feeding" from his supervisor and not seeming able to see where his problems might lie in his work with his patient are really but two faces of the same coin? Or does it derive at least in part from Dr. Daniels' feeling that he must now belatedly fully catch up with issues that he should have joined earlier, when they first arose—as early as the very first session together?

Dr. T, on his part, still couldn't see any particular problem about this; he had "presented the reality situation" to the patient, and the patient responded wholly in keeping with his character. Of course, the patient had taken the therapist's presentation as a rejection and felt it as the first step to being dismissed from the hospital; furthermore he felt much too weak to go. But it had certainly not been meant as a rejection! Dr. Daniels wondered if that might constitute a problem, that Dr. T had intended a communication one way, and the patient perceived it otherwise—as another rejection by a malevolent fate. Dr. Daniels wondered, could this outcome have been influenced in any way by the manner in which this entire matter had been presented? Dr. T thought not; it was again the patient. He was that kind of guy who takes things in a paranoid way. Dr. T didn't see at all where he himself could have done differently. He had said nothing deliberately rejecting; he really couldn't see where he had any specific problems for discussion in this material.

At this point Dr. Daniels seemingly quite accepted this and said that maybe Dr. T really had felt none. Dr. T then counter-asked, "Well, maybe *you* see some problems that I have." Dr. Daniels wondered now how well that would work. He said: "If it were me or were my therapy, maybe I would see the patient's misperception of what I thought I intended as a problem, but that would be my problem, not yours." Dr. T said that all this was very confusing. Maybe there was a real problem here. Suppose he did raise that point about the misperception as a problem, what about it? Dr. Daniels wondered then whether Dr. T felt this as such or was it more an intellectual game.

If it did represent a problem he felt, it could certainly be discussed as such. Dr. Daniels then went on to state his own feeling, however, that Dr. T just had a contrary conviction that the patient was hopeless and psychologically immovable, and couldn't be affected no matter how Dr. T approached him or dealt with him. Dr. T said slowly that, well, he guessed that was so. The patient *is* that way. Dr. T didn't see how he himself could have done otherwise. He had just presented it all straight, and even if it had been different, he didn't think it would have made any difference. He said, "I guess I still don't really see the problem here."

Dr. Daniels said that that was O.K.; perhaps Dr. T just felt no problem about this at this point. Dr. Daniels said, however, that one thing puzzled him about all this. In some of the previous supervisory sessions together, when he himself had actively pointed out Dr. T's problems for him as he had seen them, there always seemed to be plenty. Now that a share of the responsibility for this task was shifted back to Dr. T, no problems were apparent. Yet the therapy wasn't that different. Had Dr. T never really felt as particular problems the kinds of things the supervisor had been pointing out?

Here we can see Dr. Daniels' technical mistake. He attempted to bring the full impact of the meaning of having to learn by "spoon-feeding" home to his student, by suddenly stepping out of this role and shifting the burden of finding the problems, the things to be discussed, to the student. Such a real change in a learning pattern cannot be effected by fiat in this abrupt manner, and hence the frustration, and perhaps irritation, too, engendered in the supervisor. Dr. T responded with his own sense of frustration and puzzlement, "Oh, no, I could see the problems very clearly when you pointed them out." Dr. Daniels said perhaps so, but wondered how helpful all that had been. Dr. T stated that he had gotten all his previous supervision that way the first two years here.

At this point Dr. Daniels recalled what had been stated by Dr. T the very first time they had met together, as to how little help he felt his previous supervision had been as a learning experience. Perhaps this was a chance for things to work out differently. But then Dr. T queried, "But I have scotomata just where my problems are. How *can* I see them?" Here Dr. Daniels called on a clinical analogy for help. He said that in that case it might indeed be difficult to find things that could be fruitfully tackled together. It's sort of like when a patient comes for psychotherapy, we expect him to come because he experiences problems—he is not expected to come with solutions (that's the job of the therapy), but with awareness of the problems. Maybe that is the first step. Maybe Dr. T was being like the patient who comes but who feels "no problems." How can we figure out ways to help such an individual? . . . At the end of this supervisory hour Dr. T left, saying, "I'll have to do a lot of thinking about all this."

Here in this hour, we have (albeit, abruptly) highlighted the learning dilemma of Dr. T, developed through the several months to this point of explicit awareness. He said, "I don't know where my problems are. They are scotomata by definition. And if they're scotomata, how can I ever see them?" Counterposed against this statement of his own inadequacy was his conception of the wise and helping supervisor, "You know everything. So just go ahead and point things out and teach me everything. Tell me concretely where I have made mistakes with my patient. You can see my scotomata, so it's really *your responsibility* to tell me where they are." And Dr. T had underlined this conviction by appearing for each supervisory hour, not with questions to ask, but with a receptive attitude, paper in hand, pencil poised in air, in order to write down whatever the supervisor might say about the case.

In the mid-period evaluation this had been called the need to learn by "spoon-feeding." Dr. T had recognized that he had certainly been accustomed all his life to a pattern of expected learning by "spoon-feeding." He had begun to see how this same magical expectation pervaded the entire relationship to the supervisory process and was now beginning to see how the "problem of finding a problem" was indeed the exact counterpart in the therapy situation of the expectation of being "spoon-fed" in the supervisory situation. And he agreed now that, yes, he wanted very much to break out of this learning pattern. For, after all, in terms of learning how to do psychotherapy, it hadn't worked—his confession in the first supervisory session was a statement of the perceived inadequacy of this kind of learning. Where he was really spoon-fed, he didn't learn effectively. And yet the effort to effect change was so difficult. When the supervisor refrained from pointing out problems, none were to be seen. The attempt to break with the no-longer-desired (and fundamentally not helpful) method of learning led to the frustration and difficulty that one encounters in any effort to make such a basic change in one's entire manner of professional functioning. And here the supervisor has his leverage for effecting change by really caring enough to want to help the therapist stop doing what he himself has become dissatisfied with.

The supervisory session four weeks later showed further delineation of the magnitude and kind of learning difficulty being struggled with. Dr. T had switched to a consideration of the work with another patient. (He had given up on the previous patient and, as a sign of his pessimism, had transferred the patient to a more chronic setting within the hospital.) The new patient was overtly hostile toward any attempt at psychological help and was able to openly express his disbelief in the whole process. In trying to help the patient to thus focus his own attitudes toward the psychotherapeutic process, Dr. T had allowed the discussion to become an argument between them, rather than being able to help the patient see it as his own intrapsychic dilemma. As in the instance with the previous patient, a presentation of a point of view by Dr. T had led to an unwanted result; it came out and was perceived otherwise than intended.

When this came up in the supervisory session, Dr. T indicated that he had certainly been aware all during the hour with the patient that he was getting into an argument—it often happened that way with lots of patients—and that this was not what he had intended. But he was also reluctant to bring this to the supervisory hour as a problem for discussion. He went on to say that this tendency was so universal with so many patients; how could he admit a total failure? Dr. Daniels expressed surprise at this. Was having a problem an admission of "total failure"? Dr. T said that maybe it shouldn't be; maybe this was just part of his own resistance; part of why he never saw problems in himself; why he just never saw problems.

Dr. Daniels said that it seemed true that Dr. T could see conflicts and problems in the personalities of his patients, but seemed not to have the same psychological perceptiveness in regard to his own mental processes, even when the two situations were somewhat parallel. Here the patient was in the dilemma of needing and wanting help with his distress and yet not seeing any psychological problems. Dr. T was saying that he could not deal with this as effectively as he would like. Maybe because he was struggling with quite similar problems in himself and, hence, could not really help the patient with them. Dr. T smiled and said that he hadn't seen it that way before. He then went on to say that maybe one of the real difficulties was the way he thought of the word *problem.* If you didn't know how to tie your shoelaces and had to run around barefoot as a consequence, *that* would be a problem.

And here we have a full measure of the dimensions of the learning dilemma introduced as the "problem of finding a problem." With his shoelace analogy Dr. T showed the concreteness represented to him by the word *problem.* Perhaps asking him to conceptualize the abstractions of psychological problems had been truly too burdensome a task. No wonder all the anxiety.

At this juncture what kind of supervisory help can be offered? Perhaps all this can be turned fruitfully into a real demonstration, in terms of his own present discomforts, of what a psychological problem is. Suppose the supervisor acknowledged this difficulty in conceptualization as indeed a problem and the demand for it as too difficult a task before which Dr. T had been wont to retreat in helplessness. And every time he had been confronted with this task throughout the supervisory process he had thus retreated. *That* is a psychological problem, which, incidentally, patients have in exactly the same way . . . And this inhibiting paralysis expressing such deep anxiety has effectively covered up the specific lacks in technical psychotherapeutic skills and has prevented student and supervisor from ever really helpfully tackling specific skill problems.

Two weeks later Dr. T came to his supervisory hour (now near the very end and just prior to the final evaluation) and said that before he began to discuss the patient's material he had something he very much wanted to tell. It was so obvious, but it had just occurred to him. The previous week Dr. Daniels had asked him whether he had gone over the material with a particular focus (that they were discussing together) in mind. He had not. Here the supervisor had been reading the material pretty carefully—in advance—week by week, and he himself had never looked at the notes once after dictating them. Dr. Daniels said that this was certainly right and perhaps this was a psychological problem. Dr. T said he could see all this as part of his own resistances to this process much as he had thought he wanted it. And he had repressed it all along. He was just becoming aware of it. This week for the first time he had taken his own notes home and reviewed them pretty carefully for this conference. Somewhat later in the hour Dr. T said, in regard to a reminder of this same problem, that it all made him wonder. Was that his characteristic reaction? That the repression lifts at the last minute when it's almost too late? It's as if this discovery —and confession—could be made only under the pressure of ending, like the examination anxiety liberated in even the well-prepared student by the finality of the examination process. Perhaps here Dr. T has made his first real step away from the expectation of being "spoon-fed"— the receptivity of poised paper and pencil.

As is apparent by now problems about learning can be pyramided on end, in as bewildering a variety as individual differences in characterological configurations assume when measured along any other major dimension. Perhaps at this point a number of other patterns that have emerged and have assumed significant and interesting forms among the students seen in our program can be stated here in summary form without the same kind of detailed spelling-out as those dealt with to this point.

These include, for instance, the problem of the student who became overinvolved in so many other conflicting interests and claims on his time that psychotherapy training was only one among the many goals to which he was committed—to be gotten "on the run," as were all the others, because adequate time could not be found for any of them.

A commonly expressed problem, stated usually as a complaint, is that the supervisory process acts to inhibit the spontaneity and the full effectiveness of the therapist's work. This problem is usually stated in such terms as "I have much more trouble in my work with the patient whom I carry in supervision than I do with the rest of my case load." When the student thus says that he makes more mistakes with this particular patient, what he usually means is that his awareness of his mistakes is greater, that the exposure arouses anxiety, and that the pressure for change creates conflict. This also has the meaning that the same mistakes with other patients, being hidden, somehow do not count. The supervision, then, evokes an affectively highly charged situation for the therapist, who with one of his patients at least has to confront his own dilemma about whether he will go on being his old professional self, or try to become some new self, with all the struggle and anxiety which goes along with this conflict about making a change. This is often handled by blaming the supervisor, or the structure, or both. "It's you—and your function—that inhibit me." Ultimately, before learning can proceed effectively, the externalization must be taken back and the problem internalized as an inner psychological dilemma. The opposite situation of the beginning therapist who has but one patient helps engender the problem of all the meaning for him if he does not do well, if he loses his one patient, or has a difficult time in the supervision.

Another, not infrequent, problem is that created where the patient improves, though the therapist shows no real progress in his psychotherapeutic work, no growth in skill. Such a student can point to the seeming progress of the patient as evidence of the adequacy of his own work and as resistance against the need for insight and change. Yet this whole improvement on the part of the patient may be built on an intuitive, albeit static, use of himself by the therapist who does not grow to where he adds insight and conscious control to the natural gift or the display of lively interest and warmth that have elicited the initial favorable response.

Another manner of expressing the inner struggle around supervision is posed by the problem of "skepticism vs. faith" in the psychotherapeutic process. The student may state that he works without any faith in psychotherapy as an effective method in the treatment of mental illness. He may elaborate with any number of examples—often from his own experience. Or he may express it somewhat differently as "I really have no faith in all of this, nor that anything you propose will be any better than my own methods. If I do apply your suggestions (because you say so), it can only be a mechanical application." One might directly ask such a student whether he feels able at least to try out the supervisor's suggestions, even without believing in them, and try then on the basis of this experience to decide how helpful they can be. Or does his feeling of futility at the whole extend to the conviction that he can't even try them out fairly and in such a way as to really test their workability—indeed a crucial question for many learners. For the problem of skepticism about the principles and about the method does not by itself preclude helpful and worthwhile work, both in psychotherapy and in supervision, anymore than does any other equally ingrained resistance to learning. Overt skepticism can be dealt with as a resistance just as any other—and in each of us there is a measure of skepticism, manifest or more covert. Rather than a statement that he is not teachable, the acknowledgment of this difficulty in the student is a foreshadowing of the particular way in which he will resist being taught.

A problem about learning of a different order that emerges in various guises is that stemming from the way the individual perceives the relationship between the nature and purpose of supervision on the one hand, and of personal therapy on the other. The conversion of supervision into a therapeutic experience can be both wished and feared. This can be expressed variously. It can be "I don't want this supervision, because it is treatment. I want you to be a different kind of supervisor who does 'patient-centered' supervision. I want to learn about the patient's dynamics and don't want you to help me be at all different myself. (And I will defend myself against that process by calling it therapy.)" Or the problem can be expressed just oppositely, as "I don't want supervision. I need treatment rather than supervision, and would want to turn this into the treatment I am looking for." We recall that Dr. X added a further rationalization when he confessed his real wish, not for supervision, but for therapy, "which I need more and will ultimately help my patients more." Corollary to this expression of personal anxiety and this request for personal therapy was the implied assertion that supervision itself was not really necessary (the corresponding denial of the need for help in the area in which it is specifically available).

And it is this assumption that betrays the underlying defensive character of the move to ward off supervision under the seemingly so acceptable guise of pressing one's own therapeutic need. This same wish emerged, more subtly expressed, when a student finally told his supervisor that he, the supervisor, was being quite inconsistent. He seemed to expect the student to treat the patient in a certain way and yet he, the supervisor, was not treating his student in the same way at all. The supervisor at that point asked whether the student really expected—and wanted—to be treated like a patient. Was he asking for therapy and not supervision? When thus explicitly brought into focus, the nature of the underlying plea was clarified and attention could again be paid to the proper material of the supervision.

With some students this problem can be a more doggedly persistent one, leading ultimately to the need for a basic clarifying decision—perhaps in truth to abandon psychotherapeutic work under supervision and look instead for personal treatment, before returning to the attempt to learn psychotherapy. Dr. V's work with his supervisor, Dr. Ellis, is an illustration of this. This example is taken from a point far along in his contact with Dr. Ellis, where Dr. V had lost yet another in a succession of patients. He was finally beginning to see a little the role he played in these repetitive losses of his patients. This one he had seen as an "aggressive" woman who made excessive demands on him. (Ultimately, the demand to help and cure.) Since Dr. V felt so inadequate in his capacity to handle these demands, he in turn rejected the patient with considerable counter-hostility, in accord with the model, "I am in turn hostile to you because you impose demands that show up my inadequacy." In the supervisory hour, Dr. V went further to bring this issue more personally home to himself by stating, too, that the patient in her appearance and behavior resembled his own wife, and he could only think of the poor devil of a husband. At this point Dr. V then indicated quite clearly that this identification touched off a key problem for himself and would have to be dealt with—in terms of his own inner emotional turmoil—before he could focus on problems of learning and technique in relation to his work with the patient.

In response to a question by Dr. Ellis, Dr. V acknowledged that he wanted therapy, *not* supervision, because "supervision does not go far enough." Behind this was his resistance to learning. "Make no supervisory demands on me in terms of work performance. Do not try to hold me to any standards. Because you can see I am sick and need therapy." Dr. V went on to state resignedly that not being able to do psychotherapy because of inner inhibiting difficulties was like having brown hair. Once you found out about it, it was diagnosed, and nothing could be done.

And through subsequent supervisory sessions the same pattern was reiterated. When confronted with difficulties in his work, he seemed constantly to say, "Diagnose me, but don't try to change me; leave that to my (future) therapist." He revealed grave doubts about his current clinical assignment and expressed the need for a more constraining structure. He felt that the other residents on the service had better breaks in their assignments of case load than he himself did. He continued to lose patients. His pattern had been to handle patients in a harsh, authoritarian fashion, and he found himself to be more concerned with getting them out of the hospital than helping them to solve their problems. He over-confronted them regularly in some kind of effort to hurry the therapeutic progress and get them out of the hospital. Dr. Ellis persistently pointed out this excessive pressure toward action and indicated that in doing psychotherapy progress might be slow, and action need to be held to a minimum. At this, Dr. V expressed himself as perhaps temperamentally unsuited to doing psychotherapy. He felt that as an individual he was more "active" and that something like gardening was more gratifying to him. Dr. V finally asserted his personal therapeutic need to be an overriding one, not just a resistance to learning that might be worked through, but a barrier, at present insuperable. Shortly thereafter, at the time of his evaluation, he withdrew from therapeutic work and stated his intention to seek personal help before returning to it.

In this situation the problem about learning had become so intertwined with the over-all character difficulties, of which the learning difficulty is but a particular manifestation, that the boundaries and purposes defined by the supervisory relationship could not provide sufficient help to the student. At this juncture the student turned to a different relationship—personal therapy for himself—in which the new boundaries and purposes would enable the kind of consideration of these difficulties that would promise more usable help. Though students in the course of their therapeutic work and in considering the problems about learning that arise in the supervisory relationship often come to an enhanced awareness of difficulties in over-all functioning that then impel them to seek personal therapeutic help, it is much less frequent that the difficulties in functioning necessitate the cessation of clinical therapeutic work while the treatment of the inhibiting personal difficulties is going on. Except for such extreme outcomes, it is our conviction that consideration of the problems about learning that arise within the supervisory relationship will provide sufficient leverage for the supervisor to help the student achieve significant shifts in his professional self, to the unraveling then of the learning problems he has with his patient, and through that, to the acquisition of increased therapeutic skills. How this process operates in the relationship between therapist and patient, and in the tackling of the learning problems within that relationship, will be the subject matter of the next chapter. For the problems about learning (problems between supervisor and therapist along line S–T of the clinical rhombus), when viewed within the framework of the relationship between therapist and patient (line T–P of the clinical rhombus), can often be seen there as the learning problems of the student and the technical-skill questions that stand behind these.

X / *Therapist and Patient—Learning Problems*

Vergebens, dass ihr ringsum wissenschaftlich schweift,
Ein jeder lernt nur, was er lernen kann.
("In vain, that you scientifically explore all around,
Each only learns what he can.")—GOETHE

The "learning problem," the problem the therapist has in responding appropriately and helpfully to his patient is the final justification of the entire supervisory and training structure. The student comes to his supervisor in order to acquire psychotherapeutic skills. He discovers in his work with his patients that at times he acts and responds within the psychotherapy situation in ways that are determined, not by the objectively demonstrated needs of the patient, but by characteristic, automatic, and inappropriate patterns within himself. These he discovers to be his learning problems.

In the preceding chapter these problems were projected into the student's relationship with his supervisors as problems about learning. In this chapter they emerge in the psychotherapy situation with the patient, and are brought from there—as learning problems—for discussion with the supervisor. All this could convey the impression that these "problems" are to be regarded as impedimenta to true learning, neurotically based obstacles to be gotten rid of so that proper learning can proceed with optimum efficiency. Actually any process involving personal change is impossible without affective components and the consideration of these components—inevitable in the most "normal" of interpersonal relationships—is what is meant by working with the learning problems. Put another way, working out and solving the learning problems (and the problems about learning as well) is the very process of learning—it is itself the learning that is sought, and not just the necessary preliminary.

Such a view differs, of course, from the many attempts to consider as learning problems (and hence appropriate to the supervisory process) only "intellectual" problems—problems where the difficulties are presumably lack of knowledge of either theory or technique—whereas "emotional" problems which carry charges of affective and therefore drive-influenced behavior are to be excluded from supervision, and to be considered necessarily analytic problems or therapy problems. We feel that learning is not just conveying the technical tricks of the trade, any more than it is just the removal of blind spots that impair the therapist's objectivity in his relationship with his patient. The skill that is acquired consists essentially of the capacity to integrate factual knowledge with appropriate emotional responses. True learning therefore combines cognitive and affective levels of experience into new and enduring integrations. Learning that results in the acquisition of skill, and that therefore requires change, necessarily involves strongly charged affective components. This is especially so when the vehicle of the learning is the interpersonal process between the supervisor and the student, wherein the student reports what transpires between himself and his patient and gradually becomes aware of the characteristic patterns of his relationships, to his supervisor on the one hand and to the patient on the other. Where these characteristic patterns determine and limit the manner of professional performance and the level of professional competence, they are focused upon as learning problems within the supervisory context.

Perhaps this can best be elucidated by turning to an example of a learning problem common to many beginning therapists, the problem of the therapist's overidentification with the patient expressed in the formula, "I can't treat this patient because I am too much like him. He has the same problems that I have and I'm not sure that I can solve mine. How can I help him solve his?" The problem here of establishing a real *difference* between the therapist and his patient—between the help-giver and the help-seeker—and using this difference to promote the psychotherapeutic process can be seen clearly in the work of Mr. Y, the student whose initial psychotherapeutic work was discussed in the chapters on the beginning process. There we followed his contact with a patient, which lasted only two hours when the patient decided to leave the hospital. In the study of those sessions we could see in detail Mr. Y's defensive maneuver counterposed as a protection against the demand implicit in the patient's plea for help. With this depressed patient he had depreciated himself. He had stated his own lack of skill and his beginning status, thereby asserting, "Don't look for much help from me with your feelings of dejection and lack of self-esteem, because I have those selfsame feelings myself." Here Mr. Y was stating the doctrine of "there's no difference between us, so how can I help" to the patient; and he was simultaneously thereby stating to the supervisor, "Don't expect much of me. I'm just a beginner—hardly good enough even to begin to think of treating a patient."

Toward the end of the supervisory hour with Dr. Baehr in which some of the many meanings of this need to overidentify with the patient through trying to wipe out the differences between them were discussed with Mr. Y, attention turned to the question of securing another patient for him to work with. Mr. Y expressed some reluctance in regard to some of the patients currently available, and when questioned about the basis for this, stated, "Well, I guess what I wanted is a more compliant patient than either of these. But that would be more like myself and I don't suppose I could learn as much, in terms of my own goals of wanting to be a therapist." Actually, Mr. Y is hardly compliant. Rather, he means by compliant a patient who will be willing to stay in treatment. But he also means that he must see each prospective patient in terms of how alike and how different he feels himself to be. While he states his desire to hold on to the difference, he has acted counter to this desire, by assuming an identity with the patient that then supposedly justified his inability to help.

Some two months later Mr. Y was with his third patient. He had in the interim "lost" a second patient. His constant anxiety now was lest he "lose" this one, too, and he wondered how much longer the supervisor would allow such repetitive losses to go on. He coped with this anxiety by the, to him, familiar technique of trying to be as much like the patient as possible, and thus to be completely devoid of any even fantasied threat to—or influence upon—the patient. In the session under consideration both the patient and the therapist began by exchanging apologies and guilt feelings as to who was to be held responsible for the short period that the patient had been waiting before his appointment. The patient was an obsessional, ruminative individual, who would flit anxiously from topic to topic. He presented a wide gamut of life difficulties and of disabling symptoms, jumping from one to another, never stopping to allow for focus on any aspect of the material, and putting everything, the meaningful as well as the more trivial, on the same level in a garrulous, anecdotal way. His constant need seemed to be to deny and to apologize for any possible aggressive intent, and to go on to what he hoped might be another, less anxiety-provoking topic, whenever the danger of having to discuss such impulses arose.

Through all of this Mr. Y flitted with the patient, following every change, and at no point injecting a difference of any kind. Just as he had been depressive with a depressed patient, so he was now obsessional with an obsessional patient. Even Mr. Y's process notes were in keeping with these qualities. They were long and rambling—seven pages for one interview—and unfocused. The list of topics covered in any one interview was a long one. When he came to his supervisory hour Mr. Y said apologetically, "I certainly gave you a lot of material this time." He said, too, that a lot of it was repetitive and he had begun to wonder where he was getting with all this. Dr. Baehr said that the question, "Where is this getting?" had likewise occurred to him. He had followed the various turns of the material, and had nowhere seen evidence of any active intervention on the part of the therapist, no effort to bring order and meaning into any part of the voluminous material. Where did Mr. Y feel that he, as the therapist, came into this process at all? Mr. Y said, "Well, I really felt like saying something like 'Slow down! There's too much here. What part of it shall we pick to deal with?' " Dr. Baehr asked then why he hadn't said something like that.

Mr. Y responded that this kind of remark struck him as too much like the "over-confronting" that he had been doing with his first two patients, and that he had come to see during the process of the supervision as having contributed importantly to his loss of those patients. And so in each situation Mr. Y gave his reasons. Being self-depreciatory with his first, depressed patient was a question of honesty. Being fearful and willing to flit obsessionally with his present, obsessional patient was a result of having learned that his tendency to be "over-confronting" had already helped precipitate the loss of two patients. Whatever the expressed reasons, in trying to present himself to each patient as no different, Mr. Y was effectively precluding any real helping activity. In his anxiety to hold onto his patient, he in effect gave up any effort to help him (and any possibility of learning more about how to help him); for in order to be helpful, the therapist must pose a difference to the patient that the latter can come to grips with in the course of the therapeutic process. Around the discussion of this issue at this time Mr. Y could begin to see his learning problem as one of how to express a difference between himself and his patient and yet not "confront" the patient in the way he conceptualized confrontation—as a hostile assault on the integrity of the other.

Such a learning problem has, of course, a complex structure and ramifies widely into a series of related, though distinct and separable, problems which we can see in the further unfolding of Mr. Y's therapeutic work. The patient began to display an expectant—and to Mr. Y, troublesome—passivity during the therapeutic sessions. Mr. Y brought this up in the supervision, stating, "One of my real problems is going to be this patient's passivity and how to handle it." The supervisor, perhaps mistakenly and in any case prematurely, seemed to take this as a statement of the student's own passive inclinations, his own passive asking what to do about this turn of events. Reacting to this cue, Dr. Baehr began to tell his student just what had gone wrong. That is, rather than exploring with Mr. Y the exact ways in which *he* had felt that the patient's passivity made for treatment difficulties and how he thought he could meet them, Dr. Baehr turned to the material and pointed out a number of examples of how he, the supervisor, felt that Mr. Y had responded to the breach left by the passive patient by his own authoritative reactions and active interventions, thus reacting to the patient's neurotic expectation, rather than attempting to interpret it. Dr. Baehr pointed out that in so doing Mr. Y had blocked the patient's possible movement out of the passive position, and had precluded even clarifying to the patient the meaning which the passivity had in the context of the therapeutic relationship. What Dr. Baehr overlooked, however, was that his own active intervention and response might, in the same way, block his student's own willingness to explore the possibilities he could see as available to him at this juncture.

And Mr. Y reacted to "being told" with a qualified acceptance. He would say about each point being made something like, "Yes, I see that and this is not to deny any of what you say, but I think in this particular case that I can explain it as follows. . . ." And he would then proffer some such explanation as that the patient's specific character pattern made any other kind of response less appropriate at the particular moment; or that he was merely trying out some principles he had seen applied in a didactic course on psychotherapy where they were discussing a similar sort of patient; or "I had to get myself in edgewise right there to show him that I was in this situation, too"; or that "I am doing this sort of thing less than with the last patient, anyway." That is, Mr. Y "accepted" the supervisory interpretations about his assumption of the role of the directing and all-seeing therapist in response to the patient's pattern of neurotic passivity, and yet in accepting, he qualified and denied and "proved" that the supervisor was not quite right in the way he saw it.

In looking at both the therapeutic process and the supervisory process at this point, we are perhaps left to wonder whether the facet of the therapist's problem currently to the fore in his work with the patient and with the supervisor is his own propensity for passivity (as the supervisor seems to have presumed) or an opposite tendency toward authoritarian, controlling interventions.

By the next supervisory hour Mr. Y had swung from these active efforts to control to an overcompensating directionlessness in his contact with the patient, and again fell into the familiar pattern of obsessional hedgehopping with the patient. Mr. Y was bending over backward to avoid controlling and "overconfronting," the kind of thing he had learned from his supervisor he had been doing too much of. Dr. Baehr said then that it seemed as if Mr. Y had to keep gravitating between two extremes in his conception of the psychotherapeutic process—(1) that of confronting, of directing, and of clever interpretations in which the therapist constantly jumped in with his conceptions and conclusions, or (2) that of just following and reflecting the patient's feeling, tone, and communication. Perhaps each of these concepts, Dr. Baehr said, were both true and yet not true, that neither was the "psychotherapeutic answer."

At this point Mr. Y expressed his confusion; he felt as if he had been buffeted by contradictory advice in successive weeks, each of which he had been trying in turn to follow, only to have new difficulties arise. Dr. Baehr said that Mr. Y must then feel quite inhibited in what would be his natural and spontaneous bent by what he must feel was constant pressure and critical supervisory review. Mr. Y said that he certainly did feel that what the supervisor had said and might say did influence his therapy. But that was as it should be; after all, he was here to learn and to apply and test out the things talked of in the supervisory sessions. He certainly *had* become aware of his tendency to intervene too authoritatively and cleverly, and that he was bending over backward to try and correct this. He didn't really feel that it made him do things unnatural to himself. Dr. Baehr wondered a little at that and whether or not in trying to apply advice in blanket, Mr. Y wasn't going to an extreme where the advice would prove unworkable (such as not trying at all to focus the flow of material because that would be in the category of overconfronting), and thus perhaps "prove" that the advice was not so sound.

In thus picking up what we have noted before as the student's need to "prove" that the help offered was not as good as it might be and should be, the supervisor has chosen, perhaps unwittingly, to project the problem out of the psychotherapy arena (the problem of "learning by overdoing") to the supervision arena (the problem *about* learning of the student). It is this very problem about learning (the impulse to show the defect in the supervisory suggestion) which we saw foreshadowed in the first contacts with this student, who came initially with the expectation of being "a little bit disappointed" in what he found.

Mr. Y, however, was not ready to acknowledge his difficulty as a problem about learning. He said, "I deny that. I'm not trying to 'prove' anything. I do want to use these things and test them. I am too far on the other side, now; that's all." He went on to say that as a matter of fact he had come to see for himself, too, that he couldn't just treat this passive patient by going along. He had himself come to the decision that he ought to try to focus the material more; he had, in fact, started to do just that in his hour of this very day, the material for which the supervisor had not yet seen. (Because of a necessary shift in appointment time that week, the supervisor was one hour behind on the material). Mr. Y then ended the supervisory session thoughtfully, "I guess I *am* trying to prove something—that I came to the same conclusion, even before you." Here Mr. Y thus restated his "problem about learning" in another way; that whatever good idea the supervisor had, he himself had it first.

The next week Mr. Y began by stating that he felt that now the patient was moving, although slowly; that he had applied in part what had been talked about the previous week about focusing; but that the patient had slipped away from him again in his usual garrulous manner.

Dr. Baehr asked where the difficulties had arisen. Mr. Y said that he had applied what had been talked about, but not fully, and it had worked somewhat—but not fully. He said that there were various contributing circumstances; somehow the discussions of the previous week seemed not quite appropriate in the context of the hours this week; the patient had gone off on some more rambling associations, and Mr. Y had "held off" because more "material" might come to light. This brought up some theoretical questions about therapy, such as, "Do we deal primarily with content or defense?"

Dr. Baehr said that more than theoretical issues seemed to be involved. For this kind of thing had happened more than once. The previous week suggestions had been made in the direction of trying to help focus the diffuse and rambling material. At that time Mr. Y had indicated that he had, in fact, thought of it himself and had just not done it because he had felt that it might be deemed "too confronting." Now he had gone ahead and "focused," but perhaps focusing was looked at somewhat differently by the two of them. Dr. Baehr said that he had not intended to convey a concept of focusing as being a matter of getting the patient to talk only on one topic at a time rather than many (because within that he could be just as garrulous and rambling—as indeed he was), but rather that focusing was meant in terms of the relationship between therapist and patient and the relating of the patient's material to the therapeutic interaction. Now both of them seemed to be saying that this had not really been done in the way that had been discussed and that might have been helpful. What could they together do about this?

Mr. Y said that one thing was suddenly clear to him, that it really seemed as if he were trying to anticipate the supervisor. This was all right, except he wondered to what extent he was intent on "proving" that he had thought of it all first. Dr. Baehr said that this might be part of it and another part might be that suggestions made in the supervision could never be fully applied (even where Mr. Y had himself also thought of them) and never seemed to work out quite as well as had been anticipated. Was there something wrong with the suggestions or with the way in which they were made that rendered them less applicable by Mr. Y? Dr. Baehr added that he had tried to raise the same point—maybe somewhat awkwardly—the previous week. Mr. Y answered, "You did raise it last week and I denied it then. I deny it again. I'm not aware of anything of the kind." Dr. Baehr recalled that when they had first started working together, Mr. Y had expressed a feeling of being a "little bit disappointed" in many aspects of the training program and in many of his clinical experiences. Could this be more of the same? Here Dr. Baehr not only again raised a question in terms of his student's problem about learning, as it arose in this particular instance, but he also linked it explicitly to the general expectation of the student, expressed in his initial contact with supervisor and supervision.

To this Mr. Y answered, "I see our difference now. I just look at this relationship much more positively than you do. I've gotten so much help here, especially help in conceptualizing my difficulties. I can't see ahead very well. After each time with you, I'm able to go ahead on three more interviews with the patient, and then I need you to talk it all over with again. If I have trouble in applying some of these things, it's not something between us. It's me. It's my own insecurities. That's why I have to keep coming back for more guidance . . . This is good."

Here we see a complex interplay of the problems of both supervisor and student in reaching a productive working relationship. As an expression of his pique that his supervisory suggestions were constantly being undermined by his student's impulse to disprove their value, Dr. Baehr felt driven to try to "counter-prove" to his student how much he (the student) still had to learn. In his turn Mr. Y reacted by "proving" what a good student he had been and how much he had indeed learned. At this moment it would seem as if the technical problems with the patient have become obscured by the interplay of the teacher's and the student's problems with each other.

By the next week, however, the focus was again directly on the learning problems with the patient. In the interim Mr. Y had *really* applied all that had been spoken of in the supervisory sessions—and with a vengeance. He came in wondering whether he hadn't even "focused" too much on the relationship; in the very last hour the patient seemed to feel somewhat annoyed and pushed. Dr. Baehr agreed that he, too, felt that all this might have been overworked. Mr. Y said, "Yes, that's the word, overworked." He was overapplying the kinds of things that before were only half done. And he could himself give examples from the material where he was again too directing. And he could see Dr. Baehr's point that he swung from extreme to extreme, and yet each time could see what he was doing. What did it all mean?

At this point Mr. Y stated that he "knew" it now, but he guessed the evidence kind of had to pile up before he could really recognize it.

Dr. Baehr said that he was struck that each time Mr. Y worked on a problem or a suggestion that came up in the supervisory hour, he tended to swing to an opposite extreme and raise another—opposite—problem. Must it be that way? Mr. Y reiterated that he was making progress, learning this way, bit by bit. Dr. Baehr said that maybe that was an expression of his learning pattern and for him the best way he had so far devised to learn. Maybe, though, there might be better ways for him?

Perhaps this is developed enough to reveal the intricate pattern of the problems being grappled with by Mr. Y; the eagerness to learn, and to learn by adapting himself imitatively to the perceived virtues of the more experienced supervisor; to look for, take, and apply every suggestion that he could elicit, and yet simultaneously to indicate that most of these ideas he himself had already had, and to prove that, besides, when he used them they didn't work out quite right; to be, in fact, a "little bit disappointed," and yet to prove that it was a good relationship in which he was learning a great deal, and in which he was such a good student. Under cover of these difficulties in learning he faced the problem with his patient of steering a course between the Scylla of directionless diffusion and the Charybdis of "focusing" and "confrontation." In his work with the patient he swung between the two extremes. The working through of such an intricate complex of interlocking problems in learning is—inevitably—a slow and patient process. In following Mr. Y's material as far as we did we could see the constant interweaving of his problems about learning (his particular ways of responding in the supervisory relationship that determined the kind and extent of use he could make of it) with his learning problems (his ways of responding in the therapeutic relationship that determined the kind and extent of help he could offer his patient).

At this point we can perhaps delineate more sharply the distinction of learning problems from problems about learning by turning to briefer representations in more "pure culture" of a range of typical learning problems as these emerged in work with a variety of students. One kind of learning problem, widespread among psychiatric residents, and reinforced certainly by the traditional role of the physician in accepting quite naturally the patient's trusting dependence ("I put myself in your hands, Doctor"), is the automatic assumption of the role of a well-intentioned, controlling father who with greater wisdom can rechannel the patient's life into more satisfying molds.

An example of this can be drawn from a sample of Dr. S's work with Dr. Field, in which the student came to the supervisory hour with material that he was at a loss to understand. For example, the patient presented her therapist with a reality event and tried to obtain a change in her appointment arrangements involving the missing of some hours—she said she wanted to go with her boy friend to the funeral of a distant relative of his. Dr. S felt that, regardless of the reality (which need not have forced so large a shift in appointment arrangements as the patient asked), the request was an overdetermined one. A number of possible meanings occurred to him. The patient might be expressing her feelings about how unimportant the therapy hours really were to her. Or she might be probing Dr. S to see how important *he* thought them. Or it might be a reactive hostile impulse ("You're about to take off and miss an hour—I can miss hours, too"). Whichever it was, Dr. S felt peculiarly helpless to determine. He said, "I can't just guess at what goes on. I have to be able to take this up with her and explore all these possible meanings."

Dr. S was asked then where he felt all the difficulty in doing this resided. He was not sure. He felt, though, that it was a function of his own "poor timing" in the therapeutic interviews. He said, "All these things came up right there in a big rush at the end of the hour. They were so jumbled that I did not have time to deal with them at all." Dr. Field asked, if this were so, why then had Dr. S waited literally to the very last minutes of the hour to bring up such an important matter to the patient as the fact that he would have to be away and would miss the next appointment—which released counter feelings with no time left to handle them. Dr. S said that that was just it. That was an example of how he had gotten all mixed up on timing. He was going to tell her about the session he would have to miss. The hour with the patient turned out to be such a desultory one and there were so many fruitless interchanges that he was quite surprised when she "suddenly opened up" after forty minutes had gone by and began to talk quite volubly about her family. Dr. S had thought that he was going to draw another blank with his question about the family, but instead she did what she *shouldn't have*. She opened up. Dr. Field at this point questioned the words "shouldn't have." He asked, "Do you really mean that *you* decide what she should and should not talk about?" Dr. S became flustered. He said that he had had ten minutes allotted to this matter of his necessary absence at this time, but the patient had encroached on this allocation. When asked whether he really felt that he could control the interchanges and manipulate the hour that way, Dr. S was indeed embarrassed. He suddenly said that that was the same thing that they had been talking about again and again in the supervision, that he always did with the patient—like constantly outguessing her or putting her thoughts in for her. It was just another way of trying to control her. He had seen that he did it in the other interviews when it had been previously pointed out. But here it was startling, it was so clear. He was *really* learning about it, he said.

And yet, though he was *really* learning about it, Dr. S's problem of control—of making the patient into a predictable mechanical doll to which he had the key—was by no means worked out as much as he thought, and it is instructive perhaps to see it in another manifestation in the subsequent supervisory session. The following week Dr. S came in much troubled. The patient had spent a whole hour talking about her family and, with an unusual degree of vehemence, complained of their hostility and rejection, their interest in her only for her pension check, etc. Yet Dr. S had felt at a loss as to how to enter helpfully into any of this. If he would try to relate to any of these themes, she would constantly slip away to another example rather than face more fully the impact of any one. He said, "So then I tried a short cut and brought it to her direct and told her I felt she must be depressed today. But it didn't work. She couldn't make the connection to all the material she had been dealing with and just denied the feeling." Dr. Field said that he felt that this was quite right; the patient couldn't make such a connection, it was much too remote from the manifest material. Dr. S said that he had done this deliberately. He had been getting nowhere following all her complaining material. So he had in effect deliberately changed the subject completely. At this point Dr. Field asked did he mean that, as a result of feeling that he was making little contact with the patient on her themes, Dr. S had felt that this ought best be handled by changing the subject completely—to *his* theme. Wasn't this more of the very control they had been talking of? At this point Dr. S was again embarrassed. Yes, it certainly was. He could see all that now.

This problem of the need to control can, of course, reveal itself in a variety of ways, as we can see from a contrasting example from the work of another student, Dr. R, where the control was differently manifested—in the intellectual realm of control by knowing rather than in the active realm of control by doing, as with Dr. S. Dr. R had a need to constantly "know" the whole structure of the unfolding psychological terrain—and to know it in advance. He tried each time to reformulate the "structure of the case" and to predict ahead the development of the therapeutic process. He came to the supervisor, Dr. Daniels, as to a compendium of greater knowledge and experience, to fill in gaps where his own knowledge was insufficient. His questions of the supervisor were usually requests for further elaborations of the dynamics of the patient. And in his hours with the patient he very carefully selected all of his questions, and chose the themes that he would respond to, in terms of selecting pathways that promised to lead to the preconceived theoretical formulations. This all came up most clearly when, in response to some speculations during the supervisory hour about what the patient may have intended by a particular kind of behavior, the supervisor asked why Dr. R had not asked the patient. Dr. R was suddenly at a loss. It had not occurred to him to ask the patient—it was the kind of thing that he counted on figuring out during the supervisory hour. It would have made him uneasy to ask the patient, since he himself had no idea what it meant or where it would all lead, or how to deal with what might come next in response to his question. And around this issue Dr. R was able to see for the first time his avoidance of open-ended questions, where he would really be asking things that he didn't know and wanted to find out about and have clarified. He said somewhat lamely, "I guess I only really ask questions where I feel I already know what kind of answer to expect." The need to "control" the therapeutic situation—and one's own anxiety—by always "knowing" in advance had prompted this student to ask questions only where he already knew the answers!

A very different learning problem characterized the work of the action-oriented Dr. Q who, with his patients, constantly fell into the role of the "therapeutic acter-outer." A sensitive and gifted individual, Dr. Q demonstrated a quick and intuitive grasp of his patient's material, which he tended to react to by acting to thwart the neurotic expectation, without, however, helping to expose the mechanism involved or to bring the insight that would enlarge the patient's own effective area of control. For example, his patient once came to him complaining of her difficulty in getting a friend, whom she had allowed to share her apartment for a while, to move out. The patient complained of the friend's stubborn passivity in the face of which she felt helpless. She had no idea as to what to do, and in her helplessness turned to her therapist for advice as to what would be the best way to handle this situation—to rid herself of her undesirable tenant. Dr. Q, empathically grasping that his patient was turning to him with the same stubborn passivity of which she complained when she was its victim, indicated that, no, he would not advise her in this situation. It was best that she figure out the alternatives in such a dilemma herself. The patient was frustrated and angry. She called her therapist unhelpful. What had Dr. Q done? He had felt his patient imposing the selfsame demand on him that she correctly felt as an unwelcome "neurotic" demand when it was made on her by her roommate. Feeling this as his patient's neurotic demand, he had avoided gratifying it—and hence perpetuating the neurotic interaction—by taking a strong counter-active stand. In so doing, however, he had failed to help his patient see that what she was describing as her roommate's passive-hostile behavior likewise characterized her very own behavior and represented her own inappropriate expectation and frustration in the therapy. Rather than interpreting in this way, Dr. Q had reacted.

Useful as such techniques may be at times with many categories of patients, they are singularly limited when applied to classically neurotic patients, candidates for truly insight-aiming therapies. And it was with the difficulties created in work with just such patients (of which this was one), with the many opportunities for therapeutic progress that were not fully consolidated, that Dr. Q, our therapeutic acter-outer, could himself come to see the inappropriateness of his own response-patterns, and to institute delay mechanisms between impulse and action. Somewhat further along in his work with the same patient he reported to the supervisor that his patient, a teacher, had maneuvered herself into a position where she would have a teaching relationship to her therapist's young son. Mindful of how the patient's previous therapy had disrupted shortly after the patient secured professional contact with her then therapist's child, Dr. Q's immediate impulses were to one of two actions. One was to forbid his patient to take on this new position. The second was to withdraw his son from the school. This time he undertook neither action, but brought the whole matter to his supervisor to be discussed as a technical problem in the therapy. At this moment Dr. Q's learning problem has—for the moment at least—matured into a technical-skill problem.

Still another kind of learning problem is operative in the student who cloaks his dilemmas behind stated theoretical and research interests. Such an individual was Dr. Z, a psychologist with a research-oriented and academic background, who came to the clinical setting primarily, he stated, with an eye to the introduction of objective, quantifiable and hence "scientific" methods to the subjective and up-to-now unprecise data of psychotherapeutic processes. He had a research interest in comparing theoretical "systems of psychotherapy" and in validating one against another. An interest was stated in "proving" that psychotherapy is "scientific"—or at least in establishing just how scientific it is or can be made to be. One can certainly postulate that this is usually not an unambivalent wish. It may cover another and deeper need to prove that no system is effective, that none is scientific and that, therefore, one can spare oneself the need for empathic closeness and emotional involvement that real psychotherapeutic work demands.

Approaching psychotherapeutic work from an opposite direction (but one equally embedded in research objectives) was Dr. P, an earnest and intellectual individual who also described his would-be role in psychiatry as that of the "objective scientist." He had come from a primary interest in the physical sciences and was much preoccupied with the "data of psychiatry" and with validating the scientific nature of its methodology to his friends who remained in other medical disciplines. As one might expect, a major kind of learning problem that served to block his fullest usefulness in his chosen role as a psychotherapist (as it also blocked his research-psychologist colleague, Dr. Z) was his need to keep uninvolved in the emotional world of his patient, lest his position, which he conceived to be that of the "scientific observer" of the clinical interaction, be undermined. In turn, Dr. P's patient was a timid and inhibited young lady, recently recovered from an overt psychotic illness, and wondering now whether in her interpersonal relationships she could dare allow herself to be more spontaneous and more emotionally involved. A main technical issue in her psychotherapy rested in the problem of helping her perceive that interpersonal involvements need not be hurtful and anxiety-arousing. It was this very technical problem in the therapy which was met, however, by the therapist's learning problem—his own need to take a detached and uninvolved stance—and it was only as this learning problem was in some wise resolved that attention could be effectively paid to the technical issues posed by the patient, and constructive therapeutic solutions worked out.

This brings us to the point that it is only through unraveling the learning problems that he experiences with his patient, that the therapist can come to see the other side of the therapeutic interaction, the technical-skill problems posed by the disturbed mental processes in the patient. This will be a rather late achievement in the training process of the young therapist. It may even seem that this achievement is not a part of the process of learning, but rather is the end-product of successful learning. The therapist can now use himself with so much freedom that he can decide on therapeutic interventions entirely in terms of the patient's needs, revealed through the structure of his personality and of his illness, and through the strategic situation of the therapeutic process as influenced by the current transference position and by the current social reality.

This hard-won achievement on the part of the therapist is, however, also a part of the training process, just as the patient's new-found capacity for insight may represent both the cause and the effect of change. The psychotherapist, when he has arrived at this advanced stage of the training process, will use the supervisor not only as a source of greater experience and knowledge, but also as a teacher who can help him to become this very source himself. The therapist will then test his own ideas, play with various models of therapeutic strategy, and slowly take hold of the training process in an increasingly active way. He will put forth his own suggestions and permit himself a process of discovering which will lead him to independent learning. Articles on the process of supervision usually contain very little concerning this part of learning. Actually, however, one may turn to the rich clinical literature concerned with case studies for a description of that part of learning in which the performance of the therapist or the supervisor recedes in the background, and the focus is brought onto the technical (and theoretical) problems in the therapeutic process.

However, even the experienced therapist who has acquired his mature capacity will not always be able to maintain this position. From time to time he will fall back on positions which have been previously described as learning problems and as problems about learning. This should not be considered a form of retreat, but rather as a peculiar aspect of any emotional growth process which—like a spiral—climbs higher and higher, but returns again and again to similar relative positions. As the therapist becomes more fully aware of his own automatic response tendencies in the therapeutic situation, he will also become increasingly able to modify these responses in terms of the objectively determined needs of his patient—to acquire, that is, increased therapeutic skill. As his skill increases, his need to fall back on outmoded automatic responses will diminish, or will reach different, more subtle levels of automatization, and require of him and his teacher a more subtle, a more involved, but also a more deeply enriching way of working together.

At this point, rather than catalogue an increasing variety of learning problems, it may be well to turn to a specific problem that arises in this kind of supervised work with learning problems, with its inquiry into so many affective, drive-determined aspects of functioning; and that is the need for exposure of the self in order to learn. Though as compared with psychotherapy, for example, the sector of total functioning surveyed in supervision is but a narrow one, the problems uncovered and the resolutions sought may at times be equally deep. One student expressed his great fear of this process by his concern that, if he were really open and free in his discussions of the many dilemmas he experienced in trying to carry out psychotherapeutic work, he would be placing himself in a very dangerous position where he could be "stabbed in the back," if not by the supervisor, then by the administrator who might have access to this material.

Certainly the knowledge revealed in discussions on problems in doing psychotherapy can be extremely intimate and private. Much of the material that emerges in the process of supervision exposes significantly the infantile aspects of the individual's functioning, at times almost equally so as in psychotherapy. Teachers can well ruin the confidence of their students by betrayal of such intimate material and have, moreover, a clear ethical duty to avoid doing so. A guidepost might be that the process itself be understood to remain quite confidential. The final evaluation, however, which is a series of derivative judgments based, to be sure, on that process, is, as fully as possible, a mutual understanding and a shared conclusion. This material, including its judgments and prognoses about the effectiveness of the learner's work, should be, in a fully responsible organization, shared with the administration. It is shared and known equally to all the participants—student, supervisor, and administrator.

It is also, and over and again, one of the core resistances to learning that one must expose his weaknesses and dilemmas in order to learn, and to do this in the face of so many possible consequences to job, status, salary, professional training, and advancement. Analogously with the patient who comes to psychotherapy seeking help, the therapist coming to supervision must display his weakness for which he desires the help. Just as one tries to teach the therapist to do with his patient, so the supervisor must *demonstrate* to the therapist his realization that the weaknesses displayed are *not* all there is to his total professional functioning. It can even be said paradoxically that in displaying their weakness the patient and therapist, respectively, show us a side of their strength, which consists in their ability to focus on their weaknesses and bring them to another person, rather than to deny or conceal them. This self-exposure, then, despite the fear of possible consequences, is in itself a considerable forward step. It must be emphasized and seen by each participant that in each case the aim is not to "infantilize"—what is seen at any one time is merely a phase of a larger process. In subsequent stages of the process we can be sure that the therapist will come to relate with different facets of his personality functioning.

In this entire consideration through these two chapters of what constitutes a proper "problem about learning" and a proper "learning problem," questions both of separateness and of interrelatedness with personal (and therefore therapy) problems on the one hand, and with technical (and therefore skill) problems on the other, insistently require definition. The conviction that they can be clearly defined and helpfully worked with is the rationale for a system of supervision that is neither personal therapy nor just a conveying of didactic information on theory and technique. Since these various kinds of problems ramify into one another so widely, however, and are separately perceived largely in terms of the frame of reference within which they are viewed and the purposes to which these perceptions are to be put, it cannot be denied that help in any one area can result in overlapping effects on another. For instance, the kind of change that stems from the resolution of troubling personal problems through therapy cannot fail to facilitate the tackling of problems about learning and learning problems in supervision. In some cases (and one object of beginning supervision would be to help detect these early) supervised therapeutic work should not be carried out at all until a measure of personal help is attained through therapy. But no matter what the extent of resolution of personal problems through therapy, this does not solve or substitute for, but will merely facilitate, the working with the learning difficulties—the core of the supervisory process. And this, the psychoanalytic institutes whose students have been the recipients of such an intensive help-giving process (their personal analyses) specifically acknowledge in the requirement that ultimately learning comes from doing—and doing under supervision geared to focus on the problems in doing and in learning.

XI / *Supervisor and Student—Therapist and Patient—the Parallel Process*

Quis custodes ipsos custodiet?
("Who takes care of those who take care?")

Throughout the clinical examples of the preceding chapters we have seen how attention to the meaning of events occurring along one axis of the clinical rhombus (say, line S–T, Supervisor-Therapist) has illuminated difficulties existing along another axis of the rhombus (line T–P, Therapist-Patient). This, of course, is to be expected since the one individual, the student-therapist, remains the same in both situations, and brings his specific abilities and attitudes and his problems in learning to each. The beginning student especially, with his very small armamentarium of consolidated technical skills, frequently seems prone to respond particularly to those aspects of his patient's problems that highlight his own specific learning problems as these are activated around his expectations in the supervisory process.

This *parallel process* carries with it a never-ending surprise element as if we should not expect things to turn out as they usually do, as if the occurrence of such parallels is chance rather than the rule. The surprise, we believe, depends on the teacher's perhaps irrational expectation that the teaching and learning of psychotherapy should consist primarily of rational elements. It is expected that these rational elements would express themselves in the modes of teaching and learning which, according to this view, would be primarily didactic, and would permit us thus to bypass the powerful affective aspects of the supervisory process. The hope that a mere prescription—a technique-giving method of instruction—may suffice never ceases and is responsible for the experience of surprise and for the necessity to constantly rediscover what actually should be quite obvious. Even the rational questions of the student, for which a mere didactic answer may suffice, are often based on specific affective problems the student has in both processes. The therapist's growing skill is reflected not only in an increase of general knowledge about patients and the nature of the therapeutic process, but also in a new and fuller use he makes of himself.

The development of the professional self of the student depends on his specific and unique ways of seeking help and of helping—two faces of the same coin that have a definite functional relationship to one another. These idiosyncratic ways are decisive in patterning the interview with the patient as well as the conference with the supervisor. Such observations can be made more clearly if a teaching method is utilized that does not deny the affective, the interpersonal, aspects in the teaching as well as in the therapeutic situation. Other teaching methods, particularly those that are based primarily on information-giving—the authoritative transmission of technical advice—will tend to obscure these patterns, since both the interview with the patient as well as the conference with the supervisor will be dominated by the supervisor's way of doing things.

Teaching then will not be geared to the student's specific needs and will be likely to succeed only in those cases where the student can adapt his ways of learning to the needs of the teacher. While most mature students are likely to have a large capacity for adaptation and can learn through almost any system of teaching, their being able to do so does not justify avoiding the search for the optimum teaching method, which must inevitably be based on the individualization of the teaching process.

As we look at such different students and their ways of working with a patient, we may liken them to the blind men who try to "see the elephant." These different students, by distilling the material of the patient through the fabric of their own past experiences and their own problems in learning, would no doubt record the very same interview with a patient much differently. More importantly, with different students, the interviews themselves, even if they could conceivably be conducted with the very same patient (as if he were able to wipe the magic slate clean and start afresh with each interviewer), would emerge altogether differently. Psychotherapy is an interpersonal process and what emerges as the therapist's perception of the interaction and of its meanings is a reflection not only of the presenting anxieties and psychopathological manifestations of the patient, but of the level of competence and the problems in skill and in learning of the therapist.*

This difference in interviews between different interviewers (so inherent in the nature of two-way interpersonal processes) was graphically illustrated by an exchange in a supervisory session in which the therapist was describing a most difficult dilemma he had gotten into with a patient. After recounting the whole of the problem he turned to the supervisor and asked what *he* would have said in this particular situation. The supervisor responded that he was at a loss as to what he might have said in just this situation, but one thing he was sure of—he would never have gotten into precisely that situation. The question, then, as refocused by the supervisor, was whether the student could have kept from getting into that situation.

Should we therefore wonder at the surprise of so many a beginning therapist, selecting the patient's material, distilling it through the vehicle of the emphases dictated by his own needs, and presenting it thus to the supervisor, when he discovers that what he sees and presents often so closely parallels comparable problems he himself experiences in supervision. Whether it be of beginning, of termination, or of process in between, therapist and patient *seem* to be constantly working on the

* That the personality attributes and therapeutic style of the therapist importantly affect the course of the psychotherapy, even when comparable (and advanced) levels of therapeutic skill are available, is again demonstrated by the experience quoted by Anna Freud ("The Widening Scope of Indications for Psychoanalysis: Discussion," *J. Am. Psa. Ass.*, 2:607–620, 1954): "Years ago, in Vienna, we instituted an experimental technical seminar among colleagues of equal seniority, and equal theoretical background, treating cases with similar diagnoses and, therefore, supposedly similar structure. We compared techniques and found in discussion—not only as Dr. Stone put it today—'that no two analysts would ever give precisely the same interpretations throughout an analysis,' but more surprisingly still, that such uniformity of procedure was never kept up for more than a few days in the beginning of an analysis. After that, the handling of the material would cease to run parallel, each analyst giving precedence for interpretation to another piece or even layer. These differences in timing would influence the emergence of the next material and this, in turn, influence the trends of interpretation. Even though the final results might be the same, the roads leading there were widely divergent."

same problems. Only as the student is helped in the resolution of such difficulties in himself, will he be able to see objectively enlarging aspects of the patient's problems. It is as though we work with a constant "metaphor" in which the patient's problem in psychotherapy may be used to express the therapist's problem in supervision—and vice versa.

Clinical examples of this frequent phenomenon can be widely varied. An example of a situation in which the therapist presented a pattern of interpersonal expectations similar to that of his patient can be taken from the therapeutic work of Dr. R, a beginning therapist, who was most struck by his patient's marked passivity and "oral dependency." This emerged very clearly in the therapist's presentation of the patient's account of his life situation. The patient spoke resentfully of his mother's intense need to keep infantilizing him. He chafed at these attitudes in her, yet he could not bring himself to move from her immediate vicinity, nor did he really seem aware of his own strong feelings of dependency on his mother. He pointed out that, now that he was married, it was no longer really his mother's job to take care of him; it was now his wife's privilege. He expressed concern over the intense rivalry between his mother and his wife in vying to take care of him, each accusing the other of being insufficiently attentive. It appeared almost as if he must continually choose between them and always risk hurting the feelings of the one not chosen. That he could always turn from one to the other was the weapon he used constantly in his relations with each.

Not only in the historical material, but also within the context of the transferences in the therapy setting, the therapist was alert to evidences of the same dependent strivings. The patient indicated in a rather indirect and very polite manner that he had some misgivings as to the possible purpose of these therapy sessions. He assumed that the purpose was to give the therapist a better understanding of the patient which would enable the therapist to semi-magically cause the patient's many phobic and anxiety symptoms to disappear.

The therapist, Dr. R, was much concerned about the patient's passivity. He wondered how to handle it helpfully. Mostly he matched it with his own passive avoidance. Thus he wrote the following representative passage into his process notes: "Looking back on the interview, it appears at this time that it might have been desirable to make some comment to the effect that . . . However, instead of doing this, I *listened rather passively* while the patient listed some of the pros and cons concerned with . . ." He was, however, unaware that he also brought to the supervision hour a passive expectancy as marked as that evidenced in the therapy hour. He had come in unprepared. He did not remember what was in his process notes (which he had submitted to the supervisor the day before the conference). He stated that he had dictated them several days ago. He had no idea as to what he might want to talk about this hour; he "sort of expected" the supervisor to *tell him*, by a process of making *ex cathedra* judgments on the basis of the submitted material. He confessed all this in an embarrassed way when the supervisor asked him what problems he wished to discuss and he in turn asked to see the supervisor's copy of his material to refresh his memory. (He had not brought his own copy.)

Dr. R then stated that maybe his biggest problem had to do with the patient's overwhelming passivity. How might he have handled it? The supervisor replied that, yes, passivity did seem to be a real problem—in every aspect of this relationship. Dr. R wondered what was meant. The supervisor mentioned Dr. R's own comment (which was one of several in his material) on his own passivity vis à vis the patient. Dr. R explained that this was his way (deliberately chosen) to "force" the patient out of his passivity into a more "active" role. The supervisor questioned how "deliberately chosen" this passive role in the interview situation had been and wondered if the therapist had really had such a range of choice. Dr. R again asked what was meant. At this point the whole tenor of his approach to the supervisory situation itself was brought into focus. Dr. R became uneasy. He had certainly not looked at his own conduct in the supervisory hour that way. Nor had he seen that it could be linked in any way to his conduct in the therapy hour. He said, "This is the first time I have been *accused* of passivity"—and he was struck by the thought.

The use of the word "accused" by Dr. R is indeed revealing, as a restatement, even while defending himself against the implication, of his own passivity in the process. Too, it had a number of other revealing ramifications. It betrayed his own derogatory attitude toward the patient whom he had described solely in terms of his passivity. It gave a clue to his concept of his relationship with his supervisor in which statements intended to clarify were perceived as threatening accusations. And it was clearly a danger signal to the supervisor as to the distrustful and suspicious core in his student. Since this occurred in the beginning of the supervisory process, none of these observations was taken up at this point. The focus of this particular supervisory session with this beginning student had been on converting the completely externalized problem of "handling the patient's passivity" into the very personal struggle of dealing with his own passive tendencies. Only as this problem was coped with, was the student freed to learn to deal in a technically more effective manner with the marked passivity in the patient, which Dr. R had indeed identified correctly.

In other supervisory situations the parallel with the treatment situation of the patient can be seen in the simultaneous display by the student-therapist of opposite expectations in the two interacting, interpersonal processes in which he is engaged. In pairing opposing impulses, bound together in uneasy union in the psychic life of an individual, the differing relationships assumed toward the hierarchical structuring upward (being supervised) and downward (doing therapy) evoke in one direction an attitude that is the antithesis of the one displayed in the other. Here, too, the phenomena of the supervisory hour can be used to reflect the problems of the therapy hour, but in a somewhat different manner.

An example of this derives from the work of Dr. U, an earnest, intelligent, and gifted student, given, however, to intense introspection and self-condemnatory ruminations. He will be followed through a succession of supervisory conferences taken from the beginning period and the mid-period of his work in supervision with Dr. Gabel. In the first of these hours Dr. U presented interview material in which he directly played an intervening and controlling role in relation to the patient. He would steer the patient away on to topics of his (the therapist's) choosing; he would be educative in his presentations of dynamic formulations to the patient; he would moralize as he enjoined the patient to relax his overstrict superego standards—"Be more selfish and less Christ-like. It'll do you good"; and he would play the part of the omnipotent father in promising by implication to have the answer to any problem the patient might pose, if the patient could but give more information in relation to it. As this material came up for discussion in the supervisory session, Dr. U became confused and embarrassed. With his ready psychological-mindedness he could quickly perceive these facets of his work, but he saw them only as expressions of his own aggressions which he tried hard, but unsuccessfully, to control. He exaggerated these failings and saw in himself a hypertrophied model of cruelty, controllingness, and authoritative omnipotence. Actually a major protective maneuver on his part was to keep ahead of the supervisor in diagnosing his own "psychopathology" and in assuming a total *mea maxima culpa* attitude. How could anyone else find fault or demand change where the unwilling sufferer was already seemingly so aware of the difficulties?

In the supervisory session the following week Dr. U unexpectedly tried to reverse the psychologic climate. He was disgusted with his interviews with the patient during the intervening week. He felt he had handled many situations awkwardly. And he felt that he had also gotten some ideas as to where the difficulty might lie. He thought that he and the supervisor differed in their attitudes toward the patient. The supervisor, Dr. U felt, was basically unsympathetic to the patient, and Dr. U saw himself in effect playing the role of protecting the patient from the hostility of the supervisor. Dr. Gabel replied that it must then all seem to Dr. U that he, the supervisor, was funneling a lot of bad advice and restrictive control through Dr. U which was having a harmful effect on the therapy. Dr. U was unwilling to go that far. He paused. He surely knew that there was considerable hostility involved and he was reasonably sure it was not his. The supervisor suggested that they look at the patient's material to try to see where this hostility came through to the patient and how it affected him.

Dr. U did this reluctantly. How would that help clarify the issues? In the ensuing discussion of the patient's material, it emerged that Dr. U had on at least two occasions "warned" the patient about the possible consequences of some contemplated behavior, conjuring up the image of jail as the likely outcome. Where had all these visions of jail come from? From the patient or from the therapist? Dr. U was embarrassed. At another point Dr. U was asked about a technical maneuver he had attempted with the patient, asking him to "think hard and concentrate and tell me the first word or picture that comes to your mind." Dr. U grinned and said it was a trick. He had seen a senior therapist do something like it in a psychotherapy demonstration session. Dr. U was asked what deep-lying material he was after and what he expected to do with it when it came. He suddenly said that he had an image of himself standing there wringing the patient's neck trying to extract information from him. He was beginning to catch an uncomfortable glimpse of fantasies stirred in himself in response to the patient.

Dr. U then smiled. In a "confessing" manner he said, "It's true. It's really me. I didn't know how you would do it. I didn't know how you'd turn the tables and bring it all back to me, but you have . . ." Suddenly everything was undone. Dr. U had come in, this time divesting himself of his hostile impulses by projecting them onto the supervisor and assuming himself the role of their unwilling victim. In so doing he had maneuvered a situation that he knew the supervisor would not let stand; somehow it would be brought back to himself. When this happened and Dr. U felt himself capitulate, he seemed to experience an almost conscious masochistic gratification at this reversal. He was "congratulating" the supervisor on having brought about his discomfiture. At this point we see the other side of the coin; we see his hostile and aggressive impulses, so evident in their effect on his therapeutic work, beginning to emerge in the expectation of being made to suffer in his work in supervision.

The next interview to be quoted occurred some months further along, in the mid-period of the work in supervision with Dr. Gabel. These same problems, as one would expect, had continued to dog both the therapeutic work and the supervisory relationship all the way along. In the hour at hand there was considerable discussion, with ample illustration from the patient's current material of Dr. U's tendency to lecture the patient with elaborate intellectualizing, psychodynamic formulations. Through this discussion Dr. U confessed to a growing confusion as to the essential nature of the psychotherapeutic process and an increasing sense of disquiet in the supervisory relationship itself. He was disturbed and didn't know whether he wanted to discuss the whole matter. It had to do with all the "mixed feelings" he had about the supervisor. Maybe he just ought to keep quiet about it. He had already told too much within the context of the supervisory relationship that could be used for "ammunition" against him. Maybe he didn't want to say any more at all but just challenge the supervisor to help him, if the supervisor could. "I could just sit here and let you produce, and nod and say, 'yes, yes,' and be a passive obstructionist. Only I don't get any help that way. I have to decide for myself how much help and what kind of help I want from you. I just don't know." The hour ended on this troubled and depressed note. Dr. U had a lot of things he wanted to think over.

The next supervisory session brought many of these strands together. Dr. U tried in a summary way to list his many long-term problems that had come up over and over again with the patient. He enumerated all those previously discussed and added examples from the current week's material. He interpreted them all as varying manifestations of his tendencies to be controlling and educative. He was puzzled, though, in his material, at instances where he suddenly seemed to act quite otherwise with the patient. In fact, he had gone to the other extreme of avoiding coming to grips with the patient's material at various times; of having to say, "I don't know," in answer to questions Dr. Gabel asked him about the patient, questions that Dr. U had never even thought to put to the patient. He was aware of this and wondered why. Dr. Gabel suggested that it might in part reflect a feeling of Dr. U that he had gotten burned too much; often when he did go into a situation with the patient it had come up for critical scrutiny in the supervision as reflecting aggressive and controlling impulses. Maybe Dr. U was just being less spontaneous and more guarded. To this he assented eagerly. At times he would withdraw from the patient and risk losing contact with him because he was now so anxious and inhibited about doing things that he had come to regard as bad therapy, and it was getting harder to discuss all this within the supervisory setting. His work was under too much scrutiny. He felt exposed. He was consciously beginning to experience the supervisory sessions only as criticism and censure. And he didn't like that.

Dr. Gabel stated that, perceiving it that way, naturally Dr. U wouldn't like it. And this was the very thing that supervisor and student had been talking about all along, in the same way the patient had so often experienced the therapy—as a hostile assault to be warded off. Dr. U said that there was no analogy in this sense between the two processes. After all, he, as a beginning therapist, had made a "contract" to be criticized, so that with him it was amply justified. Dr. Gabel said, "Not really. You made a contract to learn, just as the patient made a contract to be helped, not to be criticized." Dr. U said quietly that he wondered whether he had an inner need always to experience teaching as criticism—and not just here.

It was at this point, after months of laborious and often circuitous work together, that the supervisor was able to help Dr. U to effect a meaningful first level of closure on this problem. Here was the structure of the problem as they came to see it together. In the one situation (doing psychotherapy) Dr. U was trying to cope with the problem of being too controlling and directive, and of censuring the patient—which the patient perceived as a hostile assault; and in the other situation (being supervised) Dr. U was trying to cope with the opposite problem of feeling on the receiving end of control, direction, and censure. From this juxtaposition of the problems of supervision and therapy came a deepened awareness of the areas in which the therapist needed help. At the end of this particular supervisory session Dr. U was somewhat relieved.

Perhaps at this point we should shift our focus to the psychotherapeutic work and the supervision of Dr. S, where a similar problem—that of seeing psychotherapeutic work and being supervised in terms primarily of controlling and being controlled—was somewhat differently handled by a student of different personality. Dr. S was an intense, eager student (like Dr. U), one who gave the impression of rushing into things with great enthusiasm but usually without stopping to reflect and assimilate (unlike the more reflective Dr. U). This was particularly so in his easy compliance with supervisory suggestions. Unlike Dr. U, who saw his own behavior as a therapist and his own responses to his supervisor in terms of the hostile elements of the struggle to control and against being controlled, Dr. S tended to see this more in terms of its benign and helpful intent. When various facets of his obvious impulses to direct the flow of the patient's material, and to manipulate her reality decisions in accord with his concepts of what was to her best interests, were discussed with Dr. S, his responses were in the nature of, "Yes sir! You're right!" And with this need to please and conform, without ever stopping to reflect on how all this fitted together and what it all meant, Dr. S succeeded in stilling any inner restlessness stirred up by the psychological processes in which he participated. Also, with his easy acceptance without reflection, Dr. S kept from focusing on the problems that were being raised and from facing the impact they might have on his whole professional personality. By complying, Dr. S was successfully avoiding—avoiding an awareness of the kind of learning pattern he showed in the supervisory relationship, and avoiding a real appreciation of the nature and scope of the control he constantly exerted in the therapeutic situation.

This problem can be highlighted in describing how Dr. S handled a characteristic episode from the patient's therapy. The patient had wanted to go on a trip for a week to attend a niece's wedding in a distant city. It would be the first time this hypochondriacally crippled patient would have been out of the hospital in two years. Dr. S was not sure, however, whether her desire to go was a reasoned decision or "just a flight from therapy." Whenever he asked the patient to discuss the reasons, pro and con, she could only come up with reasons against the trip; yet she still insisted she wanted to go. Dr. S's attitude began to crystallize—it was very much a flight from therapy. He tried to get her to see that point. He reasoned that for the first time the patient had a "positive transference" to a therapist, and that this made her uncomfortable and frightened her so that she had to run away. He tried hard to get her to see that. He "almost had her" when she admitted that it was easy to tell people when she disliked them (like her previous therapist) but hard to acknowledge feelings of liking them. But Dr. S's approach did not quite work out.

Dr. Field, the supervisor, said that Dr. S had "almost had her" but that she didn't bite. This must have made him really frustrated (Dr. S smiled at this) and angry too (from the way he had banged his fist on the desk in telling all this). Dr. S said that that was just the way the hours had been—like arguments. She had banged her fist many times. He was after answers that she just wasn't giving. Sure, he was pursuing an objective. He just did not think it was a good idea for the patient to go on that leave to the wedding. He was sure she couldn't make it. She'd get to Kansas City and turn back (the trip itself would be 1,000 miles farther). On a recent week-end pass to a nearby city she had had several "heart attacks." And besides it would be time away from his therapy.

Dr. Field said that maybe all this was becoming a little clearer. Instead of being able to follow the psychological implications of whatever decision the patient made, Dr. S really had an axe to grind—for a variety of reasons he did not want the patient to go on the trip. Yet he was ostensibly offering her freedom of choice. "Let's discuss the pros and cons so you can make the best possible decision." Dr. S wanted her to choose all right—so long as she chose not to go. What kind of choice was that? How did he expect the patient would react? Dr. S said he could see that now—he was certainly prejudging the issue. It was true that he didn't want her to go. It could "mess up" the therapy. Dr. Field agreed that it might alter the therapy. Was "mess up" necessarily the correct appraisal of this move? What was really against her going in terms of her illness or the state of her treatment? This was discussed back and forth. Dr. S brought out that she might get "sick" on the way and have to come back. In that case, what was lost? On the other hand, it was to be her first trip home for two years, the first time she felt actually able to make such a trip, and also the first time her family seemed to want her. Wasn't this a good sign? Dr. S expressed concern that once she got home she might stay there and not come back. Dr. Field said he kind of doubted this; but if she did, would it not be a real achievement for this heretofore invalided hypochondriacal patient? Dr. S agreed that it "sure would." He had been pursuing a single idea. It had been his idea. He guessed it was the same old problem, which had been discussed so many times, about "controlling" the patient.

Dr. S came to the next supervision conference much perturbed. In the intervening week the patient had accused him of not wanting her to go on the trip, of never intending to let her go, and of taking covert steps to prevent it. Her final decision not to go, she stated, was less a reflection of any lack of desire on her part, but rather a consequence of feeling so pressured by the therapist. Dr. S wanted to know first how much of this was the patient—her psychopathology—and how much he himself had contributed to set it up. He had seen in the supervisory hour the previous week how, up to that point, he had indeed been trying to influence the patient and to influence her toward a decision not to go. But that had been "resolved" in the discussion last week, and the continued trouble over this point must be the patient.

Dr. Field agreed that the patient certainly externalized, and projected onto Dr. S her own inner dilemma about her proposed trip. But to what extent had she perceived Dr. S's feelings (against the trip) and used these to project onto? Dr. S was not so sure. After all, much of it had been worked out. Where did it show in the work? They turned to the week's material and Dr. Field asked Dr. S how he would take the following if they were said to him, and then read back half a dozen statements from one interview with the patient, all designed to throw doubt on the wisdom of the planned trip. Dr. S said he thought he had only been trying to elicit the negative side of the patient's feelings and her anxieties about the trip. Dr. Field said he wondered whether it was a question of: (1) "Look how anxious you are. Can't you see how ambivalent and paralyzed and really unable to go you are?" or (2) "You are so very anxious and have so many fears. Can you face this trip despite them, or is it too much?"

Dr. S said he could get the point. It was still the same problem. But it was certainly getting subtler in its manifestations. He had never been aware of all this as a problem before, but he certainly was now. Another instance just came to mind. He remembered the first time this patient spoke of her psychopathic boy friend. Dr. S had not said much. He had written into the record all kinds of rationalizations as to why he had reacted so passively. But they were none of them the real reason. The real reason was that he had had an impulse to berate the patient with, "Why the hell don't you get rid of that good-for-nothing boy friend? He's not for you." He could see this, too, with other patients. It was quite a problem with him. Dr. Field agreed that it was indeed quite a problem with him and wondered how much help the supervision had been with it so far. Dr. S protested that it had helped. He had never even had it pointed out as a problem before. Up to now "control" had always been, "Do this my way—do this and do that!" He had tried to do exactly what the supervisor wanted, and he had never found out his own problems. Dr. Field said that maybe just this was the crux of the difficulty. Dr. S had always experienced supervision—which he called control—as, "Do this my way"; and he transmitted the same controlling attitude on to his patient.

Dr. S said somewhat heatedly that that was the way supervision always was. The prevailing theory around here with each staff member seemed to him to be a matter of, "While on my section, you do it exactly my way. Incorporate it. And at the end of your training you can fuse all these incorporated images." Dr. S said that he had never believed in that kind of teaching and yet that was certainly what he felt he had always been exposed to. Dr. Field responded that Dr. S felt that this was the kind of supervision he had always had and that consciously he rejected it. Yet maybe he, too, operated in this very manner that he so deplored. Dr. Field then recalled a question Dr. S had raised in their very first session together (before he had even started with the patient) about how Dr. Field's views compared with another staff man's "system" for treating a hypochondriacal patient. Dr. S said that it was all suddenly dawning. He had evidently come to the supervision with enthusiasm to apply someone else's—not his own—"system" in the treatment of a hypochondriacal patient. Dr. Field then also reminded Dr. S that he had also wanted to know whether his new supervisor had some *other* "system" that he wanted used—as if every act in the therapy would be directed. Dr. S said that this was just the thing he thought he didn't want. His complaint about some other supervisors had been that he thought them too dogmatic and controlling. He experienced this everywhere, and he always complied—and rebelled inside. Just as last week in the supervisory hour. He had been angry. Something had been pointed out to him critically. Dr. S's first thought had been that he was only trying to do exactly what the supervisor had himself advised on a previous occasion. What more was wanted? He could see all this in wider and wider circles. He had never previously discussed with the supervisor his own plan to devote his career to the psychotherapy of hospitalized psychotic patients. With psychotic patients there was always a necessary element of control involved. At some point in the treatment the therapist would have to be able to give this up, however. Would it be possible for him?

This was certainly a serious question. It came up again in still clearer form some four months later, toward the very end of the supervisory time together, and in a manner to indicate that only then did its real impact, and the consequent felt need for change, really become evident. That hour Dr. S began by stating that he had some questions that were troubling him. He had been comparing notes on his supervisory experiences with another resident who worked with the same supervisor, as well as with one who had a different supervisor. The three of them together had figured out that Dr. S seemed to have a different relationship with the supervisor from either of the other two. With the others, much of the therapeutic work with the patient seemed to be related by the supervisor directly to the supervisory process, and both students agreed that they felt this to be not always appropriate, stretching material to fit theory, etc. But Dr. S had felt none of this. Many of his problems in working with his patients had come up and been dealt with, but he had not felt that they had been constantly related to the process between himself and the supervisor.

So the three of them had figured out that supervisors are different with different supervisees. It was all part of an educational experiment. Half of the supervisees are treated by the officially enforced system, the way the supervisor "has to"; and the other half are treated differently, the way the supervisor wants to. This latter way was of course the better way, and Dr. S felt that he was indeed fortunate to be among this half. The other two therapists felt more frustrated. They were angry and did not feel helped. Dr. Field said in response to all this that since he himself was the same person, perhaps the differences in the two supervisory situations might well rest in the supervisees, who were different and had different kinds of problems. Dr. S said that he had thought of that but felt convinced that the differences were in the supervisor. Dr. Field stated that he would then himself be in a peculiar position. With at least one supervisee he would be using a method without much conviction in it. Could he really be helpful to that fellow in that case?

Dr. S said that he hadn't thought about all this from this point of view. One thing was certain: somehow he didn't constantly feel that everything that went on between himself and the patient was always related in a one-to-one way to the situation in supervision. Dr. S had certainly seen his own problems in doing psychotherapy emerge. For instance, he had become very aware of his tendencies to "control" the patient. He had seen so many examples of it. He could certainly accept it as one of his major problems and try in his work to do something about it. But that problem had *never* had its counterpart in the supervisory sessions together. Except that in the mid-period evaluation, the supervisor had seemed to "hint" at the existence of this same problem in the supervision, but Dr. S couldn't really see it then and he hadn't seen it directly brought up in supervision at any time.

Dr. Field responded that indeed he had more than hinted at it at that time but that Dr. S hadn't seen it. It was true that it had not been explicitly in focus as such since then. Maybe it hadn't been ready to be dealt with very much before in the supervision. Maybe that wasn't for the best at all, and perhaps now Dr. S was stating that he wanted to examine the same problem as it might emerge between himself and the supervisor. What would be the counterpart in the supervision of this problem of control? Dr. S said that he guessed the other side would be a constant looking to be controlled; a looking for the answers, etc. There was a pause and then Dr. S went on to say that that was exactly what he did do all the time. He himself was always looking for the answers from the supervisor and then trying to go out and apply them exactly. As a matter of fact, when at times he had been questioned in the supervisory sessions about some of the things he had done in the therapy, Dr. S had had the feeling that he had only done what the supervisor had previously said he should do. Dr. Field reminded him that Dr. S had actually verbalized this thought on one occasion. Dr. S said that he had a feeling, too, when the answers were not forthcoming as specifically as he had desired, that the particular hour had been pretty "useless." He then said that this was exactly the attitude with which his patient constantly confronted him during their hours together. She constantly looked for the answers, wanted to be told, etc.

Dr. Field said that now perhaps they were seeing together the other side of the problem that they had been dealing with all along. Up to now they had been concentrating together on Dr. S's tendencies to control the patient. Now they were seeing how both Dr. S (and the patient) looked for control. In relation to herself, the patient provoked and accentuated just these tendencies in Dr. S. Dr. S said that the patient certainly set it up that way and that he tended to fall right in with it. She would look for answers and be angry when they were not forthcoming. And yet when he tried to give her such specific "answers," she seemed to organize herself to disprove them, and rebel against them, and accuse the therapist of not allowing her real freedom of choice. Dr. S was certainly struck by all these evidences of the "parallel" between his relationships in the therapy process and in the supervision process. Maybe it wasn't so different from the process with the other supervisees after all. But how could we proceed from here? Dr. Field said he guessed that Dr. S was saying that there was still so much ahead to be worked on. Dr. S agreed that there was and this time did not ask for a "specific" answer.

In tracing in some detail these episodes from the supervisory work with Drs. R, U, and S, we have sought to characterize through these striking clinical examples the way in which the problems of the supervision hour can shed light on, and in fact often stand for, the problems of the therapy hour—and vice versa. That this is so should occasion no real surprise, for it merely restates the principle of psychic determinism that underpins all our psychotherapeutic work and our psychological understanding. That it can be used helpfully, both in the learning process with the student and through our influence with him in the therapeutic process with the patient, has been seen in part in the working out of the episodes depicted. Perhaps a number of other—and briefer—examples can illustrate some specific possibilities for helpful use, if we constantly approach our material from within this conceptual framework.

Sometimes the stumbling block in the therapy can be cleared up only by reference to the parallel dilemma in the supervision. Dr. W, for example, with a very depreciated picture of his therapeutic competency, was anxious lest the patient might perceive the "real" him inside. He had constantly to hide behind the transference image of himself as a powerful and awesome father, and foster the maintenance of this illusion. He thus used the transference as a way of perpetuating psychological distance from the patient and being secure from the threat that the patient might see that this transference image expressed a fantasy, not a reality. That is, the therapeutic outcome, ordinarily felt to be desirable, that the patient come to a more reality-centered appraisal of the therapist, was to Dr. W an anxiety-arousing threat of exposure of his own inner weakness. To know him was to see his weakness, so the "fantasy" of his strength had to be constantly reinforced.

When this grouping of attitudes finally came to light within the supervisory session, it was dealt with in terms of its analogy to the very problem between Dr. W and his supervisor, Dr. Baehr. For Dr. W had the selfsame image of the supervisor—as a powerful and threatening father figure—that he desired to maintain at all costs as the patient's image of himself. Dr. Baehr suggested that, after all, in the course of the work in supervision together, Dr. W would be faced ultimately with the very same problem of discovering that the fantasied difference—and distance—between himself and the supervisor was not that real either. At this point Dr. W protested. It was his conviction, he stated, that the difference between himself and the supervisor (in terms of competence, prestige, authority, etc.) was very "real" but that that between himself and the patient was a "transference fantasy" that might be found out. It was only when Dr. Baehr indicated that whatever the difference and distance between himself and Dr. W, it was by every objective criterion so much less than the differences between Dr. W and his quite sick patient, that Dr. W was first able to see his dilemma as an inner psychological problem rather than a reality problem. With that, he experienced for the first time a feeling that something could possibly be done about it.

Or, in another clinical example from the supervisory work with Dr. W we can see how this parallelism can be used to pinpoint the technical difficulty in a phase of the psychotherapy, as a reflection of a basic problem about learning, and not just a lack of technical "know-how" which could be solved by appropriate instruction alone. Dr. W's patient was constantly flouting the hospital structure and defiantly ignoring every rule that was called to his attention. Dr. W felt unable to cope effectively with this behavior which evoked feelings of anger and frustration in him. He wondered how he could be helped both to cope with these feelings in himself and to deal therapeutically with the patient.

It was pointed out by Dr. Baehr that this problem that Dr. W was having in regard to the patient (holding him to the hospital structure) was the very one that troubled Dr. W so much in regard to the supervision, which he so often saw as a constraining and unwanted structure that constantly provoked his own rebelliousness. Here a problem that had been talked of all along in the supervision was coming up in a new guise—as a direct problem with the patient. Dr. W could now see why he had so much difficulty coping with his patient's acting-out behavior. The intensity of Dr. W's own struggle with this issue and the reiterated recognition of his own continued need for help with it were simultaneously manifest.

If we look closely enough at both the patient's material as brought to the supervisory hour by the student, and at the student's own productions, we can see, again in this "parallelism," constant indications of the changing patterns of the learning relationship as its various problems are uncovered and dealt with. Dr. V was an individual who in his work with patients was harshly confronting, meting out to them the same stern dictates, which he constantly felt that he experienced at the hands of his various supervisors. He felt uncomfortable with his patients as well as with his supervisors. He tried to escape all expressions of warmth from whatever source and felt most comfortable when evoking—and responding to—hostile feelings. He excused his discomfort at getting involved in any way other than a hostile, punitive one, by citing an instance where he had gotten more closely involved with a patient who then went through a number of suicidal attempts and psychotic episodes. To Dr. V each patient and each supervisor was a projected image of himself—an angry individual to be struggled against. Supervisors especially were individuals who sought to "beat him over the head with his mistakes," to trap him into speaking his mind and giving himself away, and then to take retaliatory punitive action against him.

When the time for the mid-period evaluation of his therapeutic work came around, Dr. V "steeled" himself for a rough session. Dr. V felt the need to focus much of the evaluation discussion around his "problem with authority figures." He stated that he suspected that Dr. Ellis' kindly manner was but a subtle attempt to "tear me down" and cited a number of supporting instances from his work with other supervisors. Through the ensuing discussion Dr. V was able for the first time to see both the way he *had* to perceive the supervisory authority and how little reality basis for this view could be derived from his present experience with Dr. Ellis. At the end of this hour Dr. V mentioned, incidentally as it seemed, that there had been one solitary exception, a supervisor who had treated him kindly and with understanding of his difficulties.

The next week Dr. V was away on assignment to a state children's institution where all the psychiatric residents were sent in rotation, in part to see the working of such a place, and in part to help as much as they could in the minimal time toward the assessment and treatment planning for the patients. Dr. V came to his next supervisory hour straining to tell about his experience at the state institution. It was quite a mess. The administration was poor, there was lack of proper personnel, physical facilities were obsolete and overcrowded, etc. But there was a new hopeful atmosphere down there. There seemed to be some spirit and will to do something about it all. It was a tall order. It would easily take several years to clean up the mess. If we transpose these sentiments to the supervision situation and the evaluation just gone through, we can read in it not only the acknowledgment of the many difficulties ("the mess") but also the new feeling that despite the difficulty, something could be done, though "it would easily take several years." Dr. Ellis responded in tune with the metaphor that even large problems could be dealt with, though indeed it might take lots of time, and there was always danger that the interested parties might lose heart and patience.

Sometimes the metaphoric statement of the change in the nature of the relationship comes not in the productions of the therapist, but once removed, in the material of the patient as recorded by the therapist. Dr. W, like Dr. V, constantly saw his supervisor as a stern, demanding individual, who held up standards of work performance that were impossible of attainment. Following a full discussion of these attitudes in the supervisory hour, Dr. W reported in the next hour a change in his patient's material. The patient had always talked much about his commander in the navy whom he associated importantly as a central figure in his own neurotic reactions. The commander had always been described as being strict to the point of harshness, perfectionistic, intolerant in his demands in regard to work performance, and cruelly vindictive toward those who failed to fulfill these expectations. For the first time the patient reported a kindlier version of the commander. All his driving demands were for the good of the men, he was loyal to them and looked out for their interests in a variety of ways—indeed in certain ways, he was a benevolent father figure. This statement, reflecting the therapist's new capacity to see a broadened spectrum of interpersonal patterns of his patient, seemed to parallel precisely the changed state of the supervisor-therapist relationship at that moment.

This parallelism can work in reverse as well. All changes in supervision are not necessarily in the direction of improved functioning nor is all the supervisor's work itself without difficulties, both technical faults stemming from lack of supervisory skill and experience, and teaching problems anchored in the supervisor's own unresolved conflicts surrounding his role as teacher. The alert and flexible supervisor can sometimes detect and work out his own problems in teaching, as he sees them revealed in the difficulties imposed upon the student, which then reflect in his therapeutic work with his patients. The full awareness of these parallel processes and their imaginative use can thus both illuminate many of the problems being dealt with in the day-to-day work of supervision, and be a powerful vehicle toward their resolution.

Students and their supervisors will work together best if each of them have active insight, achieved frequently only after struggle, into both parallel processes. This insight will be most productive if it is not only insight into the behavior of the other person in the respective relationship, but is concerned as well with the part that each himself plays in contributing to the total problem and its solution. In many treatment situations we are satisfied with the notion that a specific patient is untreatable, and in many teaching situations we satisfy ourselves of the student's inability to learn. Observations of the parallel process show that we need not only good patients and good therapists but also effective supervisors. Our teaching philosophy insists that we look not only at the problems of the learner but also at the problems of the teacher which frequently can be best observed in the interactions of these two parallel processes in intimate functional relationship to one another.

XII / On the Psychology of Emergencies

Time in itself is a purely arbitrary category of man's invention, but since it is a projection of his innermost being, it represents so truly his inherent psychological conflict, that to be able to accept it, to learn to admit its likeness to one's very self, its perfect adaptation to one's deepest and most contradictory impulses, is already to be healed, as far as healing is possible or applicable, since in accepting time, one accepts the self and life with their inevitable defects and limitations.—JESSIE TAFT

Siegfried Bernfeld, in discussing the nature of the psychoanalytic process,* once used a simple example from everyday life to illustrate the task of the patient and the analyst. An acquaintance called him one evening, expressing considerable upset and conveying a real feeling of emergency. The acquaintance requested an appointment as early as possible and the urgency of his request forced Dr. Bernfeld to agree to arrange time the very next morning during his office hours. At the appointed time the person arrived, sat down in the office, and in a leisurely way began to talk about the weather, a picture on the wall that caught his eye, in every way giving an impression entirely different from that transmitted over the telephone the previous evening.

* Siegfried Bernfeld, "The Facts of Observation in Psychoanalysis," *J. of Psychology*, 12:289–305, 1941. The paper does not make clear whether this story is real or invented—a point not relevant, of course, to its meaning.

When reminded of that phone call and asked whether he did not wish to talk about something more important, his friend told him that there was actually nothing important on his mind. The friend had just wished to come by and chat with him. Dr. Bernfeld was puzzled and did not quite know what to say as he compared the memory of the importunate call with the person chatting with him at the moment.

Since there was a little too much draft in the room, he got up and closed the door, which by chance had been left open when his acquaintance had arrived. As he sat down again, he noticed that the behavior of the other person suddenly changed. He looked with relief at the closed door and with renewed insistence wondered whether he could borrow $50 from his friend.

Using this example, Bernfeld then suggests that the task of the analyst, as well as of the patient, consists in finding out how to close the open door that prevents the patient from talking about his problem. Only the closed door secures the intimacy required, in order to talk freely about the problems that bother the patient. For the sake of simplification, the example does not explicitly state the fact that the closing of the door refers not only to the patient's conscious desire to withhold information, but also to his unconscious defensive devices which will operate as long as the door is kept open.

At first glance this analogy to closing the door seems to run counter to the natural assumption that it is the "open door" that symbolizes accessibility and unobstructed communication. At least in everyday parlance the phrase, "my door is open to you," is used to stress such freedom. But when we think of who uses such a phrase, we generally have in mind paternalistic deans of colleges, benevolent business executives, and communication-minded administrators—all of whom tend to substitute affability and geniality for deep, confidential intimacy. That is, when the door is always open to you, too often it does not get closed when you enter, so that the relationship is always superficial, and the open door is used to preserve this psychological distance—to preclude real closeness of relationship and freedom of communication.

As the therapeutic process proceeds we frequently find, however, that the door cannot always be kept closed. From time to time the patient and therapist revert to conditions of work which do not seem to provide the type of intimacy that is required. Renewed analytical work has to be done on the "open door" to make sure that it is closed again. This open-door situation is frequently introduced or comes to the attention of therapist and patient by way of an emergency situation. The urgent telephone call of the evening before, and the inability to state over the phone what it was really all about, as well as the inability to talk in the consulting room about other than superficial subjects as long as the door is left open, is a simplified example of the kind of stalemate that frequently arises in psychotherapy and that requires skilled technical handling if it is to be resolved. In this example a feeling of emergency was experienced, and this feeling dissolved as soon as the request for the $50 could be expressed. As long as the door remained open and as long, therefore, as others could overhear it, this request was experienced as a forbidden wish, the expression of which would evoke a feeling of shame.

Psychotherapeutic situations are usually more complicated, in that, though the patient may be fully aware of the sense of outer emergency, he may at the same time be quite unaware of the nature of his unconscious request or of the open door which blocks its expression; he may truly feel that he has nothing to talk about. We must therefore keep in mind, if the example is to be turned to our purposes, that the open door did not just happen to be left open by chance, but was arranged by the patient, as it were, consciously or unconsciously in order to permit him to talk about inconsequential things and to thus keep the forbidden request out of awareness.

As long as the flow of material during the psychotherapeutic process creates no particular difficulties for the patient, no guilt or shame, he will tend to make the therapeutic situation one that is governed by the policy of the "closed door." He will tend to create an intimate situation in which what goes on between him and the therapist is maintained as a sort of private domain between the two of them, and in which no attempt is made to bring other persons into the process. The carrying of treatment material, of the experiences and insights from the therapeutic session, outside of this experience to other people can usually be considered an effort to give up the closed-door policy, and is usually based on the anxiety that the existing intimate process might lead to a dangerous situation. The patient who thus opens the door and attempts to break out of the intimacy of this two-body situation can be compared to the young woman who wishes to bring a chaperon to her dinner meeting with a male admirer. The danger situation, of course, consists not only of forbidden sexual temptations, of disturbing erotic thoughts, but concerns a wide range of difficulties that can arise in the course of the psychotherapy.

Thus, the mounting emergency, the sudden necessity to have the door open, to have someone overhear what goes on inside, the bringing in of the outsider (in spite of the feeling that the outsider is unwelcome) is frequently an attempt to keep material from coming to consciousness which would otherwise emerge. Many therapeutic emergencies are but acute defensive maneuvers against emerging unconscious material.

The emergency then becomes a way of pleading with the other that the normal process of communication, the therapy behind closed doors, no longer helps, and that outside assistance must be introduced. The panicky patient who suddenly feels that he cannot trust the therapeutic process anymore, that psychotherapy cannot help him, seeks to destroy the situation of intimacy between himself and the therapist, and attempts to restore his equilibrium by calling the outside helper. In Freud's famous Dora case, Dora is described as being erotically involved with Mr. K. Behind the closed doors of the therapy situation she shows similar erotic interests. As she misinterprets the analyst in terms of her transference preoccupation, she dreams of the father who is to awaken her and to save her from the burning house of her projected sexual desires. In order to ward off this erotic temptation, she breaks up the intimacy of the analytic situation, sees herself rescued by the third person during the emergency (actually her emerging, burning sexual desires toward the analyst), and reports the dream, her indirect announcement that she will interrupt her treatment.

Emergencies, of course, are not specific to the psychotherapeutic process. They occur in other interpersonal helping processes as well, and they are of particular significance, since it seems that the attempted solution is so frequently one in which the intimacy of a situation between two people is to be broken up by the emergency wish for rescue through some third person. In fact, professional processes on all lines of communication, as they are presented in the clinical rhombus, are characterized by the fact that they are beset from time to time by situations of emergency, of crisis, of a seeming crying need for immediate intervention.

These emergencies can be created and felt by the patient, by his therapist, by the therapist's supervisor, and also by the administrator.

Each of these four may experience a situation as an emergency, and may then use his characteristic patterns of dealing with such events. Each may feel himself to be the victim of an emergency, or the one who has engineered an emergency, or who needs to help the other with an emergency, or who is utterly immobilized in the presence of the emergency. As we turn our interest to the students of psychotherapy, we will find that they often have a double problem in the face of emergency. They are frequently confronted with the emergencies that their patients bring to them. They are also often faced with their own inner feeling of emergency which they may bring to the supervisor or, since it is an emergency, to the administrator.

It is in the nature of emergency situations that they usually do not permit reflection. They are usually seen not as inner psychological constellations, but rather as external crises for which an immediate answer must be secured. This "must" creates anxiety, strong feelings of inadequacy and dependency, and tends to move one to seek outside help. So strong is this feeling that one is coping with an outer reality that it is almost impossible to dilute enough of this experience, in order to permit delay, some reflection, and solutions that are not just rescue missions in an externalized sense.

It is typical for many learners that for long stretches during the process of learning they may only bring emergency situations to their supervisors. They may present their learning problems in a way that gives the supervisor little choice but to take over the emergency, as it were, to move in the crisis which the student cannot handle, to enter the open door of the psychotherapy situation and become the rescuer. Such emergencies indeed are tremendous temptations to the supervisor and seem to invite his invasion of the privacy of the psychotherapeutic world between the student and his patient, an invasion which the student usually welcomes, since it allows the type of dependency in which not he, but the supervisor, must cope with the existing problem.

The reader who has been following this train of thought must have been thinking, meanwhile, of the many emergencies that happen in the lives of people that seem so clearly reality-bound. He will think of the kinds of external events and pressures that make our model seem inapplicable. The student of psychotherapy will quickly join him, and mention example after example in which he has been confronted with emergencies based on a reality-situation that must be changed, rather than lending themselves to the type of psychological solution which is implied in our figure of speech of the closed door. The young psychotherapist will confront us, as he attempts to refute our notions, with the patient who suddenly must interrupt treatment and leave the hospital because of an emergency at home, the sickness of close relatives who need him. He will tell us about the patient who suddenly threatens suicide, or attempts some kind of desperate, violent measure which seems unamenable to psychotherapeutic intervention. The therapist may tell us, too, about other reality-situations which bring emergencies into the lives of his patients and undermine his therapeutic effectiveness. He may talk about interfering relatives who are threatened perhaps by the progress shown by the patient, or about hospital personnel who, out of lack of training and lack of insight, undermine his efforts and create emergencies for his patients. He will tell us about the patient who expresses emergency needs which, if not met, will lead to the patient's discontinuing psychotherapy against medical advice, and may wonder with us as to how he could possibly meet this type of emergency.

There may be a good many situations where one faces the kind of crisis in psychotherapy that does not seem to allow a constructive answer. Perhaps the best available answer, while having no direct bearing on the specific handling of the situation, may consist of a psychological post-mortem in which one can do no more than study what actually led up to the crisis, in order to find out what might prevent such an event were it to threaten again. Each training setting is full of examples of such unresolved emergency situations, of failures of treatment, of premature terminations, and of technical mistakes for which as yet no answer is available, either in the psychotherapeutic armamentarium of the therapist or in the teaching skill of the supervisor.

It is typical for one who experiences an emergency situation to tend toward solutions in which the problem is placed in the lap of the helper. The "Can you do something about it, Doctor?" approach might be the expected solution of the patient when coming to the therapist, as well as of the therapist when he asks the supervisor for help. The social work slogan "Helping people to help themselves" is actually a reflection on this natural tendency of help-seeking people, and the model for a kind of help that consists not in taking over the problem, but rather in strengthening the other person so that he can cope with the problem himself.

At this point we can look at an example of a specific crisis situation and the modes of solution that could have been attempted by the various participants involved. Dr. O, a highly regarded and sensitive individual, was beginning his formal psychotherapy experience in the outpatient setting of a psychiatric hospital. The patient had come to the outpatient department ostensibly in order to apply for urgent psychiatric help for his wife. He was seen by the intake social worker and he recounted to her the history of his wife's symptom, repeated severe vomiting, and incidentally volunteered information about his own troubles in his personal relationships. The intake worker, recognizing the clear plea for help for himself, recommended the husband for psychotherapy, as well, and he was assigned as a patient to Dr. O.

When the patient came to his first interview, he arrived with a heavy bag full of groceries, which he laboriously set at the side of his chair, and a folded newspaper which he kept under his arm. Although Dr. O was quite struck by these symbolic modes of expression and recorded them in his process notes, he made no response to them. Dr. O apparently did not yet see at this point how the patient was trying to tell him that, even in this one hour which was to be devoted to the patient's own problems, he was not free of the heavy burden of household chores he felt imposed on him, and which he periodically attempted to defend himself against by retreating behind a newspaper. He had not initially come for help for himself, but really wanted help for his wife, or rather wanted to solve the problem that he felt with his wife by putting the problem, his wife, into the hands of the clinic doctors. He had accepted help for himself only half-heartedly, and the load of groceries and the newspaper indicated well the pressures he felt under. His home emergency had brought him to the outpatient clinic, and his plea was to let him be with his newspaper, while others would carry the burden and change his wife.

When asked about his problems he thought that many of his inner psychic difficulties could be ascribed to the indoor nature of his work, and he wondered whether a switch in jobs to outdoor employment might not relieve much of his stress. Dr. O, a new psychotherapist, felt he had no ready answer to the problem posed in this way, and withdrew to a sort of pseudo-neutrality, suggesting that he would need more information before he could give the hoped-for advice. That is, rather than relating directly to the situation which the patient had described so well, Dr. O responded to his own preconceived stereotype of what the psychotherapeutic situation was supposed to be. When the patient remained silent Dr. O complained that he was withholding information and began to press him about what was "really troubling him," seemingly oblivious of the fact that the patient had already been telling him exactly what troubled him even before he had started to talk at all. When confronted by the demand to tell, the patient acknowledged that he found it hard to talk in such a situation, and he literally began to read his newspaper. He thus responded to what seemed to him the unreasonable demands of the therapist in very much the same way that he did at home to those of his wife.

The whole of this interview was transcribed in a verbatim account recorded by the therapist during the hour, reflecting in yet another way the separation between the patient and the therapist that existed in place of the psychological process. The therapist became increasingly frustrated in his anxious attempts to elicit information and was aware of his emerging irritation with the patient. The more irritated he felt, the more he urged the patient to give information and the more unsuccessful he was in getting it. It soon became clear to him that he might fail to establish effective contact with this patient, that this patient might not come back, that he faced a possible emergency situation. How could he hold the patient in the face of the latter's disinterest, even open resistance?

The therapist, Dr. O, brought this emergency situation to his supervisor and wondered what he could do in order to keep this patient. He needed quick advice, a way of keeping the patient from disrupting the treatment. How could he hold on to the patient? How could he get the patient to bring up psychological problems? The patient had, by this way of presenting himself and his problems, created a situation which the therapist experienced as an emergency, with an implicit threat of treatment disruption. An answer seemed to be demanded that Dr. O felt at a loss to give. He, in his turn, tried to transmit the same sense of emergency to his supervisor, demanding an answer—an immediate prescription—which would enable him to cope with the emergency at hand.

Put another way, the patient has seen the solution of his dilemma in the answer of the therapist, while the therapist in turn has seen the solution of his dilemma in the answer of the supervisor. The therapist, rather than being able to deal with the problem within the therapeutic situation, sought to step out of the therapy situation and have the supervisor take over from him. In this regard he was not unlike his patient who felt he did not know how to deal with his marital situation and hoped the psychotherapist would take it over from him. Both did so with feelings of anxiety, a sense of emergency, and with the expectation that the outsider could indeed help best through taking over.

The supervisor now had an interesting problem. What choices did he have? He could respond to the request by stepping into the situation and giving detailed advice to the therapist as to how to alter his techniques, how to respond more appropriately to the patient's very manifest communications, so as to enable the patient to give expression more freely to his inner tensions. If he were to do so, he would have taken over the emergency, would have excluded the therapist, or rather just have used the therapist as an extension of himself, and would thus have indirectly become the therapist of the patient, although he would have continued to use the student as his mouthpiece. This kind of solution is used by supervisors more frequently than one might think. The rationale for such a taking-over of the therapeutic function consists in the very legitimate worry that the patient might otherwise not be helped. The supervisor may rationalize, especially with beginning students, that only if he takes over himself can he safeguard the patient against the therapist's lack of skill. The supervisor will now have fallen victim to the transmitted feeling of emergency, arousing his legitimate feeling of responsibility toward the service function of the institution. He will be trying to carry out this service function, at the cost of giving up his teaching function.

But, one will ask, are there not true crises, in which the supervisor must take over through direct advice (even though the student may not be able to use it most effectively), in order to save the therapy situation from total collapse? Of course there are, and intervention in such a crisis may become mandatory upon the conscientious supervisor. How far it is justified to conduct teaching at the risk of losing patients is both a practical and ethical question. However, in any way of working, even with the most direct advice-giving, beginning students "lose" patients. (Parenthetically, the "loss" of a patient in such a way need not always be an emergency. Though treatment disruption can be a serious problem, often having to do with the skill and sensitivity of the therapist, there is also such a thing as a patient not being ready for the helping process and using any possible leverage to break it off. And "losing" a patient does not necessarily mean that the patient is lost.

Such an assumption would presume the omnipotence of the therapist.)

It is, indeed, an inherent dilemma of any responsible system of supervision, that though the supervisor has a major responsibility for the training of the student, he has also accepted a concomitant responsibility for the welfare of the patient. Therefore, we speak of "supervision" more frequently than of "teaching." The concern of the supervisor is, however, most directly with his student and it is through him that he has his only sustained, effective leverage. The basic problem of the supervisor is to help the student with his difficulties in learning, keeping in mind, however, that there is always the possibility that the student should not be allowed to go on with the treatment of the case.

With this in mind, what other avenues of entry into the threatening therapeutic impasse were open to the supervisor in the illustration under consideration? He might, for instance, have entered the situation by helping the therapist become aware of his growing irritation with the patient, against which the patient felt he had no way to defend himself other than to barricade himself behind his newspaper, just as he did with his wife. The supervisor might also have helped the therapist to face his own mounting anxiety in not being able to bring "significant material" to the supervisor, to fail with his first patient, and thus to face a possible emergency in his training situation. As the patient brought a heavy bag of groceries to his psychotherapy, the symbol of the constant demands of his wife, the therapist brought a sense of emergency, the symbol of his feeling that the task he had undertaken was too great and that the supervisor ought to relieve him of it. Too, by complaining to the supervisor of his difficulties in getting the patient to bring up his problems, Dr. O could also have been indirectly pleading his own difficulty in bringing up his problems in learning within the supervisory hour. Hence, the "emergency" plea for the other to take over.

The supervisor had a range of choices. He could identify with the feeling of emergency, see the therapeutic situation as one that might collapse at any moment, and take it over from the therapist. Or he could wonder why the student needed to represent his learning effort as a crisis situation; what in the learning situation made him try to blot it out by his appeal for direct rescue.

Frequently, the emergency situation that is presented seems to be of an entirely different nature. There are examples where the psychotherapist delineates his inability to help the patient against the background of a chaotic hospital situation, the destructive behavior of personnel, or the sabotage of the relatives. He describes situations with which the patient is truly unable to cope because of his illness, and presents the request that the supervisor ought to do something about the actual reality-situation which has created the specific emergency. The supervisor ought to see the ward doctor, the administrator, or whoever else is felt to be responsible for whatever has created the emergency for the patient. The patient has presented his problem as one of helplessness in the face of this reality. The psychotherapist, in identifying with the helplessness to this degree, brings his own helplessness to the supervisor and asks the supervisor to take the problem over. Again a psychotherapeutic impasse is experienced as a reality-impasse. Many of these reality-impasses are so powerful, so convincing that we fail to see their psychological roots within the psychotherapeutic situation. These kinds of impasses are particularly frequent in psychotherapeutic work with severely disturbed and hospitalized patients, and with children; as a matter of fact, with all patients who are in dependent situations, whether of confinement or of dependency on parents and educators. Such impasses readily permit one to overlook the fact that a specific problem in psychotherapy has its roots within the therapeutic situation itself rather than in the external obstacle.

The supervisor might frequently be tempted to overidentify with the therapist's request, and to go out to fight the therapist's battle. He might see himself as the link between psychotherapist and administrator and might try to change a situation rather than help the therapist to cope with the situation himself. The supervisor's task would, however, rather be to help the therapist close the open door again. He should help the therapist go back to the consulting room, in order to resolve the situation which exists between him and the patient.

A further aspect of this problem of the temptation to the supervisor to take over in times of crises lies in the interaction of the natural impulses of the supervisor with the expressed wishes of his student. Just as the student, out of his sense of inadequacy as a therapist, may try to wipe himself out so that the supervisor can "directly" treat the patient, so the supervisor may fall in with this request out of his own greater skill in, and more intense identification with, doing psychotherapy than with teaching it. He may be all too willing to wipe out the therapist (in ways that can be rationalized as helping the patient) by proffering direct advice as to what should and even what must be said in the therapeutic situation with the patient.

When seen in this light, true emergencies requiring an active intervention over the head of the student-therapist become much less frequent. And often when they do occur, they are already beyond the point of recoverability through this kind of intervention. An example of this occurred when two patients, both in intensive psychotherapy within an institutional setting announced their firm decision to marry within a very short time. The therapists, cognizant of the individual psychopathology of each of the prospective marital partners, might have been tempted to actively discourage this wedding (even to the point of possibly making the continuation of the therapies contingent on the postponement of the wedding plans) and thus try to stave off what could easily be seen as a double piece of transference acting-out. The danger in such a therapeutic course would have been twofold. The therapists would have automatically been repeating with each patient the characteristic pattern of neurotic interaction with the forbidding parent of infancy. And the intervention itself would have been likely to fail and, with its failure, to endanger the continuation of each of the therapeutic situations. In fact, only by taking a psychotherapeutic position, with its offer to try to understand and to interpret the unfolding psychological life of the patient, could each therapist maintain his effective contact with his particular patient.

Basically, the problem of the handling of such "crises" becomes one of heading off the crisis before it develops, through an awareness of the many determinants that go into building up the crisis situation, with a responsible acknowledgment at the same time that minimal acceptable standards of performance must be enforced.

Such decisions, as to the degree of freedom of movement and experimentation to allow the therapist, and the amount of "protection" to be afforded the patient, are not always easy to make. A case in point will illustrate the real crises and the problems incident to their handling that can arise in a so-called extreme case. Interestingly, this arose as a form of inverted emergency with a therapist who, rather than claiming that an emergency existed for which he wanted supervisory help, constantly claimed that there was not only no emergency but even no problem. Dr. N was to treat a youngster in a child guidance center. He had seen the child for two interviews prior to his first supervisory session with Dr. Heath. Dr. N had not prepared himself by going over the available work-up material before seeing the child, and through both interviews held himself at a distance from the child by a noncommittal passivity. He stated that both of these moves had been recommended to him by another staff man (other than the supervisor), and if they were to be questioned, they were in no wise his own doing. He pseudo-submissively suggested, "I only do what I'm told. If it's not good advice, you fellows fight it out." And he then tried to solicit additional information and "advice" from his supervisor, using the pseudo-passivity displayed toward both the patient and the supervisor to bind the anxiety experienced with each.

When Dr. Heath raised questions about part of the psychotherapy material dealing with grossly inappropriate remarks made to the child, Dr. N would admit no problem, since it was "only a case of happening to focus on a different level." This denial of any need for supervisory help was underscored by Dr. N's statement that, after all, he understood the patient quite well because he had a child the same age. Thus at his first meeting Dr. N revealed his very deep-seated resistances to any kind of learning, and primed the supervisor well on the limited goals toward which to aspire. Dr. N ended the hour with an onslaught on the supervisor's administrative arrangements, contending that the bureaucratic requirements imposed by the structure interfered with his therapy. Dr. Heath, in response, tried to get across the point that Dr. N felt in a real dilemma between getting supervisory help and the desire to help the patient, the only resolution of which he could see as loosening the structural requirements. Dr. N ignored this somewhat obliquely made point, and left, stating gaily, "This will be fun!" The supervisor was perhaps left to wonder, "Fun for whom?" and, "At whose expense?"

In his second supervisory conference Dr. N brought very short notes on his conduct with the child, stating as the reason for this the supervisor's previous advice to abandon note-taking during the interviews. He stated that the therapy posed no special problems, but he did want to discuss his growing feeling that the child needed no therapy at all. Both these points he attempted to document, and whatever effort was made to show him how much this child needed help, he brushed aside. Dr. N came to the next conference with a myriad of complaints about the administrative chaos in the agency and the mishandling of personnel. He was now sure that the child did not need treatment and that really it was the mother who needed the treatment; no one else could see it (they were all so incompetent). He felt that with this case he was, in fact, relegated to the role of a baby-sitter, rather than that of a therapist.

By now Dr. N had succeeded in externalizing the whole of his problem in the relationship with the child and had created a series of perfect alibis behind which he could hide his real lack of skill (as well as his awareness of this deficit) and through which he could rationalize his passivity. At this point he felt clearly that his only problem was to secure permission to stop seeing the child, and thus avoid having to focus on any of the difficulties in the therapeutic situation which by now was beginning to get rapidly out of hand. When Dr. Heath tried to focus on what was happening to the young patient in the meanwhile, Dr. N stated that if the child suffered as a result of these wrangles in this (in his eyes) very incompetent agency, that was "the way of the world."

While the student thus denied any existing emergency or even any therapeutic problem at all, the supervisor could not help but see the growing emergency being created by the therapist. By his gross neglect of therapeutic responsibilities and the denial of any existing therapeutic problems, Dr. N was enabled to deny his own emerging awareness of therapeutic incompetence, and thus ward off painful insights in the supervision. The more he felt that the child needed no help at all and the more he claimed that he had no real questions, the more the supervisor felt that something external needed to be done in order to handle the emergency and to meet the organization's responsibility to the child.

The supervisor thus sought action outside of the existing relationship between himself and the student by an appeal to the administrator. The administrator, too, had his problems created by Dr. N's activities. During one session when the child was supposedly in the therapy office, she was actually in the yard on the swing, inadequately clothed for the winter weather. Dr. N had permitted this, as the child "was free to use the hour any way she wished," a literal application of a therapeutic principle to a nontherapeutic end. The mother, aware of this episode, and conscious that something was amiss, complained to the administrator, who was thus in the unenviable position of being responsible for another person's irresponsibility.

We can thus easily understand the administrator's readiness to have the supervisor open the door of the supervision conference and call upon the administrator to help deal with a situation in which there seemed no possibility for teaching, no willingness to learn, and no way to guarantee effective service to the patient. We see here an instance where there seemed no other way but to open the door. There was no psychological leverage for the resolution of this emergency, even though enough knowledge was available about the student to allow an understanding of some of the psychological roots of his difficulties. There was, then, no other choice but to handle the emergency as a reality and to discontinue the student in psychotherapy training. Even at that point Dr. N could see only dimly how his anxieties and problems as a beginning therapist had generated the emergency situation. Rather, he attributed the unsuccessful outcome of his therapeutic efforts and his supervisory experience to the unsuitability of the child, the uncooperativeness of the mother, the lack of understanding of the supervisor, and the inefficiency of the administration. He had labeled the child a "no-treatment case," and in so doing had warded off the need to look into his problems in trying to carry on the treatment.

Emergencies can, of course, be created at any level of organizational functioning and then transmitted through the many interacting clinical processes. We have indicated how the patient can generate a state of emergency through his difficulty in entering the treatment situation, and the implied threat of withdrawal and treatment disruption that is introduced. We have also seen how the therapist can induce the state of emergency through *his* difficulty in entering the treatment situation, and in undertaking a treatment program which he rationalizes as not indicated anyway. Sometimes it is the supervisor who sees an emergency situation as based in reality, and who then seeks outside solutions as a defense against his own emerging difficulties in teaching. Likewise in such instances, opening the door and calling for the external solution may be but a denial of a psychological difficulty for which there should be a psychological solution.

A case in point occurred in a guidance center where a therapist, Dr. M, resigned his job, in order to leave shortly and go out into private practice. The resignation was actually in large part an outgrowth of Dr. M's increasing awareness of the dissatisfaction of his superiors with his work, although he had not fully accepted these judgments of his supervisors and employers. He came to his supervisor, Dr. Irving, to discuss with him the disposal of his current therapy cases. His handling of these situations with his patients was rather ambiguous, reflecting the lack of resolution of a conflict situation with the supervisor. Since Dr. M did not really accept his supervisor's judgments concerning his inadequate level of performance, he saw no need to give up all his cases, but hoped to take one or two of these patients along with him and treat them in private practice. Dr. Irving, who had a negative judgment of his student's work, felt this plan to be irresponsible, and felt it his duty to the institution to protect the patients, and not allow the therapist to take them along.

The supervisor indicated this decision quite clearly to the student. Dr. Irving found another staff member in the organization who would be able to take over the cases, and demanded that his student state quite explicitly to his patients that he would not be able to continue privately with them. Dr. M did take this action with his patients, but in a very indecisive way, reflecting his own inner struggles over the many unresolved meanings that attached to this step. This indecision on the part of the therapist evoked an open confusion in the patients as to what they would do when their therapist left—go along with him, or stay with the agency and the new therapist.

Dr. Irving, no longer trusting the therapist, tried then to hurry the transition period on the basis that the patients needed to be protected; he wanted to be sure that the transfers were effected and the patients already being seen by the new therapist before he himself went on vacation. This pressure from his supervisor evoked a counter struggle from Dr. M, who kept insisting that he was only trying to terminate his relationships with his patients as constructively as possible, to show them that he was concerned with their welfare and their continued treatment. The attempt on Dr. M's part to have as much time as he felt he needed to effect this transfer, in order to work out such problems as much as possible with the patients, was opposed by Dr. Irving. At this point Dr. Irving appealed to the administration for help and made this appeal in terms of the need to safeguard the welfare of the patients.

We have here an urgent situation which was created neither by the patients nor by the therapist. In this instance the feeling of emergency was created by the supervisor who found it difficult to cope with his own resentment toward the therapist, and used the feeling that it was necessary to invade the therapy situation and to rescue the patients from the therapist as a way of rationalizing the resentment. Since the supervisor obviously did not feel quite comfortable with the solution and must have sensed somewhere the inappropriateness of his emergency feelings, he appealed to the administration for advice and help. This appeal, however, was experienced as a wish for complete endorsement. The administrator's position in such a case is, of course, a rather difficult one, since he would be inclined to identify with the supervisor and to back him up in a way that would estrange the therapist even further, and would not offer maximum help to the patients. The administrator's problem would require, however, that he not overidentify with one function or the other. Rather, he would need to help the supervisor go back to the supervisory conference room, to talk things over with the therapist once more, in order to find a solution in which the recourse to the open door and to the outside person becomes unnecessary.

Administrators, too, sometimes create emergencies, frequently under what they feel to be the pressure of the community or the governing board of their institution. They might tend to try to curb situations with many good reasons which, however, might not always be justifiable. Administrators, not unlike relatives, may feel certain reality-events in the life of the patient so pressing, or his behavior presumably so intolerable to the community, that they feel they need to intervene with the therapist. They will then want the therapist to consider the reality not as a psychological one, but as an external one, for which he ought to feel responsible and which he ought to change, in order to make it possible for them all to function properly.

There is thus hardly a helping process which is without its emergencies, since there are always new situations emerging with which the one to be helped, or also the helper, frequently cannot cope. Our examples are not designed to show that emergencies can always be avoided. Some emergencies no doubt can be avoided if we can see the determinants of the crisis clearly ahead of time. As one therapist once reported to her supervisor: "If I had been more alert to the chaos in myself, rather than complaining to you for weeks on end about the chaos in the hospital, I would have been able to help the patient more, and to get help from you in those areas where we could do something together, rather than keep demanding that you intervene in a situation that neither you nor I could change."

The greatest danger of emergencies, of course, is that he who feels confronted with one must plead in such a way, must ask for help so "convincingly" that he frequently wipes out the very source of help by involving the helper in the spreading panic. The helper, in over-identifying with him, may show sympathy but no true understanding, which cannot be achieved unless the helper keeps his objectivity in the crisis. The more convincing the plea for emergency help is, the more suspicious the helper must be that it may not be the reality of the emergency which causes the problem, but rather the emerging of inner reality which frequently comes first to the surface as awareness of a quasi-nonsolution problem.

We assume of patients that to a large extent they create their realities and their emergencies. May we not likewise assume that the therapists to a large extent also create their realities and their emergencies when they attempt to treat patients? If that is so, we must then help them to see how and why they create these realities and these emergencies and thus help them to find an inner answer which frees them for appropriate technical choices, rather than to see the answers in opening the door for external help. If the door can be kept closed, it becomes possible to share the true problem on the highest possible level, rather than only as a primitive plea for help.

While this may be an ideal attitude, the realities of training, like the realities of therapeutic work, do not always allow the application of the ideal model. There are phases of training, just as there are phases of psychotherapy, where there must be the kind of direct help which takes over for a while before there is again a readiness for a way of working which does not depend on emergency measures. The emergency situation may demand that one take over the total problem. A more fruitful way of helping, whether in the realm of therapy or in the realm of teaching, is one where only that much of the problem is taken over as is necessary, so that the one to be helped can find his own way for the rest. Our discussion of the psychological nature of the emergency highlights in a magnified way the nature of the whole training process. True learning requires of the student the willingness to give up emergency methods of asking for help, and how can one better help him with this task than if one is unwilling to accept the emergency as he presents it. Rather, one would help the student break the emergency up into its component parts, so that he himself can search for solutions to each part. The emergency is an expression of helplessness, but helplessness has frequently been used to show the helper up as equally helpless. He who fully accepts helplessness does not trust in the inherent strength of his student. If he cannot trust the inherent strength of his student, should one be surprised if one were to find out that he cannot trust his own?

XIII / *Following the Process of Supervision*

He who hopes to learn the fine art of the game of chess from books will soon discover that only the opening and closing moves of the game admit of exhaustive systematic description, and that the endless variety of the moves which develop from the opening defies description; the gap left in the instructions can only be filled in by the zealous study of games fought out by master-hands.—SIGMUND FREUD

Study of the nature of ongoing interpersonal helping processes tends to focus around certain groupings of discrete and readily isolable aspects that contain identifiable generic problems, toward the resolution of which considerable technical know-how has been accumulated. Thus every supervisory process—like every therapeutic process—has its problems around beginning, the use of time, the meaning of structure, the handling of crises, the impingements of external reality, and termination, to mention some that are more widely recognized. These can be studied in each instance as the individualistic patterns of expression of a universal problem. To formulate more explicitly what transpires in the interacting process of supervision, much time and thought has been devoted to a careful study of these isolable problems which are more easily perceived. The broad sweep of the supervisory process—the long "middle game" of chess—that encompasses the ebb and flow of the manifold factors entering into the interrelationship—skill differences, learning problems, the transmission of knowledge, and the gradual growth in the professional use of oneself, etc.—is less clearly delineated.

Yet, though less specifically charted, this "middle game" constitutes the major bulk of the actual work. It is what goes on in a supervisory relationship when there are no special crises, either externally imposed or internally experienced, and when the focus of the supervision can be clearly on the content of the therapy and the skill and learning problems that arise in the process. Actually, one soon learns that the recurrent "crises" around problems in learning cannot be separated at all from the content of the material and the skill problems faced. For not only does the student manage to use supervision to acquire skills, but the recurrent crises—the learning blocks, the problems in learning and in teaching that arise—are themselves an essential part of the total process that must be worked through in order to make the most fruitful headway in acquisition of experience and skill. Thus the dynamics of the process are analogous to psychotherapy, where the "learning block" (resistance and defense and transference, if you will) is not to be narrowly seen as the obstacle to "learning" (therapy), but the vehicle through which meaningful therapeutic progress is made. The process of supervision itself thus becomes a stepping stone back to the patient and to the content of the therapy material.

To illustrate some of the intricacies in working out such a complex process, we chose a longitudinal record of the work in supervision of the therapist, Dr. W, with his supervisor, Dr. Baehr. This particular example was selected for a variety of reasons. Dr. W was a beginning therapist, with the full gamut of anxieties, problems and aspirations, and the intense eagerness to know more that characterize many a beginner. Moreover, he had very open inhibiting difficulties which were consciously focused upon early in the supervisory process. He was at the same time an individual who, despite his difficulties, was able to work through to successive levels of partial resolution, with the consequent consolidation of technical skills. In addition, the supervisor, being a relatively inexperienced supervisor (much as Dr. W was a beginning therapist), made his quota of technical "mistakes" because of his own problems in teaching, as well as his own insecurely consolidated supervisory (and psychotherapeutic) skills. Lastly, Dr. W is someone with whose initial work we have already become familiar. We first introduced Dr. W (and his supervisor, Dr. Baehr) in Chapter VI ("The Supervisor Meets the Student"), and discussed the initial supervisory interview as an example of the "diagnostic" use that can be made of such a first conference—"diagnostic" not only from the point of view of predicting the learning patterns expected to emerge, but also of foreshadowing the possible supervisory pitfalls. In the prediction of the difficulties ahead, the nature of the obstacles that Dr. W erected against the possible impact of the supervisory process was delineated. At first he forgot: he forgot the first meeting, he forgot to free his schedule, and only after two broken appointments did he find it possible to come at all. Next he seemed overly confused and constantly asked to have this or that aspect of the training setup explained to him again. He then denied that any of this was different from anything he had had before. Lastly, he saw the whole problem in the patient when he wondered whether his *patient* was motivated. Certainly, as indicated in our discussion, the question must arise as to what progress in learning such an anxious individual can achieve through supervision.

In Chapter VII ("The Therapist Meets the Patient") we followed Dr. W again as he, in turn, met with his new patient for the first time. The patient, a hypochondriacally suffering individual, was a type that Dr. W had seen often in his medical practice, but was now confronting for the first time in his new role as a psychotherapist. His account of this first interview showed he perceived that the patient had come to the first hour a little resistant and certainly cautious as to what the new doctor would be like. We already know that Dr. W, too, was quite resistant to starting (especially something new) and was troubled about the problem of motivation. Dr. W tried to empathize with the patient, to "start a relationship," while sidestepping the issue of the essential difference between a psychotherapeutic relationship and a social relationship, since he himself had no conviction that psychotherapy did represent a difference from the more usual kinds of social interactions with which he was familiar. He was therefore frustrated by the patient for whom this was *all* different and confusing. Were not his symptoms somatic and were they not sufficiently cared for by the attending internist, according to the conventional model of the doctor-patient relationship? The patient wondered how this new intervention by the therapist could help. And the therapist wondered how to involve the patient in a psychotherapeutic process, and that involvement to stem from a faith that it would help.

Such were the problems brought by Dr. W to his second supervisory hour with Dr. Baehr, which we followed then in detail in Chapter VIII

("The Supervisor and the Student-Therapist Discuss the Patient"). In presenting and discussing the problem that he experienced in his first week's interviews with the patient, Dr. W followed the pattern forecast from his first encounter with the supervisor, in which they had met (with no patient material) in order to program their work together. When questions were raised by the supervisor about handling the issue of whether one could "start a relationship" without clarifying the nature and purpose of the relationship, Dr. W replied that there was really *no difference*. The many possible avenues suggested by the supervisor had all been explored. Maybe it just hadn't come out properly in the material. Again he depreciated whatever difference the supervisor might try to offer, which had been so characteristic of the first supervisory hour. And indeed, as one interview with the patient after another was discussed, whatever was offered by the supervisor was "no different" from what had been known and said before.

At this point we can well see that whatever accretion of technical skill the supervisor might offer fell on the rocks of the student's unwillingness or inability to see the newness, or his need to wipe out the difference. Dealing with this was the problem of the supervisor, a prerequisite to reaching the student. This was perceived and faithfully recorded by the supervisor who, however, in his actual response seemed hesitant.

Here we see the supervisor's own teaching problem, his gentle acceptance and his hesitation to enter actively into the psychological world of his student even at the point where ostensibly he was asked to—when the student-therapist demonstrated his clinical inadequacy and lack of skill. Yet the supervisor knew this was precisely what had to be done, if any help were to be forthcoming to his student, and, incidentally, if any growth in his own supervisory capacities were to take place.

In the ensuing week the patient abruptly terminated his psychotherapy (though he chose to stay on in the hospital), and it was for the discussion of these terminal events in this abortive psychotherapeutic relationship that supervisor and student came to their third session together. Dr. W began by not remembering the hour and came at the wrong time. When he finally did get together with Dr. Baehr, he went into a detailed discussion of how the whole management of the therapy had been constantly troublesome to him. He had been beset by so many difficulties. Dr. Samuels, the internist on the case, had been constantly changing the somatic therapy, and Dr. W felt like a flunky carrying out the internist's requests; he could hardly regard the patient as his own, there had been so much interference. And, unknown to Dr. W, a social worker had been seeing the patient all along through an arrangement that had been made prior to instituting the psychotherapy and for reasons that were still unclear; this Dr. W had just found out about. Then the patient would wander over to the internist's office and discuss his "childhood" with him; Dr. W reflected, "The patient doesn't come and discuss his childhood with me." All these things troubled him very much, interfered with his relationship with the patient, and probably accounted for his own "bungling" that had led to the rupture of the treatment.

In response, the supervisor acknowledged the special complexity of carrying on psychotherapy with a patient with physiologic disturbances who was likewise undergoing somatic investigation and treatment by the internist; and acknowledged, too, that maybe the channels of communication all around had not been the best. But, Dr. Baehr went on, reality aside, perhaps Dr. W was expressing, as well, a more general psychological problem of his own in accepting and working within the structural limitations of a particular clinical setting—in this case one that treated "psychosomatic" patients. Just as every patient faced the problem of whether he could accept help within the psychotherapeutic structure in which it was offered, so every therapist had the problem of whether he could work within and offer help within that same structure. Dr. Baehr then said, "Your problem seems to be whether you can work effectively within *this* structure—both in your therapy and in your supervision with me. Look at the difficulties you've had with me so far. We've had trouble getting together on appointments. Part of our structure here, too, is that we submit notes in advance, so that we can both study them before the hour; and yet, last time you presented interviews for discussion that had not been written up as yet."

Here we can switch our focus to our neophyte supervisor, Dr. Baehr, struggling to hold his student to the "structure" and perhaps more than a little annoyed at the memory lapses by which the student kept juggling the rule concerning the regularity of their agreed-upon meeting time. Here Dr. Baehr probably saw in his student's complaint, about how the "others" upset the rules, his opportunity to turn the tables and drive home to the student his own difficulties with this selfsame problem. In his eagerness to do this Dr. Baehr made quite a jump from what the student had told him. The student might feel that he had to accept this–since he knew somehow it was true–but not without a measure of resentment at this abrupt turning of the psychological spotlight away from his question and back onto himself. Perhaps Dr. Baehr's overly forced confrontation derived, too, from another source. We have noted his propensity to observe and record, but to refrain from action–and interaction. We have seen in another instance how this usual inhibition of action could give way to a sudden excess of action, especially as he confronted this problem in himself in his study of his own supervisory work.

Dr. Baehr continued on with his student and raised one other question–he wondered at all the importance attributed to the internist as the major block to Dr. W's psychotherapeutic endeavors. Did Dr. Samuels really loom so large in the psychotherapy? Dr. W confessed that he was likewise troubled by this. He wondered why he perceived the internist as such a great interferer. Some of it was indeed real. But he recognized, too, that some of it was irrational. The internist was a staff man; that meant he represented authority. It was always hard for Dr. W to relate to authority. Dr. Baehr agreed that, indeed, some of this feeling might be real. But might not much of it be meant for the supervisor rather than the consulting internist? For Dr. Baehr also was on the staff and had *more* authority in relation to Dr. W than did the internist; this might represent a real problem in the supervisory relationship. And the advice that Dr. W had taken the previous week, and which when applied in the therapy situation had not seemed to help, had been advice from the supervisor, not from the internist. Whatever pressure there was in this regard was from the supervisor. Maybe Dr. W felt that Dr. Baehr's way would not work. Maybe much of the difficulty in the relationship revealed in the therapy process notes had stemmed from these feelings between student and supervisor.

At this point Dr. Baehr had struck his second heavy blow, but this one somewhat closer to what his student could acknowledge and work with fruitfully–though not without distress. We see this in Dr. W's slow and uneasy response, "That's a very shrewd–and accurate–observation." Then even more uncomfortably, "I have a confession to make–I did this once before and it didn't help then, but I think I should now. May I have a cigarette first?" He then said, "Well, here goes. There's something about you that I can't like or accept. I don't know all that it is. There's a lot of jealousy and envy. After all, we came here to this setting together, and now you're the chief and I'm the student . . . I've had supervision before and I had troubles with it then, too. I presented a patient to a group control once. Whenever I felt secure with the patient and seemed to be doing well, I never took their advice. When things weren't going so well, and I *did* do what they suggested, it just never worked out. It was no help . . . In my first year I had a control with Dr. Ellis. I was exposed so often. And then he said one day, 'You've made every mistake in the book, but your heart is in the right place, and you haven't hurt the patient.' I'm still trying to work that one through . . . With my patients, I've always tried to be a nice guy and friendly, and I can see how nontherapeutic that is, yet I don't know what else I can do . . . Boy, have I messed up this whole deal."

In responding to this confession of his student, Dr. Baehr restated the therapist's dilemma as follows: "You say, on the one hand, 'I realize that I'm not so hot as a therapist. I've been attempting a lot of therapy that hasn't turned out to be very therapeutic. I've been too busy being a nice guy and friendly to my patients,' and yet, on the other hand, 'I'm not able to accept help in learning to be different, and when I do try to, as with the group control or here, it always works out badly.' It's as if you act out against it and mess it up." Dr. W said that they had come to his chief obstacle to learning. He kept repeating this a few times, slowly and thoughtfully. Then he said, "But now that we know what it is, what can be done about it? It's there. It's conscious. But there doesn't seem to be anything I can do about it."

Dr. W had passed the first hurdle in his work in supervision. A major learning problem of his was "diagnosed" and quite apparent. He had then posed the next question: "Now it's conscious and out in the open. So what! What can I do about it?" To this Dr. Baehr responded by stating that he was not exactly sure what Dr. W had meant. Was he saying that he himself was so rigid that he couldn't possibly change (and such a self-evaluation could hardly be taken literally this early in the course of the supervision), or that Dr. Baehr was such an inadequate teacher that he couldn't help effect a change? Certainly, Dr. Baehr had many choices of words in dealing with this oft-recurrent complaint—that the problem is now conscious, but what can be done about it. He might have said simply, "Yes, but we have time"—with its counterimplication that something *can* be done about it; or conveyed the same idea by turning the statement into a question, "You can't change?"; or he might merely have acknowledged that "Having it conscious by itself doesn't seem to help very much." Each of these is a variant on the same theme, leaving the issue open as a question between student and supervisor. To what extent could they, through bending their best efforts to the task, work out this problem together?

But the tension had not yet gone out of their hour together. Dr. Baehr presented to Dr. W the possible alternative paths that were available. They could go on with another patient and keep on working together on just such problems, which could be a helpful turn; or it might be too difficult and they could break it up, which would be too bad because it wouldn't really result in the help that Dr. W came seeking.

Perhaps in the events of this hour lay one answer to Dr. W's query as to what this supervision was all about. And other answers would come as other learning problems would come to the fore and be worked with in the continuous process ahead. But none could be dealt with as long as this one precluded Dr. W's accepting any kind of help. At this point Dr. W exclaimed, "This is a *different* sort of supervision"—the first frank acknowledgment of any difference in his new experience and the first breach in the protective wall with which he had tried to shield himself. It was hopeful, too, for the supervisor, who had taken perhaps too pessimistic a view from the seeming stubbornness of his student's defensive and provocative maneuvers in their first supervisory session together.

Certainly, out of this hour came a feeling of crisis met and surmounted on the part of both participants. The supervisor's "strategy" had paid its dividends, though his "tactics" were indeed somewhat heavy-footed. Dr. Baehr had felt impelled to enter the fray with all his heavy artillery, airtight arguments and conclusive confrontations. He had waded in and overwhelmed Dr. W. Perhaps this was not necessary to effect the results achieved. Dr. W had been left no alternatives. The same confrontations expressed tentatively as questions would have provided outs, had Dr. W needed them and would perhaps have reduced the crushing weight of the proffered insights, or even turned these blows into potential cues for self-discovery.

But where there was earnestness and integrity and a modicum of good will on both sides, the teaching faults of the supervisor and the barriers to learning in the student and the lacks of technical skills that each brought to his task were overcome. Help was both given and received in the interaction, clumsy and heavy-handed as it was. For, teaching and learning can proceed and be effective under conditions that are far from ideal so long as there is a differential in skill and knowledge that is to be transmitted, and an alertness to the barriers that stand in the way of its transmission. Though certainly the more skillful the teaching, the less "traumatic" and uneven the process will be.

And Dr. W did not let the hour close without a protest against what he perceived as an assault. At the very end of the period, after a brief pause, he suddenly blurted out, "The thing about this discussion is that it has been so *intellectual.*" Dr. Baehr was surprised at this rebuttal. The tension in the air during the hour had been very real. Both participants were emotionally very involved. And he stated this surprise and this feeling. To which Dr. W responded that yes, that was so. What he had thought to be intellectual was Dr. Baehr's confronting him with "choices" in this dilemma. Dr. Baehr, the student thought, was pretending that Dr. W could move in the one direction or the other, when actually Dr. W felt that he had no real freedom of choice. It's as if he were saying, "It's so intellectual of you to offer me choices as if I truly have free choices. Each of these is so emotionally loaded, so compelling in its implications, that I don't have objective intellectual choices. This is my great problem. Recognize it, won't you?" What Dr. W actually said to his supervisor was, "As you offered me each 'choice,' I was automatically saying to myself—almost because you said it—no, I don't want it." Here again is exemplified the selfsame problem, phrased by the supervisor at the end of the session, "It's so difficult for you to accept anything from me." The hour ended with Dr. W's stated desire to go on with supervision and to follow another patient, and with his vow to keep his time schedule straight.

Considering the immediately preceding interchange between supervisor and student, one may wonder whether this final resolve on which the hour closed represented a true growth in insight or rather an unwilling submission to the new power arrangements. It probably contained elements of both. For most learning—as most other kinds of change in interpersonal processes—proceeds in the same fashion, through working out obstacles and holding onto the old at the same time one incorporates the new.

Following this very tense session, the supervisory atmosphere "quieted down." Dr. W was punctual the next time and gave the supervisor a "follow-up" on the previous patient (further somatic investigations were still in progress), but made no direct reference to the previous supervisory hour. Rather, he stated the difficulties he was encountering with the new patient, an inhibited and constricted hysterical individual. Starting was again a real problem. Mainly, Dr. W felt guilty that he was "confronting" his new patient too severely and too early, and he feared that this was not "the proper therapeutic approach." He kept wondering whether he had "done right." Dr. Baehr said that they could perhaps clarify this question of the appropriateness of Dr. W's "confrontations" by going over the material together, trying to look at Dr. W's statements in terms of both his intent and the way it might have seemed to the patient.

Considered in this framework, many of Dr. W's comments, he could see, might be perceived by the patient as cold and rejecting. Dr. W was dismayed by this accumulating evidence. He protested, "I didn't mean it that way" or "It isn't really like me to act in that kind of fashion." At one point the patient told Dr. W about previous psychiatrists who had helped him and "told" him things, and in contrast pointed to Dr. W as someone who didn't seem to tell him anything. Somewhat later in the interview, when the patient began a series of associations centering around his difficulties in interpersonal relations, especially on his job, Dr. W responded with an interpretation ("told" him something) very directly (and brusquely) linking these frustrations to the patient's vomiting, one of his chief symptoms. The patient could only respond to this interpretation by denial, change of subject, and the blocking of further associations. Dr. W said at this point again that he had felt uneasy about this, that his need to say something—to interpret—had probably represented his answer to the patient's previous challenge, that needing to respond in this way was "not at all like me."

When Dr. Baehr inquired about these feelings, Dr. W went on to state that he had always tried to be a "nice guy and friendly" with his patients—to build social relationships with them—and though this was spontaneous and easy, he was coming to feel now, on the basis of this supervisory experience, that it was nontherapeutic. He was now becoming aware that there was something definite to psychotherapy; that it was a serious business and demanded skill; that, in it, patients often had to be confronted and to be made uncomfortable. In doing this, he was not as "nice" a guy to the patients as he used to appear and as he actually was; he had to be different from himself.

Certainly, Dr. W was stating his new dilemma as he saw it. One was either a "nice guy," a "pal," or a coldly impersonal psychotherapist, confronting harshly for the patient's own good. Dr. Baehr stated that this seemed quite a dilemma. Was it really necessary to lose one's warmth and spontaneity in acquiring psychotherapeutic skill? Dr. W said that he *was* coming to the gradual conviction that for good to result from psychotherapy it must be uncomfortable. He then referred to the previous supervisory hour which had been "hellishly uncomfortable," but which had done him a lot of good, and that was the way it had to be. And here the student-therapist harked back to the "showdown" supervisory session of the previous week. That was the way it was supposed to be. Dr. W now saw himself doing to the patient exactly what he himself had experienced at the hands of the supervisor.

Here we see how the teaching problem of the supervisor (his reaction against his own tendency to inhibit action resulting in the opposite of excessive action, excessive "confrontation") has been perceived by the student and in turn projected by him into the therapeutic situation, with his patient as a *technical* problem in psychotherapy. Acting imitatively, Dr. W only repeated what had been done to him, and then defended himself against accepting responsibility for this new position by avowing that he personally was not at all like that. At this point Dr. Baehr became painfully aware of his own role in the process and tried in a cautious way to reverse the trend. Yes, he agreed, the previous supervisory session had been tense and uncomfortable, but out of it perhaps a better working relationship had emerged. Maybe it should be the same in psychotherapy—the discomfort experienced should be within the relationship between therapist and patient, not at the expense of it.

Dr. W agreed that, yes, this was a problem with him. He could either be a "nice guy" or a cold and objective psychotherapist, and he kept splitting it that way. Here Dr. W was also right. For this way of behaving was not just a reflection of what was experienced in the supervision (though Dr. W would have liked to rationalize it that way). It was also a learning problem of his own that had thus come to light. He said that he felt himself vacillating between his desire to return to his earlier state of just being a "pal" to the patients (though he could no longer really do that, for he had come to see how "nontherapeutic" it was) and his desire to go on in this learning, though it put him in a most uncomfortable situation where suddenly nothing seemed to work.

Thus we see that by tackling Dr. W's *problem about learning* in the previous supervisory hour, we have caught a glimpse of the emergent *learning problem* behind it. Dr. W's own final questioning comment in this hour was, "But what can we do about this? All right, now I know it, but how can I do differently?" This is, by now, a familiar sequel to the exposition of a problem in the process we are following. This time Dr. Baehr answered that he just didn't know. They would have to keep on going and see what questions continued to come up.

The warning signs had, however, been insufficient. By the next week this second patient was also "lost." He had decided to leave the hospital. In reviewing the patient's material, Dr. W saw with increasing clarity the nature of the problem he had created for himself in the image of the therapist as a harsh confronter. At first he saw this only as a technical problem, essentially one of tact and timing. Confrontation was an essential, even the pre-eminent therapeutic tool, but Dr. W felt that he didn't always handle it properly. "I time it wrong or something, so it isn't good the way I use it. I should learn to time it better when I have a better relationship, and then use it. Because it is important. Whenever I have done it well, important material came out." (He pointed to several examples.)

Dr. Baehr wondered how valuable the "material" was if at the same time the patient was lost. Mostly, he again wondered about this dilemma which Dr. W had seen the last time between being a "nice guy" and being a therapist (able to "confront severely," albeit with better timing). Dr. W said that he had been thinking about this problem. Didn't psychotherapy require "confrontation"? Wasn't this inherent in doing it? If he timed them appropriately, when the patient was ready, and after "establishing a good relationship," the basic harshness might be lessened but never eliminated. Dr. Baehr said that to him there were two main aspects to this matter. One was the technical problem, the question of timing, which had been discussed—and which Dr. W felt he had not handled well. The other aspect seemed to be in the affective charge with which Dr. W invested the word *confrontation*. It was as if it had its colloquial rather than its technical meaning, in which people are usually confronted when caught in wrongdoing. And using the word *severely* connoted the "bad value" he attached to the process.

Dr. W said, "I guess you're right. To me, confrontation does have this flavor. The other week when you confronted me severely, I felt chastised. All my life, when I've been confronted, I've felt chastised.

And if I get mad about it, I turn around and take it out on my patients." He then brought up a memory of when he was a Freshman in high school and was assigned to a debate for the first time. He knew little about debating. He had prepared his talk and delivered it. Right after that some girl got up and spoke, ripping his talk to pieces. He felt stunned, and was speechless for an answer. This experience, which kept returning to mind, he associated with the word *confronted.*

Such a statement presents a temptation for the supervisor to turn into a psychotherapist in turn, rather than to see it in the light of its present import: as a displaced way of indicating (and at the same time diverting attention away from) a learning problem. Dr. Baehr avoided this pitfall and allowed Dr. W to go on to wonder whether he could learn to use "confrontation" differently—not only with better timing, but in a different spirit. Would he learn from this experience and "do better" next time or would he be just the same? Probably Dr. Baehr was considering at the same time how best to use the supervisory process between himself and Dr. W to help his student fathom the many-sided complexity of this problem of confrontation, both as receiver and as giver, and in its range of meanings from technical tool to hostile weapon. During the hour, as they focused together on the problem of "confrontation," Dr. W seemed to exude a good feeling, as if to say, "Now we've got a good relationship and are getting somewhere."

By the next supervisory session (after a two-week vacation taken by the supervisor) Dr. W was already well along in his work with his third patient, this time one whom he was able to hold and to work with in a helpful manner through the balance of his period of formal supervision. The patient was an intelligent, ambitious young man of a somewhat obsessional turn, bogged down by his barely suppressed hostilities which impaired all his relationships, and suffering, as well, from a very troubling physical symptom, a severe torticollis (wryneck). Dr. W had a wealth of material covering three weeks of therapeutic work and many problems to discuss. He was most concerned, he felt, with the problem of specific choices of therapeutic techniques in the different hours. Was he "hitting them right"? How does one determine which technique is best where?

Dr. Baehr tried to focus this problem of "technique" in terms of what the patient was trying to say, and whether Dr. W related himself to this in terms of making it easier—or more difficult—for the patient. Certainly this relationship had begun very differently—and better—than the last, in the directness with which Dr. W helped clarify the mutual expectations and conditions of both himself and patient. The patient was immediately involved in the helping process. He began to express his difficulties in terms of his bad school adjustment, talking freely about his various "school" difficulties and the different aspects of his own personality functioning that were thereby revealed. In this process Dr. W experienced an increasing discomfort. He tried to interpret the school metaphor in such a way as to make the patient more explicitly aware of these problems as projections of his own inner dilemmas. He tried to push the patient not to talk so much about school and more about "himself" (in a "don't-waste-our-time-with-irrelevancies" manner). Many examples of this came up, and in discussing them, Dr. Baehr took occasion to explain what metaphors are in psychotherapy, and how problems can be worked with solely in terms of the metaphor, if that is the level on which they are presented.

Following this explanation, Dr. W said that perhaps he, too, had something to explain. In the supervisor's absence he had discussed the case with a senior colleague who had, as he understood him, given him a "different kind of psychotherapeutic advice"—to "handle the patient very directly"; to "tell" the patient, whose chief symptom was torticollis, that his bent neck represented a bent penis and that he was afraid to have an erection. Dr. W felt that he could not use so "direct" an interpretive approach; he "would not have been comfortable," although it must have influenced the kinds of things he *did* do. Dr. Baehr said that it seemed that Dr. W did have a problem, having different psychotherapeutic "schools" presented to him, and left thus to choose—or to obsess—between them. However, in seeking out advice from a colleague whose many ideas Dr. W knew to be deviant from the prevailing institutional climate, Dr. W had, in fact, set up this problem. Dr. W confessed that this was true. He mentioned still other variant points of view acquired by contact with a number of different colleagues, supervisors, and staff men. How could one choose from among them all? How could one pick the right technique for the right place?

Dr. W had now shifted his ground and was projecting his inner struggle against identifying with the psychotherapeutic point of view represented by his supervisor into the broader arena of competing psychotherapeutic "schools," each with its differing technical interventions stemming from differing ideologies. Of course, one can also see Dr. W's now familiar conception of confrontation as an inherently aggressive and destructive process, emerging in another guise as the invocation of his senior colleague's recommendation to "shake the patient up and give it to him straight." Thus the old defense is concealed, and also revealed, in the new. We can, too, examine how this apparent shifting of ground had come about.

In discussing the therapist's process notes of his material with the patient (which *had*, by the way, shown considerable improvement in skill and in technical handling as compared with the work considered in the very first interviews together), Dr. Baehr had been led into an explanatory discussion in an area where his student showed gross lack of knowledge (in this instance, the meaning and use of metaphor by the patient, the metaphoric use of his school difficulties to represent his over-all interpersonal frustrations). And, of course, this is a necessary component of a process that seeks to impart technical skill and knowledge. However, one can question its full justification in this particular situation because it served to help the student-therapist attempt to cover his very real problems in accepting supervisory help, problems which precluded his objective acceptance of such didactic explanation at this time. And this Dr. W himself realized when he responded to the explanation with an "explanation" of his own, that he had solicited competing technical advice and then been left to wonder how to choose between these conflicting schools of thought, each, as he wanted it in his fantasy, offering its wares and competing for his favor. It is not only the patient who has a "school problem" and needs to use a "school metaphor."

Here Dr. Baehr stayed with the metaphor as he had counseled his student to do, but refocused it in terms of the underlying question being asked. "There are so many psychotherapeutic schools; I get help from so many and such different sources; how do I know which is right, if any? How do I know if what you are trying to teach me is true or worth-while? How can I know how much I can trust you?" And thereby, Dr. Baehr placed the whole dilemma back where it was most keenly felt. At this point the problem could then be approached in various (not at all exclusive) ways. These could include the questioning statement, "That is quite a dilemma. Is there any way in which you think I can be of help with it?" Or a sharper and clearer question concerning the implications for subsequent action, "Well, I see if I were to try to teach you one more system, it would only add to the confusion and the difficulty of the choice. Perhaps you are already perplexed enough, so that you wonder whether we should go on." Or the more challenging confrontation, "I guess you are wondering whether I know what I'm doing or whether you can trust my supervision—whether my system is as good as all the others, or as bad." In this last question the supervisor would be harking back to his student's initial presentation of himself as someone who could see no difference between the old and the new, no change, no growth, and hence no improvement.

In such a situation with a learner who feels impelled to run for advice from one to another, the supervisor can only focus the process helpfully by appearing at that moment to represent dogmatic conviction, against which the therapist can be brought face to face with his doubts, not only about systems in general, but about his own supervisor in particular. This situation is similar to the problem of the student who wants only the best supervisor, in order to quiet his own inner doubts about all supervisors. Of course, the very positive aspects simultaneously reflected in this frantic behavior should not be overlooked. The therapist actually seeks out lots of supervisors; he *does* want all the help he can get. He only has to come to see the self-defeating nature of the *methods* by which he tries to obtain it. Lastly, one can look at the difficulty the supervisor experiences in dealing with this—in having to sustain the blow to his ego when such a student doubts the value of his supervision.

The supervisory session the next week was opened by Dr. Baehr's statement that he wished to defer until later discussion of Dr. W's three very interesting—and instructive—interviews with his patient, although he certainly did want to discuss them and would, if necessary, give an extra hour to Dr. W this week for that purpose. Dr. Baehr wanted to talk first about the formal evaluation of Dr. W's work, which had been discussed before as something in the future, but which was now upon them, with two weeks to go before the three-month mark. There were in Dr. W's case some special problems in that he had only a three-month assignment to his present service, rather than the six months that all the others had, and that would therefore make this a final rather than a mid-period evaluation. That would certainly raise questions as to how in this case they could go about it in a way most helpful to Dr. W. Dr. Baehr wondered what thought he had given to it.

At this point we can wonder at the way in which the supervisor raised this whole issue. The whole evaluation process seems suddenly to be somewhat awkwardly and apologetically introduced. Does our new supervisor himself feel ill at ease with this structural device which he feels obligated to use, perhaps against his own inner feeling that it connotes on his part the same kind of aggressive and unpleasant "confrontation" that he has been trying to help the student modify in his therapeutic work with the patient? Does he, in fact, tend to handle his own unfamiliarity with his new role and his relative insecurity in his new supervisory responsibility by an overly rigid and stereotyped application of this device (the evaluation) in a way that indeed would be harshly confronting? Is he in danger of being caught up by his student's drive to do battle with him, which could lead to the use of the evaluation as a handy and potent counter-weapon rather than as a helpful mutual assessment of the progress of an unfolding process?

Administratively, too, this is an awkward situation. It is as if the clinical arrangements had been made only with regard to the need to cover all the available assignments, seemingly unmindful of the therapeutic needs of the patients or the training needs of the students. This administrative awkwardness, however, only serves to magnify a problem which every supervisor and student must face at some time as they learn to work with rules not created by them.

In any case, Dr. Baehr coupled his statement that the forthcoming evaluation should be discussed with the offer to devote another hour that week to discuss the *really important* material from the interviews with the patient. Perhaps the patient's material of that week did require this immediate attention and could not be deferred another week, but the manner of saying so certainly tended to undercut the importance of the evaluation procedure which our supervisor was trying—ambivalently, it seems—to maintain. Then, too, Dr. Baehr might have felt it necessary to offer a compensating gift to his student, out of his guilt at the administrative requirements by which Dr. W would have only half the usual clinical and teaching assignment to the particular service. The supervisor's inability to identify with the administrative rules in this instance thus served to hamper his fullest psychological use of the evaluation procedure.

The student for his part stated that he had not given much thought to the evaluation per se, but he had certainly been thinking about his leaving the service soon, and wondering both about what would now happen between him and the patient, as well as about the possibility of going on in this supervision. He said that he would like to continue with this patient, and he would very much like to continue the supervisory experience with Dr. Baehr, if possible, since he now felt it to be such a valuable one to him. He realized how busy the supervisor was; and failing to obtain more time with him, Dr. W wondered if he could perhaps by "shopping around" get supervision on the same case with some other staff man. He had not actually gone out to try to find anyone.

Dr. Baehr expressed his willingness to explore these various possibilities. He stated that he felt more and more how treatable this patient was and how much he was asking for help. He felt it essential that they, of course, keep the patient's interests very much in mind in whatever planning they did. Certainly, the "shopping around" for some other staff man who would be willing to take this supervision on as an extra, unofficial arrangement, would be undesirable in many ways, not the least of them the absence of any administrative responsibility of the off-service, unofficial supervisor in relation to the patient and the patient's therapy. Short of discontinuing the present supervision and treatment situation, and transferring the patient to another therapist, Dr. Baehr saw two possibilities. The one (if this were to be the joint recommendation of supervisor and student) would be to request an administrative arrangement by means of which Dr. W could go on treating the patient officially in supervision with Dr. Baehr, even though Dr. W would now be working in another facility within the same over-all clinical setting. In view of the fact that there were therapists who had not yet started because of the tightness of supervisory time, it was uncertain whether this could be approved. The other possibility would be for the two of them to go on personally, as a private arrangement between them. Here, again, we see Dr. Baehr's willingness to consider making a compensating gift to his student as a way perhaps to assuage his own guilt about the harsh confrontation he believed inherent in the evaluation process, and without either thinking through himself or exploring with his student all the implications—the possible uses *and* abuses—of this changed arrangement. We can see, thus, how this same *technical* problem about the nature of confrontation reverberates at different hierarchical levels as both a learning problem of the student and a teaching problem of the supervisor. The supervisor, too, prefers to give and be friendly, rather than to withhold and "confront" as he feels he is compelled to do by his administration.

Dr. W said that he was well aware of these many difficulties. He had no solution to propose; he did want to continue. Certainly it was the best supervision he had had. He had been made to deal with such important and hitherto unrecognized problems in his own psychotherapy as: (1) Whom was he emulating? What "system" was he trying to apply in mechanical fashion? (2) Why did he have to feel that "confrontation" must be an aggressive and threatening experience? (3) Could he "find himself" and his own individual psychotherapeutic potential? In thus formulating his questions, Dr. W indicated the *learning problems* that emerged into clear focus as work was done to clarify his *problems about learning.* Dr. W himself went on to state this in terms of time sequences. He said there had been two major periods in the supervision thus far, in the first of which problems between supervisor and student had been dealt with, and in the second, they had "shifted focus" onto his problems in dealing with the patient. He didn't know now which had been the more helpful. Didn't the supervisor see it the same way? Wasn't this worth-while enough to go on? Dr. Baehr said that he had tried to deal with problems as they came up, one leading to another. He certainly hoped that the process had been helpful.

Dr. W said that for his part he wanted to go on. He was passing the problem back to the supervisor; could Dr. Baehr arrange it? Dr. W knew that if the supervisor said, "no," it would indeed be a realistic decision; nonetheless, he would still feel rejected. He would think "We could meet in the evening," etc. At this point Dr. Baehr for the first time in this hour turned the issue back to the potential technical problem in the psychotherapy. He said that just as the student wanted to go on, and in view of the existing schedule difficulties "hated to ask for it," so the supervisor for his part would like to go on and hated to end up saying "no," and that these were the separation difficulties of the two of them. This would give them some idea of what Dr. W's patient would experience in the same process yet to be dealt with.

Dr. W, rather than thinking about his work with the patient, took this as the harbinger of a final "no" to his own request and said, "Well, we can hide behind the system and say that's all we can do." Here he voiced his complaint and his disappointment at not getting immediately the asked-for reward; and this was certainly the other side of his constant struggle against the impact of this teaching experience in which there might indeed be something "new" to learn. Dr. Baehr said that they did, in fact, have the problem of doing the most that they could in the time allotted and within the framework of what the structure allowed. He stated that he thought it would have been bad, however, to have said flatly, "That's all there is; and there's little likelihood that discussion can change it," because that might have precluded all these feelings coming into conscious expression between them—feelings of separation, rejection, not being loved, etc. These were important to see in their relation to such situations—and especially to the ways in which they would make it harder to deal with the selfsame problems as they might emerge with the patient.

Dr. W finally took the cue and likewise turned his attention more to the patient. It seemed as if he'd be giving him up, yet he wasn't sure just how he would present this to the patient—they had begun so recently. This they discussed together, how the patient could be approached in terms of this having been a trial of psychotherapy, a mutual testing. Now that it was apparent that the patient needed and was ready for more far-reaching help involving a longer stay in the hospital, he could be transferred to a therapist who would be able to follow him through all the way. Dr. Baehr said this brought them back to their original problem of preparing themselves for their evaluation conference. Dr. W said that he would be thinking about this for the meeting next week. Meanwhile an appointment was made for the following day to discuss Dr. W's clinical material from the week's interviews with the patient.

The formal evaluation meeting was set for the next week. Yet in anticipation of that, and of the many possible conclusions that could stem from it, both supervisor and student had jumped the gun, so to speak, and had already been discussing possible future directions as if the consensus about the evaluation itself was so definitely predetermined. Here was the largest compensating "gift" that the supervisor made to his student; in so doing he restricted not only his own full freedom of action and exploration in the evaluation conference ahead, but that of his student as well. Together, they had de-emphasized the evaluation itself as if it were indeed only an empty ritual imposed by an administration bound by its own red tape.

In the additional supervisory hour the next day supervisor and student discussed the sequence of the week's interviews with the patient. Dr. W expressed how bewildered he had been during those hours. Dr. Baehr indicated his awareness of this and wondered about its source. He felt that the essential nature of the patient's communication was equally clear both to himself and to his student. The content centered around the patient's preoccupation with a question once raised by a previous doctor about his lack of desire to get well. The patient wondered whether that was true. Did that mean that he was largely responsible, that he had the illness *and* the cure largely in his own hands? Dr. W was "bewildered" by this. The supervisor wondered why. Dr. W said that he had kept trying to get *beyond* this preoccupation with the previous doctor's remark to get the patient to express *why* this bothered him, *why* he had such feelings about it. Dr. Baehr asked why, with the patient making such a confession of inner psychologic responsibility and in view of the confused and ambivalent feelings that this stirred up, Dr. W did not relate to that, but felt that he had to "go further," asking "whys" that the patient was not ready for and could not answer. Dr. W said he could see this now as just another case of his own racing ahead and not meeting the patient on the level at which he was "dragging behind." Yet he didn't know what impelled him to do this.

Dr. Baehr suggested that they turn in detail to the interactions in the therapeutic situation that puzzled Dr. W. The patient had been talking about a previous doctor whom the patient found to be "about the most difficult person to talk to that he had ever tried to talk to, because every time he said anything the doctor always asked him why he said it. He said that even one time when he saw the doctor downtown and asked him if the children with him were his own, the next day the doctor called him and asked him why he said that. He said it hadn't bothered him so much when the doctor first told him that he was willfully resisting treatment, but it did later on. . . . It was because of this remark by the doctor that he didn't return to that hospital this time. He stated that the way he was treated there was the reason he had such difficulty getting started in our interviews here, and said it was the reason that he didn't know what to expect from me and why I had difficulty in getting him to talk. Then I asked him why it was so important that he had to know just what this doctor meant. . . ."

What has transpired in this interaction? The patient has complained about the previous doctor who has always either asked why ("why did you say that?") or has accusingly confronted him ("you are willfully resisting getting better"). He was saying that he could not go back to such an individual and was warning his new therapist to avoid these very tools, the aggressive confrontations that Dr. W had always assumed to be an essential part of the psychotherapeutic armamentarium. Deprived of his major tool, Dr. W had responded with the same irritated "why" that his patient had so explicitly warned against, and then was puzzled that his patient would not—could not—respond on this level. He said to his supervisor that he didn't know what impelled him to try to "go further" than the patient. And in his statement about the interview with the patient he said, "I didn't understand at all what the patient was trying to do." In his counterreacting to the patient, Dr. W did, of course, give evidence of understanding all too well, but not yet in a way that could be turned usefully and therapeutically.

Dr. W could suddenly see a pattern emerging in his three therapy hours with the patient that week. The next hour he now felt was occupied with the same problems and he felt discouraged over it. The lack of "being with each other" had degenerated into an argument between himself and the patient. The patient, too, felt this quite consciously and had said as he left that "he was sorry that things had gone this way this hour, but that maybe we can get something done next time." During this hour Dr. W had taken notes with the patient, though he had never done so before. He explained this to his supervisor by saying that he had become upset at the "sloppiness" of the notes he reconstructed afterwards. But now that he had taken them, he wasn't so sure that they were any more helpful. Dr. Baehr said that he was struck by the fact that immediately after an interview in which Dr. W felt bewilderment at what was going on, he resorted to taking notes, as if to master the source of confusion in this way. Dr. W guessed that that was so; he had certainly not been aware of this.

Dr. W said that all of this was somewhat depressing; he had missed so much. This problem of confrontation, of what it was, and the place it occupied in psychotherapy ramified widely in all his efforts. He now felt both bewildered and deprived. Dr. Baehr responded to this feeling with words of encouragement. Surely there were these problems, but on the other hand this patient (unlike the first two) did stick and did keep coming through, and a stronger relationship with him was being forged all the time. At this point Dr. W described his discussion of the case with Dr. Williams, the surgeon, centering around the question as to the kind and timing of whatever surgical intervention might be indicated for the patient's very severe and disfiguring torticollis. He commented on what a "good egg" Dr. Williams was, how easy it was to come to agreement with him, how willing Dr. Williams was to accommodate himself to our psychiatric handling. They had together outlined a program of physiotherapy with ultimate surgical correction, if necessary, and Dr. W had said that it would be worked out with the patient one step at a time. Thus, metaphorically, Dr. W reinforced the statement he had made directly to his supervisor the previous day, that these staff men and authority figures could be worked with, and that one could even learn from them. That he said this on the eve of his formal evaluation gives a clue to the mixed motivations of the statement. How much is it a real working out of inhibiting difficulties and how much is it a reluctant submission to the supervisor, who with all the difficulties in the process is proving that he has something "new" to offer? At the very end of this supervision hour Dr. W said that he still had to take up his possible leaving and the transferring of his patient. He didn't know why he hadn't yet, but he had at least five more hours with the patient. He supposed that would be time enough.

The next week the formal evaluation conference took place, marking the completion of the first three months of working together. The supervisor began, before they read and discussed their separately written assessments of the work done to date, by stating that he had taken up the whole problem of available time with the administrative authorities and that it would be possible, if it were desirable, to maintain Dr. W's work with his patient, and with official supervision for it, for another three months, just as with the other students. The evaluation material could be discussed in this framework. If they were to decide on recommending to the administration that they go on together, they could discuss the patient, whether Dr. W should stay with this one, and if so, how to backtrack on a termination process already set into motion.

They then turned to the evaluation statements. There was a real concordance in the discussion of the technical aspects of Dr. W's work; his learning problems were delineated around his increasing awareness of his characteristic reaction tendencies in dealing with his patients, and his increasing consciousness of his conceptions of the nature of the therapeutic process. But there were also real differences—in the discussion of Dr. W's problems about learning. Dr. W put it this way, "The thing that strikes me most is your freedom to discuss the problems that have existed between *us* and my own reluctance to do so." Dr. Baehr said that he was likewise struck by this. He wondered what it might mean. Did Dr. W feel that these difficulties had been resolved to the point where they no longer affected the teaching situation? Or could it be, rather, that they were currently reactivated, perhaps around the threatened termination of the supervision and the evaluation process?

Dr. W said that evidently all these things were still active. He had very much felt that in their tense third hour together, they had brought out some of these feelings to the point where a workable—and profitable—relationship between them became possible, but the problems he knew were still present, and he had sought in a sense to leave well enough alone, not raise them again by writing about them in the evaluation report. So he had confined himself strictly to a discussion of his own capacities—and improvement—in his work with the patient. He raised, too, the question of confidentiality. He hesitated to put down on paper things that were so revealing about himself and how he related to his supervisor. Dr. Baehr responded that here Dr. W was raising a question that he had to take on the basis of faith—faith in the supervisor's integrity and his use of such material only within the framework of increasing his possible help to his student in this learning situation. That these records were as confidential and inviolable to possible misuse as any others would have to go without saying.

Dr. W then went on. He said that he had looked on that "showdown" hour as valuable "therapy" for himself. He said, "I mean it seriously. I learned a lot. I could see that, just as I had affect in the situation, so did you. But you were able to keep your problems, whatever they are, out of it. Maybe you got help with it, too. I don't know, but in any case, as far as I was concerned, you could keep yourself out of it and still help me. I learned a lot from that, not only here, but for my work with patients. . . . But I figured that was enough therapy. Not that I can't use more, but I figured that now I was able to focus on my problems with my patients and I wanted your help with that."

In saying this, Dr. W, of course, was stating that an affectively-charged process in which he learned something about himself and his own interpersonal relationships was "therapy," and as such to be gotten out of his learning situation just as rapidly as possible. He was also divorcing his problems about learning and about working with colleagues from his learning problems in working with patients, rather than seeing how what was perceived in one way in one relationship was projected into another relationship with a different purpose under another guise. Dr. W would indeed have liked to make a clear separation, and focus henceforth on only one side of the coin.

To all this the supervisor responded that the reason he was raising this issue again was the fact that he again felt it to be threatening the most effective use of their time together. He mentioned that for the last three appointments Dr. W had come a little later each time until he came twenty minutes late that day. This did cut drastically into their time together. Dr. W said slowly, "Yes, you're right. I've been aware of the latenesses. I have a good excuse for each time, I suppose, but they're really all irrelevant. I don't want to offer excuses." He went on, "What it comes down to is, yes, this problem is still there. What I think I have learned is that it's not just you personally, but a general discomfort with people in your position who I feel have more on the ball than I do intellectually. When I was preparing my paper on 'Headache' for the Journal Club, I read that article on the subject by Fromm-Reichmann. She makes the point that, dynamically, headachy people often have tremendous repressed hostility against people who they feel have superior mental endowments. My immediate thought was of my relationship with you and all the headaches I have around here. And then there was the day I had that terrible headache and I told you I wanted some sympathy. We went to lunch together and I just kept talking to you about all kinds of things, and by the time lunch was over my headache was gone."

Dr. Baehr said that with all these difficulties it was quite something for Dr. W to be in the position now of trying to decide whether he wanted to go on and be exposed to more of this—in addition to keeping up with all his obligations—time commitments, progress notes, etc.—while he was carrying a full clinical load in his new assignment. To this Dr. W stoutly remarked, "But I do want to go on. This is the most meaningful supervision I ever had. I want more of it. There's really so much to learn compared with what I know." Which is indeed a long way for this student—who denied the difference, who could see nothing new and nothing to be learned—to have come.

And out of this discussion came a joint decision to recommend to the administration that they go on for another period together, at which point the conference focused back on the patient. Dr. W wanted to continue with the same patient, but wondered what he could say to him. Dr. Baehr said that Dr. W could tell the patient that, contrary to what he had originally thought, more time was available (just as his supervisor had done with him), and he could then give the patient a choice. They could spend an additional three months together, with an opportunity to work out as much as possible in that interval, and, if still necessary, to be transferred to another therapist then, as against being transferred right now to someone else who could promise him a more stable time arrangement. Dr. W wondered how the patient might react to this threatened deprivation and then about-face offer of additional time together. Dr. Baehr said he didn't know. A variety of ways were possible. The patient could look at Dr. W as a rejecting and uninterested individual who took away and gave back with no consideration of how upsetting this was. Or he could look at his therapist as someone with so much interest in him that he went to bat to secure more time for the patient. Or anything in between. One doubts that the analogy to the supervisory situation was lost on Dr. W. In any case, the supervisor went on to make it more explicit, stating that whatever it was, it could be used in the situation between therapist and patient, just as a similar threat of termination and then reversal of a tentative decision had been used in supervision to set the whole discussion in focus. Dr. W smiled at this.

Of course, there is much in the above that was administratively avoidable. In many clinical centers with psychiatric training programs six-month shifts in assignments are the rule, despite the difficulties this creates for sustained psychiatric, especially psychotherapeutic, treatment. On top of this Dr. W was in the odd position of having but a three-month assignment to a clinical service where psychotherapy training and supervision were available. Added to this was the fact that it was not grasped until almost the last minute that this could be less rigidly worked out, so that he could continue with at least the one patient and the supervision for that experience. But even with these far from ideal administrative arrangements, helpful psychological use could be made of the turn of events, as supervisor and student by now agreed.

The session was then up and the student said, referring to the evaluation, "That was very hard to do." The supervisor indicated that he knew it. The student had one final—technical—question; he asked about his newly acquired habit of taking notes when he was with the patient. Dr. Baehr indicated that this must have some real meaning in terms of what Dr. W was trying to tell both his patient and his supervisor. They could discuss it at length in the next supervisory hour if Dr. W wished. Dr. W got up to go and said, "This has been a good hour."

At this point of evaluation and review we can take leave of this process that we have been attempting to follow in sufficient detail to convey an appreciation of the ebb and flow of this "middle game" of chess. The variations in its further working out in this case, and in all others, are, of course, numberless—limited only by the myriad problems and hiatuses of the student and the skill, ingenuity, and forbearance brought to bear on them by the supervisor. The particular example we have chosen seems to us to have lent itself especially well to a study of the complex interplay of the component aspects of the supervisory relationship. On the one hand is the constant struggle with the problems about learning mobilized by virtue of the process entered upon. On the other hand is the attempt to solve technical learning problems of therapeutic skills. As these reveal themselves to be different faces of the same coin, seen differently in each setting as the purposes of the setting differ, we also see how they at times mirror the teaching problems of the teacher—both his technical problems in teaching and his problems with the effective execution of his teaching function. And in this case we have seen the additional problems of having to deal with external administrative rules designed with broader considerations in mind than the learning and teaching situation that they regulate. All these complexities create difficulties that will persist all through the supervisory relationship, but despite them (or better, because of them), meaningful learning with development toward an increased level of competence can nevertheless take place.

XIV / *Supervision vs. Psychotherapy*

Since in the so-called psychical mode of cure, one personality has to act upon another . . . the treatment in most instances demands a second education of the physician.
—Baron Ernst von Feuchtersleben *

The history of training in psychotherapy has produced a rather curious dilemma for those who are responsible for present-day training patterns. This dilemma has led to efforts at resolution of the existing problems which often seem to be irreconcilable. A number of examples presenting different historic positions, which were taken as training convictions and have been developed in the various clinical professions, should suffice to acquaint us with the range of current notions concerning psychotherapy training and the role of supervision in that training.

It is approximately forty years since formal training was established in the European centers of psychoanalysis, particularly the first Institutes in Berlin, in Vienna, and in Budapest. The first pioneers, the founding fathers of psychoanalytic training, as it were, had themselves almost no formal training, only a rather short analytic experience with Freud, and certainly very little academic training compared with the extensive four- and five-year academic programs that modern institutes have developed. Almost from the beginning, however, strong emphasis was laid upon the personal analysis, the training analysis or didactic

* Von Feuchtersleben, an Austrian medical psychologist, wrote this in 1853, three years before Freud was born.

analysis, as it was called, as the essential ingredient of training without which the psychoanalytic practitioner could not really be developed. Reading seminars and course work were underemphasized, and the personal therapeutic experience that would demonstrate to the future psychoanalytic practitioner "the existence of the unconscious" was held to be the cornerstone of training.

This original tradition, or rather basic conviction, of those responsible for training has had a long-lasting effect, which even today, when the notions about the nature of the training analysis have entirely changed, can still be found strongly entrenched in the minds of those responsible for training programs. The personal analysis is the *sine qua non* on which all factions agree, regardless of how much they otherwise differ, and which they frequently use as the solution to any kind of training problem that may arise. The advice, "The candidate needs more analysis," seems to be a frequent answer to almost any question that one may raise about training difficulties. The historical fact, then, is that it was recognized very early that a personal therapeutic experience is necessary for one who wants to devote his professional career to doing analytic work, and that this personal analysis is an essential element of training. One might say that in the early days of psychoanalysis the personal analysis constituted the major training vehicle and this training requirement was the one most relied upon to prepare the future analyst for his vocation. Many psychotherapeutic groups of varying theoretical persuasion have by today espoused the desirability of the future therapist having a therapeutic experience himself. Training for therapeutic work is looked upon with distrust in many quarters if a personal therapeutic experience is not one of its basic requirements.

As the European psychoanalytic training centers developed further, they instituted a series of more academic requirements and soon introduced what is today usually called supervisory analysis but is frequently still referred to as control analysis. The American term "control analysis" is a somewhat misleading translation of the German "Kontrollanalyse," since it gives the impression that the young analyst must be controlled, which is just one of the meanings of the German concept of "Kontrolle."

Very early during the history of analytic training a now classical debate, which is of particular interest to us, highlighted two different points of view regarding training. The Hungarians at that time, while endorsing the idea of control analysis (that is, the supervision of the analytical work of the young analyst), developed a special concept about the nature of this control analysis. Their feeling was that one could supervise the young analyst properly only if one really knew him well.* Most of his problems with the patient were considered reflections of residual problems he had with himself, countertransference problems; and who could help him better with these than his own analyst? It was proposed, therefore, that the first analytic control ought to be carried out most usefully by the candidate's personal analyst. This first control analysis was thus really a continuation of the candidate's own analysis, but with a new slant to it. His thoughts would now turn to his work with his patient, and as he would develop these thoughts while working with his own analyst, he would analyze his difficulties with his patient, that is, he would analyze his countertransference difficulties, see his blind spots, and thus become a better analyst. Control analysis was thus seen as a form of personal analysis, perhaps an advanced form, in which more stress would be laid on bringing in selected free associations, as it were, about the work with the patient. Such a philosophy indeed would make it very difficult to differentiate between the personal therapeutic experience and the supervisory experience. One grew out of the other, and could not be seen apart from it. That position, of course, hardly permits any attempt at clarification of the difference which is our concern here.

The opposite position was taken by the representatives of the Institute in Vienna who thought that the personal analyst should preferably not control the first case of his candidate. The candidate ought to be exposed to different points of view and should work with a person who would teach him rather than analyze him.† It was suggested that this control experience, rather than consisting of the analysis of his blind spots, or his countertransferences, should be strictly a didactic experience. The controller (in our language today, the supervisor) was to be strictly a teacher who would explain, correct, and direct; and he was to use an entirely didactic approach without touching the affective problems of the beginning analyst. If such problems arose, they would be referred back to the candidate's personal analyst (or he might be

* See Vilma Kovács, "Training and Control Analysis," *Int. J. Psychonal.*, 17:346–354, 1936, for a full statement of the Hungarian position.

† See Edward Bibring, "Report of Four Countries Conferences: I.T.C., Methods and Technique of Control Analysis." *Int. J. Psychoanal.*, 18:369, 1937, for the opposing position of the Vienna group.

required to go back into analysis), as though this indicated that he could not make proper use of a didactic teacher.

What has basically changed in modern-day psychoanalytic training can perhaps be summed up as follows: The original personal analysis, the "Lehranalyse," training analysis, or didactic analysis, as it was called, has changed into a therapeutic analysis. The literature abounds with illustrations which stress that the training analysis is essentially a therapeutic analysis. Some argue justifiably that the fact that this personal analysis is a training requirement creates certain therapeutic difficulties for the training analyst, and they have even thought of replacing the requirement of a personal analysis with a system in which the completed personal analysis is to be considered a prerequisite to acceptance for training rather than a requirement of the training itself. Unfortunately, this would not really alter the problem, since one who wanted to enter psychoanalytic training would create the very same psychological problems for himself as well as his analyst while in a "prerequisite therapeutic analysis." The fact, however, is that the original very short therapeutic experiences that analysts went through at the beginning of formalized psychoanalytic training has given way to longer and longer analytic experiences. The stress is no longer on the "didactic," but rather on the "therapeutic," and it has become clearly recognized that one who is to practice psychoanalysis all his life may actually need a more thorough therapeutic analysis than other patients, because of the special provocations to which he is exposed in his work.

At the same time, the original notion that supervision and the personal analysis should not really be separated has given way to a basic conviction, certainly in the United States, that these two phases of training should be separated, that they have different functions and should be carried out by different people. On the other hand, a large number of teachers in our field no longer claim that supervision—that is, the "control analysis"—should be simply a didactic form of teaching. Supervisors or control analysts agree more and more, even though there still are wide divergences of opinion, that counter-transference problems, the relationship of the candidate to the supervisor, and the affective problems of learning and of treating patients, must all be considered by therapist and supervisor. The divergences of opinion are today more over specific methods which the controller should use in order to solve difficulties as these arise during the course of the "control analysis."

A parallel historical development that has greatly influenced present methods in psychotherapy training has taken place in social work. Social work schools, which have trained casework practitioners, have made especially valuable contributions to the development of supervisory techniques. While psychoanalysis early put great emphasis on the personal analysis as the keystone of training, teachers of social workers have put the main emphasis on supervision. We think of one outstanding social work leader who, at a time when it seemed important for him to stress the difference between social work practice and psychotherapy, insisted that the social worker does not need a personal analysis. He felt that the personal analysis was the training requirement for the psychoanalyst, while personal supervision stood in like stead for the social caseworker. He saw personal analysis for the social worker not really as an aid to training, but rather as a potential therapeutic necessity for a sick person.

These two extreme positions, while having developed independently in two different professions, nevertheless represent the present-day range of conviction about training in psychotherapy. There are some residency programs for psychiatrists where the belief is firmly held that no psychotherapeutic training can be undertaken unless the young psychiatrist undergoes a therapeutic experience himself, a personal analysis as a basic requirement which will enable him to do therapeutic work. There are other training centers that stress supervision as the chief requirement, although it is conceded in these centers that a therapeutic experience may frequently be useful and at times perhaps essential. Thus, modern training has at different times placed different emphases on the importance and significance of the personal therapeutic experience for the future practitioner on the one hand, and the supervision of his work on the other. The tendency today seems to be to emphasize the desirability of both forms of experience as a part of clinical training.

In actual practice, however, different centers have developed training patterns which indicate differences in conviction concerning the importance of the one or the other. These differences are in part natural expressions of practical developments. Training requirements, after all, are not simply a function of inner conviction as to what is really essential, but are also a reflection of specific historic situations in different parts of the country. Newly developed areas will need to rely on many practitioners who may not be able to meet the exacting requirements of areas that have had more time to elevate their standards. One needs only to look at job descriptions for the main clinical professions in the different parts of our country in order to realize that the question of adequate training requirements is in part a problem of supply and demand. We all know that training of clinical personnel in no way meets the existing needs, and this very fact must influence training patterns as they exist. The vast social needs and the rapidly expanding programs to meet them make it necessary to make concessions to the practical.

One who becomes a teacher in a specific training center, then, cannot work effectively if he wants to function only in terms of the ideal personal training requirements that he would like to see enforced. Rather he must become the representative of the training system and identify himself with its existing requirements, even though he may want to contribute toward change designed to improve its standards. Such a point of view is not to imply that training convictions are only pragmatic issues, adaptations to existing realities, but it does stress the necessity of identifying with the existing reality to the extent of accepting the fact that such conditions can only be changed slowly.

Our own practical experience, and we speak now not about psychoanalytic training but about the training of practitioners in psychotherapy as it is undertaken in psychiatric residency programs, indicates that most psychotherapists who wish to learn the techniques of "intensive psychotherapy" will benefit greatly from a personal analytical experience. It is not likely that many people can be found who can function independently and adequately as psychotherapists unless they do have such an experience. We have, of course, found some extremely gifted people, "naturals" as it were, who could do very well without such a personal experience. And it is hard to believe that in the present state of affairs our training programs for psychotherapy, whether they concern psychiatrists, social workers, or clinical psychologists, will make personal analysis a standard requirement.

For the present we are highly in favor of such an experience, and hope that means can somehow be found to help the future psychotherapeutic practitioner carry the financial burden of such a program. At the same time we must point out that many a clinician has been doing fine psychotherapeutic work without such an experience, particularly if he was trained to recognize his own limitations and only to undertake treatment programs within his competence. The lack of personal analysis can frequently be made up through the continued help of supervisors and consultants, as well as through the opportunities afforded when working in an institutional setting rather than in private practice.

Whenever one subscribes to training standards, basic requirements that seem to be the most useful for the large numbers of trainees, one should remember that such requirements at times represent an undue harshness to the few for whom a more flexible, more personalized training program ought to be instituted. This is, of course, true of all training, since all training standards must have the "average student" in mind, rather than exceptional persons.

The personal analysis, in both its therapeutic effect and its training effect, has been discussed in numerous contributions. It is suggested that one can only work with the unconscious of another person when he has learned to work with his own, has relived his infantile neurosis, freed himself from its terrors, and has resolved his basic conflicts. He will have identified with his analyst and through this identification will have acquired a method of understanding himself; and he will have worked as well toward a method enabling him to understand others. It has frequently been argued by people less disposed toward this requirement that such personal experience may also foster indoctrination, the feeling of belonging to a select group, of being one of the initiates and therefore different from the others. These group phenomena are true for any form of training and do not make the personal analysis any less valuable, although it is of course desirable that the personal analytical experience yield more than this. And the danger is not denied that such identification with a teaching elite may frequently make the future practitioner uncritical, overidentified with orthodox opinion, dogmatic, and resistant to scientific experimentation. The purpose of the personal therapeutic experience is not to inculcate the faithful, but rather to open the way to genuine new insights into a method. There will be times as the young practitioner is going through his personal experience when he may feel like an initiate to a religion. Only a thorough analysis, a thorough therapeutic experience, will free him from such aspects of dependency, faulty group allegiance, and lack of the internal and external criticism so necessary in a young science and a young profession.

The question might also then be asked as to whether the student of psychotherapy might benefit from "analytically-oriented psychotherapy" alone without having to go through the expensive and lengthy standard analytic procedure if he did not plan to become a practicing analyst. This question might be prompted by the feeling that the general psychotherapeutic practitioner, like the medical general practitioner, can do with a less thorough therapeutic experience. This stand is fortified by the social fact of the large number of human sufferers who ought to have some form of help, even if it is very little. A poorly trained person is therefore considered better than nothing. This point of view is a perfect rationalization for the lowering of standards, and we cannot subscribe to it.

Another feeling behind the question asked might concern the psychiatrist's personal psychotherapeutic experience, not in terms of the social need, but in terms of his own individual need. He may need a form of help different from what is indicated in a program of classical analysis. In analytic training centers it is, of course, felt that one who cannot make use of the classical analytical experience and is in need of a modified psychotherapeutic program should not attempt to become a psychoanalyst. One might take the same stand as far as the general psychotherapeutic practitioner is concerned, and would then argue that the psychotherapist ought to be analyzed with the standard procedure. This answer, however, overlooks the fact that there are a variety of individuals with whom certain modifications are indicated, at least for certain phases of the therapeutic experience, and who nevertheless are gifted people who can do excellent psychotherapeutic work. There is no question that a number of very sensitive clinical practitioners have developed out of students who brought serious emotional problems into their own therapeutic experience. Some of these sensitive individuals, perhaps because they had a brush with severe mental difficulties, have made extraordinary contributions to our field. The problem of the proper selection of psychiatric students, in spite of all the research that has been done in this area, has not yet been solved; there are no answers as to what kinds of pathological problems should exclude a person from training. We have been able to give answers for certain definite signs of mental illness, of severe psychopathology, but we have insufficient experience in many wide areas.

The third possible interpretation of the question asked, namely, that many psychiatrists cannot afford during their training period to undertake the responsibility of a personal analysis, may be countered by pointing to his future excellent earning power. A more severe difficulty, of course, arises in those areas of our country where an intensive analytically oriented psychotherapy may be available but where there are no analysts for the student. The lack of availability of analytic time may make it necessary for the resident to move to centers where analysis is available; or he may have to use whatever is to be had in his community.

We are quite aware that our stand on this issue will be considered by some as biased, and we want it understood only as a general answer which may not necessarily be true for every student of psychotherapy. In spite of our wish to improve standards and to define training requirements, we feel equally strongly about the necessity to keep the field open and flexible, to be ready for exceptions and for changes, and to take a point of view which, rather than insisting on the dogmatic strengthening of training convictions, is based on constant experimentation, on constant re-evaluation of training results, and on a constant readiness to learn from experience.

The question under discussion could also take another form such as: Suppose someone wanted to do non-directive ("client-centered") psychotherapy, would he possibly benefit from a personal psychotherapeutic experience? Should his personal psychotherapeutic experience likewise be nondirective? Or psychoanalysis? Or individual psychology? Or a Jungian analysis? These questions hint at some of the problems that exist today in psychotherapy training. We would usually assume that the best psychotherapeutic experience would be one that is more or less based on the same theoretical principles that the psychotherapeutic practitioner will himself use. If this is the case, then, one cannot help but wonder at times as to what the true purposes of this personal experience might be. Most, if not all, "schools of psychotherapy" or "schools of psychoanalysis" would insist, we believe, that the personal therapeutic experience be within the framework of the same "school of thought." Is this an ideological or a political conviction? How much does this reflect the merely political needs of the group that carries out the training? How far do we want the young psychotherapist to be identified with the views of the one who treated him? How can one block the type of school formation that precludes collaboration between different schools of thought, exchanges of opinion, experimentation, and prevents us from having an open mind? But are there not also equally strong dangers in the development of an eclectic point of view, which actually destroys the creative search and sees virtue in the notion that there is something good in everything, and that no strong beliefs must be held? It was once jokingly remarked,

"In my father's house there are many mansions but it must be understood: My father is an analyst." This suggests that tolerance in itself is no virtue if it is not structured by a clear purpose and a clear understanding of the function carried. Tolerance with purpose and with strength is certainly preferable to a chaotic ideological confusion hidden behind a front of pseudo-scientific respectability and a pseudo-democratic attitude which accepts everything except a clear identity of purpose.

It is our opinion, then, that the personal psychotherapeutic experience is, with but few exceptions, essential for the psychotherapeutic practitioner, and should be highly recommended to him, although most training centers are not as yet ready to make it an explicit requirement. But we favor a recommendation instead of a requirement, since the development of training patterns has not yet yielded sufficient experience to back up our impressions with reliable statistics. The personal supervision of the psychotherapist-to-be should not compete with his personal therapeutic experience. Neither experience is to take the place of the other.

This brings us then to the task of discussing the place of personal supervision within the system of psychotherapy training. If personal supervision were simply a didactic experience in which a body of knowledge is transmitted, not much would have to be said at this point about its function. Our purpose though is to describe supervision—that is, the supervisory process—not simply as the transmission of knowledge and skills, but rather as a complex process that goes on between the supervisor and his student. This process is a helping process in which the student is being helped to discover his problems as a psychotherapist, to resolve them with the help of the supervisor, and to develop toward higher integrations as a learner and as a psychotherapist. This process includes affective problems, interpersonal conflicts, problems in being helped, as well as in helping, and is therefore truly itself a helping process.

The central issue of this chapter can be understood, then, as a question as to whether the supervisory process is not really a hidden form of psychotherapy, since so many of its elements as described in our other chapters are the very same elements we find in therapeutic processes. The affective relationship to the helper, the wish to change coupled with the resistance to change, the struggle about being dependent, the unconscious repetitive ways of taking hold of a problem and of attempting to master new experiences, the link of past helping experiences with the present helping experience; all these issues seem to find their counterparts in the therapeutic process on the one hand, and in the supervisory process on the other. The one who would claim that there is no difference between the two processes could quote example after example from this book, in which the beginning student seems to be pictured as a person suffering from severe psychopathology, and in which the solution to his problem seems to find him then in a less pathological state. Could one not claim that supervision really was disguised psychotherapeutic help? One might say that the supervisor's suggestion to the student, "What do you want to discuss today concerning your case?," is not too different from the analyst's suggestion that the patient talk about whatever comes to his mind. One could go on and suggest that transference and countertransference manifestations, identifications with the helper, even the repetitive working through of problems, are alike in both processes. Both processes are described as affective processes. Such observations would seem to wipe out the differences between psychotherapy and supervision.

In delineating the essential differences between the psychotherapeutic process and the supervisory process, perhaps we can turn first to a similar problem of conceptualization raised by Bertram Lewin in a recent publication * where he discussed the various uses to which the method of free association can be put. Usually one thinks of free association as an intrinsic part of the psychoanalytic method, and assumes then that its purpose would necessarily be to uncover the unconscious. It is indeed true that free association can be used toward this purpose and will yield results which are defined by the purpose, as well as by the method employed. Lewin convincingly shows, however, that the *method* of free association can be put to many other uses—to many other purposes.

Let us, therefore, consider a solitary individual who is contemplating his own thoughts, feelings, memories and impulses. Let him approximate Freud's idea of free association by having him limit action to a minimum and by letting him put his mental processes into words with no care for style or form. That he should report these words to anyone is, for the time being,

* Bertram D. Lewin, "Dream Psychology and the Analytic Situation," *Psa. Quart.*, 24:169–199, 1955. The portions quoted are condensed from pages 180–184.

irrelevant. In any event, we have as yet no "analysis," not even a self-analysis, for many persons have used very much this method of introspection for many purposes.

Freud tells us that he came upon this method of giving free rein to the contents of consciousness in the writings of the German author, Boerne. In an essay, The Art of Becoming an Original Writer in Three Days (1827), Boerne concludes his exposition with the following words: "Take a sheet of paper and for three days in succession write down, without any falsification or hypocrisy, everything that comes into your head. Write what you think of yourself, of your women, of the Turkish War, of Goethe, of the Funk criminal case, of the Last Judgment, of those senior to you in authority—and when the three days are over, you will be amazed at what novel and startling thoughts have welled up in you. This is the art of becoming a writer in three days." Boerne evidently intended to use the scribbling as the raw material for his literary work. He had as his purpose the liberation of the imagination, or as we might prefer to say, the exploration of the preconscious system, for the advancement of literary composition. In *The Interpretation of Dreams* (Standard Edition, IV, p. 102), Freud calls attention to Schiller's use of a method very like free association for the same purpose. *We see, therefore, that from the start analysts have known that there was involved not merely a way of thinking, but also purposes and intentions that determined its use.* (italics ours)

These intentions may be various. . . . As Boerne took notes for literary composition, so Jung (and in part, Silberer) used associations and reveries for metaphysical and mythological constructions. . . .

Given any fantasy which arises during free and solitary ruminations, such as Silberer's while he gazed into his crystal globe, it is clear that one or another feature will be more likely to impress the observer when he retrospectively assesses them, and that he will be guided by his purposes, special interests and education. One observer will be struck by the similarity of the given fantasy to ideas he held as a child or which possibly he has heard expressed by children. Another person, with little empathy for children but well-versed in cultural history or anthropology, will be more aware that the fantasy resembles a certain series of myths. Consequently, the first observer would ultimately try to construct a psychology of the child, while the second might contribute to anthropology or the history of culture. A third observer, departing from the principle of putting the fantasy into words and running into complex reveries and unusual absorbed states, might come to accept these manifest, processed, ideas and qualities as the final desiderata of the method. Still another observer could ignore all the frames of reference mentioned; in fact from Zilboorg's account (1952) of Francis Galton's use of the method, an academic psychologist of the old school, interested in the study of the mind according to the old canons of the science, might view the associations simply as novel, static "enlargements of consciousness." Clearly, all such observers have brought to the field their own measures and coordinates. . . .

There are doubtless many other purposes that free association might be made to serve. Those mentioned are: 1, literary creation; 2, psychological science; 3, mystical experience; 4, ethical and philosophical guidance or inspiration; 5, therapy. As a drug is only *materia medica* in itself and variously utilizable for experiment or therapy or pleasure, so are free associations capable of varied employment. They can be elaborated, superseded, used "anagogically" for moral illumination, or permitted to lead to buried memories, according to the interests and intentions, conscious or unconscious, of the self-observer.

This same kind of distinction holds true, as well, for the essential difference between supervision and psychotherapy. Lewin has cogently shown that the therapeutic process of the psychoanalyst and the creative process of the writer can each make use of the very same element—free associations—and weld this element in accord with its own purposes. In the same way, both supervision and psychotherapy are interpersonal helping processes working with the same affective components, with the essential difference between them created by the difference in purpose. Though both are helping processes, the purpose of the helping experience is different. Whatever practical problems the patient may bring to his psychotherapist, they are always viewed in the light of the main task: the resolution of inner conflict. Whatever personal problems the student may bring to his supervisor, they are likewise always seen in terms of the main task: leading him toward greater skill in his work with his patients. While it is true that the patient may occasionally benefit in practical matters, or perhaps even from direct practical advice, and while it is equally true that the student will frequently benefit in a personal sense, they have made these gains in the course of following the main purpose of their relationship with the helper. If the main purpose of a relationship is maintained throughout, the difference is clearly apparent between the type of relationship called psychotherapy and the one called supervision.

Why is it that the one who becomes acquainted with a training method such as that described in these pages so frequently feels tempted to think of it first in terms of psychotherapy? We believe that this has to do with a special learning problem which is perhaps typical for most of us. The one confronted with something new will try at first to reduce the new to the familiar. The psychotherapist who becomes a teacher of psychotherapy will frequently be tempted to fall back on skills that represent prior acquisitions. He will thus try to convert the teaching relationship into a therapeutic relationship. Or he may defend himself against this temptation by rigorously avoiding any aspects of a "therapeutic" relationship and by becoming a teacher who remains simply "didactic." However, as he learns to truly identify with his training purpose, which is to teach psychotherapeutic skills, he will not deny the student as well as himself the opportunity to make maximum use of what goes on between them, of what blocks or frees learning and teaching, just because these same elements are put to a different purpose and in a different light in the psychotherapeutic process.

In accord with the difference in purpose is the manner in which the different goals of the two processes are determined. In psychotherapy the patient essentially sets his own goals, with the clarification afforded by his consideration of them jointly with the therapist, and with the proviso always that these goals may change as the therapeutic process itself develops and makes for change. The therapist has no vested interest in any particular degree or direction of change. In supervision, on the other hand, the clinical setting, whose representative is the supervisor, sets both its requirements and its goals in terms of standards of professional performance and clinical service currently rendered and to be attained. The institution thus furnishes the external yardstick which both supervisor and student must measure up to.

To fulfill his side of the contract, the supervisor has a quantifiable body of knowledge that he wishes, through this process, to convey in such a way that it becomes usable to the learner, part of his therapeutic armamentarium; and in coming to supervision, the student states his desire to acquire this body of knowledge. The teacher in that sense has a mission and an investment in the student. Though the patient can quit the therapeutic situation almost whenever he so desires, the student cannot leave the supervisor without significant professional consequences. When the patient asks, "What are you trying to do to me?" this question is seen as a reflection of his transference expectations and fears. The same question on the part of the student, though it must likewise be understood within the fabric of his interpersonal expectations, has at the same time a reality-determined answer—to try to make a better therapist out of the student as enjoined by the contract under which the two came together. The student is, after all, a professional colleague—someone who, it is hoped, will take his place alongside the supervisor as a co-worker; who will ultimately do the things the supervisor does, including possibly supervision itself. Herein lie the particular gratifications of the supervisory task, which differ from those of therapeutic work in their more explicit focus on the mutual achievement of a designated outcome. (And herein lie, too, the pitfalls created by the vested interests of the supervisor and by his susceptibility to outer pressures.)

These differences in the nature of the two relationships which flow from the essential difference in purpose can perhaps be best demonstrated if we utilize a case illustration of supervisory work with a student who had just completed her personal analysis. She had considerable clinical experience, was well versed in psychotherapy, but was starting her first analytic control case. Her psychoanalytic experiences had helped her considerably in a personal sense, and she was felt to be indeed ready to undertake the next part of her analytic training, the psychoanalysis of a patient under supervision.

In choosing this example, we have departed from our more usual procedure in this book, where we have been using clinical material gleaned mainly from the work of psychotherapeutic beginners, who for the most part had not as yet had a personal therapeutic experience. These beginners frequently gave the impression that they had to cope with a degree of personal pathology that could rightly necessitate a prior personal therapeutic experience and might indeed make one feel pessimistic about the usefulness of supervision for them. Their "pathology" at times seemed to be of such high degree and so inappropriate that the temptation must have arisen to treat them rather than to teach them, and to confuse the supervisory process with the psychotherapeutic process. While it is clear to one who has worked with many beginning students that what looks like special pathology is often just the appropriate, although frequently exaggerated, reaction to typical learning situations, it may nevertheless prove helpful to show a learning problem which confronts an analyzed candidate for psychoanalytic training while in supervision. In this case there was no question, we believe, of any need for further analysis (as could also be confirmed from the later training record of this particular student). Nevertheless, problems arose which are crucial for this discussion, whose aim is to clarify the differences between the supervisory and the therapeutic processes.

The psychoanalytic candidate, Dr. L, had assumed responsibility for the treatment of a young woman with a basic hysterical personality patterning, with severe symptoms of hysterical vomiting, and complicated phobic arrangements to avoid situations that might stimulate her symptoms, which made eating in the presence of others all but impossible for her. During the early phase of the analysis an important problem, which the candidate frequently reported in her control hour, concerned the fact that the patient never referred in any way to the analytical situation, to the relationship between herself and the analyst. She made no comments whatsoever about the analyst and seemed "to show no signs of transference." It was as if transference feelings in fact did not exist. However, the patient did talk a great deal about her aunt, who had played a considerable part in her upbringing, the mother having died during the patient's infancy. But even when she talked about the aunt, the patient succeeded in keeping out all reference to personal and intimate feelings, just as she did within the analytical situation itself. The aunt was described in a pseudo-objective way, and even if one would want to use the patient's associations about the aunt as a displacement from the analyst, the fact remains that this shadowy displaced transference was empty, without feeling, and the aunt was not seen as significant in any way in terms of the patient's problem.

It was quite clear from the content of the patient's material that the dynamics of this behavior and of her acting-out were that the analyst was so important and so very much the object of many conflict-laden wishes and impulses that this constricted, inhibited patient dared not talk about her, lest the vomiting as well as the phobic arrangements themselves be brought into the analytical situation. While it was clear, then, to the observer of this process as to just how immensely important the analyst really was for this particular patient, the patient succeeded, through directly ignoring her therapist in the overt material and in thus implying that the therapist was of no great importance to her, in striking a responsive chord in Dr. L. Within the supervision with Dr. James, Dr. L acknowledged how she had started to feel that maybe the patient was right. Dr. L did feel that she herself was really unimportant. On this particular level she experienced the patient's implications, not as a description of a specific phase of the transference neurosis, but as an accurate estimate of herself. She was unimportant. Much as she understood the theory of the transference reaction, she wondered how she herself could really ever bulk so large in the psychic life of another person. And perhaps, too, she was afraid to be "important," to be the recipient of the patient's infantile projections. We frequently refer to such reactions on the part of the analyst as countertransference reactions and can understand quite well how such reactions would make it impossible for Dr. L to interpret the patient's behavior correctly and with conviction, so that both would find it impossible to move out of the therapeutic impasse.

Thinking of our young students who for the most part had no therapeutic experiences of their own, one might easily suggest that the tendency of our young analyst to depreciate herself should be considered an unresolved personal conflict of hers. One could say that the patient merely tapped the latent predisposition to this difficulty, which became manifest as soon as the patient's material—in this case, lack of direct reference to the therapist, and indications that she, the therapist, just like the aunt, did not count—corresponded to the present low self-estimate of our candidate. This would be an effort to cast the problem as a personal problem, requiring perhaps again a psychotherapeutic resolution. Should this candidate be sent back into analysis?

This same incident, however, also lends itself to a variety of other conceptualizations, whose range can perhaps clarify some of the basic issues of personal therapy as against the supervision of therapeutic work. For instance, the problem could also be seen as one that has to do with the inexperience of our analytic candidate in the technique she is to learn, as a problem of just "not knowing." If this were the case, didactic information on the part of the controller would suffice to turn the trick. Our first answer that she ought to have more treatment for herself would correspond to the early conviction in psychoanalytic training that the personal analysis really was the essential preparation for the future analyst. The second solution would correspond to the notion that supervision ought to consist only of the giving of technical information in a didactic form.

Neither solution is quite applicable, however, since, actually, as it turned out in the supervisory situation, the therapist did indeed "know" what the transference situation was in this particular case. She had accurately perceived the nature of the psychologic dilemma of the patient. She had correctly understood the patient as saying, "Keep away from me. If you stay uninvolved, then I can control myself and my symptoms on my own. I have never allowed myself direct feelings about my mother's early death, about the meaning of my aunt for me.

I could master the loss, as well as the intruder into my life with father, by denying any affects, any direct involvement, and I repeat now in the transference a situation which permits me to keep buried the very problems which feed my symptomatology." Dr. L had even understood that she had acted in accord with the patient's neurotically-determined request. She had stayed away. She could see this and "knew" it. However, instead of using her understanding for interpretation in the direction of showing the patient the nature of the dilemma, she seemed to act out the patient's indirect command, and did so because she felt paralyzed by a feeling that, in spite of all, the patient was perhaps correct in her estimate of the analyst.

When Dr. James wondered with her about the discrepancy between the lack of true therapeutic action and the candidate's actual insight into the total situation, and then questioned its sources in her own self-depreciatory impulses, Dr. L discovered that these self-depreciatory impulses had more to do with her attitude toward the controller than toward the patient. She saw herself as the beginning student who could learn only—as actually she had also done in the past—when her respect for the teacher went hand in hand with self-depreciating attitudes. This indeed had been a problem in her own analysis and, while essentially settled in her private life, came up again from time to time, particularly in work situations in which she attempted to learn from another person. Her pseudo-ineffectiveness, her lack of freedom and spontaneity in using what she knew about the patient, when understood by her in the light of her attitudes toward the supervisory situation, gave way to a more spontaneous use of herself and to a more effective handling of the case.

The difficulty of this student was at that time primarily anchored in her beginning a new learning experience. It is quite typical for such new experiences, in beginning with a new teacher, that one may present oneself in the way that she did. In effect, she told Dr. James: "I am unimportant. You are the expert who will control things properly and you will keep me from making mistakes." Her feeling experienced with the patient, namely, that the patient was right, that she, the analyst, was unimportant, that she did not count and had no role in the life of the patient, as conflicting as it was with her theoretical understanding of the psychoanalytic process, can be considered here as the displaced feeling of her own attitude toward the supervisor. When viewed one way, we might suggest that the analyst had a problem, a countertransference problem with the patient whose transference depreciation of her she seemed to have to accept as realistic. When seen another way, we might suggest that she actually had, as well, a problem, a transference problem, with the supervisor; that she had to experience him like teachers of the past, or the parents of the past—big, powerful, all-knowing—with herself as unimportant, incompetent, and only daring to act when she had his permission and his direction, lest she lose his acceptance.

We have by now offered four different choices. We could consider Dr. L to be sick and suggest to her that she needs more personal analysis. We could consider her as uninformed and then provide her with didactic instruction. We could consider her ineffectiveness and her particular way of reacting to this kind of material as a particular kind of learning problem (or, in other language, a countertransference problem) aroused in the work with this patient. We could see the material as a reflection of a problem about beginning, about learning, with her teacher (a transference to the teacher). Inasmuch as Dr. James intended to supervise his student rather than to treat her, we would prefer not to use the language of transference in this context. We would rather restrict the concept of transference to the treatment situation where it is put to appropriate technical use as a vehicle of therapy; and in the supervisory situation with its different purpose we would cast interactions into the framework of problems about learning.

Each of these various answers that has been offered yields a model for the handling of the situation. In this particular instance, the fourth answer, that is, the clarification of feeling existing in the analytic candidate toward her supervisor during the beginning phase of learning, freed in her the spontaneity she needed, in order to make actual use of her past experience, as well as her theoretical understanding of the case situation. She could, then, discuss with her supervisor the actual skill problem of the best technical handling of the situation when the patient tries to keep the analyst out of effective contact with her.

This particular student had no need for personal help in the therapeutic sense. She did, however, have need for help in relation to the other areas presented. Supervision will be primarily concerned with the three areas which are implied in the second, third, and fourth ways of viewing our material. A reaction to a patient may actually turn out to be a disguised reaction to the teacher. These two reactions are nothing but two sides of a coin. It may occasionally be that by just flipping the coin we may find it more effective to treat the student's material, the student's questions which he brings into supervision, as a problem with the patient or as a learner's reaction to the supervisor.

Most supervisors, though, do not usually flip this coin. Rather they tend to use one or the other method as an expression of their personal predilections and their personal comfort. Some supervisors prefer to remain aloof, uninvolved, and somehow do not allow a direct consideration of the relationship between themselves and the students. They will prefer to discuss the problem with the patient, the "countertransference" difficulty. Some teachers might even prefer to take the matter completely out of the realm of learning problems and refer the discussion of this difficulty, seen only as a countertransference reflecting unresolved personal problems, back to the personal analyst of the candidate. Finally, there are those teachers who are unafraid of the direct use of the student-supervisor relationship and are willing to use it in the way indicated in our example.

We would hope, though, that a flexible generation of teachers could make choices among these four models of operation which derive from the specific problems and needs of the learner rather than from their personal preferences and their personal security as teachers. In this instance Dr. L found it easy to make use of the fourth method described, and thus could resolve the conflict she had about having to start again with a supervisor. Had she been a highly neurotic individual, unanalyzed, or very incompletely analyzed, this particular intervention of the supervisor, indeed, might not have been effective. The specific choice of method depends, therefore, on the particular problems of the student.

Experience with our students has shown us, however, that the model which was employed in this particular instance can be used much more frequently than is usually assumed. The dissolution of the existing difficulty between the supervisor and the student (the problem about learning) will often free the latter to consider didactic (technical) problems, and very frequently will also free him to look with more spontaneity, with more capacity for insight at his "countertransferences" (or his learning problems, depending on our frame of reference). He learns to realize that "countertransference," just as the transference manifestations of the patient, need not necessarily be a hindrance, a resistance to successful treatment, but frequently, if used correctly, takes on forms which lead to insights on the part of the therapist and actually help the treatment. It was stated by Freud that no treatment is possible without transference. Transference is the track on which treatment proceeds. One may indeed say the same about counter-transference. The free discussion of the student's relationship with the supervisor, and of the particular nature of his reactions to the patient, frequently forms the necessary groundwork which makes possible the discussion of theoretical and technical problems, and thus reintroduces the didactic issue. Occasionally it will become clear to a student that in spite of all learning, in spite of all progress that he is making toward enhanced skill, certain basic difficulties cannot be resolved outside the first of our four models, namely, the personal psychotherapeutic experience of the student, which then becomes essential should he wish to grow beyond the beginnings he has made.

We have suggested earlier in this chapter that the original solutions in teaching psychotherapy consisted in stressing the first two possibilities: the personal analysis, on the one hand, or technical, didactic instruction, on the other. The supervisory philosophy which is propounded here sees these answers as essential elements of learning and teaching. But it seeks to enrich these two methods through two additional technical models, and to synthesize all four models into a spontaneous and flexible method of psychotherapy training which is constantly reassessed and applied in its different variations in terms of the specific needs of each student. These needs, of course, will change as the learning process continues through one phase after another toward a goal which ultimately permits the student (with his teacher's help) to separate himself from learning and to arrive at a point of professional self-development and continued learning which can be carried out independently. This is analogous to the psychotherapeutic process in which we hope to help our patients to a point at which they have received sufficient help to continue alone, to use the acquired insights and the new ways of viewing themselves toward a better life, unaided by the personal helper.

We are no longer surprised that a psychotherapeutic experience cannot be considered final and that frequently our patients, and also we as therapists, need to go back into further treatment. The same may be true for the learner. He may need to go back into supervision again for a new experience of growth. A correct estimate of the nature of psychotherapeutic help and of supervisory help, as well, would be one in which such a return to a helping situation is not experienced as a defeat, as a loss of self-esteem, but rather would be a part of our *identification with the nature of helping*. One who is genuinely identified with helping other people in a way that does not make it necessary for him to look down on those whom he helps does not mind being helped himself if necessary. Only when helping, be it in the realm of psychotherapy or supervision, is beset by hidden attitudes of a condescending nature, or a sadistic nature, will this philosophy of being truly able to identify with both positions be impossible.

The teachers of psychotherapy should preferably be people who are identified with a philosophy such as we have described. Their students will then identify not only with their techniques, but also—and frequently this is much more important—with their basic attitudes toward the process of helping and of being helped. The true helper has humility rather than power motives toward the helping process. Such humility is a part of genuine self-acceptance, the basic ingredient without which the best of techniques will not bear fruit. Had Dr. James enjoyed Dr. L's feelings of unimportance, her admiration of the powerful teacher, and her dependence on him, he might have left untouched the very source of her difficulty, and might have driven her back into a situation where it might have appeared to her, as well as to him, that she was dealing with an ingrained neurotic pattern rather than a situational reaction with which both could easily cope. He might have then defensively considered her reaction as a neurotic one, in order to remain unaware of certain neurotic needs in himself which made it necessary for him to maintain an authoritarian position. Our philosophy of supervision depends then also on the capacity of the supervisor to have insight not only into the dynamics of the patient, the dynamics of the learning psychotherapist, the dynamics of the situation between the psychotherapist and the supervisor, but also into himself and the complex nature of his own needs which made him aspire to become a teacher of psychotherapy. This will help him to maintain the true purpose of the complex relationship between himself and his student: to teach psychotherapeutic skills within a helping relationship which evokes problems in each participant that are to be made a part of the total process.

IV / The End Phase

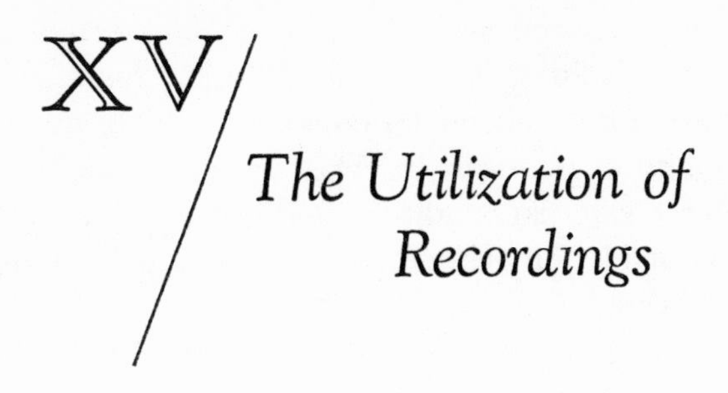

XV / *The Utilization of Recordings*

The only good histories are those written by those who had command in the events they describe.—Montaigne

---

Throughout the different chapters of this volume we have especially emphasized the fact that the structure of the organization within which the learning of psychotherapy takes place will vitally influence the kind of teaching process which can be carried on in it. Many readers will be tempted to interpret our discussions of this concept of structure as a plea for an ideal table of organization, for well-defined administrative channels, and will think of us as proponents of the idea that unerringly wise political decisions are the essential underpinnings that make training in psychotherapy possible. There is no question, of course, that those who are entrusted with the responsibility of devising and organizing the administrative structure within which learning is to take place will do well to read some of these chapters just in this spirit. They will read with the eyes of the administrator, with his primary identification with the administrative corner of our clinical rhombus.

Those who are primarily interested in the problems and techniques of teaching, as the authors of this book are, will not look at structure as something ideal that must be built up and defended, but rather as an ever-present reality, an important fact of life which should be skillfully used by the supervisor who works within the given training setting. The ideal structure does not really exist and is at best a thought model against which to measure the advantages and disadvantages of existing opportunities. We are usually tempted to think of structure as the supporting basis of our endeavors, very much like the steel frame which supports the total building with all its different functions. Our concept of structure is not understood completely, however, if one thinks only of its stability or permanence. The supervisor who looks for these features wants the external conditions and guarantees that would make his functioning at his job easier but he has not fully understood our concept of structure.

There are learning situations, and this is generally true of new teaching centers, that are characterized by rather chaotic administrative arrangements. These disorganized settings with their many unformalized (and hence unpredictable) features also represent a variety of structure; that is, they, too, create a specific psychological atmosphere and specific psychological opportunities and difficulties for the supervisor.

In a sense, the position of psychiatry and of psychotherapy today reminds one of the American frontier days. The frontier, too, had its legal officer who had to carry on his function within the boundaries provided by frontier society, regardless of how much he may have longed for the kind of legal order existing in an older, more settled society. The settled communities of the East had a type of legal structure differing from that of the "Wild West." In the same way, psychiatric training in many of our clinical centers today depends on types of organizational structure that are far from the structural refinement which might be of maximum help in the development of teaching facilities.

Though the teacher must thus operate within the structure at hand, at the same time he participates slowly and indirectly in the evolution of different structural conditions, as was illustrated in our chapter on "The Clinical Setting and its Structure." Some of these conditions he may change through his own efforts, while some others will be more enduring, since the leverage for change is not entirely in his hands. He must learn, then, to use what he has to the best advantage. Each structure offers certain opportunities, and only as the supervisor recognizes these does he become the master of the structure.

Certainly, there are proponents of the idea that "structure" is an inhibitor of freedom and creativity, and that the less structure, the better. But even the deliberate absence of formal structural requirements (the usual meaning of the word "structure") would nevertheless be some kind of structure, if only the structure of anarchy. The small child who is suddenly told that he can have all the candy he wants, and finds that all parental restrictions in this respect are lifted, discovers to his dismay that there is a limit after all—the capacity of his stomach and his sense of bodily well-being. The dropping of all explicitly stated limits does not lead to greater freedom, but to greater anxiety. In order to be free to grow one must have limits within which to function and around which to anchor one's basic security.

The whole problem of structure can in this sense be restated as one of "what kind of structure? How explicitly are its component aspects thought through and formulated?" And mostly, "Is it conceived as a hindrance—albeit an inevitable one—to good functioning, or can it be used psychologically in a way to further the clinical operation and the teaching process?"

Ordinarily, the supervisor works within a structure characterized by both stability and flexibility. Certain of its features are defined by the total setting and the administration, while other features may be defined by the supervisor and occasionally also by the student. Most of our training programs have a variety of basic arrangements which are binding upon the supervisor, but which still leave room for his imaginative work and for him to create certain structural elements with his students.

These basic requirements may include the fact that he will supervise a student who may treat a number of patients. He will see the student regularly, the most common arrangement being once a week, and the student will present his material to him for discussion. There may be specific arrangements about the assigning of cases, and about the veto power of the supervisor or the student. There will probably be arrangements concerning the length of time during which the supervisor is to work with the student, about the frequency and nature of evaluations, and concerning the rules of transfer from one supervisor to another. There should be arrangements for the handling of extreme situations, such as when the student proves entirely ineffective, and some intervention by the supervisor on behalf of the patient becomes necessary. Beyond all this a good many settings benefit from the fact that the group of supervisors is usually united by a more or less common theoretical frame of reference, a certain philosophy about the helping process. But even if this is the case, an advantage indeed for the student who ought not to find himself caught in the crossfires of ideological warfare, we shall still find conflicting interpretations of certain structural elements, and consequent differences in the application of these structural devices. This is indeed all to the good, since the best training system is one which combines stability and a shared viewpoint with room for flexibility, individual difference, and an opportunity for creative and imaginative work on the part of the teachers.

One of the most important structural aspects of every training center and clinical organization has to do with the system of recording clinical material, the system which defines the communication between the student-therapist and those to whom he is responsible. One may be inclined to look at clinical records as a bureaucratic ritual, a necessary administrative and legal device but essentially an unproductive use of time, and thus not see at all its true psychological meanings and uses. Since some system of clinical record-keeping exists in every organized setting and is agreed to be an essential part thereof, this structural device lends itself well to illustrate the psychological uses to which any structural device can be put. Thus we can examine the use of clinical records to generalize about the problems of structure in their psychological meanings and implications.

One of the chief uses of clinical records is in the supervisory process, which is most frequently based on the submission of clinical material by the student to the supervisor. The student, for example, submits process notes to the supervisor which the supervisor uses in order to teach. The structural arrangement which has been established by the training group may ask for just that. The supervisor conveys this requirement to the student, and both may have many ways to interpret this particular rule and to use it in the learning process. The stable rule permits many flexible (and also inflexible) interpretations on the part of both the teacher and the learner. The way that this rule is interpreted by both, the way that it is carried out, will instantly convey something about the nature of the teaching and learning process that can go on, and will have many consequences for the training relationship that is established.

Ideally, supervisors will be quite flexible about the use of the written material. They will tend to give the student considerable latitude, though some will feel that some students need a tighter structure—students who procrastinate and never have their material up to date, or others who report obsessively in endless repetitive pages. As usual, it is the experience of the extreme case that affords the supervisor the justification for a strict and inflexible requirement, which may be expressed in an explicit definition of how the clinical record must be prepared. Anyone who has been instrumental in bringing some degree of uniformity into a medical records department or the recording system of a social agency knows how we tend to replace spontaneity (and hence variety) of recording by a very necessary, but occasionally overdone, uniformity, beginning with the type of case study and the system of diagnostic classification, and proceeding to the monthly progress note, and perhaps the recording of the process of treatment itself.

This uniformity of the recording system and the creation of basic rules to govern the recording is, of course, unavoidable, and is indeed one important reflection of the professional standards of the clinical organization. The recording system of any clinical setting will frequently give us decisive clues as to the kind of clinical work done in the organization, and as to the kind and level of competence of the training which is carried on, as well. This tendency toward a uniform procedure, stemming from the healthy desire to create workable minimum standards of service and of training, may, of course, become overritualized, and may then inhibit the student's development rather than aid it. An example would be a social agency that forbids its case workers to use technical psychiatric terms in the description of their intake interviews, lest they forget that they are social workers and think of themselves as junior psychiatrists who have the right to "diagnose" clients. Another agency might insist that the worker, in describing his interviews, refer to himself with the personal pronoun "I" rather than the more indirect description, "the worker," in order to stress the interpersonal aspects of interviewing and to preclude a kind of objectifying that might help the worker disclaim personal responsibility for his interview behavior. Another organization might insist on a formal recording in which the candidate refers to himself always as the "analyst" or the "therapist" rather than by the personal "I." Through such ritualistic devices the belief is expressed that somehow the ritual itself will create the atmosphere. But the atmosphere ought to be the cause of the ritual rather than its effect.

The good training center will insist on a certain basic uniformity, but will nevertheless leave sufficient leeway for supervisor and student to develop that specialized adaptation of the standard recording method most beneficial in terms of combining maximum service to the patient with a maximum learning opportunity for the student. We believe that the supervisor who informs the student about the basic requirement that the case he carries must be recorded will do best if this information is given in general terms and avoids overly specific directions. If the student asks what kind of record is expected from him, the supervisor will do best if he suggests maximum freedom—"Record the process in whatever seems to you your own best way of describing to me what happens in each psychotherapeutic interview."

There may be students who insist on very specific directions as to how and what to record, and others who will take their cues from records that they have taken out and studied; but most students will choose a manner of recording that is specific and individual, and will thus permit the supervisor to get his first cues concerning the student's learning patterns, and concerning his ideas as to the nature of the psychotherapeutic process. The student's way of recording will be his own interpretation of this particular structural device and will represent his effort to adapt the structure to his particular learning needs. Unwittingly, he tells us much about himself, about his work with the patient, and about his expectations in the supervision through the form of his recording in addition to the content that he records.

We have already mentioned the student who gives us a message about himself and about a problem he has in the learning situation through the very fact that he tends not to have his material ready in time for the supervisory conference. He may attribute the difficulty to secretarial deficiencies or to specific emergencies that have arisen in his work, or he may have discovered rather early that he has a special problem with having his work prepared on time, and about describing the content of his interview with the patient. With this type of student, long phases of the supervisory work may have to center less around the content of his therapeutic endeavors and more around his inability to master the clerical aspects of his clinical responsibility. For this may represent a serious statement of his inability to accept the ordinary routines of communicating with the supervisor. He has a problem in living up to the regulations of the organization which he may attempt to cover by warding off inquiry into his difficulty, and by defying the requirement as an overly rigid insistence on bureaucratic red tape. He may feel that he would rather talk about his patient without written material, and if one helps him try to bypass his difficulty in this way, one may discover that such a student finds it equally difficult to account verbally for what he is doing with the patient.

On the other hand, there is the student who does just the opposite, that is, relies on a conscientious and objective, an obsessive and over-complete collection of data which—aside from the not unimportant point that it overwhelms the clerical staff—is also designed to over-whelm the supervisor. This ritualistic faith in "complete data," so easily rationalized as a desire to know everything about the process and to tell the supervisor everything about it, is frequently an obstacle to the dynamic interpretation of data, in spite of the fact that it seems to be the sign of the perfect student. The more such recordings approach "verbatim accounts" in pursuit of the illusion that thus everything is captured, the more they tend to ignore the therapist's inner affective and cognitive responses to the patient's material, as well as all the elements that comprise the emotional climate, the feeling of the impact two individuals make upon one another that the written words (even if absolutely complete) do not by themselves convey. Many researchers in pursuit of this ideal of complete recording, particularly in studies of the psychotherapy process, have added electric recording devices to their investigative armamentarium. Useful as the data are for many purposes, most workers recognize, as well, their inherent limitations; what one wants most to know of the therapist's conceptualization of the case and of the strategy that underlies his efforts is not expressed in his verbalizations.

A somewhat related difficulty is encountered in the type of recording in which everything is accounted for that the patient has allegedly done or said, but in which one finds no trace of what the therapist has done. While the communications of the patient may have been recorded quite sensitively, the therapist has so removed himself from the account that one cannot quite make out his place in the therapeutic process or what difference it made that he was in the room with the patient at all. Other students will "objectify" the data by an over-rich use of technical and theoretical terms that may hide a lack of sensitivity, or an anxiety and lack of knowledge concerning the process. Some recordings betray in their form a wish to alibi for therapeutic actions or for the lack of action, a wish to justify rather than to examine and to learn.

One could go on endlessly describing the many first sins that beginners usually commit and that are illustrative of various types of difficulties expressed through the form of recording. Rather than hoping to bridge these difficulties by giving the student a very early prescription as to how to record, the sensitive supervisor will allow freedom in recording. The difficulties that are then expressed can and must be used as one of the many psychological vehicles of his work with his student. As he permits the student to discover some of the meanings of his specific methods of recording, and some of the specific learning difficulties thus expressed, and permits the student, as well, to experiment with new forms of communication, the supervisor helps the student grow toward sensitivity in describing the psychotherapeutic process and toward skill in communicating with the supervisor.

There is, in fact, no absolute concept as to what ideal process recording is that could be imposed on every student. What is ideal in each instance depends on the student's present capacity, on the specific use of certain recording methods in specific learning situations, and perhaps also on some of the capacities of the supervisor himself. Communication is a two-way process. What may be ideal recording in one particular situation and for one particular student will be less ideal if applied with another supervisor whose way of making use of communication is different from that of the first teacher. This variability in what constitutes proper recording and proper communicating with the supervisor will go parallel with the discovery by each good psychotherapist that his style of communication with his patients varies from one to another, because of the different communication skills and methods of different patients.

Moreover, the student's development of skill in communication through process recording will represent—at least in part—his adaptation to the teaching method of his supervisor. Any specific teaching method will require its own method of communication, its own variety of recording. The same holds true for the effective supervisor. His teaching with each particular student will improve, his skill will change, as it were, as he discovers the particular learning problems of his student, the specific ways that the student must use in order to communicate to the supervisor the nature of his problems as a therapist. This mutual process of adaptation can best be aided if a flexible structure is maintained in matters of recording. The student who has outstanding difficulties in having his recording up to date may for a long time need a sensitive and specific handling by the supervisor to help him surmount this obstacle, rather than be allowed to use it as a permanent wall between himself and the supervisor.

There are many ways that students and supervisors will utilize in order to benefit most from the recorded material. A supervisor may, for instance, request that the student read his material to him and may then critically review the material and make certain suggestions. This way of being briefed, as it were, by the student will stress certain aspects of the relationship—the preference for a didactic form of teaching—and will convey to the student the role the supervisor wants to play, as well as cue the student as to what is expected of him. The student may rebel against this method. His opposition might not emerge overtly, but be expressed in an inhibited and obedient mechanical reporting with an anxious awaiting of approval. The situation could slowly develop into one where only what is expected by the supervisor is reported, and where both never move closer to the real problems of the therapist. The imitative and cue-taking propensities would be augmented through this particular use of recorded material. Frequently a supervisor will be confronted by a student who interprets recording in this very way and acts as if the supervisor wanted only to be briefed and had nothing in mind but to approve or disapprove the work produced.

In some instances the supervisor may read the material ahead of time, which, of course, puts an extra time burden on him, but clears the entire conference time for full discussion of all relevant problems. The supervisor may or may not choose to read the material together with his student at the beginning of the conference and then suggest that the material, now fresh with both of them, be the basis for discussion of the questions of each. Most supervisors will leave the initiative up to the student, and will encourage him to ask specific questions about the material. Others may feel that the record in itself already implicitly contains the questions of the student and may themselves take the initiative after having acquainted themselves with the facts described.

It is a commonplace that no recording can be a faithful rendering of the total therapeutic experience even if the recorder uses the objectifying aids to data collection described earlier. Most supervisors feel that there is certainly no advantage in taking notes during the therapeutic session, although for some therapists this seems to be a necessary stage in the development of their skills, the only way they seem to have at the beginning of retaining enough about their experience to start learning from it. They may be so paralyzed otherwise that they cannot be immediately weaned from a method that shields them from the opportunity—and the necessity—to react spontaneously to their patients. But even in these cases where notes taken during the interview are used for the final recording, while the interview presented to the supervisor may represent honest reproduction, it will never constitute a truly comprehensive record.

Some schools of training, therefore, propound the view that any kind of process recording, no matter how detailed, is really inadequate and should be replaced by electric recordings which would be utterly faithful, reliable, objective, and thereby enhance the possibilities for true learning. Some supervisors have experimented with the use of verbatim electric recordings, even listening to the sound recording while working with the student, with both student and supervisor able to turn the record off at any point to discuss any suggested problem, or to replay any doubtful passage. There are even supervisors who prefer to watch their students through a one-way vision screen. These devices are still experimental, and convey something specific about the kind of communication the supervisor desires. Teaching methods based on such objective, mechanical recording systems lend themselves much less well to a truly dynamic interplay in the learning relationship and lose many other important advantages offered by the record which the student himself prepares.

This is not to say, of course, that such experimental devices should not be used. As a matter of fact, they are excellent devices for auxiliary use from time to time in almost any training situation, and may be especially instructive for the more advanced and better trained student. It may be an informative experiment to have the advanced student compare his own process recording with the electric recording, and have him discover the nature and meaning of his omissions, his distortions, and his elaborations.

The lack of absolutely faithful recording, the likelihood even that a beginning student will consciously distort the record in order to try to please the supervisor, actually has definite advantages for the learning process. There are things that the verbatim record cannot offer us. The mechanical sound record does not lead us to the motivations of the therapist—anxiety reactions, inferences about himself and the patient, technical alternatives he chooses, and general impressions of the over-all process which he records. The process record may distort the actual events that transpire between therapist and patient, but it will more faithfully record the way the therapist sees his experience and wishes to communicate it to the supervisor for the purpose of making a particular use of supervision.

We may liken these efforts in the supervision to the comparison of the material that the patient brings into the therapeutic session with the actual events that he is describing.

It may help from time to time to know what actually happened with the patient, but we have found from experience that it is more important to see *with* the patient just *how* he remembers his experience and reproduces it for the purpose of therapy. From time to time an actual and completely objective account might be useful, but most of the time the supervisor will benefit more from the kind of recording which is individual for each student. It is the student's device of language, his choice of interpretation, and his posing of certain questions through the record that lead to those aspects of the truth of what went on between him and the patient that are truly important for the teaching and learning process.

It is, then, a selected truth, and frequently a somewhat distorted truth, but nevertheless it is that part of the student's interaction with his patient which is within his reach for technical consideration and for theoretical discussion. We find, then, that he frequently remembers only those fragments of the therapeutic interview which have been particularly meaningful to him, and that he tends to leave out other aspects over which he has as yet no mastery, and which he is not yet ready to bring to supervision.

These early distortions that enter into recording will then give way later, after the initial period of work, to more faithful, more sensitive, and more useful recording. But even then, as we know from the comparisons among our various students, we will see vital differences in recording which will teach us something about the nature of the student's problems and his ways of communicating. As the student's skill increases, the necessity for recording changes. As he goes on in supervision, he will slowly develop different uses of recording, of communication with the supervisor, provided that he works with a flexible teacher who can adapt himself to his changing needs. The student may still record, but his power of abstraction may have changed so much that he will bring in short summaries of his work and may come to depend on an entirely spontaneous use of conference time. This development is given impetus not only by changing levels of competence, but by the practical considerations of the great expensiveness of elaborate recordings in terms of both professional and secretarial time. Worth-while and essential to the teaching and learning process as this detailed recording is, as growing skill permits, it should give way to simplified and less burdensome methods of record taking and communicating.

This method is, of course, not possible for the beginning student. Some neophyte therapists despair at the thought of having to remember an entire hour's interview. They are not yet ready to make any spontaneous use of material and are overwhelmed by the many events between themselves and the patient and must slowly learn to distinguish what is relevant. They have not yet the power to select typical or decisive situations from the total therapeutic context, and are not free enough to allow themselves an entirely unprepared and spontaneous use of conference time. Only as they reach advanced stages will they allow themselves a kind of useful summary interpretation of certain therapeutic problems, and be able to communicate problems of this kind to the supervisor without having to give all the data as they see them.

Such varied and increasingly spontaneous uses of supervisors require that the supervisory functions be exercised by experienced and skilled clinicians. Only experienced teachers can adapt themselves flexibly to advanced and spontaneous methods of teaching. If the teachers are young clinicians just beginning to carry the teaching function, they will themselves have to depend on more formalized ways of communication, in order to make maximum use of the teaching and clinical skill they have available. The group structure will support the still weak professional personality and professional skill of the beginning supervisor and will, in fact, make it possible to use new and relatively inexperienced supervisors in a helpful way. A price, however, will be paid in the more circumscribed ways such novice supervisors have of using themselves helpfully and in their need to hang on more rigidly to formal lines of structure. It cannot be stressed enough that the kind of recording system used in supervision is a function of a two-way process that depends as much on the capacity of the supervisor as on that of the student.

The essential factor about any structural device is that it is not simply a voluntary arrangement, but rather that it defines certain limits of a process in accord with decisions made and given sanction by the group. Chess players may take delight in developing different versions of the chess game by simply redefining the value of certain chess pieces and the moves which these pieces can make, but nevertheless they will have to agree on mutually accepted rules, a mutually accepted structure, if they are to play together. The same holds true concerning the rules that govern recording as it is used in a clinical setting. We advocate a system that allows for some experimentation and that may slowly change its rules according to the progress of the learning situation.

It is not possible, however, to develop a structured learning situation in which many people are trained that is so flexible that it can adjust to every given individual need, or to any given wish expressed by the student or the supervisor. Any structural arrangement will impose certain limits which will perhaps preclude training certain individuals who might be successfully trained elsewhere. Any clinical organization will have to stand for certain regulations which might make it impossible to use certain teachers who cannot fit into its basic structure and philosophy. The supervisor will make difficulties for himself and for the student if he insists on creating rules that are too individualistic. Unless he can adapt himself to the group climate, he will constantly, regardless of his very best motivations, undermine the structure and harm the total setting, including ultimately his own freedom of teaching.

The task of the supervisor, then, is to work through a given structure, rather than in spite of it or against it. This, too, is the task of the student. The student will frequently have the greater difficulties in learning how to make use of what a given setting provides for his learning. Many of these difficulties will come out as the supervisor makes use of whatever structural elements the given situation contains. There are some aspects of structure that cannot be moved, and there are others that permit subtle adaptations to the needs of both learner and teacher. The system of recording, the most vital element perhaps in establishing responsible communication, represents a part of structure that lends itself well to a flexible use, and provides illuminating insights into the kind of learning process taking place.

This is not to say that the skillful use of structural elements in itself *is* teaching, or that a clearly delineated structure with an awareness of its psychological consequences by any means guarantees good teaching. Though it is felt that the clarification of mutual responsibilities, which is the function of structure, must precede any effective day-to-day work on the operational level, it is obvious that "rules are not enough." And, of course, rules and function *can* be used destructively, if rigidly adhered to in a way that chokes off consideration of possibilities in areas other than that specifically provided for by the structure. One needs both an awareness and an acceptance of differentiated function and responsibility as well as an on-going process between the two participants. If function is handled so as to block process, the result is a self-defeating one.

We have to this point omitted a very important aspect of recording. Recording serves not only as the basis of communication between supervisor and therapist, but serves many other functions, as well. We record for the administration, which needs our system of records in order to make proper administrative decisions, in order to evaluate constantly the quality of the work of therapists and supervisors, and in order to be able to account legally and professionally for the work of the organization. Records are also necessary to safeguard the interests of the patients about whom we need information on file, in order to insure their total treatment program, their re-evaluation, if indicated, and their transfer to other therapists when necessary, as well as to make communication about them possible with other physicians and other clinical organizations. Records may also be used for research purposes and thus provide data for the scientific work that is carried on.

This multifold function of recording will reflect itself within the supervisory process, since it will frequently be true that a specific record is made for more than one purpose, for more than communication with the supervisor, and will be written with these other people and purposes in mind. One might almost suggest that each clinical record will have on it the invisible imprint of the total clinical rhombus, and all the functions that it serves.

This creates additional difficulties for the student who has to record not only in order to learn from the supervisor, but also in order to collect data that insure better treatment, facilitate research activities, and provide evidence to the administration that effective work is being done. This leads then to a special problem which actively influences the supervisory process. We refer to the fact that students, and for that matter usually staff members, as well, are directly or indirectly evaluated in terms of the work that they are expected to do. Our whole evaluation and selection system depends on reliable recording, and necessitates the use of this structural device for this purpose in a way that permits the best professional judgment, scientific insights, and an identification with a total responsibility toward the patient, the young therapist, and the training organization.

It is this total professional and ethical responsibility that creates a special problem for our system of clinical recording. We speak, of course, of the problem of the confidentiality of the knowledge we acquire. The psychotherapeutic process requires confidentiality; it demands of us that what transpires between therapist and patient be kept secret. Training and research, as well as maximum service to patients, require, however, a system of recording that seems to undermine the confidential nature of our work by making some of the material "semipublic," as it were.

A part of the therapist's difficulty in recording adequately, in giving the secret away, stems from this wish not to betray the patient's confidences; part, however, relates to the fear that his own confidence entrusted to the supervisor could be betrayed. What will the supervisor do with the material? Such discussions leave many questions open as to who ought to have access to clinical records, and how can one insure maximum confidentiality, in spite of the necessity for a certain amount of necessary dissemination of the data. Each organization will need to devise its own safeguards to insure that the recording system is used only for legitimate technical purposes. This concern with confidentiality relates to the secretarial, as well as the professional staff, and in certain larger clinical organizations specific secretaries may be designated as "confidential secretaries" to handle certain particularly confidential records.

Perhaps again it is the trained supervisor who, through his own behavior and through his own reactions to aspects of the therapeutic process, will be instrumental in helping the student to identify with the function of professional secret-taking in a constructive way that could never lead to situations which would prove harmful to patients and their relatives, or to colleagues. The student is in a vulnerable position, especially if he is a beginner, since he exhibits "secrets" about himself which he must tell the supervisor sooner or later if he wishes to learn, and which he wants to see used in a constructive way that will benefit rather than harm him. What he tells the supervisor is not only an aid to the process of teaching him skills and insights, but also is information that will lead to graduation or failure, to employment, promotion, or demotion. The whole problem of the evaluation and selection of psychotherapists through the system of supervision hinges, then, on communication, on the kinds of structural devices that are expressed in our recording system. How this works in practice and the problems that are encountered will be discussed in the following chapter.

XVI / Evaluation and Selection

> Just at this moment Alice felt a very curious sensation, which puzzled her a good deal until she made out what it was; she was beginning to grow larger again, and she thought at first she would get up and leave the court; but on second thought she decided to remain where she was as long as there was room for her.
>
> "I wish you wouldn't squeeze so," said the Dormouse, who was sitting next to her. "I can hardly breathe."
>
> "I can't help it," said Alice very meekly; "I'm growing."
>
> "You've no right to grow *here*," said the Dormouse.
>
> "Don't talk nonsense," said Alice more boldly; "you know you are growing too."
>
> "Yes, but I grow at a reasonable pace," said the Dormouse, "not in that ridiculous fashion." And he got up very sulkily and crossed over to the other side of the court.
>
> —Lewis Carroll

A characteristic misunderstanding of structure as it was discussed in the last chapter is to see only its external and "tangible" aspects rather than its inner meanings as part of the psychological matrix within which the process of learning takes place. Our stress on different methods of recording is an attempt to demonstrate that even so seemingly mechanical an arrangement as the manner of record keeping, rather than being a bureaucratic detail of clinical organization, represents in each instance a particular way of working, which helps define the subtle nature of the relationship of student and teacher to each other, and to the administrators of the training setting.

An additional example might elucidate this point more fully, and will at the same time help us to crystallize our thinking concerning the problems of evaluation of work in supervision, as well as the problems concerning the proper selection of psychotherapists. This recording device consists of advising the student to make a written summary of the conference between himself and his supervisor. The student is asked to describe the way in which he understands the material after the conference with the supervisor, the insights which they have gained together, the technical problems that were discovered, and the technical suggestions that were made during the discussion of the previous week's clinical material.

Again, directions are given in a not too specific way, in order to permit the student considerable latitude in interpreting the supervisor's recommendation. These conference notes will demonstrate the degree of clinical and theoretical understanding which the student has attained. They are useful to clarify misunderstandings, and also to show how much of the understanding that is reached becomes an integrated part of the student's knowledge and skill, and how much of it is simply seen as an external suggestion by the supervisor about which the student has no consolidated conviction. One can observe, too, his capacity for the use of the newly gained insights as one studies the succeeding material. It is also possible to detect in these conference notes specific problems that the student has in using the supervisory conference.

However, one colleague who learned of this method criticized it by suggesting that such conference notes, if required of the student, would "create a transference towards the supervisor," since the student is asked to put primary emphasis on what is discussed in the conference between himself and his supervisor (rather than what specifically had gone on between himself and his patient). One may guess that this colleague must be in favor of a form of supervision which, at least on the surface, is more explicitly didactic and authoritative, and avoids, insofar as possible, making any direct use of the affective components of learning. With such a supervisory method, any problems that the student may have with his supervisors will be relegated to the student's own analyst or therapist, if he has one. The supervisor would be afraid that a "transference" might develop if affective aspects are touched upon at all, and he therefore would try to keep the relationship on a strictly "didactic" level.

The use of the word "transference" in this connection confuses the issue, since it seems to suggest that supervision is but a form of therapy. The word "transference" is really legitimate only in those types of relationships in which appropriate technical use is made of this phenomenon as it occurs. In the situation described the student is encouraged, rather, to account for the use of the supervisory time, to integrate for himself and to clarify what he has worked on with the supervisor, to demonstrate to himself and to the supervisor how he understands the material. Rather than drawing on the regressive features which may occur and develop in the learning relationship, the student is here encouraged to do independent thinking, and to constantly check on what he and the supervisor have been working on. He thus evaluates his own understanding and the supervisor's understanding, the usefulness of the technique employed and the technique suggested. He is in a position constantly to check his work with the patient, his work with the supervisor, and to check, as well, on what is offered by the supervisor. He is encouraged to interpret actively what he gets from the supervisor, rather than to take the supervisor's techniques and interpretations passively without intellectual critique.

It is true that many students will need considerable help during the supervisory process, in order to develop the strength to use these notes in this more ideal and mature sense. It will take supervisors who do not mind that the study of the psychotherapeutic process will be utilized as a constant check on their suggestions and on their understanding. They will have to stand ready to revise their opinions and to admit fault when they are wrong. This process, this constant re-evaluation, which actually is a mutual process, can, of course, not proceed on an intellectual level alone, and will be accompanied by interactions on every level, which would be described, were they to occur in a therapeutic context, as transference reactions of the one and countertransference reactions of the other. These reactions, however, will in this case constantly be geared to the purpose of developing increased skill in the treatment of the patient in question. The decisive difference between a therapeutic process in which "transference" is therapeutically utilized and a supervisory process in which affect and distortions of all kinds take place consists in the purpose which, in the latter case, is to help the young therapist develop workable therapeutic techniques with specific patients.

Such conference notes would have different meanings in terms of a variety of different purposes to which they could be put. The student will be helped to learn better, to integrate systematically the material which he brings to the supervisor, to see whether he understands the supervisor, to learn how to ask meaningful clinical and theoretical questions, and to see whether he can use his new insights in actual clinical application. The supervisor will use this material to watch the learning patterns of the student, to measure his own effectiveness, and to improve his teaching techniques. The material of these conference notes could also be used to reach a greater clinical understanding of the patient and to study the theoretical implications of these clinical data. In the hands of more advanced students such conference notes can become a valuable source of data for research into the psychotherapeutic process. In fact, one way of surmounting the problem of the complexity and hugeness of the data accumulated when one is engaged in research into the psychotherapeutic process, especially with long-term intensive psychotherapeutic and psychoanalytic treatments, is to use such weekly summary conference notes as a chief source of data, rather than the detailed process notes of each session with the patient.

As we know, learning and teaching never take place in a vacuum, but rather within a given social environment, which always implies requirements that define the success or failure of the work done. The supervisor is responsible not only to the student, but to the training center, as well. Has the supervisor successfully taught the student? Was the student able to make adequate use of the supervisor or did he fail at this task? In what manner is the supervisor to communicate to the administration whether the student has failed or succeeded? If he has succeeded, what is the next step in his training? Does he need an additional supervisor? Can he work with more complicated patients? Is he ready to take on cases without supervision? Is he to graduate? Or, on the other hand, has he failed and should he be discontinued from the program? If the student is also a staff member, is he to receive a salary increment? A promotion? These problems of evaluation are always a part of supervision and are always playing on the mind, as it were, of both the teacher and the student. For the supervisor in this situation has not only a teaching responsibility to the student therapist, but a service responsibility to the institution he represents and to its patients. He teaches and he simultaneously enforces, through his demands, standards of minimal acceptable performance, always keying these appropriately to the degree of capacity brought by the student and the amount of training received.

We have heard many a teacher say that it becomes thereby more difficult to teach their students, since the latter are constantly over-anxious that they may not get credit, that they risk being discontinued from the program, that in effect they cannot expose their weaknesses and their mistakes to the person who must make responsible judgments about the adequacy of their performance and their learning. Such teachers would prefer to teach in an ideal vacuum in which there are no problems of evaluation and no decisions required concerning success or failure. These teachers forget that even if they were given such an opportunity they would discover quickly that the external administrative requirements are but structural devices which express an inner psychological reality; an inner reality that would continue to exist even in a setting free of external codifications, examination boards, licensing agencies, etc. One may also suspect that some teachers who yearn for such ideal conditions are less worried about the students than they are about themselves and the execution of their own function. It is not only the student who is afraid of examinations; it is also the teacher who is anxious about having to examine, about having to make authoritative decisions concerning those for whom he is responsible. Examination fears and neurotic attitudes toward evaluations are common to students and supervisors alike.

The supervisor will in these instances be concerned not only with the decisions which he has to make as he evaluates the students, but he may worry, too, about the fact that at the same time he is likewise being evaluated by the students and by the administrators as to his effectiveness in his job as a teacher. And this is true even for the most dogmatic teacher who is sure that any failure of a student must be caused by the student's laziness, lack of talent, resistance to learning, or all of these combined. Such teachers are actually even more sensitive to the criticism of students and less able to endure any form of revolt on the part of students than those who permit themselves some self-awareness, some questions about their effectiveness as teachers.

Teachers who seem to have no doubts about their own talents, who seem to be absolutely sure about their own technical skills, and who expect therefore to be taken for granted by their students, will always have difficulties with evaluation procedures that leave room for an expression of the student's reaction toward them. Conference notes, as described above, which would allow for some check on their recommendations, which would perhaps force them on occasion to revise opinions which they thought to be correct, might indeed be a problem for them. Teaching for them is essentially a one-way process, and the evaluation of students is for them nothing but an authoritative and, occasionally, an autocratic verdict, rather than a part of the total teaching process in which the student should naturally participate.

Every training center will sooner or later develop some mode of evaluation procedures which will require of the teacher, and frequently also of the student, some form of communication concerning the progress that has been made during the supervised work. Sooner or later there will be occasion for the formal evaluation of the work. This evaluation takes many forms in different training centers, and is usually organized through a variety of formal procedures or requirements which teach us a great deal about the psychological meanings that are attached to the evaluation procedures. A few of the possible methods will be presented here, in order to show the range of specific psychological usefulness—as well as the potential limitations—of each.

Most training centers start out, when evaluation procedures first become formalized, with expecting reports from their teachers which are one-sided statements about the students that are to be kept secret from them. The students are given only final decisions concerning outright passing or failing, and get at best some further hints from their teachers as to where they stand and what is thought of their work. We know of training centers where it is explicitly forbidden to the teacher to communicate his judgment to the student. This judgment is reserved exclusively for the organizational files and for the teachers and administrators who make final decisions about the student. Such a structure, we feel, will create very specific tensions between supervisors and students. It will create an authoritarian (and secretive) atmosphere in which there will be considerable anxiety that will hardly ever be touched on in the supervisory situation, and which will make the student dependent on the supervisor in a very specific sense. He will feel that he needs to live up completely to the requirements and the demands of the supervisor; and for him compliance might become more important than actual intellectual and affective mastery of the material.

Psychiatric training centers, as their organizational structure strengthens and their clinical and teaching philosophy evolves, and as the teachers learn to work together cooperatively, tend to get away from this method of "secret" files. There are, of course, transitional phases. The responsible psychotherapy supervision committee may slowly devise methods which will encourage the supervisor, before he has filed and discussed his specific report on a student, to let the student in on the essentials of this report, but there still may be an immense gulf between the version which is filed and the view of it which one is ready to share with the student. Usually the one that is filed is more strict and more truthful.

The student is usually a younger colleague, and what one is able to tell him depends a great deal on the strength of the total training system. Supervisors will be disinclined to share opinions with the student-therapist that may be negative and highly critical if they feel that they are not backed up by the administrative authority. Serious evaluations which are to have consequences, positive or negative, can only be fully and frankly shared with a student if there are provisions in the system which offer both the student as well as the supervisor protection against the potential arbitrariness of hierarchical one-to-one relationships. Both the young psychotherapist and the supervisor must have recourse to outside administrative authority. The supervisor will not dare to fully evaluate the student if he is not sure that he will be backed up. Why should he create a personal enemy for himself? The student will not dare to be frank with the supervisor if he does not feel that in the extreme case, for example if he feels unjustly treated, he could have recourse to an outside source, someone who would fairly and justly administer the program and protect the total training situation, rather than simply arbitrarily back the supervisor's authority and judgment.

Occasionally, even with the full support of the training system whose delegated representative he is, the supervisor will still retreat from the logical consequences of his own judgment. For instance, in one case the supervisor wrote an evaluation that was logically followed by the administrator with a move to change a student's clinical assignment—removing him, at least for the present, from further psychotherapeutic work. When these consequences became apparent, the supervisor backed down from his judgment, claiming that the "punishment" was too harsh. He told the administrator, "I'm sorry you took that attitude and went that far." That is, a supervisor, initially judgmental and condemning, experienced such guilt at the logical outcome of his judgments that he could only counter his guilt by disassociating himself from the administrative decision that followed from his own recommendation, and siding then with the student in his complaint against the administrator. A responsible (and non-judgmental) supervisor will feel no need either to apologize for—or attack—an administrative decision, but can use it helpfully in his work with the trainee. He has a real responsibility to do so—to both help the student and to uphold the standards of the agency. Occasionally this may mean helping someone out of the field. It is too glib a generalization to say that, if sensitively handled, this is usually experienced as a relief by the person who is leaving work that he is really unfitted for. It is also a severe narcissistic blow, and it is not easy both to stand firm and to continue to be helpful through such a crisis.

As the training system continues to strengthen, both student and supervisor will feel increasingly secure in it. Their enhanced security will lead to greater honesty with each other and also to more self-discipline, since they will realize that whatever they do together can and must be accounted for to an administration that has the ultimate over-all responsibility. At this point training centers can develop structural devices that include evaluation procedures based on a full sharing of opinion between student and supervisor, evaluation procedures that then become an integral part of the training process. Such training centers will develop formal arrangements that require that the supervisor and the student submit reports to the leadership of the school after stated periods of time, reports which are at the same time fully used in the process between teacher and student.

An experiment which was carried out with evaluation procedures, though it may seem costly and overdone, and overritualized, too, may nonetheless offer us a model to indicate ways in which the student's participation can be secured in the evaluative procedure.

In this experiment the students were told that there would be an evaluation at the end of the first learning period. They were themselves required to select two interviews from their process records for comparative study. The first was to be an early interview, which was to be compared with the second, taken from the later period of work. This comparison would permit student and supervisor to look at the early problems with this particular case, the progress that was possibly made, and the present state of skill of the psychotherapist. Both the supervisor and the student independently would study the material which the student had selected, and each, again independently, would write an evaluation of the supervised work as it was reflected in these two interviews. These evaluations would then be studied and discussed in a joint evaluation conference, the result of which would be a final summary, prepared by both together, in which an attempt would be made to integrate the two evaluations and to formulate recommendations to the administration on the future training status of the student.

This evaluation process thus went on under the pressure of the anticipated decision that would be based on it, and evoked characteristically different responses in different students. The evaluative ritual thus established would not in itself produce these varying reactions to evaluation. The reactions would also exist if there were only a "secret" evaluation submitted by the supervisor to the administration. What the evaluation procedure established here did was to *bring out* these reactions, to utilize them in the process of arriving at decisions that were truly mutual, and that avoided one-sided, authoritarian decisions.

Most students will not be able to undertake this responsibility without experiencing considerable anxiety. This anxiety, stemming from many previous experiences of being marked, of being selected or rejected, of having reason, realistic or neurotic, to expect negative and destructive administrative or parental reactions to evaluation reports, will have its influence on the process. The student may experience the process itself as anxiety-arousing, and may attack the structure and charge that it is devised to evoke anxiety. Actually, it merely brings into focus an anxiety that is already there, but which the student can first perceive only in a projected manner when he accuses the supervisor with "you make me anxious." Only slowly does he discover that the very process of evaluation that he and the supervisor go through together works to alleviate his anxiety, and helps him to gain insight.

The supervisor, too, now the representative of the training organization and not simply a private individual who sits in judgment on a colleague, is equally supported by this arrangement. As private individuals we are rightly loath to pass judgment on our fellow men and to help shape decisions that may influence a whole career, no matter how seemingly clearcut the indications. As the representative of an organization we cannot avoid such a responsibility, and the nature of the supporting structure behind the evaluation procedure makes it possible to reach such decisions and to make such judgments without arousing undue feelings of guilt on the part of the supervisor. The difficult task of one individual letting another know directly what he thinks of his work becomes possible. This is far kinder than the commonly employed gossip by which professional judgments are circulated in the absence of a structure that draws this material into the process. Since so much is shared (and so continuously) between supervisor and student, gossip tends to become superfluous as the medium for the handling of professional relationships.

Though most students select one of their earliest interviews and one of their latest for this review of their work and learning, they are given wide latitude in this choice. Since it is the student who chooses the interviews for this evaluation procedure, the supervisor is in a position to gain an understanding of just what areas and manner of problems the student is ready to deal with, as well as what he has selected as significant in his learning experience. The complete freedom of movement given to the students makes for the clearest expression of determinism—and demonstrates most exactly the student's capacity for criticism, his readiness for change, and his ability to participate in future planning.

As one watches a variety of students, one notices that different patterns emerge around even such aspects as the time sequence of the two interviews chosen. One student selected two interviews, one week apart, both from the very latest period of his work with the supervisor and the patient. He was an individual who struggled constantly with his open doubts about psychotherapy as a helping process, and his suspicion was that possibly there was nothing to it and, consequently, little to learn. Through his choice of interviews he practically said: "You see, I really learned nothing at all during these weeks, so that the first interview that I choose (from right near the end) is just as much a beginning interview as any of the many preceding it. And for the second, I chose an interview a week later. The little change between the two, just a week apart, is the full measure of what I have learned from you. It isn't much, is it?"

Another student, a very conscientious person, overwhelmed and almost paralyzed by the many problems that emerged during psychotherapy, ruminated for a long time as to just what interviews he ought to select, in order to illustrate which of the many problems he had experienced. He finally stated impulsively: "Oh, let's just use the very first and the very last interview. That way we can consider the biggest degree of change I've reached." A third student wanted to have the supervisor choose the interviews for him. He said, "Look, it doesn't make any difference. Why don't *you* choose for me. To me, they're one just the same as another." Perhaps this was his confession that he saw the very same problems unchanged all the way through, in one form or another, and that therefore he could not feel that it would make any difference which interviews were chosen. He must have been wondering quite seriously whether he had been helped at all with any one of his technical problems. Still another student picked two interviews from the first five weeks of work, thus implying that all that he had learned had been acquired during these first weeks, and that all the rest had not helped additionally.

As we look beyond the time placing to the specific content of the interviews chosen for the evaluation, our understanding of what the whole learning experience has meant to the student is immeasurably extended. From the choice the student announces those of his learning problems that he is prepared to deal with. Evaluation is always a selective process. In it, the student does not describe all that is possibly important, all that he has learned or ought to learn, but rather he chooses those aspects of his total experience on which he has really gotten together with the supervisor, those problems which were mutually perceived and experienced and possibly solved.

Our experience, tried on many a student, has shown that the selection of these two interviews usually sufficed, without any further communication on the part of the student or the supervisor, to provide an adequate cue for both to write evaluations which were usually very similar in focus and in content. Whenever there was—and this actually only happened once or twice—real dissimilarity in the evaluation which the student wrote from the one that the supervisor provided, one could conclude that little that was useful had gone on between the student and the supervisor, and the dissonance, as it were, disclosed that the learning was as poor as the teaching.

This experience, in the final conference, of "togetherness," of having "said the same thing," was often surprising to both the supervisor and the student—and rewarding, particularly in those cases where the supervisor was required by the very facts of his experience with the student to be rather critical and perhaps "negative," as it were, in his recommendations. As he discovers that the student sees things pretty much as does he, he no longer experiences his own criticisms as destructive, but comes to see the whole evaluation process and outcome as a joint achievement truly helpful to the student.

The following is a sample illustration of such evaluation work. The student, Dr. K, submitted two interviews, approximately three months apart, representing work with his first psychotherapy patient. The first formal evaluation of his work for which these two interviews were submitted took place some six months after he started. In these interviews the therapist's remarks are printed in italics, in order to afford a clearer picture of the types of responses which the therapist characteristically used at the beginning and at the end of this particular learning period. Following these two interviews with the patient is the evaluation of his work which the student himself wrote, based on this interview material.

First Interview, August 18

Mr. H began the hour by telling what occurred in psychodrama the preceding hour. He felt it was an important session and that it brought back to him something he had not thought of since childhood. The drama somehow got on the subject of knives and from there to the telling of castration threats and fears. Mr. H then remembered the following incident which he told to the group and which he repeated to me.

He thinks he must have been three or four years old at the time. He was doing a lot of thumb-sucking at the time. His mother tried all sorts of methods to break him of it, like tying his hands and putting axle grease on his thumbs. In desperation she asked an "ugly, big Indian" hired man what to do about it. He promised to break him of the habit. He threatened to cut off the boy's ears, his nose, his thumb. "When my mother wasn't around, he also said he would cut off my penis." The patient would run screaming to his mother, the Indian following, pretending he was going to cut off his ears.

I said something I shouldn't have (I've repressed it now). Anyway, it got him off the subject and he started telling of another visit from his sister. He was in the photography shop when they arrived, trimming some pictures. It annoyed him that they came and he showed his annoyance by finishing the job before going to see them. He said the visit started out well enough, but that he got upset when he heard that the brother-in-law was trying to get a job here at the hospital. He would prefer not to have them around. He was also upset by the fact that they talked so lightly of the brother-in-law's frequent job-changing. It made him think of his own difficulty in holding a job and he felt it was not a joking matter. He was very happy that they did not stay long and hopes there will be no job here for the brother-in-law. He also resents that they want him to hold the baby, to goo and smile at him. "I have enough trouble smiling anyway without making a damn fuss over a kid."

I tried to get him back to the castration story, asking whether anything else occurred to him concerning it. He couldn't remember anything but said that he had terrible fears as a kid and that he still has. As a child he was afraid of the dark, afraid to sleep alone. While in high school he still had deathly fears when alone after dark. Just before he went in the army he was terribly afraid to go to the chicken house after dark. He told how his father publicly made fun of him for being so afraid. He also told how at times he would run to his parents' bedroom to get in bed with them. He would always get between his parents, saying he felt safer with one on each side of him. *I asked what else was accomplished by that.* He responded immediately, "It also kept them apart."

He says he doesn't know what he feared—maybe that someone would kidnap or hurt him. "Now I wonder if it all started with the fear that someone might come and cut off my penis." He then recalled an incident when he was sleeping with his brother. His brother had been out late; Mr. H, alone and afraid, had been trying to stay awake until his brother arrived. But he dozed off, wakened in a cold sweat when someone had thrown his arm over him and "started going to work on me." He hurried on to say that although his brother often did that, he still wasn't sure it was his brother. He felt his arm "but it didn't feel like my brother's." *I questioned the "going to work"* and he explained "like he was screwing me." "I can't remember but I wonder if I used to play around with him. I can't remember doing it but maybe I even used to get my mouth down on it." He has always shied away from talk about his brother. *His way of telling this incident makes me think* that he has had homosexual relations with his brother which he remembers clearly but cannot bring himself to tell them.

He then told of his trumpet playing in the school band but "didn't blow" the trumpet at all. He would hold it to his mouth, pretending to play it "but I didn't blow it." After a while he smiled and said, "I was just thinking about the way I said that—about not 'blowing' the trumpet." *I smiled with him and said that I had thought about it too. I pointed out that he had also stopped singing, that he had been forced to stop thumb-sucking, that everything that used the mouth, he felt he had to stop. "Do you feel there's something bad about the mouth?"* He related how he had been told that thumb-sucking would affect his health, would deform his face, might even drive him crazy. *I remarked that still a strong desire to use the mouth continued and wondered why he thought that might be.* He didn't know and *I couldn't keep quiet and so asked: "When did you first use your mouth?"* The answer came rather quickly, "When I sucked my mother's breast." He added, "You know, I sometimes think I can remember sucking her breast—I just seem to get a picture of lying on her lap and her having one breast out and me sucking it." *So then I didn't know what to say.* He went on to tell how even the thought of thumb-sucking made him think of taking a penis in his mouth—that the word suck bothered him. *I said that it bothered a lot of people, that many mothers were upset over their children's thumb-sucking for that reason; also, that's why the word is included on the test he had some time ago.* He said, "I probably said 'dick' to that." *I had the test folder, checked and assured him that he had not.* He seemed relieved that being bothered by the word "suck" was not something peculiar to him.

Mr. H used the last few minutes of the hour to run himself down, saying he wasn't very smart. This stemmed from the above reference to the tests. He remembered missing some easy arithmetic problems.

Second Interview, November 26

Mr. H wore his worried look when he arrived today and he immediately began to demonstrate verbally that he was disturbed. He said he was very upset and confused. He thought much of the disturbance was due to the psychodrama session of the previous hour. Last time it bothered him that no one praised the way in which he played his role. This time he felt neglected because his role hadn't been discussed at all. He jumped from one topic to another, however, *suggesting to me* that it was not really the psychodrama that was bothering him. He said that he seemed more confused, that his head was hurting more this week. *I thought he had gained some insight into the problem his mother had posed for him during the last two sessions. If he had, now I felt he was trying to shut out all understanding.* Then he asked, "Can't we try hypnosis—I think it might help clear things up more quickly?"

K. "*This has become pretty painful and you feel hypnosis might return us to a pleasant, painless situation.*"

H. "I just want to move faster." There was a pause, followed by, "I asked Dr. O'S this morning if I could have an hour with him—I think that might help speed things up."

K. "*You've really gotten angry with me, haven't you?*"

H. "Well, we didn't accomplish anything last session, and we don't seem to be getting anywhere now. I guess I should be angry at myself. It's my fault I'm not getting anywhere. Maybe there's something else sticking that should come out."

There was a long pause during which Mr. H fidgeted, was very uncomfortable. His stomach was growling loudly. He smiled and commented on the noise it was making. *I had to laugh.* Mr. H became angrier, saying, "Go ahead and laugh. It's not funny to me."

K. "*I laughed because I thought you knew why it was growling and that it amused you too.*"

He continued to look sour and unamused. Nothing was said for a few minutes. Mr. H rather exploded with, "Now you're trying to torture me again."

I guess he must have gotten me angry now. I didn't recognize it at the time I said it. But his reaction and my later reflection on it showed how aggressive my next comment was. The sarcasm must have been obvious when I said, "Would you like us to talk about your plans for the weekend?" Mr. H really exploded: "I don't want to talk about any goddam plans for anything. I might as well leave—I can't think of anything to say."

K. "*Well, that remark of mine wasn't very nice. I think you're really angry with me because you feel I've gotten you to say some unpleasant things about your mother—your one friend in the world. You put it on a physical basis, but you told me she stinks. Now you feel I attack and criticize your mother. You told me your father did something like that and you hated him for it. Now I'm doing it, and you hate me for it."*

H. "Well, I do feel somewhat that way. I felt you couldn't be very good —you don't know what you're doing. I guess that's why I wanted Dr. O'S."

K. "*Or hypnosis or some other painless process.*"

Mr. H got going on a review of much that was told at the previous session, adding a few details here and there. This time he made many of the "interpretations" *I had made previously*. Several times he said, "I can see it better now" and concluded with, "I think I understand it now. I guess we were getting somewhere in the last session." Then, in a rather self-conscious manner, he said, "It's funny—now I keep thinking what a swell guy you are—a little while ago I really did hate your guts."

I had said earlier when talking about the pain connected with this, that the confusion might be a good thing. Looking for a closing, I guess, I said, "Maybe our confusion has turned into a good thing today."

I feel now that he really had insight on Wednesday. In the interim, this insight became unbearable. He had to reject it—to blame me for a stupid error. By reviewing it, by reaching the same conclusions, he has come to accept it and to gain relief in acceptance. *I think he knows better now the origin and meaning of his aggression and why it frightens him.* He begins to see that more understanding of it can lessen the conflict over it. It is no longer a crime to think that even mother can occasionally do wrong. He seems to see how similar his present confusion is to the confusion of his adolescence.

Dr. O'S told me later that Mr. H said, "I won't be needing that hour with you—I got things cleared up."

Evaluation of Supervised Work in the Psychotherapy Training Program:

The process notes of August 18 illustrate at least two of my major shortcomings as a therapist. The notes of this session epitomize all those which preceded it and many which followed. This report was selected because it made so obvious an error which my supervisor tried in vain to get me to recognize earlier.

My first difficulty, then, was a willingness and eagerness to flounder around in the patient's past to see what dark and startling secrets I could unearth. Early success at learning things which he had never told anyone else made me confident that I was a "born" therapist. The patient felt quite safe in remaining with childhood experiences and so required little urging to go back there. He learned quickly what sort of things to bring from psychodrama in order to keep us in the past. The "castration" topic (first two paragraphs) is an excellent example of this.

Then, in the third paragraph, when the patient tries to come back to the present, I consider this an error and get him back to castration as quickly as possible, in an awkward way. Incidentally, the interpretation at the end of the next paragraph was obviously put in the patient's mouth and was not as spontaneous as the report might suggest. I'm sure this is also true for other "interpretations" during that interview. The patient was not gaining the insight I attribute to him. I was trying to demonstrate my skill at discovering and explaining his oral development in one easy lesson. The lecturing nature of that paragraph is also clear and illustrates another tendency of mine which I find it difficult to avoid.

But, I was proud of this session, as I was of others in which "discoveries" were made. I was provoked when Dr. James was not impressed by any of it. Previous suggestions to keep the patient in the present were ignored. If I could do in two months what usually required a year of psychoanalysis, then it should be continued. There was real hostility toward the supervisor up to this time and a desire for a supervisor who would recognize my worth. With the notes on this session, however, he was able to open my eyes and to demonstrate that I was permitting and encouraging the patient to indulge in schizophrenic-like fantasies of homosexual and breast-sucking activities. With this incident, supervision sessions began to be cooperative rather than competitive affairs.

The second major criticism of my therapy technique is illustrated in the last few lines of these notes. It is the tendency to be the kind, approving, reassuring, sympathizing father figure. I mustn't make him angry at me; I must do and say things which will make him like and think highly of me. I must be careful not to cause him any pain. This difficulty, though now less pronounced, had been a persistent hindrance to the patient's free expression of feelings. Even now, when it is possible for the patient to show anger at me, I find it hard to refrain from comment which is aimed at dispelling his anger.

It is difficult to find favorable points in this report. A review of this period suggests that I did develop a relationship with the patient which was strong enough to withstand the dangers of anger and the pressure of reality when I was ready to bring him and myself to it. When I could avoid interpretations, I was able to provide some support. Giving opportunity for catharsis helped relieve some of the patient's guilt.

My greatest gain in this period was a slow but certain insight into the need for structure in a therapy situation. The structure is flimsy and wasteful if it consists only of an aimless exploration of childhood. I began to see that we could spend two more months or a year in similar wanderings without one bit of improvement in the patient.

I also began to see in this period that the supervisor was able to get a better picture of the process from my reports than I was able to get from writing them. I reached a point at which my attitude toward him changed from "How can I avoid his criticism?" to "How can I make most use of his supervision?" As this transformation took place, it was pleasantly surprising that the patient shared in the benefit.

The interview of November 26, although not free of some of the criticisms made above, shows a better ability to remain in the role of a therapist. It should be noted here that this session took place about two weeks after time structure had been applied to the relationship by setting a date for discharge. That was a sign for the patient to retreat into his childhood again. Now I was able to permit such a retreat because I had advanced far enough to keep the focus in the present, both for the patient and for myself.

This report shows a better ability to avoid lecturing and intellectual explanations, and in this avoidance, a better recognition of the feeling behind the patient's verbalizations. Earlier I answered the patient's request for hypnosis with an explanation somewhat like Freud's reasons for abandoning hypnosis. This time I was able to recognize the meaning of hypnosis for him and to respond appropriately.

The first page of the report suggests that my fear of hurting the patient has lessened. Consequently, he is able to express true feelings of hostility. However, after needling him into an angry outburst, I became apologetic and tried to smooth matters again. Undoubtedly I am relieved when he says he likes me again.

In general, I believe with this interview, and particularly since then, I have reached a period in which continuing therapy training and supervision will be of greatest benefit. My roughest spots have received some smoothing but much more needs to be done, not only to become a skilled therapist (and not a preacher or explorer) throughout the therapy session. This can be accomplished with further practice and supervision, and with a variety of patients.

With present academic and work demands, such a program of training does not seem feasible or practical for me. In order to maintain my other work commitments, I will have to forego further psychotherapy training at this time. My patient is to be discharged soon. I would like to continue with him on an out-patient basis. Some supervision will certainly be necessary. Perhaps the hours with the patient and with the supervisor can be reduced. I am by no means ready to say that I want to do therapy exclusively. To be a good therapist I believe such a final decision is necessary.

* * *

It will be interesting for the reader to compare this evaluation of the supervisory experience submitted by the therapist with the evaluation of the same experience contributed by the supervisor. In terms of the mere mechanics it is of interest to note that in our experience, with all types of supervisors and all types of students, the evaluations written by the supervisors were usually considerably longer than the self-evaluations written by the students. We don't know if we should infer from this that the supervisor is always more worried about his part of the proceedings and therefore gives a more detailed account, or whether we ought, rather, to infer that the student who is in the less powerful position is somewhat less free in his expression and therefore does not feel able to describe the situation as fully. The material that this student contributed is perhaps typical of the kind of student who is genuinely able to look at himself. Occasionally, one receives evaluations from students that say practically nothing about themselves, written as if they were college questionnaires concerning the effectiveness of a course. There are other students who write about themselves, but do not dare to mention anything that has to do with the supervisory experience itself. They are willing to analyze the records, the case examples which they offer, but will not say anything about their relationship with the teacher. All these ways of using the written evaluation report, in order to say something about themselves and about the supervision, can, of course, be used in the final evaluation conference.

As one compares the following evaluation, which was written by the supervisor, with the one that was submitted by the student therapist, one should note the very high degree of concordance between the two. Even in the choice of their examples, supervisor and student have picked the same incidents from past supervisory conferences, as if they both independently rediscovered which examples were most instructive and had most decisively influenced the total training process.

Evaluation by Supervisor

The following material constitutes the supervisory evaluation of the psychotherapeutic work of Dr. K, covering the period from July to December. This report will be supplemented by Dr. K's own evaluation, and a few concluding paragraphs which will be the result of a final conference between supervisor and supervisee based on these two reports.

During the last six months Dr. K had 18 supervisory conferences with me. His conception of psychotherapy before his experience in supervision can best be exemplified perhaps through a few paragraphs he wrote during a course on psychotherapy. He, as well as all other class members, was given a psychotherapeutic situation in which a patient comes to the doctor for help, feeling panic-stricken about his being unable to control erections in the men's shower-room. The students were asked to write down spontaneously what they might have said to the patient. Dr. K gave the following response:

"I think we might be able to learn what causes you to have erections at such times and, by so doing, free you from such an embarrassing situation. It is not something we can accomplish with a secret formula in a few minutes. So let's arrange for times when I can see you, and then we will start working on the problem. I think we might have our first appointment this afternoon." Dr. K adds then the following comment: "I feel this is too big a problem to try to solve in five minutes. I will try to give reassurance, as above, and some encouragement that our course of interviews will alleviate his difficulty."

I could not help but note his use of the words: "course of interviews," since this perhaps was his conception at that time as to the nature of psychotherapy. He had done considerable interviewing during his army experience and had felt—and I think with justification—that he was a helpful person. A good many people who experienced having received help from him remained in contact, and sent him, later on, appreciative letters. One of his ideas of psychotherapy, then, was that the patient learn something in a course of interviews (parallel to the way in which one could learn something in a course on psychotherapy), and the other motive in his way of reacting to patients was that he wanted to be appreciated and loved, and hoped that the patient would understand his wisdom. During our supervisory conferences we developed a private language, such as saying that he acted toward patients as if he had to be their kind and clever uncle.

It seems to me that Dr. K had exactly these two points in mind when suggesting, as the basis for our mutual evaluation procedures, the interviews which he had with his patient on August 18 and on November 26. While actually his psychotherapeutic work started in July, he chose a later interview, since he felt that this was the end of the early period where he had really "diagnosed," with the help of supervision, his interviewing problem, and wanted to see if he could change it. The second interview is neither his best, nor his latest, but falls in a period where he felt that he had experienced for the first time his ability to change toward a new way of doing psychotherapy, of using himself.

At the point of dictating this, I do not have the exact diagnosis of the patient on file, but I conceive of him as a very disturbed person and, while I feel that the word "borderline schizophrenic" does not say too much about him, it is at least an indication that Dr. K got a difficult situation as his first one. The situation was made more difficult because the patient had to be transferred from his former therapist who left Topeka. The former therapist worked with this patient, if I'm correct, without control, and Dr. K felt impelled, I suppose, to use himself as much as possible in a way similar to the patient's previous experience, since he did not want to lose the patient and had not yet confidence enough to trust his own professional self.

The first interview of August 18 is a good example of the kind of psychic material which has dominated hour after hour the sessions of the patient's contact with the former therapist and later on with Dr. K. It was as if the therapist pushed the patient away from the present situation, did not make use of the interpersonal relationship that existed between patient and therapist, and encouraged the patient to wander off into childhood, to delve into schizoid fantasies. In spite of the terrifying nature of some of this fantasy material, both patient and therapist felt more comfortable in the realm of castration threats, seduction of mothers, homosexual fellatio experiences, and the like, than in coming to grips with each other about the problem of help.

Dr. K's use of himself, to quote from his first interview, was to get the patient "off the subject," "to get him back to the castration story," to ask him for explanations, to question the patient, to reassure him, to point out to him, to give him reassurance in terms of genetic explanations, to tell him that others do similar things, and that he wasn't really so bad, since in his test folder he did not respond with "penis" to the stimulus word "suck" in one of the association tests. His idea was to lead the patient back to pathological material of the past to reassure him about it, and to avoid any hostility that the patient may express toward him during the therapeutic situation.

He truly was a good uncle full of wisdom who knew everything very well, who forgave, and who was moralizing and helped the patient to speak about everything except the present situation, except the psychotherapeutic situation, except the future, and except the real problems he had in taking help from this particular psychotherapist. Whenever the patient made a reference to receive such help, to get nearer to the psychotherapist, Dr. K "got him off the subject."

It is, of course, only for the sake of pointing out the learning problem Dr. K had that I am magnifying his difficulties in this way, thus almost indicating that Dr. K was not a helpful person during this initial period. I do not want to give this impression, and the best proof for his helpfulness consisted of the fact that the patient stayed with him and improved. It is not the basic helpfulness of Dr. K, his basic integrity, his desire to help, that is questioned, but the psychotherapeutic skill, the conscious use that he made of himself during his beginning months of therapeutic work.

The interview of November 26 demonstrates striking changes in the use Dr. K made of himself. When the patient wonders if hypnosis could be tried to clear things up more quickly, Dr. K did relate this to the painfulness of the psychotherapeutic experience, to some of the doubts that the patient had about Dr. K. He did dare to relate to the anger of the patient and, rather than avoiding the subject, was able to point it out to the patient without feeling uncomfortable; he could even stand the patient's attack when the latter suggested that he had arranged an interview with another doctor. He did not have to avoid the past in this new use he made of himself, but was able to tie up the patient's past with the present therapeutic situation. He had thus learned to live and to work with the patient's ambivalence and also to face his own ambivalence.

It might well be useful to point out that a similar change did occur in Dr. K's use of his supervisory experience with me. He was always a pleasant student, who asked careful questions and avoided conflict within the supervisory situation. Once during a meeting of the whole group, while sharing the anger of one of the group members, he did not express it when the evaluation procedure was discussed. Later, however, he was able to tell me how he had felt about it. In facing and in expressing his own ambivalence he learned to make different use of the supervisory conferences, of me as a teacher, and of himself as a learner. At first, I suppose, he had hope that I, too, would be a good uncle full of wisdom for him, who would always keep him in kind spirits. I think he has learned now that he can use me differently and without danger, and in turn has made a beginning step in a different use of himself as a psychotherapist.

Dr. K's use of the supervisory experience was adequate, very adequate. I certainly feel that he should be given continued opportunity to do supervised psychotherapeutic work if he so desires. The experience with me was too short, I think, in order that Dr. K know how much of himself he was to put into psychotherapeutic work. He has interest and growing sensitivity for it. I understand from the new rotation schedule that Dr. K will be working on the neurology section, where there will be no direct opportunity for psychotherapy. He should be given an opportunity to finish his work with the present patient under supervision. I would be quite willing to undertake the responsibility of supervision if the psychotherapy supervision committee will allot the time for it. However, it is important, I think, that Dr. K think of this new method of supervision as not only a learning experience, but also as one that might help him more fully to decide how much psychotherapeutic work he wants to do in the future.

It is at the present time my impression that Dr. K can and should do such psychotherapeutic work if he develops at the same rate. His future work assignment would have to be adjusted to this plan, or is it possible perhaps that he may be assigned to cases outside of his particular ward? As soon as Dr. K feels ready for it, he should let us know. I have also no objections to his taking more than one case.

Finally, I would want to add that mine was a very pleasant experience with him, even though the going was rough at times. I hope that the psychotherapy supervision committee sees fit to accept the above recommendations.

* * *

During the final evaluation conference, the supervisor and the student read these evaluations together. Each has an opportunity to react to the material of the other. They discover how much they are together in their assessments and where the differences may lie. In this particular case, the therapist decided that he would not continue his psychotherapy training beyond finishing this case. The training experience had helped him to realize just what he would need to do, in order to identify himself fully with a therapeutic function. At that time he was not ready for it and he chose to withdraw. The final summary reflects what went on during the conference when both supervisor and therapist try to reconcile whatever differences exist and come to a final decision which is to be submitted to the administration.

Final Summary of Evaluation Conference

In our final evaluation we shared the material which we had prepared and we feel that there is consistent similarity. Dr. K said that he felt about it as if we had written these evaluations together and at the same time.

We used this session in order to discuss one difference in these evaluations which relates to the future work of Dr. K. While the supervisor spoke of the possibility of Dr. K doing continued supervised psychotherapeutic work with one or more patients, Dr. K expressed in his evaluation the feeling that his present work obligations would not allow him to continue psychotherapeutic work at this particular moment. We discussed some of these external pressures which would prevent Dr. K at present from allowing himself to bear the "internal pressures" that supervised psychotherapy would put on him. He is also not quite certain about his professional future, employment or private practice, in Topeka or in another community.

While it is important for us to have the psychotherapy supervision committee know about the work done, and to acknowledge in terms of the choices it gives Dr. K for the future, it must be stated that the practical decision for the moment will have to be that Dr. K will do no more than finish his present case with me. Of course, if certain aspects of his present training, his present placement, work assignment, etc., might change, he and the psychotherapy supervision committee may want to rediscuss this decision.

* * *

This particular evaluation is of especial interest, since it demonstrates that even successful performance, evaluated as such by both the supervisor and the student, can lead to the discontinuance of training as the learning experience permits the student to become aware of what he would need to do in order to identify himself fully with therapeutic work. Evaluation of students, then, frequently raises as a major consequence the problems of proper selection for a profession. In this case it was self-selection on the part of the student. The procedure discussed certainly permits us to consider selection as a mutual process, rather than as a one-sided decision that is reached by designated selection experts. Evaluation and selection are in effect two interrelated aspects of the training process.

The problem of selection has always been an extremely baffling one in the clinical professions. Professional schools continuously try to devise screening procedures which will permit them to select students with a maximum expectation of success, of suitability for the profession. As one reads the existing literature on selection and screening procedures, one realizes the enormous difficulties in trying to pre-select for these very expensive and time-consuming training programs those who will successfully repay the investment of energy, time, and space on the part of the training organization. This is as much true for the specific issue of psychotherapy training as it is for training in psychiatry in general, in the different forms of social work, in psychoanalysis, and in all similar clinical professions. In recent years, intensive studies have been undertaken, in order to investigate the problems of selection for training in clinical psychology and in psychiatry.* These studies which report on years of responsible and painstaking research seem to indicate that, despite careful and systematic scrutiny, using all the currently available testing tools, selection in these fields is up against the fact that it is hard to select if one does not know much more precisely what one selects for. The fields of psychiatry and clinical psychology, for example, are so wide, differ so much in varieties of potential application, and leave so much room for all types of gifts, and perhaps also for all types of lack of gifts, that those who select are in the position of a surveyor of land who, while knowing all of its features, does not exactly know what it is to be used for, but nevertheless must make decisions concerning its suitability.

A second serious problem with the process of selection has to do with a central theme underlying all such selection research, namely, that it would be desirable and should be possible for a small group which comprises the élite of the profession to decide the fate of those who wish to be trained, to have enough wisdom and power and the God-given right, as it were, to play Saint Peter at the portals of the professional heaven. Most admissions committees of clinical centers, in order to protect themselves against this kind of potential power complex, develop attitudes of humility and try to cope with the problem of the power delegated to them by using it sparingly and letting everyone get by unless there is an outright indication that he definitely will not succeed. There is, then, the "laissez-faire" school of selection committees who take everybody but the extreme borderline student or delinquent student, and those who dare to act on their fantasy of having to select for the élite and who then use the "genius clause" as a guide to their decisions.

* See E. L. Kelly and D. W. Fiske, *The Prediction of Performance in Clinical Psychology* (Ann Arbor: University of Michigan Press, 1951); and R. R. Holt and L. Luborsky. *Personality Patterns of Psychiatrists: A Study in Methods of Selecting Residents* (Vol. 1, New York, Basic Books, 1958; Vol. 2, Ann Arbor, Edwards Bros., 1958).

The field of psychotherapy is no exception to these considerations. The question of who is to be admitted to practice psychotherapy (whether under private practice conditions, or under the conditions of a clinical setting where private therapeutic responsibility is constantly related to some form of public responsibility) is, of course, first of all a question of public policy. Those who have the power to make such decisions may choose to operate with the philosophy of "laissez faire" or with that of the "genius clause." These decisions may be governed largely by the interaction of supply and demand which varies in the different parts of our country.

We are, however, not concerned here with the political problem in itself, but rather with certain psychological issues which must become a part of the training process if training is to be dynamically oriented. We are concerned with the psychological use of selection procedures, and we believe that selection based on an evaluation process in which both the student and the teacher participate will be more effective, and will yield more scientific reward than selection based simply on a sort of diagnostic appraisal, a screening of prospective candidates who are looked at rather than worked with. This has to do not only with the state of our present clinical knowledge, which we believe yields less in diagnostic appraisal than it does in the psychological process itself, but also has to do with our conviction that selection as an outcome of a process of growth, a process of mutual participation consciously utilized as training goes on, will permit us to change the power issue into one of shared responsibility between student and teacher.

Finally, as far as training for psychotherapy is concerned, it will make it possible for the young practitioner to participate in the solution of the issue mentioned earlier, namely, the issue of what one selects people for. The basic professions that train psychotherapists today are indeed broadly defined, and must develop practices that permit the individual practitioner to find out for himself whether he is ready and able to identify himself with any specific application within the field he has chosen.

Selection procedures in which the student does not participate are comparable to decisions upon the birth of the baby as to what kind of occupation he is to have when he grows up. Selection which grows from evaluation procedures, as has been described earlier, stimulates growth.

Evaluations written on the work of students are therefore not simply mechanical statements about the quality of the work, passing or failing marks, but rather are qualifying statements through which we try to understand how each student is learning, and how we can best help each to make the appropriate next step in his training. Evaluation is in this sense always future-directed. The student and the supervisor talk about the work done in the past, in order to help determine what ought to be done next. This next step is not entirely up to the student and his supervisor. Both are responsible to the administrative authority in the setting. This fact disciplines both. In some ways they can be freer with each other, since they know that the final decision is not up to them alone. And in some other ways their relationship will be a more professional one, since the mutual responsibility includes also a responsibility to the larger setting. The teacher is responsible for the training, not of "his" student, but of a student who is enrolled in the training program of an organization which delegates certain authority to the teacher, in order to enable him to discharge his delegated function.

Whenever the training process has proceeded satisfactorily it will be improbable that the decisions reached at the end of the evaluation period will be one-sided, or will be experienced as arbitrary by the student. Successful teaching must create insights in the student sufficient to permit him to judge himself in the very same light that the teacher is most likely to see him. It is for this reason that evaluation and selection procedures of the kind being discussed create a mutuality that makes it rare for one-sided decisions to be taken against the student. Even those students who ultimately prove to be unsuitable for the practice of psychotherapy will have grown during the supervision process and, rather than having been selected for the profession or banished from the profession, will be able to experience themselves as individuals who have made valuable discoveries about their capabilities.

The supervisor who works with this method, but is not yet fully familiar with it, may think of these devices as manipulative. Actually, he thus tells us that he has not yet learned to use the tool of evaluation, the structure described, in a truly dynamic sense, but must rely heavily on secret manipulation, on suggestion and the like, in order to get the student to comply with the authoritative opinion which he, the teacher, secretly holds.

It is interesting that even experienced psychotherapists, when put into the position of the teacher, seem to forget a great deal of what they have learned about processes of interaction, and fall back on methods of teaching, and on methods of decision-making, that they themselves experienced when they were students. The student is in many ways much nearer to the supervisor than the patient is to the therapist. The involvement of the supervisor with his student, the emotional investment the supervisor has in his student's change, makes it difficult for the two to keep a sufficient distance so that an evaluation process can take place that is neither manipulative nor overprotective.

One of the protective devices that both student-therapist and supervisor can utilize, in order to maintain the objective training atmosphere, is the recourse to administration. The supervisor does not have the final authority. Both therapist and supervisor know that the authority is vested in the psychotherapy supervision committee or the education committee, or the specific administrator of the clinical setting. It is for the administratively responsible group or the top administrator himself to decide whether the recommendations contained in the evaluation material are to be sustained or not. These recommendations may be concerned with the question of whether the student ought to devote more time to psychotherapy, ought to be allowed to carry more difficult cases, needs more supervision or a different supervisor, ought to have a second supervisor along with the first, etc. If the therapist being supervised is a staff member of the organization, the evaluation may likewise be concerned with recommendations concerning change in status, increase in salary, widening of the scope of his work, or restriction or discontinuance of his psychotherapeutic responsibilities.

One very important problem that is of considerable interest to us as supervisors has to do with the optimum length of supervision. Social work practice, for example, has often been to overextend supervision through many years of service of even the trained and fully competent worker. Other clinical professions, such as psychiatry and clinical psychology, which have developed supervisory practices much more recently, usually make much less use of them, perhaps too little. Psychoanalytic training centers count their supervision period in terms of control hours and finished cases, and are currently at work to supplement the mechanical application of training requirements counted in hours and in cases by a training philosophy that is also concerned with the individual student and not only with general rules. Whatever training requirement is worked out concerning supervision, it will need to be a mixture of general procedures and individualized applications, in order to maintain clinical standards and at the same time meet the specific needs of given students.

We will have, too, to develop steps which lead from supervision to consultation. The latter is a form of advanced training and practice which can be introduced at a time when the practitioner of psychotherapy knows his basic job, when he can do independent work, but needs occasional help. Much later, perhaps, even consultation may cease, to be replaced by the occasional sharing of clinical experiences with other experienced colleagues who are partners in clarification, rather than supervisors or consultants.

Another problem of evaluation concerns the decision as to when a given student is ready for research and should participate in the research or training activities of his organization. Again we know from historical experience that practice varies widely. Clinical psychologists, because of their academic backgrounds, have frequently assumed, and wrongly so, that the young psychotherapist should start "research" instantly, as soon as he starts his first case. One still searching at that time for a professional identity, trying to acquaint himself through direct experience with new methods of working, would be forced prematurely into the position of the researcher. This mistake of introducing a step in training too early is about as dangerous as the mistake of those social work agencies that maintain dependency on supervision forever.

Supervision, of course, is a constant struggle within the student and the teacher, as well as between the student and the teacher. The student wants to be dependent on someone who knows more, he wishes to learn from him and at the same time to develop toward independence. The teacher, too, wants to help the student to mature; at the same time he has difficulties in letting him go. It is perhaps for the administration to introduce the proper balance. The ending of formal training, regardless of how careful we are with our evaluation procedures, will always remain a somewhat arbitrary decision, even if completely agreed upon by both partners. It is as arbitrary as the ending of a psychotherapeutic experience, since in both we realize that the decision depends on a selected definition of what constitutes the achievement of emotional health or the achievement of the capacity for independent psychotherapeutic work.

Evaluation in the final analysis, then, builds toward termination of training, toward some form of graduation, toward some form of the replacement of the relationship between student and teacher by one where they are now truly professional colleagues, co-workers who have to learn to work together on a different basis. If the student were to continue in the clinical setting, let us say as a staff member, he would usually move up through the ranks and become in time a teacher and researcher himself. He will then suddenly find himself in a position where he repeats the total training process in reverse order. He will be confronted with the anxieties of the young teacher, and will have to learn to identify himself in a new way with his profession, for which he has selected himself and for which he was selected through the evaluative training process we have been discussing.

XVII / Guide to the Literature

In assembling a guide to the literature on the supervision of individual helping in the clinical professions, one is faced with many decisions as to which contributions are directly relevant. The problem is how to separate out those articles dealing specifically with the supervision of individual clinical work from those concerned with the many convergent training and therapeutic problems in the field. In part, any such decisions necessarily and properly reflect the writers' theoretical convictions and biases as to what is most germane to the thinking embodied in their own position. We can do best here if we state the bases for our particular selections and, equally important, the criteria that have governed our exclusions.

We have included in this guide, insofar as our search could locate, all those items in our professional literature that deal with individual supervision of individual clinical work in the specific techniques of psychoanalysis, social casework, and individual psychotherapy. We have left out the voluminous literature on supervision and personnel problems in industry and management and have left out as well the literature on supervision in areas very closely allied to our primary focus, such as group work and group psychotherapy, institutional and community agency work, hospital and ward management of psychiatric in-patients, psychological testing, and psychiatric nursing. Though there may be much to be learned from the experiences of supervisors in these closely overlapping areas of interest, we have nonetheless held to our decision to list only contributions concerning the individual teaching of individual helping. Once our field of inquiry is broadened into processes involving group interactions (often within complex institutional settings), the supervisory problem is simultaneously more complicated and less elucidated. How applicable principles derived from individual helping processes are to such group situations is a much argued point.

The articles that have been included have been listed under five separate headings as follows:

1. General problems of training in clinical work
2. Training in psychoanalysis
3. Training in social casework
4. Training in psychotherapy
5. Administrative aspects of clinical training

The breakdown by areas for items 2, 3, and 4 is in terms of the specific technical skill that is being taught, rather than in terms of the primary profession of the one who teaches or the one who learns the skill. That is, under "training in psychotherapy" we have listed all relevant items concerning the training of psychiatrists, of clinical psychologists, and of social workers that has to do with their specific training as psychotherapists. We do this because it brings together contributions relating to the theoretical and technical problems that people share when acquiring a specific skill, and it separates the consideration of the problems involved in the learning of such different skills as conducting an analysis, doing individual psychotherapy, or giving casework service. Though we thus recognize the qualitative differences involved in the learning and doing of such disparate clinical functions, by including them all together in this chapter we also acknowledge that they have actually borrowed from one another as far as modes of training are concerned, and share to a large extent a common philosophy of the helping process.

What is specifically included (and excluded) in each of our five subdivisions warrants somewhat fuller statement. The first category, "general problems of training in clinical work," contains general articles on the dynamics of learning, on clinical training programs and clinical training problems, with more specific articles on training, say in psychiatry or in clinical psychology—apart, however, from special training in individual therapeutic work, which is listed in categories 2, 3, and 4. With the exception of a few survey articles, we leave out the whole related literature on problems of didactic curricula in formal training programs, questions of training standards and requirements, and the closely linked political considerations of who should be trained for clinical and, specifically, for therapeutic work, and what the basic background and prerequisites should be.

An important clinical concern, and one even more closely linked to training for therapeutic work, is the use of the consultant in clinical training. Rather than include such items in our bibliography on supervision, however, reference is made to a workshop entitled "The Use of the Consultant" at the 1955 meeting of the American Orthopsychiatric Association, published in the *American Journal of Orthopsychiatry*, 26:223–251, 1956. The third of that series of three presentations contains a bibliography of 17 items covering the role and the responsibility of the consultant in clinical service and in clinical training.

The second category, "training in psychoanalysis," is primarily oriented to contributions concerning analytic supervision or the control analysis. A few more general articles on problems and trends in analytic training and on the nature of the total training setting are included. However, we specifically leave out the literature on two fundamental aspects of analytic practice and training. The one aspect is that of the training analysis itself, including the specific technical problems of the training analysis, the relations of problems of training analysis to those of therapeutic analysis, and the place of training analysis in psychoanalytic training. Though the training analysis is considered the cornerstone of analytic training and is a phase of the student's development to which much thought and study has been devoted, this has been dealt with much earlier in the psychoanalytic literature and has periodically been systematically reviewed. The second area of analytic work that we have decided to exclude is that of the problems of countertransference, in both its theoretical and technical aspects. We have done this even though a case can be made for the fact that most articles on countertransference are really disguised articles on training and supervision, since they so often refer to the countertransference difficulties of the student and are thus contributions —albeit, indirect ones—to the literature on the supervision of young analysts. Since, however, these articles do not deal with the training techniques of the control analyst in a direct way, they have been omitted from this listing. We mention these omissions in part to point up the fact that the actual literature on psychoanalytic training is by now a very large one, and that the contributions dealing specifically with the problems of the supervised or control analysis that we have listed here constitute but a segment of it.

The third category, "training in social casework," is by far the largest. One reason is that the literature on training in psychoanalysis centers around a number of areas of which direct supervision is but one; in contrast, the literature on training in social casework has from the beginning been primarily focused on the issues of supervision. Unlike the situation in analytic training, supervision is the main technical tool of social-work teaching and a main preoccupation of social-work literature. Supervision is, too, an integral function of the social agency and on one level or another, as student, worker, or supervisor, accompanies most social workers throughout their professional careers. In the social agency setting supervision has not only this training function that has already been stressed, but an administrative function as well, felt necessary to maintain the structure of the organization. Considering that the literature on social-work training centers largely around the problems of supervision, and that the number of social workers and social-work supervisors in the field is large, it is no wonder that this list is the longest.

The fourth category, "training in psychotherapy," contains articles of the most varied professional origin, since all the major clinical professions, psychoanalysis, psychiatry, clinical psychology, and social work, have begun to contribute to this specific skill. Although formal training in psychotherapy as such is available in just a few clinical centers, and although it is mostly taught within the broader framework of a more comprehensive primary professional training, it is gratifying to note that a sizable literature has already accumulated in regard to the teaching and learning of this specific skill. It is to this category that our own book is an addition.

The fifth category, "administrative aspects of clinical training," is the smallest. It is, however, an important one, dealing as it does with the very crucial problems of the relationship of administration to clinical training and to learning, particularly to that part of clinical training which is our concern: the learning of psychotherapy. This list is small because we have limited it sharply to articles that relate administration directly to teaching and learning of therapeutic skills in a clinical setting. We have therefore omitted all reference to the very large literature on general principles of administration, and the many specific applications of these to industrial, educational, and scientific institutions.

We wish to restate too that this book, and hence the bibliography, is about the supervision of treatment, and not directly about treatment. We have therefore striven throughout to include articles about the teaching and learning of psychotherapy and to exclude articles about the theory and technique of psychotherapy (and of psychoanalysis and of social casework)—which is indeed a voluminous literature of its own. With the exception of some very few survey articles, we have limited our selection to those contributions that are directly concerned with the process of interaction between supervisor and student, and those influences that facilitate or impede their fruitful collaboration toward the desired goal—increased psychotherapeutic skill.

To accomplish this purpose we tried to go quite far back in the literature. It is interesting to note that almost all of the contributions that we have found were published within the past twenty years, and that in the last five or ten years the volume has swelled to enormous proportions. This is evidence indeed that there is growing awareness of the insistent need for the clarification of training issues, for the concern with increasing technical therapeutic skills, and for the training of trainers. It is also our concern, both in this bibliography and the book as a whole, to help the teachers do a more adequate job. The increase of supervisory skills would prove the most effective way to develop more psychotherapists and better psychotherapists, in order to meet the increasingly recognized challenges of the field of mental health and illness.

General Problems of Training in Clinical Work

Anderson, Gladys L. "Procedures and Methods in Supervising Clinical Interns," *Journal of Consulting Psychology*, 15:267, 1951.

Bennett, Chester C. "Some Growing Pains in Clinical Psychology," *American Journal of Orthopsychiatry*, 22:153-161, 1952.

Berman, Leo. "A Group Psychotherapeutic Technique for Training in Clinical Psychology," *American Journal of Orthopsychiatry*, 22:322-327, 1953.

Brewer, Joseph E. "Supervision of Interns in a Community Guidance Center," *Journal of Consulting Psychology*, 15:268-270, 1951.

Cantor, N. F. *The Dynamics of Learning*. Buffalo, New York: Foster and Stewart, 1946.

Carp, A. L. "Supervision of Clinical Psychology Trainees in a Neuropsychiatric Hospital," *Journal of Consulting Psychology*, 15:271-273, 1951.

Coffey, Hubert S., and Winder, Clarence L. "Field Work in the Training of Clinical Psychologists," *American Journal of Orthopsychiatry*, 21: 303-311, 1951.

Deutschberger, Paul; Mathews, W. Mason; Pottharst, Karl; Underwood, Pauline. "Supervision in the Field Work Placement," *American Journal of Orthopsychiatry*, 21:319-324, 1951.

Ebaugh, Franklin. "Graduate Teaching of Psychiatry through Individual Supervision," *American Journal of Psychiatry*, 107:274-278, 1950.

Ekstein, Rudolf, and Mayman, Martin. "On the Professional Identity of the Clinical Psychologist," *Bulletin of the Menninger Clinic*, 21: 59-61, 1957.

Fensterheim, Herbert. "Introspections of a Clinical Trainee," *Psychological Newsletter*, 41:1-5, 1952.

Gardner, George E. "The Development of the Clinical Attitude," *American Journal of Orthopsychiatry*, 22:162-169, 1952.

Grotjahn, Martin. "The Role of Identification in Psychiatric and Psychoanalytic Training," *Psychiatry*, 12:141-151, 1949.

Harrower, M. R. (ed.). *Training in Clinical Psychology*. New York: Josiah Macy, Jr., Foundation, 1947.

Henry, William E. "The Language of Fantasy—A Problem in Instruction and Supervision," *American Journal of Orthopsychiatry*, 23:315-321, 1953.

Hollis, Florence. "Intangibles of Good Supervision," *Public Health Nursing*, 30:458-461, 1938.

Holt, Robert R., and Luborsky, Lester. "Research in the Selection of Psychiatrists: A Second Interim Report," *Bulletin of the Menninger Clinic*, 16:125-135, 1952.

———. *Personality Patterns of Psychiatrists: A Study in Methods for Selecting Residents*, vol. 1, New York, Basic Books, 1958; vol. 2, Ann Arbor, Edwards Bros., 1958.

Hutt, Max L. "Discussion of Problems of Supervision and Training in Clinical Psychology," *American Journal of Orthopsychiatry*, 23:328-331, 1953.

Kelly, E. Lowell. "The Prediction of Success in Clinical Psychology," in *Relation of Psychological Tests to Psychiatry*, eds. P. Hoch and J. Zubin. New York: Grune & Stratton, 1952. Pp. 150-164.

———, and Fiske, D. W. *The Prediction of Performance in Clinical Psychology*. Ann Arbor: University of Michigan Press, 1951.

Kelly, George A. "Principles of Training in Clinical Psychology," *American Journal of Orthopsychiatry*, 21:312-318, 1951.

Korner, Ija N., and Brown, William H. "The Mechanical Ear," *Journal of Consulting Psychology*, 16:81-84, 1952.

Kris, Ernst. "Training in Psychoanalysis and the Development of Theoretical Concepts of Clinical Psychology," in *Training in Clinical Psy-*

chology. New York: Josiah Macy, Jr., Foundation, 1947. Pp. 61-64.

Kubie, Lawrence S. "The Pros and Cons of a New Profession: A Doctorate in Medical Psychology." *Texas Reports on Biology and Medicine*, 12: 692-737, 1954. Reprinted in *Medical and Psychological Teamwork in the Care of the Chronically Ill*, ed. Molly Harrower. Charles C Thomas Press, 1955.

Luborsky, Lester. "Selecting Psychiatric Residents: Survey of the Topeka Research," *Bulletin of the Menninger Clinic*, 18:252-259, 1954.

———; Holt, Robert R.; and Morrow, William R. "Interim Report of the Research Project on the Selection of Medical Men for Psychiatric Training," *Bulletin of the Menninger Clinic*, 14: 92-101, 1950.

Macfarlane, Jean W. "The Training of Psychologists for the Community Mental Health Service Field," *Journal of Clinical Psychology*, 6: 128-132, 1950.

Mathews, W. Mason, and Wineman, David. "The Psychologist and his Clinical Role," *American Journal of Orthopsychiatry*, 22:170-175, 1952.

———. "The Supervision of Clinical Diagnostic Work," *American Journal of Orthopsychiatry*, 23:301-306, 1953.

"The Menninger Foundation School of Psychiatry: The Selection of Candidates for Training in Psychiatry, Philosophy and Methods," *Bulletin of the Menninger Clinic*, 11:77-108, 1947.

"The Menninger Foundation School of Clinical Psychology, an Experiment," *Bulletin of the Menninger Clinic*, 11:109-140, 1947.

Millar, W. M., and Valentine, Max. "Teaching Aids in Clinical Psychiatry," *Journal of Mental Science*, 98:477-482, 1952.

Newcomb, Margaret L.; Gay, Eleanor; and Levin, Barry L. "A Training Program for Social Work Students in a Psychiatric Clinic," *Social Casework*, 34:204-211, 1953.

Paterson, Donald G. "Comments on the Shakow Report on Training in Clinical Psychology," *Journal of Clinical Psychology*, 4:298-300, 1948.

Richmond, Mary E. *Social Diagnosis*. New York: Russell Sage Foundation, 1917. Pp. 349-351, 449-453.

Shakow, David. "The Worcester Internship Program," *Journal of Consulting Psychology*, 10:191-200, 1946.

Smith, Harvey L. "Psychiatry in Medicine: Intra- or Interprofessional Relationships?." *Am. J. Sociology*, 63:285-289, 1957.

Spitz, René A. "The Role of Training in Psychoanalysis in the Development of Research in Clinical Psychology," in *Training in Clinical Psychology*. New York: Josiah Macy, Jr., Foundation, 1947. Pp. 65-70.

Sutherland, R. L. "An Application of the Theory of Psychosexual Development to the Learning Process," *Bulletin of the Menninger Clinic*, 15:91-99, 1951.

Tuttle, H. S. "Two Kinds of Learning," *Journal of Psychology*, 22:267-277, 1946.

Warson, S. R.; Lewis, M. M.; and Saunders, G. M. "A Method for Teaching the Emotional and Social Aspects of Preventive Medicine," *Journal of the Association of the American Medical Colleges*, 23:131-136, 1948.

Watson, Robert I. "Training in Clinical Psychology from the Perspective of the Internship," *American Journal of Orthopsychiatry*, 22: 140-152, 1952.

Whitehorn, J. C. "Psychiatry in Medical Education: The Teacher Characteristics and Qualifications," *American Journal of Psychiatry*, 103: 446-449, 1947.

Winokur, George. "Brainwashing–A Social Phenomenon of our Time," *Human Organization*, 13:16-18, Winter, 1955. (Editorials: "Brainwashing and the Teaching Process," "Brainwashing and Reliability," *Human Organization*, 13:3-4, Winter, 1955.)

Wyatt, Frederick. "Problems of Training in Clinical Psychology," *American Journal of Orthopsychiatry*, 22:138-139, 1952.

———. "The Meaning of Clinical Experience," *American Journal of Orthopsychiatry*, 23:284-292, 1953.

Training in Psychoanalysis

Ackerman, N. W. "Selected Problems in Supervised Analysis," *Psychiatry*, 16:283-290, 1953.

Balint, Michael. "On the Psycho-Analytic Training System," *International Journal of Psychoanalysis*, 29:163-173, 1948.

Bibring, Edward. "Methods and Technique of Control Analysis" (a part of the report of the Four Countries Conference of the International Training Commission), *International Journal of Psychoanalysis*, 18:369-371, 1937.

Blajan-Marcus, Simone. "Erreurs, tâtonnements et tentations des apprentis Analystes" ("Mistakes, Gropings and Temptations of Apprentice Analysts"), *Revue Française de Psychoanalyse*, 16:292-312, 1952.

Blitzsten, N. Lionel, and Fleming, Joan. "What is a Supervisory Analysis?" *Bulletin of the Menninger Clinic*, 17:117-129, 1953.

Brosin, Henry W. "Psychoanalytic Training for Psychiatric Residents and Others; The Associated Psychiatric Faculties of Chicago Experiment," *American Journal of Psychiatry*, 109:188-195, 1952.

Eitingon, Max. "Report of International Training Commission–Chairman's Address," *International Journal of Psychoanalysis*, 18:350-358, 1937.

———, et al. "Reports of International Training Commission," *International Journal of Psychoanalysis*, Vols. 7-20, 1926-1939.

Ekstein, Rudolf. "On Current Trends in Psychoanalytic Training," in *Explorations in Psychoanalysis*, ed. R. Lindner. New York: Julian Press, 1953. Pp. 230-265.

Emch, Minna. "The Social Context of Supervision," *International Journal of Psychoanalysis*, 36:298-306, 1955.

Frosch, John. "Psychoanalytic Training and Practice," *Annual Survey of Psychoanalysis*, 1:390-398, 1952.

Gitelson, Maxwell. "Problems of Psychoanalytic Training," *Psychoanalytic Quarterly*, 17:198-211, 1948.

Grotjahn, Martin. "A Note about Teaching Psychoanalysis," *Samiksa*, 1:39-50, 1947.

———. "Present Trends in Psychoanalytic Training," in *Twenty Years of Psychoanalysis*, eds. F. Alexander and H. Ross. New York: Norton, 1953. Pp. 84-113.

———. "About the Relation Between Psychoanalytic Training and Psychoanalytic Therapy," *International Journal of Psychoanalysis*, 35:254-262, 1954.

Holt, Robert R., and Luborsky, Lester. "The Selection of Candidates for Psychoanalytic Training: On the Use of Interviews and Psychological Tests," *Journal of the American Psychoanalytic Association*, 3:666-681, 1955.

Keiser, Sylvan. "The Technique of Supervised Analysis," *Journal of the American Psychoanalytic Association*, 4:539-549, 1956.

Kovács, Vilma. "Training- and Control-Analysis," *International Journal of Psychoanalysis*, 17:346-354, 1936.

———. Report of the Four Countries Conference: "Discussion on Methods and Technique of Control Analysis," *International Journal of Psychoanalysis*, 18:369-372, 1937.

Kubie, Lawrence S. "Research into the process of supervision in psychoanalysis." *The Psychoanalytic Quarterly*, 27:226-236, 1958.

Lampl-de Groot, Jeanne. "Problems of Psychoanalytic Training," *International Journal of Psychoanalysis*, 35:184-187, 1954.

Landauer, Karl. "Methods and Techniques of Control Analysis" (a part of the report of the Four Countries Conference of the International Training Commission), *International Journal of Psychoanalysis*, 18:371-372, 1937.

Loewald, Hans W. "Psychoanalytic Curricula—Principles and Structure," *Journal of the American Psychoanalytic Association*, 4:149-161, 1956.

Luborsky, Lester, and Holt, Robert R. "The Selection of Candidates for Psychoanalytic Training; Implications from Research on the Selection of Psychiatric Residents," *Journal of Clinical and Experimental Psychopathology*, 18:166-176, 1957.

Mohr, George J. "Psychoanalytic Training," in *Twenty Years of Psychoanalysis*, eds. F. Alexander and H. Ross. New York: Norton, 1953. Pp. 235-241.

Oberndorf, Clarence P. "Historical Comments on Psychoanalytic Teaching," *Bulletin of the American Psychoanalytic Association*, 8:209-213, 1952.

Sachs, Hanns. "Observations of a Training Analyst," *Psychoanalytic Quarterly*, 16:157-168, 1947.

Sharpe, Ella. "The Psychoanalyst," *International Journal of Psychoanalysis*, 28:1-6, 1947.

Sloane, Paul. "The Technique of Supervised Analysis," *Journal of the American Psychoanalytic Association*, 5:539-547, 1957.

Training in Social Casework

Abrahamson, Arthur C. "Group Methods in Field Work Teaching," *Social Casework*, 35:68-71, 1954.

Alper, Minnie. "Supervision as One Method of Staff Development—In a Rural Setting," *Proceedings of the National Conference of Social Work*, 1939. Pp. 294-303.

Anderson, Mary E.; Pfeiffer, Elizabeth E.; Schubert, Margaret S.; and Scott, Lulu. "The Content of First-Year Field Work in a Casework Setting," *Social Casework*, 34:61-67, 112-119, 1953.

Aptekar, Herbert H. "The Significance of Dependence and Independence in Supervision," *Social Casework*, 35:238-245, 1954.

Arndt, Hilda C. M. "Principles of Supervision in Public Assistance Agencies," *Social Casework*, 36:307-313, 1955.

Aufricht, Emmy. "Control and Freedom in the Caseworker's Growth," in *Administration, Supervision and Consultation*. New York: Family Service Association of America, 1955. Pp. 46-50.

Austin, Lucille N. "Supervision of the Experienced Caseworker," in *Principles and Techniques in Social Casework*, ed. Cora Kasius. New York: Family Service Association of America, 1950. Pp. 155-166.

———. "Basic Principles of Supervision," *Social Casework*, 33:411-419, 1952.

———. "An Evaluation of Supervision," *Social Casework*, 37:375-382, 1956.

———, et al. *Techniques of Student and Staff Supervision*. New York: Family Service Association of America, 1953.

Babcock, Charlotte G. "Social Work as Work," *Social Casework*, 34:415-422, 1953.

Beatman, Frances L. "The Selection of a Beginning Supervisor," *Social Casework*, 34:285-292, 1953.

———. "How Do Professional Workers Become Professional?" *Social Casework*, 37:383-388, 1956.

Bish, Bernice. "Current and Future Trends in Recording," in *Administration, Supervision and Consultation*. New York: Family Service Association of America, 1955. Pp. 59-68.

Brown, Josephine. "Principles, Content, and Objectives of Supervision," *Proceedings of the National Conference of Social Work*, 1938. Pp. 528-540.

Chichester, C. Elizabeth. "Group Meetings as an Aid to Student Supervision," *Social Casework*, 36:264-269, 1955.

———; Finestone, Samuel; Lucas, Leon; and Scott, Dala. "Field Work Criteria for Second-Year Casework Students," in *Principles and Techniques in Social Casework*, ed. Cora Kasius. New York: Family Service Association of America, 1950. Pp. 233-246.

Clark, Faith, and Maris, Madeleine. "Supervision of Fieldwork," in *Training for Skill in Social Casework*, ed. Virginia Robinson. Philadelphia: University of Pennsylvania Press, 1942.

Craig, Mary. "Field Supervision: An Adaptation of Social Work Skills," *Journal of Social Casework*, 30:200-203, 1949.

Cruser, Robert W., et al. "Opinions on Supervision: A Chapter Study," *Social Work*, 3:18-25, January 1958.

Dailey, Wilda J., and Hogan, Virginia Pettit. "Brief Recording and Supervision," *Social Casework*, 39:278-282, 1958.

Davis, Gertrude R. "The Selection and Evaluation of the Supervisor," *Jewish Social Service Quarterly*, 26:164-168, 1949.

De Schweinitz, Karl, et al. *Teaching Social Casework*. New York: Family Welfare Association of America, 1940.

Dekker, Andreas G. "Didactic Principles and Field Work Instruction," *Social Casework*, 38:350-354, 1957.

Eisenberg, Sidney. *Supervision in the Changing Field of Social Work*. Doctoral dissertation. Philadelphia: Jewish Family Service of Philadelphia, 1956.

Engel, Dorothy. "Supervision as One Method of Staff Development," *Proceedings of the National Conference of Social Work*, 1939. Pp. 284-294.

Family Welfare Association of America. *Some Emotional Elements in Supervision; Report of a Group Discussion*. New York: The Association, 1937.

———. *Field Supervision of Casework Students*. New York: The Association, 1942.

Feder, Leah. "The Group Conference as a Method of Supervision," *The Family*, 13:24-28, 1932.

Feldman, Yonata. "The Teaching Aspect of Casework Supervision," in *Principles and Techniques in Social Casework*, ed. Cora Kasius. New York: Family Service Association of America, 1950. Pp. 222-232.

———; Spotnitz, Hyman; and Nagelberg, Leo. "One Aspect of Casework Training through Supervision," *Social Casework*, 34:150-155, 1953.

Froehlich, Hans D. "Supervision of the Foreign Student," *Social Casework*, 34:216-221, 1953.

Garrett, Annette. *Learning Through Supervision*. Smith College Studies 24. October, 1954.

Glassberg, Benjamin. "The Role of the Supervisor in a Public Welfare Agency," *Public Welfare News*, 7:4 f., 1939.

Grossbard, Hyman. "Methodology for Developing Self-Awareness," *Social Casework*, 35:380-386, 1954.

Hamilton, Gordon. "Education for Social Work: The Interaction of School and Agency," *Social Work Journal*, 30:77, 1949.

———. "Self-Awareness in Professional Education," *Social Casework*, 35:371-379, 1954.

Hanford, Jeanette. "Standards of Measurement in Staff Evaluation in a Private Agency," *National Conference of Social Work*, 1942. Pp. 531-540.

Henry, Charlotte S. "Criteria for Determining Readiness of Staff to Function without Supervision," in *Administration, Supervision and Consulta-*

tion. New York: Family Service Association of America, 1955. Pp. 34-45.

Hester, Mary. "Field Teaching in a Private Agency," *The Family*, 22:14-20, 1941.

———. "The Educational Process in Supervision," *Social Casework*, 32:242-250, 1951.

Hochwald, Hilde Landenberger. "Teaching the Principle of Self-Determination to Foreign Students," *Social Casework*, 38:362-365, 1957.

Holcomb, Emerson. "An Analysis of the Supervisory Job," *Social Casework*, 37:126-131, 1956.

Hollis, Florence. "The Emotional Growth of the Worker Through Supervision," in *Worker and Supervisor*. New York: Family Welfare Association of America, 1936. Pp. 26-38. Also in *Proceedings of the National Conference of Social Work*, 1936. Pp. 167-178.

———. "Relationship of Classroom Teaching to Field Placement," *Social Casework*, 33:91-98, 1952.

———, and Clow, Lucia B. *The Skills of the Beginning Case Worker as Evaluated by the School, the Agency, and the Worker*. New York: Family Welfare Association of America, 1941.

Hutchinson, Dorothy. "Supervision in Social Case Work," *The Family*, 16:44-47, 1935.

Indelman, Rochelle. "Supervision and the Advanced Practitioner," *Social Work Journal*, 36:18-20, 1955.

James, Sara H. "Field Supervision—Unilateral or Integrated?" *National Conference of Social Work*, 1948. Pp. 293-301.

Johnson, Arlien. "Educating Social Workers for Ethical Practice," *Social Service Review*, 29:125-136, 1955.

Johnson, Vivian, and Windau, Margaret. "The Supervisor-Worker Relationship as an Element in Training: I. Mutual Activity as a Way of Development; II. Mutual Evaluation," *The Family*, 15:184-188, 1934.

Kasius, Cora. (Ed.). *Principles and Techniques in Social Casework*. New York: Family Service Association of America, 1950. Chapters by Austin, McCaffery, Neustaedter, Feldman, Chichester, Taft, and Towle.

———. (Ed.). *New Directions in Social Work*. New York: Harper, 1954.

Kauffman, Margaret. "Supervision of Case Work Staff," *The Family*, 19:196-202, 1938.

———, and Malmud, Helen. *Evaluations of Staff Members in Private Family Agencies*. New York: Family Welfare Association of America, 1940.

Kendrew, Mary Hylan. "Group Discussion as a Supervisory Tool," *Social Casework*, 33:246-250, 1952.

Leader, Arthur. "New Directions in Supervision," *Social Casework*, 38:462-468, 1957.

Lehnert, Bettina. "The Use of Case Material in Supervision," *American Journal of Orthopsychiatry*, 21:54-58, 1951.

Lehrman, Louis J. "The Integration of Class and Field in Professional Education," *Social Casework*, 33:250-255, 1952.

Levine, Norma D. "Educational Components of Supervision in a Family Agency," *Social Casework*, 31:245-250, 1950.

Levinson, Frances T. "Psychological Components of Supervision in a Family Agency," *Social Casework*, 31:237-245, 1950.

Lowry, Fern. "A Philosophy of Supervision in Social Case Work," in *Worker and Supervisor*. New York: Family Welfare Association of America, 1936. Pp. 16-25. Also in *Proceedings of the National Conference of Social Work*, 1936. Pp. 108-118.

———. "Supervision as an Aspect of Staff Development Programs," *Bulletin of the Child Welfare League of America*, 20:1-3, 1941.

McCaffery, Miriam. "Criteria for Student Progress in Field Work," in *Principles and Techniques in Social Casework*, ed. Cora Kasius. New York: Family Service Association of America, 1950: Pp. 172-186.

Munro, Marguerite M. "Modern Casework Recording: Integrating Casework and Supervision," *National Conference of Social Work*, 1951. Pp. 206-214.

Murase, Kenneth. "Problem in Supervision in an Authoritarian Setting," *Social Casework*, 35:117-122, 1954.

National Conference of Social Work. *Administration, Supervision and Consultation.* New York: Family Service Association of America, 1955.

Neustaedter, Eleanor. "The Field Supervisor as Educator," in *Principles and Techniques in Social Casework*, ed. Cora Kasius. New York: Family Service Association of America, 1950. Pp. 200-212.

Perlman, Helen H. "Content in Basic Social Casework," *Social Service Review*, 21:76-85, 1947.

———. "Teaching Case Work by the Discussion Method," *Social Service Review*, 24:334-346, 1950.

———. "Of Records and Supervision," *Social Service Review*, 28:83-85, 1954.

Perry, Martha. "Values and Limitations of the Evaluation Process; As Seen by the Worker," *Proceedings of the National Conference of Social Work*, 1940. Pp. 638-647.

Peters, Mary Overholt. "Supervising the Experienced Worker," *Journal of Social Casework*, 30:188-195, 1949.

Regensburg, Jeanette. "Professional Attributes, Knowledge and Skill in Practice: Educational Priorities," *Social Work Journal*, 34:51-54, 1953.

Reynolds, Bertha Capen. "*Learning and Teaching in the Practice of Social Work*," New York: Farrar and Rinehart, 1942.

Reynolds, Rosemary. *Evaluating the Field Work of Students*. New York: Family Service Association of America, 1946.

———. "Relationship of Field Placement to Classroom Teaching from the Standpoint of the Supervisor," *Social Casework*, 33:99-105, 1952.

Robinson, Virginia P. *A Changing Psychology in Social Casework*. Chapel Hill, North Carolina: University of North Carolina Press, 1930, Pp. 173–181.

Robinson, Virginia P. *Supervision in Social Casework; A Problem in Professional Education.* Chapel Hill, North Carolina: University of North Carolina Press, 1936. Esp. pp. 1-50.

———. "Educational Processes in Supervision," in *Worker and Supervisor.* New York: Family Welfare Association of America, 1936. Pp. 7-15.

———. *The Dynamics of Supervision under Functional Controls.* Philadelphia: The University of Pennsylvania Press, 1949.

———. (Ed.). *Training for Skill in Social Case Work.* Philadelphia: University of Pennsylvania Press, 1942.

Sarnat, Rhoda G. "Supervision of the Experienced Student," *Social Casework,* 33:147-152, 1952.

Scanlan, Emily R. "Process in the Supervision of the Beginning Supervisor," *Social Casework,* 35:199-206, 1954.

Schafer, Philip, and Norwick, Sydney, S. "Experiment in Promoting Human Relations in Supervision," *Mental Hygiene,* 36:6-24, 1952.

Schmidt, Frances. "Values and Limitations of the Evaluation Process: As Seen by the Supervisor," *Proceedings of the National Conference of Social Work,* 1940. Pp. 629-638.

Schour, Esther. "Some Principles in the Evaluation Process," *The Compass,* 21:3 ff., 1940.

———. "Helping Social Workers Handle Work Stresses," *Social Casework,* 34:423-428, 1953.

Scott, Lyndell. "The Function of Field Work in Professional Education," *Social Service Review,* 25:441-454, 1951.

Selby, Lola G. "Helping Students in Field Practice Identify and Modify Blocks to Learning," *Social Service Review,* 29:53-63, 1955.

Siegel, Doris. "Consultation: Some Guiding Principles," in *Administration, Supervision, and Consultation.* New York: Family Service Association of America, 1955. Pp. 98-114.

Siporin, Max. "Dual Supervision of Psychiatric Social Workers," *Social Work,* 1:32-42, April, 1956.

Slear, Genevieve Sennett. "Transition from Caseworker to Supervisor," *Journal of Social Casework,* 30:25-30, 1949.

Spencer, Sue W. "Case Supervision in a Public Assistance Agency," *The Family,* 22:336-343, 1942.

Stevens, Ruth N., and Hutchinson, Fred A. "A New Concept of Supervision Is Tested," *Social Work,* 1:50-55, July, 1956.

Studt, Elliot. "An Outline for Study of Social Authority Factors in Casework," *Social Casework,* 35:231-238, 1954.

Sytz, Florence. "An Experiment in Student Training," in *Interviews, Interviewers and Interviewing in Social Case Work.* New York: Family Welfare Association of America, 1931. Pp. 98-105.

———. "Professional Relations: The School of Social Work and the Agency," *Proceedings of the National Conference of Social Work,* 1942. Pp. 541-552.

Taft, Jessie. "Conception of the Growth Process Underlying Social Casework Practice," *Principles and Techniques of Social Case Work*, ed. Cora Kasius. New York: Family Service Association of America, 1950. Pp. 247-259. Also in *Social Casework* 31:311-318, 1950, and in *Social Work in the Current Scene* (Selected Papers, 1950 National Conference of Social Work).

Taggart, Alice D. "Some Basic Concepts Regarding Field Work Training for Psychiatric Social Work," *American Journal of Orthopsychiatry*, 4:365-373, 1934.

Towle, Charlotte. *Common Human Needs*. Washington, D. C.: U.S. Govt. Printing Office, 1945. Chapter 7, "Supervision." Pp. 95-122.

———. "Emotional Elements in Professional Learning," in *Professional Education*. New York: American Association of Schools of Social Work, 1948.

———. "The Contribution of Education for Social Casework to Practice," *Social Casework*, 31:318-326, 1950. Also in *Principles and Techniques in Social Casework*, ed. Cora Kasius. New York: Family Service Association of America, 1950. Pp. 260-274.

———. "Distinctive Attributes of Education for Social Work," *Social Work Journal*, 33:63-72, 1952.

———. "Selection and Arrangement of Case Material for Orderly Progression in Learning," *Social Service Review*, 27:27-54, 1953.

———. *The Learner in Education for the Professions, As Seen in Education for Social Work*. Chicago: University of Chicago Press, 1954.

Waddington, Miriam. "Student Unit: Some Problems and Psychological Implications," *Journal of Social Casework*, 30:113-117, 1949.

Wright, Helen, "Agency Contributions to Training," *Child Welfare Journal*, May, 1949.

Training in Psychotherapy

Ackerman, Nathan. "The Training of Case Workers in Psychotherapy," *American Journal of Orthopsychiatry*, 19:14-24, 1949.

Allen, David W.; Houston, Marietta; McCarley, Tracey H., Jr. "Resistances to Learning." *J. Medical Education*, 33:373-379, 1958.

Atkin, I. "Psychotherapy and the Trainee Psychiatrist," *American Journal of Psychotherapy*, 4:85-89, 1950.

Balint, Enid, and Balint, Michael. "Dynamics of Training in Groups for Psychotherapy," *British Journal of Medical Psychology*, 28:135-143, 1955.

Balint, Michael. "Training General Practitioners in Psychotherapy," *British Medical Journal*, 1:115-120, 1954.

———. "Method and Technique in the Teaching of Medical Psychology," *British Journal of Medical Psychology*, 27:37-41, 1954.

Bieber, Irving G. "Training of Medical and Non-Medical Personnel in Psychotherapy," *Bulletin of the World Federation for Mental Health*, 3:285-288, 1951.

Brenman, Margaret. "The Role of Training in Psychoanalysis for the Development of Therapeutic Techniques in Clinical Psychology," in *Training in Clinical Psychology*. New York: Josiah Macy, Jr., Foundation, 1947. Pp. 70-74.

Brody, Benjamin, and Grey, Alan L. "The Non-Medical Psychotherapist: A Critique and a Program," *Journal of Abnormal and Social Psychology*, 43:179-192, 1948.

Coleman, Jules V. "The Teaching of Basic Psychotherapy," *American Journal of Orthopsychiatry*, 17:622-627, 1947.

Dickson, John T.; Levinson, Harry; Leader, Arthur L.; and Stamm, Isabel. "The Contribution of Social Workers to the Interviewing Skills of Psychologists," *Journal of Social Casework*, 30:318-324, 1949.

Ekstein, Rudolf. "Dynamic Aspects of Training in Psychology in a Professional Group Setting," *Transactions of the Kansas Academy of Science*, 55:352-362, 1952.

———, and Sargent, Helen. "Preliminary Report on an Experimental Project in Supervision in Clinical Psychology (A. Psychotherapy)," *Transactions of the Kansas Academy of Science*, 52:232-243, 1949.

———; Brown, William; Greenbaum, Nathan; Hollingsworth, Irene; Kobler, Arthur; and Sargent, Helen. "A Method of Supervision for Psychotherapy," *Transactions of the Kansas Academy of Science*, 53: 254-267, 1950.

Ellis, Albert; Nydes, Jule; and Riess, Bernard F. "Qualifications of the Clinical Psychologist for the Practice of Psychotherapy," *Journal of Clinical Psychology*, 11:33-37, 1955.

Fleischmann, Otto. "A Method of Teaching Psychotherapy; One-Way-Vision Room Technique," *Bulletin of the Menninger Clinic*, 19:160-172, 1955.

Fleming, Joan. "The Role of Supervision in Psychiatric Training," *Bulletin of the Menninger Clinic*, 17:157-169, 1953.

———, and Hamburg, David A. "An Analysis of Methods for Teaching Psychotherapy with Description of a New Approach," *Archives of Neurology and Psychiatry*, 79:179-200, 1958.

Fromm-Reichmann, Frieda. "Notes on the Personal and Professional Requirements of a Psychotherapist," *Psychiatry*, 12:361-378, 1949.

Gans, Robert W. "The Use of Group Co-Therapists in the Teaching of Psychotherapy," *American Journal of Psychotherapy*, 11:618-625, 1957.

Gardner, George E. "The Supervision of Psychotherapy," *American Journal of Orthopsychiatry*, 23:293-300, 1953.

Grotjahn, Martin. "Training the Third Ear: Report on an Attempt at Teaching Conjecture in Psychotherapy," in *Explorations in Psychoanalysis*, ed. R. Lindner. New York: Julian Press, 1953. Pp. 221-229.

Grotjahn, Martin. "Problems and Techniques of Supervision," *Psychiatry*, 18:9-15, 1955.

Hadden, Samuel B. "The Utilization of a Therapy Group in Teaching Psychotherapy," *American Journal of Psychiatry*, 103:644-648, 1947.

Hill, Lewis B., and Worden, Frederic G. "Participant Teaching of Psychotherapy by Senior Physicians: A Hospital Program and Clinical Illustrations," *Psychiatric Quarterly*, 26:228-243, 1952.

Hora, Thomas. "Contribution to the Phenomenology of the Supervisory Process," *American Journal of Psychotherapy*, 11:769-773, 1957.

Kirkpatrick, Milton E. "Training for Psychotherapy with Special Reference to Non-Medical Fields," *American Journal of Orthopsychiatry*, 19:1-5, 1949.

Kubie, Lawrence J. "Elements in the Medical Curriculum Which Are Essential in the Training for Psychotherapy," in *Training in Clinical Psychology*. New York: Josiah Macy, Jr., Foundation, 1947. Pp. 46-54.

Lott, George M. "The Training of Non-Medical Cooperative Psychotherapists by Multiple Psychotherapy," *American Journal of Psychotherapy*, 6:440-448, 1952.

Louttit, C. M. "Training for Non-Directive Counseling: A Critique," *Journal of Clinical Psychology*, 4:236-240, 1948.

Lowrey, Lawson G. "Five Years' Experience in Supervision of Psychiatrists, Psychologists and Psychiatric Social Workers in Simultaneous Training," *American Journal of Orthopsychiatry*, 3:278-309, 1933.

Luchins, Abraham S. "On Training Clinical Psychologists in Psychotherapy," *Journal of Clinical Psychology*, 5:132-137, 1949.

———. "Patients View the Therapist: A Training and Research Device," *Journal of Consulting Psychology*, 15:24-31, 1951.

May, Rollo. "The Work and Training of the Psychological Therapist," *Psychological Service Center Journal*, 2:3-23, 1950.

Meerloo, Joost A. M. "Some Psychological Processes in Supervision of Therapists," *American Journal of Psychotherapy*, 6:467-470, 1952.

Mowrer, O. H. "Training in Psychotherapy," *Journal of Consulting Psychology*, 15:274-277, 1951.

Murphy, William F., and Kligerman, Sidney. "The Associative Anamnesis in Teaching Insight Psychotherapy," *Diseases of the Nervous System*, 11:291-297, 1950.

Neumann, Frederika. "The Training of Psychiatric Social Workers for Individual Psychotherapy," *American Journal of Orthopsychiatry*, 19:25-28, 1949.

Paul, Louis. "Introductory Teaching of Psychotherapy as Extended History-Taking," presented at the annual meeting, American Psychoanalytic Association, San Francisco, May 9, 1958.

Rennie, Thomas A. C. "Psychotherapy for the General Practitioner: A Program of Training," *American Journal of Psychiatry*, 103:653-660, 1947.

Rosenbaum, Milton. "Problems in Supervision of Psychiatric Residents in

Psychotherapy," *Archives of Neurology and Psychiatry*, 69:43-48, 1953.

Sager, Clifford J. "Aspects of Clinical Training in Psychotherapy," *American Journal of Psychotherapy*, 7:633-640, 1953.

Schwartz, Emanuel K., and Abel, Theodora M. "The Professional Education of the Psychoanalytic Psychotherapist," *American Journal of Psychotherapy*, 9:253-261, 1955.

Searles, Harold F. "The Informational Value of the Supervisor's Emotional Experiences," *Psychiatry*, 18:135-146, 1955.

Silverman, Samuel, and Cutler, Richard E. "Further Observations on Supervised Psychotherapy of Schizophrenia," *American Journal of Psychotherapy*, 11:262-276, 1957.

———, and Mutter, Arthur Z. "Supervision in Psychotherapy of Schizophrenia. I," *American Journal of Psychiatry*, 112:436-442, 1955.

Spiegel, John P. "Factors in the Growth and Development of the Psychotherapist," *Journal of the American Psychoanalytic Association*, 4:170-175, 1956.

Stainbrook, Edward. "On the Structure and Dynamics of Supervision in Psychiatric Training," *Psychiatric Quarterly*, 23:35-40, 1949.

Szurek, Stanislaus A. "Remarks on Training for Psychotherapy," *American Journal of Orthopsychiatry*, 19:36-51, 1949.

———. "Teaching and Learning of Psychoanalytic Psychiatry in Medical School," *Psychoanalytic Quarterly*, 26:387-396, 1957.

Thompson, Clara W., and Bradway, Katherine. "The Teaching of Psychotherapy through Content-Free Interviews," *Journal of Consulting Psychology*, 14:321-323, 1950.

Wagner, Frederik F. "Supervision of Psychotherapy," *American Journal of Psychotherapy*, 11:759-768, 1957.

Warson, Samuel R. "Affective Learning and the Student-Teacher Relationship," *American Journal of Psychiatry*, 106:53-58, 1949.

Weber, John J. "Some Observations on Psychiatric Residency Supervision," *Psychoanalytic Review*, 43:214-219, 1956.

Welsch, Exie E.; Bernard, Viola W.; Austin, Lucille N.; and Schlesinger, Herbert J. "Qualifications for Psychotherapists," *American Journal of Orthopsychiatry*, 26:35-65, 1956.

Whitaker, Carl A. "Teaching the Practicing Physician to do Psychotherapy," *Southern Medical Journal*, 42:899-903, 1949.

Wolberg, Lewis R. "Supervision of the Psychotherapeutic Process," *American Journal of Psychotherapy*, 5:147-171, 1951.

———. "Supervision of the Psychotherapeutic Process," in *The Techniques of Psychotherapy*. Pp. 641-660. New York: Grune & Stratton, 1954.

Woltmann, Adolf G. "Problems Involved in the Training of Psychologists as Non-Medical Psychotherapists," *American Journal of Orthopsychiatry*, 19:32-35, 1949.

Zetzel, Elizabeth R. "The Dynamic Basis of Supervision," *Social Casework*, 34:143-149, 1953.

Administrative Aspects of Clinical Training

Abramson, Eva. *The Supervisor's Job in the Public Agency: Administrative Aspects.* Chicago: American Public Welfare Association, 1940.

Berkowitz, Sidney J. "The Administrative Process in Casework Supervision," *Social Casework,* 33:419-423, 1952.

Black, Bertram J. "Some Aspects of Professional Administration," *Social Casework,* 31:326-332, 1950.

Bloch, Donald A., and Silber, Earle. "The Role of the Administrator in Relation to Individual Psychotherapy in a Residential Treatment Setting," *American Journal of Orthopsychiatry,* 27:69-74, 1957.

Cumming, Elaine, and Cumming, John. "The Locus of Power in a Large Mental Hospital," *Psychiatry,* 19:361-369, 1956.

Eisenberg, Sidney S. "Supervision as an Agency Need," *Social Casework,* 37:233-237, 1956.

Follett, Mary P. "The Illusion of Final Authority," *Taylor Society Bulletin,* December, 1926.

Hanchette, Helen, et al. *Some Dynamics of Social Agency Administration.* New York: Family Service Association of America, 1946.

Hanford, Jeanette. "Integration of the Teaching and Administrative Aspects of Supervision," in *Administration, Supervision, and Consultation.* New York: Family Service Association of America, 1955. Pp. 51-58.

Leader, Arthur L. "Administrative Conference Following Evaluation," *Social Casework,* 36:412-416, 1955.

Myers, J. Martin, Jr. "The Role of the Administrative Psychiatrist in Intensive Psychotherapy in a Mental Hospital," *American Journal of Psychiatry,* 113:71-74, 1956.

Ormsby, Ralph; Hanford, Jeanette; and Sterba, Richard F. "Symposium: Interrelation of the Executive, Supervisor, and Psychiatric Consultant," *Highlights,* 10:49-53, 1949.

Slear, Genevieve S. "Some Administrative Aspects of Supervision," *Journal of Psychiatric Social Work,* 24:20-28, 1954.

Smith, Marjorie J. "Case Work Implications of Administration," *The Family,* 22:343-347, 1942.

Stanton, Alfred H., and Schwartz, Morris S. *The Mental Hospital.* New York: Basic Books, 1954.

Towle, Charlotte. "Professional Skill in Administration," *Newsletter, Association of Psychiatric Social Workers,* 10-17, 1940.

Worden, Frederic G., and Patton, John D. "A Hospital Program for Teaching and Supervising Administrative Psychiatry," *Psychiatric Quarterly Supplement,* 28:38-53, 1954.

INDEX